Advanced Information and Knowledge Processing

For further volumes:
http://www.springer.com/series/4738

Nathan Griffiths · Kuo-Ming Chao
Editors

Agent-Based Service-Oriented Computing

Editors
Dr. Nathan Griffiths
University of Warwick
Coventry
UK

Prof. Kuo-Ming Chao
Coventry University
Coventry
UK

ISBN 978-1-4471-2534-1 e-ISBN 978-1-84996-041-0
DOI 10.1007/978-1-84996-041-0
Springer London Dordrecht Heidelberg New York

British Library Cataloguing in Publication Data
A catalogue record for this book is available from the British Library

Printed on acid-free paper

Springer is part of Springer Science+Business Media (www.springer.com)

Preface

Service-oriented computing (SOC) has rapidly become an established approach for supporting the construction and management of distributed applications. A range of tools, techniques and standards have emerged to support the construction, publication, discovery, composition and management of services. Agent-based systems are a natural complement to SOC and can provide the intelligence and reasoning capabilities that are needed to effectively support and manage the resulting systems.

The integration of agents and SOC is an active research area, and the goal of this book is to give an overview of current research and techniques, and to identify the most likely future directions. This book is a collection of chapters that discuss the main current areas of research, along with a chapter devoted to selected future directions that we see as important. We also include a chapter that introduces the basic notions of SOC, to keep the book accessible to a general reader.

We would like to express our gratitude to the authors who have contributed their research, and to Rebecca Mowat, Beverley Ford and everyone at Springer who has helped with the publication of this book.

Coventry, UK
September 2009

Nathan Griffiths
Kuo-Ming Chao

Contents

List of Contributors

Kuo-Ming Chao
Department of Computer Science, Coventry University, Coventry, CV1 5FB, UK, e-mail: k.chao@coventry.ac.uk

Fang Dong
School of Computer Science and Engineering, Southeast University, Nanjing 210096, P.R. China, e-mail: fdong@seu.edu.cn

Dieter Fensel
Semantic Technology Institute (STI), University of Innsbruck, Innsbruck, Austria, e-mail: dieter.fensel@sti2.at

Nathan Griffiths
Department of Computer Science, University of Warwick, Coventry, CV4 7AL, UK, e-mail: nathan@dcs.warwick.ac.uk

Birgit Hofreiter
Institute of Information Systems, University of Liechtenstein, Vaduz 9490, Liechtenstein, e-mail: Birgit.Hofreiter@hochschule.li

Christian Huemer
Vienna University of Technology, Favoritenstrasse 9-11/188-3, Vienna 1040, Austria, e-mail: huemer@big.tuwien.ac.at

Stephen A. Jarvis
Department of Computer Science, University of Warwick, Coventry, CV4 7AL, UK, e-mail: S.A.Jarvis@warwick.ac.uk

Arshad Jhumka
Department of Computer Science, University of Warwick, Coventry, CV4 7AL, UK, e-mail: H.A.Jhumka@warwick.ac.uk

Mike Joy
Department of Computer Science, University of Warwick, Coventry, CV4 7AL, UK, e-mail: M.S.Joy@warwick.ac.uk

Wei Li
School of Computer Science and Engineering, Southeast University, Nanjing 210096, P.R. China, e-mail: xchlw@seu.edu.cn

Kwei-Jay Lin
Department of Electrical Engineering and Computer Science, University of California, Irvine, CA, USA, e-mail: klin@uci.edu

Sarah N. Lim Choi Keung
Department of Computer Science, University of Warwick, Coventry, CV4 7AL, UK, e-mail: S.N.Lim.Choi.Keung@dcs.warwick.ac.uk

Bo Liu
School of Computer Science and Engineering, Southeast University, Nanjing 210096, P.R. China, e-mail: bliu@seu.edu.cn

Chi-Chun Lo
Institute of Information Management, National Chiao Tung University, Hsinchu, Taiwan, e-mail: cclo@faculty.nctu.edu.tw

Michael Luck
Department of Computer Science, King's College London, London, WC2R 2LS, UK, e-mail: michael.luck@kcl.ac.uk

Junzhou Luo
School of Computer Science and Engineering, Southeast University, Nanjing 210096, P.R. China, e-mail: jluo@seu.edu.cn

Simon Miles
Department of Computer Science, King's College London, London, WC2R 2LS, UK, e-mail: simon.miles@kcl.ac.uk

Sanjay Modgil
Department of Computer Science, King's College London, London, WC2R 2LS, UK, e-mail: sanjay.modgil@kcl.ac.uk

Nir Oren
Department of Computer Science, King's College London, London, WC2R 2LS, UK, e-mail: nir.oren@kcl.ac.uk

Leon Smalov
Faculty of Engineering and Computing, Coventry University, Coventry, CV1 5FB, UK, e-mail: csx211@coventry.ac.uk

Michael Stollberg
SAP Research CEC Dresden, SAP AG, Dresden D-01187, Germany, e-mail: michael.stollberg@sap.com

Ping Wang
Department of MIS, Kun Shan University, Yung–Kang, Taiwan, e-mail: pingwang@mail.ksu.edu.tw

James W. J. Xue
Department of Computer Science, University of Warwick, Coventry, CV4 7AL, UK, e-mail: W.J.Xue@warwick.ac.uk

Shanshan Yang
Department of Computer Science, University of Warwick, Coventry, CV4 7AL, UK, e-mail: Shanshan.Yang@dcs.warwick.ac.uk

Xiao Zheng
School of Computer Science and Engineering, Southeast University, Nanjing 210096, P.R. China, e-mail: xzheng@seu.edu.cn

Chapter 1
Introduction

Kuo-Ming Chao and Nathan Griffiths

Abstract The increasing number and growing complexity of distributed systems in current dynamic business environments requires more sophisticated methods and technologies to tackle the related emerging issues and requirements. Software agents, an AI-based technology, has demonstrated its potential in dealing with uncoordinated heterogeneous distributed systems. Service-oriented computing, which has evolved and learned lessons from Internet and distributed object technologies, has attracted significant interest from industry and academia for the development of distributed enterprise systems. This chapter gives an overview of the characteristics of agents and services and the relationships between them by analysing their modelling methods, supporting specifications, and platforms for system development. We argue that although the focus of these two technologies is diverse, they have great potential to complement each other to advance distributed applications. In this chapter we also introduce the remaining chapters of this book.

1.1 Distributed Systems

The increasing popularity of the Internet facilitates software accessibility and interaction. Due to rapid changes in the operating environment and increased demand for sophisticated functionality from software, centralised approaches for the management and development of large scale software becomes a less viable option. The growing number of distributed systems with associated supporting technologies, and the trend towards globalisation, has shaped the new landscape of computer system

Kuo-Ming Chao
Department of Computer Science, Coventry University, Coventry, CV1 5FB, UK
e-mail: k.chao@coventry.ac.uk

Nathan Griffiths
Department of Computer Science, University of Warwick, Coventry, CV4 7AL, UK
e-mail: nathan@dcs.warwick.ac.uk

N. Griffiths, K.-M. Chao (eds.), *Agent-Based Service-Oriented Computing*,
Advanced Information and Knowledge Processing,
DOI 10.1007/978-1-84996-041-0_1,

development, which puts more emphasis on issues such as flexibility, interoperability, reusability and Quality of Service (QoS).

Software agents are one of a number of fast growing technologies designed to cope with increasingly dynamic and complex environments. Its theory has been widely studied and the breadth of its applications range from engineering to business; from personal assistants to large-scale system integration. The emergence of service-oriented computing has provided an alternative way to design and model software systems and this has gained a large degree of support from academia and industry alike. As a result, an increasing number of companies are adopting service-oriented architectures (SOAs), and the related technologies, to implement their IT systems.

Although agent-oriented and service-oriented computing have different perspectives from which they contribute to distributed system design, they share a number of common characteristics in software development, such as raising system scalability, emphasising system abstraction modelling, increasing software reusability and distributed systems coordination etc. Software components can be orchestrated, composed or coordinated to produce a compelling distributed system that none of the individual components can accomplish alone. This, however, raises the question of whether, given that they overlap, these paradigms can work together with sufficient effectiveness to further improve distributed system design. If the answer is yes, then a further question is determining how they can complement each other. In this chapter, we examine these two technologies by looking into various aspects. We will give more background on agent-oriented and service-oriented computing. We also briefly introduce the definitions and properties of agents and SOAs, as these may lead to the various modelling methodologies and the focus of their applications. Finally, we include a brief overview of the remaining chapters of this book.

1.2 Software Agents

The term agent has been extensively used in computer science and there is no general consensus on its definition. W3C defines an agent as, "a program acting on behalf of a person or organisation" [15]. This definition gives space for developers to give varying interpretations to the definition in shaping their agents. This is understandable as W3C involves several initiatives in standardising Internet-related specifications. If the definition is too detailed and specific, it may hinder the scope of applications and development. According to this definition, some agents can possess sophisticated and complex functions, while others can be very simple which only contain a program routine. Berners-Lee et al. [2] view, for example, software agents in the context of semantic web technologies as being responsible for coordinating searches and comparing and negotiating on the web to greatly reduce a user's effort.

Bradshaw [3] concluded that the "software agent" definition proposed by Shoham in 1997 might be acceptable to many agent researchers. That is, "a software entity which functions continuously and autonomously in a particular environment, often inhabited by other agents and processes" [34]. Wooldridge also proposed a similar definition, namely that, "an agent is a computer system that is situated in some environment, and that is capable of autonomous actions in this environment in order to meet its delegated objectives" [36, 37].

Interestingly, the FIPA and OMG Agent Special Interest Group, a joint effort by two standards organisations in promoting agents, does not prescribe a specific definition to agents or explicitly prescribe their properties [6]. Instead of giving a specific definition, however, a software agent can be characterised by the four properties of autonomy, reactivity, pro-activeness, and social ability [38].

The property of autonomy drives the agent to be proactive by coordinating with other agents to achieve their common interests. Ideally, a group of agents can organise themselves by following certain social norms or ethics rules to form a community (agency) with minimum human intervention to realise their design goals. The interaction between agents is typically through communication, and as with other traditional distributed systems requires suitable protocols. Since agents are autonomous entities that have control over their internal states and actions, communication protocols such as remote procedural calls or method invocation, which allow agents to directly change states or behaviours of other agents, are not sufficient [9]. These protocols, however, can be used as a vehicle to convey messages, but individual agents have the ultimate right to decide how to reply or react. In other words, a high-level communication protocol with rich semantics sits above a transport protocol to enable the agents to interact at an intentional and social level and to influence each other to carry out actions to reach their desired intentions. An Agent Communication Language [13], a standardised communication protocol for agents based on speech act theory [33], was proposed to facilitate the higher-level agent interactions such as negotiation and coordination. Like objects, an agent has the capability to react to requests from the environment or from other agents. It also has the ability to continuously monitor the environment in which it is situated and its internal status, to ensure that its course of action will not deviate from its designated goal. If there is any deviation, then appropriate actions will be taken to correct it. An intelligent agent, therefore, is goal-oriented and focuses on task planning and execution [6].

These properties are not the only set of properties having been proposed as associated with agents. For example, Etzioni and Weld, and Franklin and Graesser, have proposed different sets of properties [12, 14]. This leads to different classifications of agents which serve different purposes. However, Nwana [21] broadly divided agent research into two strands, macro and micro, based on their evolution.

The research classified as macro-level is interested in understanding the interaction and communication between agents, the decomposition and distribution of tasks, coordination and cooperation, and conflict resolution via negotiation etc. This line of research is mainly derived from distributed AI and economics. On the other hand, micro-level research has greater emphasis on the design and development of agent systems by providing the underlying architecture. In this aspect, the introduction of software agents to computational systems enables legacy software, which has little or no capability to interact with other software, to interoperate with other agents in a consistent manner. The Palo Alto Collaborative Testbed (PACT) project, funded by DARPA [10], demonstrated the effectiveness of agents in knowledge sharing and reuse for complex engineering design. As the field of agent-based systems evolves over time, it has become a new paradigm in modelling complex software systems. The focus has shifted from intelligence and reasoning ability, to actions and modelling. According to these classifications, different types of agents with more specific functions have emerged for different agent-based applications.

In this chapter, we view agents as software programs with a degree of intelligence or autonomy to perform functions on behalf of person, organisation or other software system. The terms, agent, software agent, and intelligent agent will be used interchangeably. An agent, in this case, implies its existence in a multi-agent system, as it works with other agents to achieve a common goal. The term agent, however, does have slightly different interpretations by some authors in this book, as detailed in the corresponding chapters.

1.3 Service-Oriented Architectures

Service-Oriented Architectures are another paradigm to allow software developers to focus on the fulfilment of required enterprise functionalities at a conceptual level by providing standardised communication protocols, interfaces, workflow and service management infrastructures/policies. SOAs enable developers to compose the required services from existing ones without being concerned by the barriers caused by heterogeneous operating and hardware systems, and the syntax level differences among different software and locations [7].

Although the concept of a SOA has been backed by numerous organisations, it is similar to agents in that a number of competing definitions for SOAs have been proposed, by various industry bodies, respected researchers and standards organisations. W3C defines a service as, "an abstract resource that represents a capability of performing tasks that represents a coherent functionality from the point of view of provider entities and requester entities" [5]. A service is an abstract concept, but it is granular, as it can only provide one function. W3C further define a Service-Oriented Architecture as, "a set of components which can be invoked, and whose interface descriptions can be published and discovered" [15]. This conflicts with alternative views of SOAs, due to its narrow description of a SOA as a set of components. In addition, this definition is mainly concerned with implementation and deployment issues with less consideration of the architectural level [35].

IBM defines SOAs as, "an approach to build distributed systems that deliver application functionality as services to end-user applications or to build other services. SOA can be based on web services, but it may use other technologies instead" [8]. In this definition, the relationship between SOAs and web services has been explicitly clarified. In other words, web services are a tool which can help realise a SOA.

OASIS defines SOAs as the following: "A paradigm for organising and utilising distributed capabilities that may be under the control of different ownership domains. It provides a uniform means to offer, discover, interact with and use capabilities to produce desired effects consistent with measurable preconditions and expectations" [24]. This implies that a number of related standards and measurements are needed in a SOA, so that services can be provided and consumed in a consistent manner. This leads to different standards having been proposed for the various aspects of SOAs and web services. Regardless of the diverse nature of these definitions, Service-Oriented Computing (SOC), can be considered as a study of SOA in the context of computing.

We believe that agents and services share a number of similarities, but they also have some important differences. Agents and services, like other software modelling methods, attempt to separate concerns into agents and services in order to understand the functions and behaviours of a particular system in the process of system modelling and development. Both aim at increasing software reusability by dividing the system logic into a collection of agents and services. An agent can join different agencies to achieve different goals. A service can be part of different composite services to serve different functions. Agents are able to reuse subsystems, while services are designed to reuse functions. States and data are embedded in objects, and agents have beliefs, but services (and web services) are stateless. Both have possession of different degrees of autonomy. Services have control over the logic they encapsulate. A service can complete its prescribed functions without involving other services, and functions in one service will not interact with others residing in other services directly. Similarly an agent can fulfil its advertised capabilities without assistance from other agents, although of course assistance is permitted and is often valuable. Both have intentions of promoting loss coupling. In the next few sections, we will explore further agents and services from three different aspects, namely modelling methodologies, standardisation, and supporting tools.

1.4 Modelling Methodologies

A software modelling methodology provides a systematic approach with relevant guidelines, principles, and models to help the developer analyse an application domain and requirements, and to lead to system design and development. A development life cycle is associated with the methodology consisting of the various stages, activities and processes for system modelling. It also specifies the deliverables or models that should be produced at each specific stage of the development life cycle. This provides a matrix against which to measure deliverables to ensure that the project is on track and that software quality can be met. The process of modelling normally starts with an abstract or logical view of the system in order to capture its essence. The content of the model can be enriched by adding more detailed and concrete elements and processes. As the development process continues, along with the progressing of life cycle, more detailed specifications for implementation should be revealed and designed. At the end, the conceptual system can be realised by using suitable technologies and can be deployed.

Unlike OO which has a mature standard modelling language and related methods, UML, to support system analysis and design, there are currently no well recognised systematic methodologies for the analysis and design of agent-oriented and service-oriented software systems. However, a handful of agent modelling approaches have been proposed and adopted by researchers to develop agent-based applications.

1.4.1 Agent Modelling Methodologies

Existing methodologies for modelling agent-oriented systems originate from either knowledge engineering techniques or object-oriented modelling methods [3]. The Belief-Desire-Intention (BDI) architecture is an approach to modelling the internal states of an agent in terms of three main elements—beliefs, desires and intentions [30]. Beliefs represent an agent's beliefs about the world (including the agent itself and others). Desires are a set of possible goals the agent wishes to achieve. Intentions are commitments to goals, typically in the form of intermediate goals associated with plans that the agent has selected to perform. The benefit of this method is that it provides a systematic coherent approach from modelling logical mental states to realising BDI agents. JACK agents, a commercial tool to support intelligent agent development, is based on this approach. The authors also proposed the AAII methodology to model an agent's interaction rules with other external agents [31].

Gaia [38] is an agent-oriented analysis and design methodology for modelling both the macro-level (societal) and the micro-level (agent) aspects of agent based systems. The approach supports a number of models for each stage (analysis and design) to capture concepts from abstract to concrete levels. The whole development is an iterative process to ensure that the system has been modelled appropriately. At the analysis stage, a prototypical role and interaction model which includes key roles and the interactions between the roles in the system is identified. The outcome of the analysis is a comprehensive roles model which details the information about the key roles, interaction protocols and activities. The design stage in Gaia is to create an agent model by grouping the roles identified in the previous step into agent types and to define their relationships. The next step is to develop a service model to include essential functions to support agent's roles and activities. The final step is to develop an acquaintance model from the interaction model and agent model. After the completion of these stages, the specifications for an agent system are ready for implementation.

In Gaia, the purpose of an agent possessing a service model is to describe and support its capabilities. An agent has a collection of services that correspond to the functions required by the agent to play its role in a given environment or organisation. The activities identified at the analysis stage relate to the roles through the corresponding services. Each role will be supported by at least one service. The services that are allocated to one agent are not directly accessible to other agents.

In other words, one agent cannot directly invoke the other agent's operations (regardless of implementation platform, for example even if web services were used). The Gaia service model focuses on modelling concrete concepts, and so the issue of service implementation is not addressed [16]. For each service it is necessary to document its properties such as its required input and output as well as constraints such as pre-conditions, and post-conditions.

1.4.2 SOA Modelling Methodologies

Arsanjani proposed a service-oriented modelling approach with seven layers for the development of services [1]. The approach consists of modelling, analysis, design techniques, and activities to define the foundations of a SOA. The main task of service identification is to use top-down, bottom-up, and middle-out techniques to analyse the application domain and to decompose the domain into manageable subsystems for service identification. After the required services have been identified, the relationships between these services need to be recognised and drawn up as a hierarchical structure, so that the composite and atomic services can be determined. The activity in the subsystem analysis specifies the interdependencies and flow between the subsystems. Once the subsystems have been specified, services can be assigned to these subsystems. Prior to doing this, the component that implements the services must be documented. The final step is to realise the services by selection or custom building. Other options that are available include integration, transformation, subscription and the outsourcing of parts of the functionality using web services.

The SOA foundation life cycle is another means to guide service development [17]. The SOA life cycle consists of four main phases: modelling, assembly, deployment, and management. Another important process is governance to manage the whole process for quality of service. During the modelling phase of the service life cycle the main task is to identify candidate services and their possible interactions based on the result of a requirements analysis and an analysis of the business process. Modelling functions that meet the required business objectives in the form of services is another important task. The resulting model is designed and simulated in order to test whether the system has met the requirements or not. In the assembly phase the developers locate the available services which can be composed to produce the designated functions. If the required functions cannot be satisfied with the services in the repository, then constructing new services is necessary. Service testing before the composition takes place is an essential task to ensure system dependability. In this phase, the policies for governing the service interactions need to be determined. When the system is ready for deployment, the deployers need to configure the system for the real runtime environment. Other related roles such as IT system managers and end users etc. have to be involved to integrate business processes and information to eliminate any possible barriers. The deployed services must be managed and monitored to ensure that there are no abnormal behaviours and that they comply with non-functional QoS requirements.

1.4.3 Agents and Services

W3C states that "A web service is an abstract notion that must be implemented by a concrete agent. The agent is the concrete piece of software or hardware that sends and receives messages, while the service is the resource characterised by the abstract set of functionality that is provided" [5]. This means that a web service can be implemented by one agent and that this agent can be replaced with another, provided that the service still provides the same functionality. For example, suppose that a Google agent, that includes a Google search engine and related index database, can retrieve the required information for requests and that a Yahoo agent has a similar search capability, but it is associated with the Yahoo search engine and database. An Internet search service can be implemented using the Google agent to search over the Internet, but the service can change its underlying agent from the Google agent to the Yahoo agent. The service still has the same functionality for internet search, but the results searched by these two agents may be different and the QoS offered by these two agents could vary. Therefore, the Service Level Agreement (SLA) between service consumers and providers becomes an important instrument for SOAs [32]. The service can select appropriate agents to honour its described functions and promised QoS based on a SLA.

Agents might also be autonomous and able to deliberate to plan and fulfil the goal (tasks) a service assigns to it. A composite service is a collection of services that contain a group of agents. The agents will not communicate with each other directly, but through the associated service interfaces. If an Agent Communication Language (ACL) is the only communication mechanism for agents, then the communication between service and agent and between services will be messages that contain the ACL. A workflow will prescribe the relationships at runtime not only between services, but also between agents. A discovery and selection service could include a service discovery and selection agent to automate the service discovery and selection process. In this approach, an agent is wrapped by a service. The issue of coordinating heterogeneous agents could be alleviated, as services will be the only interface for service consumers to interact with, and so the standard web services architecture is applicable.

The Gaia methodology takes a very different approach from the W3C web service architecture to define the relationship between agents and services. The services in the Gaia service model are designed to realise the agents role. Services are one of the main building blocks to equip an agent with functions. In other words, a service is part of an agent and it can be one of the activities that an agent is able to carry out. An agent has control over the services and their interactions. In this model, an agent can adopt SOA standards to tackle issues such as non-functional QoS requirements, governance, and dependability etc., to which the community pays little attention but are important factors for business and engineering applications. We further discuss the standards issue later in this chapter. The agent can also select relevant services to not only produce the required functions, but also meet QoS requirements.

1.5 Supporting Development Platforms

There are very few software tools that have been developed for agents that comply with FIPA specifications, and some of these are no longer supported or maintained by the developers. For example, the April Agent Platform (AAP) and Language (April) (http://sourceforge.net/projects/networkagent/) and the Fipa-OS agent platform (http://fipa-os.sourceforge.net/index.htm) are no longer actively developed. The Spyse agent platform (http://sourceforge.net/projects/spyse/) has become open source software in attempt to attract input from researchers in the community.

One of popular development tools for agent-based systems is JADE which is a Java based agent platform. It focuses on the support of the FIPA agent management platform, Agent Communication Language, and underlying communication protocols, but there is no support for the intelligent mechanisms needed by an agent. Therefore, to enable agents to have intelligence or decision making, developers need to combine JADE with other reasoning engines.

JACK, a commercial tool, is not FIPA compliant but does has a sophisticated inference engine based on the Belief, Desire, Intention (BDI) paradigm [30] to support agent reasoning. It focuses on modelling agents' internal mental states, and does not provide associated communication or coordination mechanisms. This hinders its application to multi-agent systems. Recently, the introduction of JACK Teams aims to overcome this disadvantage by enhancing its capability in the modelling of social structures and coordinated behaviours. Zeus, an open source agent development tool kit created by BT and associated partners, supports a BDI like representation for reasoning and an ontology to integrate different concepts [22]. Zeus supports agents with intelligent message handling functionality for communication with other agents, such that agents can reactively respond to requests from others. The software, however, is no longer supported by the original developers.

Industry is unenthusiastic about the development of agent development toolkits. Industry and academic research communities, however, are more interested in developing tools or methods to support particular aspects of agents, such as mobility, learning, coordination and economic analysis etc. Aglets, for example, was developed at the IBM Tokyo Research Laboratory (TRL) to develop mobile agent applications [20]. It is a Java mobile agent platform, and so developers can utilise built-in libraries to develop mobile agents and embed the technology to their applications. Aglets, however, is no longer supported by IBM.

Even though agent based systems receives input from industry, SOAs gain more support from industry as the web services (WS) architecture is perceived as an industry-accepted method of technology deployment. Several large IT companies have developed software platforms or solutions to support the concept of SOAs.

For example, BEA has WebLogic Server, and the .Net Framework in Microsoft offers toolkits for developing web service based applications. Sun Microsystems also perceives the potential of service-oriented applications by introducing web service technologies to NetBeans/Java Studio Enterprise, and IBM WebSphere provides a heavy weight software platform to support service-oriented computing. There are other examples such as HP web services platform 2.0, SAP Web Application Server and Oracle Application Server Web Services etc. These are simply illustrative examples, and not an exhaustive list. Such companies envisage service-oriented software platforms as a tool to facilitate the change of company practices in business by introducing service-oriented concepts to IT systems. Therefore, they provide a systematic methodology to model business functions and processes. Enterprise Service Bus (ESB) [18], for example, supported by IBM, Oracle and other IT companies, is a reference architecture, or middleware structure, that facilitates communication among different services and applications. The ESB not only includes a collection of key services to assist the SOA developers in building and managing the services, but it also encloses a set of services to support better decision-making with real-time information. Since the main objective of ESB is to support the development of SOA applications and to provide flexible connectivity for services and applications, the components or services in ESB can be varied according to the system or customer requirements [38].

The number of supporting tools for developing agent-based systems is limited. This could raise the threshold for naïve programmers or software engineers to gain familiarity. It can also increase development costs, since it can consume more resources and time in building agent-oriented systems. The other reason for the increasing number of SOA applications and their popularity is due to the fact that commercial tools and software platforms available for developing service-oriented applications can be acquired without difficulty. So, developers can utilise these tools to gain sufficient assistance to facilitate the software development.

The barriers to attracting more investment and participation from industry in agent-based system development platforms need to be removed. One possible approach is to introduce agent features such as deliberation, intelligence, and decision making etc. to the SOA compliant development tools, so that software development time and resources can be reduced. The service-oriented applications produced can then exploit the advantages of combining agents and service technologies to achieve business objectives.

1.6 Agents and SOA Standards

In the following subsections we review the main standards for agents and services.

1.6.1 Foundation for Intelligent Physical Agents (FIPA)

Unlike the web services architecture, software agents only have a small number of standard specifications. The most widely accepted specifications e.g. agent management and the Agent Communication Language have been developed by FIPA, the Foundation for Intelligent Physical Agents (http://www.fipa.org/), which includes several academic institutions and industrial partners. The aim of the organisation is to develop and agree standards for heterogeneous interacting agents and agent-based systems by defining a full set of standards for both implementing systems within which agents could execute (agent platforms) and for how agents themselves should communicate and interact. FIPA was founded in 1996, but despite its popularity in the late 1990s and early 2000s, it never succeeded in gaining the commercial support which was originally envisaged. In 2005, an IEEE standards committee was set up to take over from FIPA. AUML, the Agent Unified Modelling Language (http://www.auml.org/) is a standardised modelling language proposed by FIPA and OMG to capture agent concepts and their interactions.

1.6.2 SOA and Web Service Architecture Standards

Four main standards organisations, W3C, OASIS, OMG, and Open Group, have had extensive involvement in specifying SOAs and web services. The working groups in W3C mainly focus on web service family standards, which have been important specifications in building enabling technologies for the realisation of SOAs. Open Standards working groups, technical committees, and special interest groups in OASIS, OMG and Open Group also have significant interest in specifying SOA standards. The following is an illustrative list of the standards that have been proposed.

- The OASIS Reference Model for SOA [23].
- The Open Group SOA Ontology [26].
- The OMG SOA Modeling Language (OMG SoaML) [25].
- The OASIS Reference Architecture for SOA Foundation [24].
- The Open Group SOA Reference Architecture [29].
- The Open Group Service Integration Maturity Model (OSIMM) [28].
- The Open Group SOA Governance Framework [27].

The SOA reference model and ontology are specified to understand and capture the core concepts within a domain and describe the relationships between these core concepts. OMG SoaML, which is based on UML with extended notations, is designed to have enabling capabilities in service modelling. The Open Group SOA Reference Architecture and the OASIS Reference Architecture for SOA Foundation both intend to provide guidelines to support other architectures in the standards, and assist architects in the modelling and decision making processes [19]. The Open Group Service Integration Maturity Model (OSIMM) is to assist organisations that adopt SOA solutions in their businesses in assessing the maturity within a complete SOA migration path. The SOA Governance Framework assumes that an organisation already has its own governance model in place. The framework provides models to help organisations define and customise their own focused SOA Governance model.

The variety of standard specifications associated with web services, "WS-*", reflect services captured as different perspectives of the same subject for different purposes and applications. Various standards bodies and industry companies have participated in proposing and specifying standards to realise SOA applications. These provide SOA developers with various choices to facilitate service interoperability at various levels and aspects. These standards, however, with varying degrees of maturity may complement, contradict or compete with each other. For example, IBM and Microsoft adopt WS-* for transaction specification, but IBM proposes the WS-BPEL extension for people, which Microsoft did not contribute to or adopt. In addition, most WS-* specifications are still evolving, and so a change of the specifications is likely take place in the future. Figure 1.1 shows an example of the WS-Policy and its relation to other specifications which utilise the specifications to define their own related policy [11].

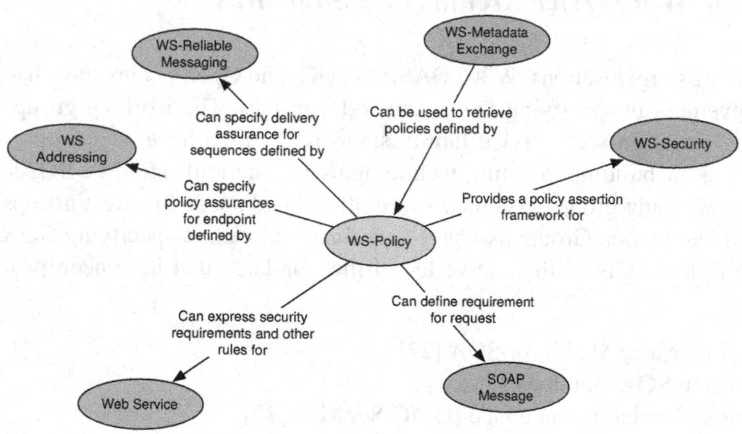

Fig. 1.1 WS-policy with other WS specifications

SOA and WS-Architecture have gained great support from industry, standard organisations, and academia, and a number of interest groups have been formed to propose and specify open standards. These standards offer guidelines in their respective areas to facilitate system interoperability for service-oriented applications built upon different development platforms to allow them to interact, if they comply with the standards. Some of these are designed to support each other to bring technological compatibility. In contrast, the agent community has a relatively small number of standardised specifications. Interoperability among heterogeneous agents using different technologies can be an issue. For example, two agents may try and cooperate, but they may adopt different coordination approaches. These two agents fail to cooperate, due to the lack of a standardised coordination approach. The large number of evolving standards for SOA and WS-*, however, might also be problematic, since only large software vendors can afford to support all of these standards. This could exclude small software vendors, as they may find it difficult to contribute and participate. In addition, some of the specifications might prove too complex and too detailed. The adoption of the full specifications becomes unnecessary for small applications, as some of the features may not be required. Standards help to bridge gaps between diverse technologies and help to advance the technology, but proof of concept for these standards can be very costly. From the above, one might even try to argue that standardisation can bring more harm than good. However, we do not believe that this is the case, since standards make interoperability among distributed systems possible. The benefits of the SOA and WS-family specifications have become evident as the number of applications adopting these standards have increased significantly. Some of the standards for SOAs might also be useful for agent-based service-oriented applications, for example, if developers adopted the Gaia service model to develop the agents functions.

1.7 Overview of Chapters

One of the key activities in service-oriented computing is service advertisement and discovery, which allows service providers to make others aware of their service provisions, and service consumers to locate their required services. Service providers need to describe their service provision in such a way that it can be published in a registry that is accessible to service consumers. A broker is typically the owner of the registry to facilitate the searching and locating of services in order to identify matches between service providers and consumers. In FIPA, the agent management platform includes agent directory services which serve as white pages for agent registration, and service directory services which serve as yellow pages for agents to register their services. Therefore, agents can use these directories to locate services for their needs. In WS-architecture, UDDI is the mechanism for service providers to advertise their services and for consumers to discover their required services.

Chapter 2 gives an overview of the existing architectures and technologies that support service discovery and advertisement, and discusses related issues. The author's view is that current popular technologies for service discovery are evolved from the various technologies for objects and components. The authors classify registry architectures into three different types, namely centralised, decentralised and hybrid registries. Each architecture has its advantages and disadvantages, and so the adoption of these architectures depends on the characteristics of the application. Agents in a SOA can play different roles such as consumer, provider, and broker etc. to perform various functions. A broker agent can be designed to carry out the essential tasks to achieve effective service discovery and advertisement. In some cases, multi-agent systems have been proposed for discovery, and so agents can coordinate themselves to discover their required services. A number of agent-based service discovery approaches are also reviewed and discussed in this chapter.

Services can be composed manually or automatically to meet design requirements. Automating the service composition process requires a software tool with decision making capabilities to link the services together in a logical way, so that the composite services can produce the desired functions. An agent with intelligence and autonomy can play an important role to facilitate this process. Chapter 3 illustrates the use of agent technologies in automating the service composition process. The proposed multi-agent based QoS-aware Service Composition solution (MQSC) is a mechanism for dynamic service composition and is able to ensure end-to-end QoS of composite services. The approach includes a number of agents such as a Portal Agent (PA), Decision Agent (DA), Search Agent (SA), Registry Agent (RA), Management Agent (MA) and Execution Agent (EA) playing different roles in the system and working together as a team to compose the required services. Even though the approach emphases the process of service composition, it is able to manage other stages of the composite service life cycle including discovery, selection, deployment and execution. Three different types of agent are introduced in order to support deployment, and a number of methods such as Ant theory and Graph theory etc. have been utilised to realise service composition.

Workflow is one of the key elements in enabling services to work together. Two well-known concepts in flows, orchestration and choreography, are abstract notions that facilitate the interactions among services. They are useful in modelling workflow, but the realisation of workflow needs a concrete representation of workflow and a suitable engine to process it. In Chapter 4, the authors distinguish between these two concepts and propose an approach to allow them to complement each other, so that the workflow modelled using these concepts can act consistently, collectively and seamlessly. One of most popular web service based workflow languages, BPEL4WS (Business Process Execution Language for Web Services) provides the syntax and a set of operators for modelling workflow. With a suitable engine the specified workflow can be executed accordingly and the relevant services will be invoked. However, the engine and the specifications do not provide facilities to cope with a change of services at runtime. The authors have proposed an approach to tackle this issue. The authors also argue for the role that agents can contribute to the realisation of flexible workflow by introducing two possible approaches, bottom-up and top-down, in combination with the concept of choreography to model the interactions between partners in a dynamic environment. In addition, the authors are interested in the issues associated with unplanned situations that have not been considered in the design of a workflow. This chapter gives a comprehensive survey on the concept of flexible workflow and uses a simple example to illustrate the concepts and the related issues.

Services contain a set of interfaces to access the functions they provide. The meanings of these interfaces and their provided functions can be misinterpreted by consumers or providers due to a lack of semantic annotation [4]. The introduction of Semantic Web services (SWS) aims to overcome the deficiency of initial web service technologies in service discovery and selection. SWS are a technology with sufficient facilities for annotating web services and reasoning over annotations in order to automate the process of service discovery and selection. Chapter 5 introduces the most prominent frameworks for Semantic Web services that have been adopted by the research and industry communities. OWL-S (Web Ontology Language-S) defines an upper ontology that consists of three elements (service profile, service model and service grounding) for annotating web services with OWL semantics. The Web Service Modelling Ontology (WSMO) is proposed to provide a comprehensive framework that can semantically enable SOA technologies. The Semantic Web Services Framework (SWSF) introduces a formal process language to improve insufficient specification models and a language for the Service Model in OWL-S. WSDL-S and Semantic Annotations for WSDL and XML Schema (SAWSDL) both extend WSDL specifications with extra XML tags to allow XML data types, as well as the messages and operations to be represented in a systematic way. SAWSDL includes additional tags that reference a domain ontology to WSDL documents. These technologies can be very useful in enabling agents to automate the process at different stages in the SOA development life cycle and to manage services at runtime.

Chapter 6 focuses on investigating various issues relating to system faults and dependability in service-oriented computing, and proposes possible solutions. A service is a software component and often exists as a group either virtually or physically, and so faults occurring in one of these components at any basic SOA step have knock-on effects on others. The author regards these steps as publishing, discovery, composition, binding and execution. Failures in each step can be further classified into different types of faults in order to assist in the design of an appropriate dependability mechanism. The choice of type of dependability mechanism is based on the types of faults, characteristics of applications, and the state mechanism in services. Fault avoidance, fault removal, fault forecasting, and fault tolerance are all mechanisms for developing a dependable system, but they are not all applicable to each step in SOA development. Fault forecasting may not be easy to conduct, when faults appear rarely in the system. In this case, artificial faults have to be introduced so that the impact of bugs on the system can be assessed. The criteria for service selection are not only based on functional requirements, but also non-functional properties. Dependability can be an important criterion for the non-functional requirements. There are a number of attributes and mechanisms that can be used to measure dependability properties. Evaluation of the dependability attributes of a service is usually achieved by performing fault injection experiments. The chapter also uses a case study to illustrate fault identification and removal in a web-based dependable system.

Service selection involves a process that measures service properties against the requirements from users. Service selection can be considered as a decision making problem, as it often needs to take multiple attributes, entries, and their relationships into account in order to form a model that can be used for assessment. In this aspect, the methods for service selection can mainly be divided into two categories: Multiple Attribute Decision Making (MADM) and mathematical programming. The criteria for service selection can be divided into functional and non-functional requirements. Non-functional requirements normally refer to a set of attributes that are related to quality of service which can be represented in crisp and fuzzy forms by users to express their subjective opinions and imprecise preferences over these attributes. The QoS profile of a service and its associated values should be derived from group consensus in order to minimise the subjectivity, if there is any. The authors of Chapter 7 propose a quality of services aware web service selection model based on fuzzy linear programming, to identify the differences on service alternatives, and assist service providers and consumers in selecting the most suitable services with consideration of their expectations and preferences. The proposed model is able to handle vague preferences or linguistic opinions for QoS attributes expressed by service consumers and providers in the process of selecting web services. It can also explore the weightings of QoS attributes in order to generate optimal solutions. The approach is capable of realistically gaining a consensual ranking on web service alternatives. Two examples are given to illustrate the proposed model.

Trust and reputation can be considered as another set of criteria for service selection. Trust and reputation have become one of the common approaches for supporting the management of interactions among agents. The authors of Chapter 8 focus on a review of existing models in trust and reputation, and their applications to agent and service-oriented computing. These models can be classified based on three different views namely socio-cognitive, computational, and reputational. The socio-cognitive based models utilise the mental states of an agent to predict and assess the degree of trustworthiness of other agents or a society. The computational based approaches use decision-making or game-theoretical methods to model trust. The trust values in this category are represented in numerical values, and so mathematical techniques such as probability modelling, numerical processing and strategic solutions can be applicable. Reputation can be used as a complementary measurement to derive trustworthiness. One agent can evaluate another's trustworthiness, even though they have never had direct interactions. The authors have carried out a comprehensive review and analysis on these existing approaches and report the results in this chapter. The authors use peer-to-peer architectures and grid computing to demonstrate the benefits that trust and reputation models can bring.

Chapter 9 reports another aspect of QoS for service selection. It focuses on the application of service switching policies to model, measure and improve service performance in multi-tier internet services. Service performance is one of the criteria in QoS that can be explicitly measured, and so performance analysis becomes an important method for effective service evaluation. The available switching policies include proportional and bottleneck-aware switching policies. The adoption of the policy depends on their revenue generation which is derived from a revenue function with a given set of parameters and input values. Two approaches, proactive switching and reactive switching, can be used to choose switching policy. Proactive switching is used to predict the workload and allocate appropriate resources to maintain performance before the performance degrades. Reactive switching is based on the data generated at runtime to make appropriate responses. These approaches have pros and cons, as it depends on the nature of the environment. An agent with built-in knowledge can make appropriate decisions to maximise the revenue (utility). The authors have conducted a comprehensive evaluation on a case study to demonstrate the benefits of performance analysis to service selection.

Finally, Chapter 10 includes a number of research directions proposed by different researchers for future work in area of agent-based service-oriented computing.

1.8 Conclusion

Software agents and services have become important paradigms for modelling distributed systems. Both have a number of similar properties, but there are also some differences. Research on software agent technologies evolved from distributed AI with some influence from distributed systems, and has focused on improving reasoning capabilities and the design of coordination mechanisms for loosely coupled systems. Researchers and developers on service-oriented architectures learned lessons from CORBA, and have put great emphasis on standardising the architectures and the related specifications in order to resolve possible differences between the distributed systems (services). Decision-making capabilities have not been the main issue for study in the area. As the technologies for SOA are becoming mature, the demand on autonomous services will likely increase. In this case, agent technologies can play an important role for services. Agent communities can benefit from the thriving applications of service-oriented architectures, as SOAs can possibly support their development. A number of authors from the agent and service communities were invited to share their thoughts and research results with us, and this book is the result, which aims to help readers learn more about the current state-of-the-art and likely future directions in this area.

Acknowledgements

We would like express our gratitude to Shah Nazaraf for his input.

References

1. A. Arsanjani. Service-oriented Modeling and Architecture. http://www.ibm.com/developerworks/library/ws-soa-design1/, 2004.
2. T. Berners-Lee, J. Hendler and O. Lassila. The Semantic Web. *Scientific American*, May 2001.
3. J. Bradshaw. Introduction to Software Agents. In *Software Agents*, AAAI Press/The MIT Press, 1997.
4. K. Breitman, M. A. Casanova and W. Truszkowski. Semantic Web: Concepts, Technologies and Applications, 219–228, Springer, 2007.
5. D. Booth, H. Haas, F. McCabe, E. Newcomer, M. Champion, C. Ferris and D. Orchard. Web Services Architecture. http://www.w3.org/TR/ws-arch/, 2005.
6. B. Chaib-draa and F. Dignum. Trends in Agent Communication Language. *Computational Intelligence*, 2(5), 2002.

7. J.-Y. Chung and K.-M. Chao. A view on service-oriented architecture. *Service Oriented Computing and Applications*, Springer, 1(2), 93–95, 2007.
8. M. Colan. Service-Oriented Architecture expands the vision of Web services, Part 1. http://www.ibm.com/developerworks/webservices/library/ws-soaintro.html?S_TACT=105AGX04&S_CMP=LP#N10053, 2004.
9. G. Coulouris, J. Dollimore and T. Kindberg. Distributed Systems: Concepts and Design, Addison-Wesley, 2000.
10. M. R. Cutkosky, R. S. Engelmore, R. E. Fikes, M. R. Genesereth, T. R. Gruber, W. S. Mark, J. M. Tenenbaum and J. C. Weber. PACT: An Experiment in Integrating Concurrent Engineering Systems. *IEEE Computer*, 26(1), 28–37, 1993.
11. T. Erl. Service-Oriented Architecture: Concepts, Technology, and Design. Prentice Hall, 2005.
12. O. Etzioni and D. S. Weld. Intelligent agents on the Internet: Fact, fiction, and forecast. *IEEE Expert*, 10(4), 44–49, 1995.
13. T. Finin, J. Weber, G. Wiederhold, M. Gensereth, R. Fritzzon, D. McKay, J. McGuire, R, Pelavin, S, Shapiro and C. Beck. DRAFT Specification of the KQML Agent-Communication Language, 1993.
14. S. Franklin and A. Graesser. Is It an Agent or Just a Program? A Taxonomy for Autonomous Agents. In *Proceedings of the Third International Workshop on Agent Theories, Architectures, and Languages*, Springer-Verlag, 1996.
15. H. Haas and A. Brown. Web Services Glossary. http://www.w3.org/TR/ws-gloss/, 2004.
16. B. Henderson-Sellers and P. Giorgini. Agent-Oriented Methodologies. Idea Group Publishing, 2005.
17. R. High, S. Kinder and S. Graham. IBM's SOA Foundation: An Architectural Introduction and Overview. http://download.boulder.ibm.com/ibmdl/pub/software/dw/webservices/ws-soa-whitepaper.pdf, 2005.
18. IBM. Getting Started with WebSphere Enterprise Service Bus V6. http://www.redbooks.ibm.com/abstracts/sg247212.html, 2006.
19. H. Kreger and J. Estefan. Navigating the SOA Open Standards Landscape around Architecture. https://www.opengroup.org/projects/soa/uploads/40/20044/W096.pdf, 2009.
20. D. B. Lange and O. Mitsuru. Programming and Deploying Java Mobile Agents Aglets, 1st edition, Addison-Wesley, 1998
21. H. Nwana. Software agents: An overview. *The Knowledge Engineering Review*, 11(3), 205–244, 1996.
22. H. S. Nwana, D. T. Ndumu, L. C. Lee and J. C. Collis. ZEUS: A toolkit and approach for building distributed multi-agent systems. In *Proceedings of the third annual conference on Autonomous Agents*, 360–361, 1999.
23. OASIS. OASIS Reference Model for SOA, Version 1.0. OASIS Standard, docs.oasis-open.org/soa-rm/v1.0/soa-rm.pdf, 2006.
24. OASIS. OASIS Reference Architecture for SOA Foundation, Version 1.0. OASIS Public Review Draft 1, docs.oasis-open.org/soa-rm/soa-ra/v1.0/soa-ra-pr-01.pdf, 2008.
25. OMG. OMG SOA Modeling Language (OMG SoaML) Specification for the UML Profile and Metamodel for Services (UPMS), Revised Submission. www.omg.org/cgi-bin/doc?ad/08-11-01, 2008.
26. The Open Group. The Open Group SOA Ontology, Draft Technical Standard. www.opengroup.org/projects/soa-ontology, 2009.
27. The Open Group. The Open Group SOA Governance Framework, Draft Technical Standard. www.opengroup.org/projects/soa-governance, 2009.
28. The Open Group. The Open Group Service Integration Maturity Model (OSIMM), Draft Technical Standard. www.opengroup.org/projects/osimm, 2009.
29. The Open Group. The Open Group SOA Reference Architecture, Draft Technical Standard. www.opengroup.org/projects/soa-ref-arch, 2009.
30. M. Rao and P. Georgeff. BDI-agents: From Theory to Practice. In *Proceedings of the First International Conference on Multiagent Systems (ICMAS 95)*, 1995.
31. M. Rao and P. Georgeff. Formal models and decision procedures for multi-agent systems. Technical Note, AAII. 1995.

32. A. Sahai, A. Durante and V. Machiraju. Towards Automated SLA Management for Web Service. http://www.hpl.hp.com/techreports/2001/HPL-2001-310R1.pdf, HPL-2001-310, 2001.
33. J. Searle. Speech Acts. Cambridge University Press, 1969.
34. Y. Shoham. An Overview of Agent-oriented Programming. In *Software Agents*, AAAI Press, 1997.
35. D. Sprott and L. Wilkes. Understanding Service-Oriented Architecture. *Microsoft Architect Journal*, http://msdn.microsoft.com/en-us/library/aa480021.aspx, 2004.
36. M. Wooldridge. Introduction to Multiagent Systems. Wiley, 2009.
37. M. Wooldridge. Reasoning about Rational Agents. The MIT Press, 2000.
38. M. Wooldridge, N.R Jennings and D. Kinny. The Gaia Methodology for Agent-Oriented Analysis and Design. *Journal of Autonomous and MultiAgent Systems*, 3(3), 285–312, 2000.

Chapter 2
Service Advertisement and Discovery

Shanshan Yang and Mike Joy

Abstract Service Advertisement and Discovery is a fundamental process in service oriented computing, which also provides a precondition for other processes such as service selection and composition (these will be covered in detail in later chapters). This chapter provides an introductory overview of the concepts, standards and current developments related to Service Advertisement and Discovery, summarised from the perspectives of system architecture, data structures, system requirements and Web Services. The incorporation of agent-based technology into Service Advertisement and Discovery is covered, and the chapter concludes with a discussion of future research challenges in this area.

2.1 Introduction to Service Advertisement and Discovery

A service is "a software system designed to support interoperable machine-to-machine interaction over a network" [73]. The purpose of a service is to "provide some functionality on behalf of its owner—a person or organisation, such as a business or an individual" [73]. The service provider is the entity that provides a particular service, and the service requester (or consumer) is the entity that wishes to make use of a provider's service. The goal of finding an appropriate service (the process of performing discovery) requires the service requester and provider to "become known to each other", and it is necessary to ensure that service descriptions are published somewhere (in a registry) before that information is available to others. This task is performed by another entity—a service broker [49].

Shanshan Yang
Department of Computer Science, University of Warwick, Coventry, CV4 7AL, UK
e-mail: Shanshan.Yang@dcs.warwick.ac.uk

Mike Joy
Department of Computer Science, University of Warwick, Coventry, CV4 7AL, UK
e-mail: M.S.Joy@warwick.ac.uk

N. Griffiths, K.-M. Chao (eds.), *Agent-Based Service-Oriented Computing*,
Advanced Information and Knowledge Processing,
DOI 10.1007/978-1-84996-041-0_2,

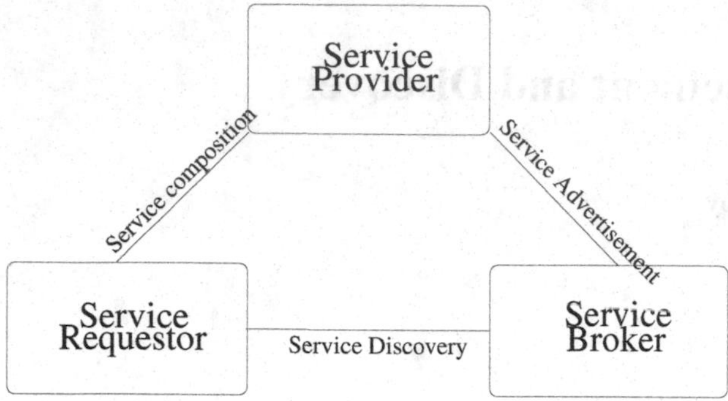

Fig. 2.1 Service oriented architecture

Most authors consider that a basic service oriented architecture consists of three different entities: services *providers* and *requesters* and a service *broker* (registry) [13,31,48,53,67], and the relationships between these entities are illustrated in Figure 2.1. Dustdar and Treiber [31] identify the role of the service provider as one of providing descriptions, and that of the broker as publishing them. The requester contacts a broker in order to locate a suitable service to fulfil a given task, and when an appropriate service has been identified, the broker will additionally provide information about how that service can be invoked. The broker uses a *service registry* (repository) to store the necessary information about services, allowing both user searches and the publication of service descriptions. Searching for and locating services, in order to identify matches between service requesters and providers, is regarded as a key issue, and service *brokers* (or *registries*) play a major role in this task. Thus the role of the service broker and its registry is central to the current model of service oriented computing [28].

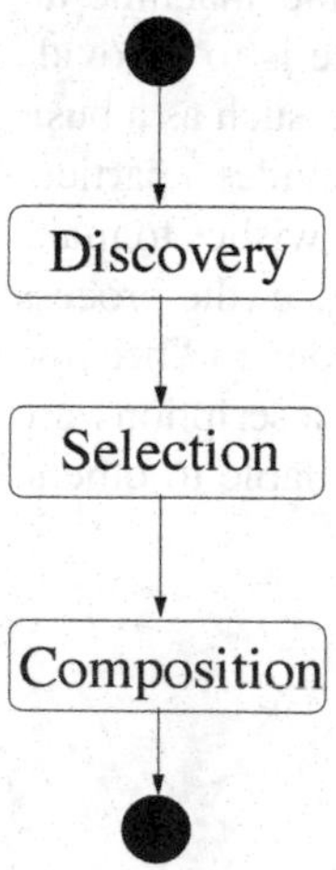

Fig. 2.2 Service execution workflow

Singh and Huhns' [75] summary (Figure 2.2) of the services execution workflow identifies the activity of service discovery as the first step, followed by the other processes including service selection and composition. Some or all of these steps can be performed offline or at runtime. Service discovery deals with finding services that meet a specified description, whereas selection deals with "choosing appropriate services from among those that are discovered for the given description" [80]. Service composition deals with combining small services into larger ones to meet a specified goal [8, 10]. As Wu [93] remarks, "As an essential SOA activity, [service discovery] paves the way for conducting further important SOA activities such as service sharing, reusing and composing in a dynamically changing environment." In this chapter, we consider the first phase—service advertisement and discovery—since in order to discover the services needed by the requester, it is necessary to specify and publish the services effectively first, which means that service advertisement provides a essential precondition for service discovery. We focus in particular on web services, that use web technologies to implement a service-oriented architecture.

There are no generally accepted formal definitions of either Service Advertisement or Discovery (or synonymous phrases), and different approaches to describing them have been employed. For example, Yu et al. [95] define *service publication* as "to make the service description available in the registry so that the service client can find it" and *service lookup* as to "query the registry for a certain type of service and then retrieve the service description." The service description is identified as containing both syntactic information (such as the data formats and protocols used by the services) and semantic information (relating to the domain in which the services are employed together with generic issues such as service functionality and quality of service). Vitvar [87] describes *discovery* as "tasks for identifying and locating services which can achieve a requester's goal", whereas Singh and Huhns [75] view discovery as "the act of locating a machine-processable description of a web service that may have been previously known and that meets certain functional criteria".

Advertising service information is normally considered at the same time as service discovery. Current research in service advertisement focuses on how web services are described, or specified, or published from a technical view, such as what standards people should adopt, or what architecture could be used effectively.

A number of researchers [12, 55, 58, 69] also suggest that agent technologies can be fitted into service oriented architectures, to improve the effectiveness of the service advertisement and discovery process. Agents can be members of multi-agent environments acting not only as brokers, but also as service providers and consumers. Details of agent based approaches will be covered after we have introduced the fundamental technologies and current developments of service advertisement and discovery.

2.2 Basic Technologies

It is commonly agreed that three basic standards are currently in use for web service advertisement and discovery [17,20,31,37,48], each with its own specific role.

- SOAP: Communication—how services can be used
- WSDL: Description—how services can be published
- UDDI: Discovery—how services can be discovered

Fundamental to the efficacy of these standards is the use of a common communications language [75], and XML is used by each. The communications protocol is defined by SOAP, and WSDL includes support for passing information about functions supported by services, including their names, parameters and result types. UDDI specifies the contents of the registry, enabling users to search for services and find sufficient information for their deployment—an essential prerequisite if web services are to be meaningful. These standards have been developed by organisations including the World Wide Web Consortium (W3C) [73], OASIS [61] and the Open Group [64] since 2000 with the latest versions published in 2007.

2.2.1 SOAP

In the context of web services, SOAP (Simple Object Access Protocol) is regarded as the standard message protocol for exchanging XML data over the Internet. SOAP is a stateless paradigm which enables complex interactions between services through request/response exchanges and other unidirectional messages. However, SOAP lacks support for the transmission of semantic data, such as routing and firewall traversal [25].

A SOAP message is essentially an XML element with two XML child elements, a head and a body. These contain descriptions of the message content and how to process it, encoding rules (for application-specific data types), and the representations of remote procedure calls and responses [86]. This information is then wrapped into an envelope, and is bound to a transport protocol for the purposes of the actual information exchange [78]. The following is an example of a SOAP message for invoking a web service for getting a stock price, which is cited from the W3C School website [88]:

```
<?xml version="1.0"?>
  <soap:Envelope
    xmlns:soap=
      "http://www.w3.org/2001/12/soap-envelope"
    soap:encodingStyle=
      "http://www.w3.org/2001/12/soap-encoding">
       <soap:Body xmlns:m=
      "http://www.example.org/stock">
           <m:GetStockPrice>
              <m:StockName>IBM</m:StockName>
           </m:GetStockPrice>
       </soap:Body>
  </soap:Envelope>
```

2.2.2 WSDL

WSDL (Web Service Description Language) formally provides a model for describing interfaces for web services [75, 86, 89]. A WSDL description specifies the location of the service, the operations for invoking and consuming the web service, and supports binding for defining message formats and protocol details. The following is a typical structure of a WSDL document, which is cited from W3C School [88]:

```
<definitions>
  <types>definition of types</types>
  <message>definition of a message</message>
  <portType>
    <operation>definition of a operation</operation>
  </portType>
  <binding>definition of a binding</binding>
  <service>
    <port>definition of a port</port>
  </service>
</definitions>
```

A typical WSDL document contains the following elements. The type element specifies the complex data types for a message, which describe the data being communicated between the web service and the requester. A set of messages and their directions (input or output) form the operations the service exposes. A set of operations then forms a port type, for each of which the concrete protocol and data format specifications are referred to as a binding. The association of a network address with a binding defines a port, and a collection of ports defines a service. In a single WSDL file multiple services can be described [92].

WSDL defines services as "collections of network endpoints or ports". The abstract definitions of messages and the endpoints/ports are then separated from their concrete implementation, such as protocols and data formats, allowing for reuse of those definitions [73].

2.2.3 UDDI

UDDI (Universal Description, Discovery and Integration) is a registry of web service descriptions, allowing users (such as businesses) to publish descriptions of themselves and their services (together with technical information about service interfaces), and clients (such as customers) to identify appropriate service descriptions and create bindings to them (using SOAP) [89, 96]. Wang [89] summarises a UDDI registry as being "similar to a CORBA trader and can be considered as a DNS service for business applications". It serves as a generic data model for providing detailed web service specifications including business entities, technical access information, natural language descriptions, keyword-based classification scheme and relevant technical specifications [25].

The initial idea of maintaining a central registry for publicly available web services by large vendors, such as IBM or Microsoft, has been abandoned because a single repository can not meet all the needs for different specific SOA systems [96]. Version 3 of the UDDI specification is over 400 pages long and contains over 300 function calls. This complexity (for end users) has led to the closure of the public UDDI Business registry and has hindered its widespread adoption, and has led to speculation that future registries will be private [93]. As Chappell [21] remarks: "the public registry UDDI is too complex for end users since UDDI specification is more driven by its primary members than feedback from the real world end users". However, Baresi and Miraz [6] also suggest that the central registry will continue to be important since not all companies will have the facilities for servicing requests locally, and Wu [93] considers that "most private registries would focus on a specific, closed domain".

Both private and public registries follow the two principals of UDDI specifications relating to the composition, structure and operation of a registry—the information provided about each service (including its encoding) and an API specifying how to update the registry and how to make queries. The information encoded by UDDI is of three possible types—*white pages* (names, contact information), *yellow pages* (categories of information based on service types) and *green pages* (technical data) [25,92].

A recent development is UDDIe, an extension to UDDIe which incorporates service leasing and replication. UDDIe includes the ability to search for services based on *blue pages* (user defined properties associated with a service). Support for service leases, by which a service is restricted to storage in the registry for a limited period of time, enhances the dynamic capabilities of the registry [74].

2.3 Web Service Registry Architectures

This section covers how a web service registry supports and implements service advertisement and discovery. Currently, a number of architectures for web service advertisement and discovery have been developed, influenced by the architectures of different service oriented systems, which can be viewed from both structural and functional perspectives. However, the technology is still emerging, and components still being developed include quality of service descriptions and interaction models.

The main structure difference between different architectures is about how the registries are distributed, and three types of architectures have been proposed, namely *centralised, decentralised* and *hybrid*.

2.3.1 Centralised Registries

In a centralised registry (such as UDDI), all web service registry entries are contained within a single "well known" central entity used by each web service provider, similar to a traditional client-server approach [22, 31, 39].

However, there are limitations on this type of architecture. First of all, a centralised registry is not scalable—it can only support small scale systems. Simple easy-to-use technologies such as UPnP, SLP and Jini [39] and the DS-1, Hawkeye and RGMA approaches for grid systems [47] have been reported as examples of small-scale centralised approaches which do not scale well. The second limitation is that it is unsuitable for dynamic environments, and Chamri-Doundane et al. [39] point out that frequent changes affect the system behaviour and its efficiency. The third is that a centralised registry does not handle fault-tolerance well, there being the possibility of a single point of failure [77].

Despite these limitations, several centralised approaches exist, and are effectively applied in situations where scalability, dynamism and fault tolerance are not paramount. Below, we introduce a selection of example centralised systems.

The ebXML (electronic business XML) standard defines a framework within which businesses can co-operate. It is similar to UDDI, but is broader in scope, being able to store arbitrary data and specifying interrelated components for business activities. Two interfaces are specified, LifeCycleManager (which handles the submission of new objects to the registry, the classification of existing objects and the removal of obsolete objects) and QueryManager (which handles the processing of client requests to locate web services using either SQL queries or filters) [33].

SLP (Service Location Protocol) is used by devices (such as printers) on a (local) network to announce services. The centralised service repository is known as a directory agent (DA), and service agents (SAs) and user agents (UAs) use the DA to register and locate services respectively [42, 70].

Sun Microsystems' Jini (now being developed by Apache as Apache River) is a networked technology which allows Java software to be accessed using a centralised service architecture. In addition to service information, lookup services store proxies which enable code to be executed either locally or remotely, thus supporting dynamic use of drivers at runtime [4].

The Salutation Consortium has created an open standard which is both a service discovery and a session management protocol. The architecture is principally targeted at device connectivity on local networks, and relies on devices communicating with a centralised repository (the Salutation Manager) in a fully distributed manner and using a message-passing paradigm. In a low-bandwidth wireless network without fixed IP addresses, the large volume of control traffic generated is problematic. The Consortium was disbanded in 2005 [71].

R-GMA (Relational Grid Monitoring Architecture) is based on a relational data model, and uses a relational database to implement the centralised GMA registry [47].

2.3.2 Decentralised Registries

As opposed to centralised systems, the localisation of services in a decentralised registry is completely distributed and diffused. This type of registry architecture has been applied to different types of modern environments, including peer-to-peer networks, mobile-ad-hoc-networks and Grids [39].

2.3.2.1 Peer-to-Peer Networks

In a Peer-to-Peer (P2P) network, each node is (in some sense) equivalent to every other node. Applications rely on ad-hoc connections between nodes (peers) without a centralised server, and the advantage lies in scalability, robustness, and ease of deployment and maintenance. An example set of protocols that supports a P2P architecture is Sun Microsystem's JXTA, which includes features such as service advertisement and messaging in addition to basic peer management [55]. Each service provider has a local registry and performs the roles both of service provider and of registry, but only for the period of time that the provider is connected to the P2P network, thus limiting the lifespan of each registry entry and enabling a dynamic registry structure with resource localisation and sharing [31,39,66].

A number of P2P approaches to web services exist. Schmidt and Parashar's architecture [72] uses distributed hash tables and an indexing system based on the CHORD data lookup protocol. Web services are indexed using descriptive keywords, and a dimension reducing indexing scheme is used. Dustdar and Treiber's [32] VISR (View based Integration of Web Service Registries) is a peer to peer architecture which combines multiple web service registries with transient web service providers in a seamless integrated system. "Views" serve as an abstraction layer which uses web service profiles as a global data model, and are supported by a simple grammar (View Description Language). The web service profiles allow extra information to supplement the registry entries without affecting the original entries themselves [32].

2.3.2.2 Mobile Ad-Hoc Networks

In a Mobile Ad-Hoc Network (MANET), cooperating autonomous mobile devices acting as router nodes form a dynamic network infrastructure. Wireless technologies are usually employed, and the use of standard protocols and interfaces ensures that the devices communicate effectively so that advertising and discovery is possible [35,54,59].

Tyan and Mahmoud [83] propose grouping mobile nodes into clusters, with one device in each cluster acting as a gateway for routing purposes, using a location-aware network layer routing protocol. The gateways also improve service discovery performance by acting as directories, and a context-aware agent-based service selection mechanism is included. This solution addresses issues of scalability and context-awareness since complex graph algorithms are no longer needed to maintain the clusters and support management of the network topology.

Carlos et al. [19] have developed a component-based service discovery framework, which can be used in both fixed and ad hoc networks, and supports adaptive service discovery middleware. This approach enhances framework configurability and minimises resource usage.

Talwar et al. [82] have developed a novel resource and service discovery mechanism for MANETs using RIMAs (Routing Intelligent Mobile Agents), which collect and index information on service availabilities as well as network resource and routing data. Each RIMA is associated with a node in the network, and each mobile node is *close* to one or more RIMA nodes. Discovery agents are used by service requesters to identify resources by using the indices contained in the RIMA nodes. The mechanism has been tested by simulating MANETs with up to 800 nodes.

2.3.2.3 Grid Computing

Issarny et al. [50] characterise Grid computing as addressing "the creation of distributed communities that share resources such as storage space, sensors, software application and data, by means of a persistent, standards-based service infrastructure". Currently used principally by the scientific community as a high-performance computing infrastructure, a Grid can support more general large-scale applications requiring substantial data processing and computation. Grid computing often requires secure resource sharing amongst multiple institutions, and this model does not fit in well with the current Internet infrastructure [55].

Globus Toolkit (GT) is an open source set of libraries and programs that has been developed over the last few years by the Globus Alliance consortium to support the building of distributed system services and applications. It addresses the fundamental issues such as resource discovery, resource access, resource management, data movement and security [36]. The architecture contains three sets of components: a set of implementation services, a set of service containers, and a set of client libraries [40].

GISs (Grid Information Services) form a key component in many Grid architectures, and S-Club is a mechanism which supports efficient service discovery on a GIS mesh network. Using the existing CROWN (China Research and Development environment Over Wide-area Network) GIS network, S-Club forms an overlay in which services are clustered as "clubs", each club providing services of a given type. A given service may belong to multiple clubs, and a service requester will initially use the S-Club overlay to identify providers by searching appropriate clubs. The overlay is constructed dynamically, and a minimum-spanning tree topology is used in order to ensure that messages are transmitted efficiently. Experimental results show that the S-Club approach improves response times for searches as well as reducing traffic overhead [47].

Bell et al. [9] propose an extension of the Grid framework to include semantic services in a real-world commercial context—a "Business Grid". An upper service ontology is used to provide the semantic context, and web services taken from investment banks have been used to validate the approach.

Yu et al. [95] propose the Grid Market Directory (GMD), a registry which manages the provision of services efficiently using a pricing mechanism. It is designed to be applied to market-oriented Grids to "support an infrastructure that enables the creation of a marketplace for meeting of providers and consumers". GMD contains two components: the portal manager and the query web service. The portal manager covers the tasks of "provider registration, service publication and management, and service browsing", and the query web service allows clients such as resource brokers to query the GMD and obtain resource information to identify those that satisfy the user's QoS requirements [95].

2.3.3 Hybrid Registries

In addition to pure centralised and decentralised architectures, some hybrid (federated) systems have been proposed, in which registry information is distributed amongst multiple entities in a peer-to-peer manner, but access to the registry information is through dedicated "super peer" nodes (peer registries). Such systems appear to users as centralised, since the use of peers is transparent and the user is unaware of the distributed implementation. This approach allows for registries to specialise in particular types of web service, although this benefit must be weighed against the increased communication overhead [31, 94].

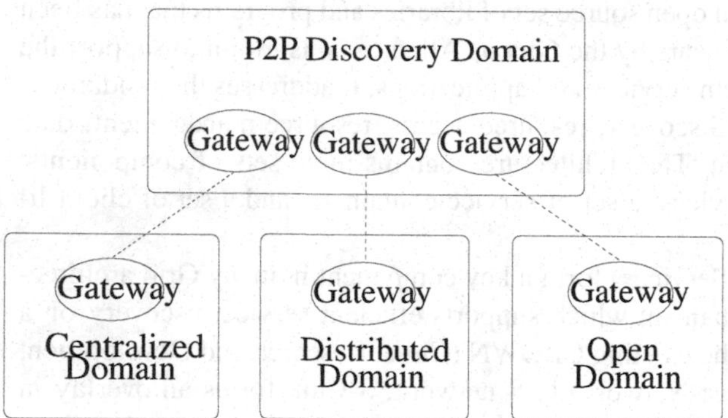

Fig. 2.3 Ghamri-Doudane's service discovery architecture

Ghamri-Doudane et al. [39] present a purely unstructured service discovery architecture containing components which include centralised, distributed and P2P discovery domains. The intention is to integrate all existing service discovery protocols but with a specific service gateway for each technology, as shown in Figure 2.3 [39].

Verma et al. [86] present a scalable, high performance environment for web service publication and discovery among multiple registries. Using an ontology-based approach, registries are organised into domains, so that web services can be classified using those domains. A semantic approach to the publication and discovery of web services is used, and it is claimed that this is appropriate for systems containing large numbers of registries. METEOR-S is an architecture which supports this environment and an implementation has been tested [86].

Papazoglou and Heuvel [67] (Figure 2.4) introduce the concept of service-syndications, where related businesses form groups based on common interests, and each group has its own UDDI peer registry.

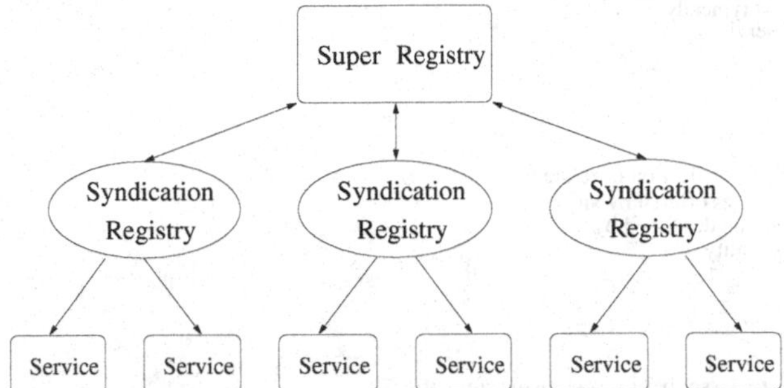

Fig. 2.4 Papazoglou and Heuvel's service discovery architecture

Caron's unstructured peer-to-peer network architecture extends traditional Network-Enabled Server (NES) by enabling tree-based service discovery which takes account of the underlying network topology. The benefits claimed for this approach include improved fault-tolerance and efficiency on wide-area networks [19].

2.4 Data Structures

Data on web services can include complex information, such as collaboration protocols and structured ontological information, in addition to more basic data such as the service name and information about the service provider.

Perhaps the most commonly used data model is UDDI, which is hierarchically structured and contains five data types defined using an XML schema [74]. The tModel data type is used to represent information about a given service, including a technical description of what the service does and how it does it, whilst the other data types contain information about the service providers, the range of services offered by each, and descriptions of the services on offer. Each entity in the model is allocated a unique identifier (UUID), and classified according to a published taxonomy [89]. In versions 1 and 2 of UDDI, the following classification schemes were used [95]:

- the North American Industry Classification System (NAICS),
- the Universal Standard Products and services Code System (UNSPSC), and
- the ISO Geographic taxonomy (ISO 3166).

The use of a taxonomy is seen as important in that it offers a structured framework which facilitates searching for services. The UDDI model is composed of four identity types, as the following diagram (Figure 2.5) illustrates [25]:

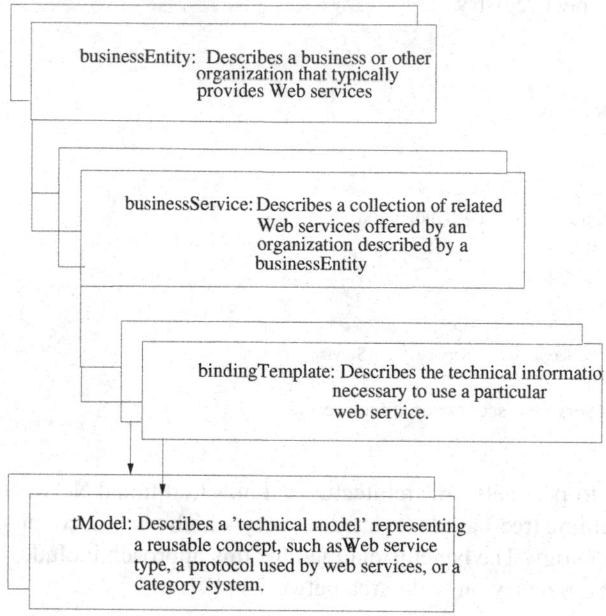

Fig. 2.5 UDDI data model

The ebXML data model is broader in scope than UDDI, and in addition to services it supports further data related to e-business. Data in an ebXML registry takes the form of metadata about objects in the registry (including, but not restricted to, web services) [33].

The Web Service Discovery Architecture (WSDA) is a modular architecture which defines services, interfaces, operations and protocol bindings, based on industry standards. WSDA has the advantage of flexibility, since the modular components can be customised easily and adapted to support a range of behaviours [46].

The Web Services Inspection Language (WSIL) is a distributed approach to the provision of data for service discovery, in contrast to the centralised model adopted by UDDI. Each web service produces a WSIL XML file containing the necessary data (which is similar to the data stored within UDDI), and that file is made accessible by (for example) publishing it using simple naming conventions on an advertised web site [91].

2.5 System Requirements

In this section, registry architectures are viewed from the angle of their common functions and requirements from the users' perspective. Interoperability and matchmaking are the only two core requirements for service advertisement and discovery systems, and the others are optional. As Doulkerdis [29] remarks: "Existing service discovery mechanisms usually focus on exact or semantic matching of static attributes". Although each system is able to meet more that one requirement, no single system meets them all. In the remainder of the section, the requirements are defined, and systems that meet each requirement are discussed.

Interoperability means "the ability to exchange and use information between different heterogeneous web service registry environments" [31]. O'Brien et al. [62] mention that "increased interoperability is the most prominent benefit of SOA", and Yu et al. [95] reinforce this opinion, arguing that, "[i]nteroperability is the core functionality that web services endeavour to achieve".

Matchmaking is "a mechanism by which service requesters can find potential web services (providers) that have capabilities for meeting their specific requirements" [93], and is explicitly supported by models such as Garg's System Template approach [38] which seeks to match instances of related services into groups.

Scalability "defines how well a web service registry responds to increasing load" [31]. An example of an architecture for which scalability has been a major motivation is AtomServ [93], which uses standard web feed technologies (Atom and RSS) accessible through ubiquitous application interfaces such as browsers. The use of UPnP is another means of supporting scalability, such as has been used in CSSD [7].

Fault tolerance is "the ability of a web service registry to continue normal operation despite the presence of hardware or software faults" [31]. Service Address Routing (SAR), which supports a "location-independent" distribution of services across a network, is an example of a fault-tolerant mechanism which has been applied successfully both to tightly-coupled networks and to a loosely-coupled Grid [72].

Reliability means "the degree to which a web service registry is capable of maintaining the service at a given service quality" [31]. This has been addressed, for example, by an extension to Web Service Repository Builder (WSRB) architecture in which a Web service Relevancy ranking Function (WsRF) is used, to modify the service discovery process. WsRF uses QoS metrics, such as reputation and compliance, together with relevancy rankings based on clients' preferences, and the technique has been validated experimentally [1].

Security means "where necessary, communications are both encrypted and authenticated" [26]. As part of the Ninja project, the Secure Service Discovery Service (SSDS) supports a high level of security. SSDS provides clients with directory-style access to services, with encrypted communication facilitated by per-session keys. Individual components are allocated certificates which can be signed by clients and by service providers, and the model then allows a client to identify services they trust based on the levels of trust the client has in the signatories to the services' certificates. Furthermore, SSDS supports signed messages (capabilities) which identify that a user has access to a set of services, thus restricting clients to those services which the system has identified as appropriate and allowed [24, 44, 76].

Context awareness is the ability "to seamlessly adapt behaviour according to the context within which the systems executes". This involves sensing the environment and adapting the behaviour of an application according to both the users' profiles and the available resources [50, 79].

CSSD is an example of a system which uses context (dynamically changing information about the services provided and the user, and the user's environment as provided by an external system) to inform the service discovery algorithm [7]. Another initiative has been the development of MobiShare—a cellular mobile resource architecture—to include Context-Aware Service Directories (CASDs) within the architecture's Cell Administration Servers (CASs) [30].

Mobility refers to the support offered by an architecture for mobile (wireless) devices. For example, the Siena architecture is implemented as an overlay on a GPRS mobile network, uses a distributed publish/subscribe paradigm, and supports a variety of Internet applications and services [18, 23, 29].

It is perhaps useful at this point to note that all systems surveyed here address the issues on interoperability and of matchmaking, most of those systems are also scalable, and roughly half consider fault-tolerance to be an important feature. The other issues are only addressed by few of the systems.

2.6 Advertisement and Discovery Services

A variety of common technologies are currently used by discovery services [85], although Hoffert et al. [45] note that "while discovery services are fairly mature and broadly applicable to today's systems much R&D remains to support emerging systems of ultra-large scale effectively, such as the Global Information Grid". This section discusses those technologies which can be considered mature.

The *Common Object Request Broker Architecture* (CORBA) is a technology which allows objects, possibly created using different languages and implemented on different platforms, to communicate across a network. The CORBA Naming Service is a database containing bindings of names and associated objects, which allows distributed objects to be located by name and accessed by clients—a "white pages" technology. The CORBA Trading Service, in contrast, allows objects to be located based on a requirements description rather than by name—a "yellow pages" technology [63].

The *Data Distribution Service* (DDS) for Real-Time Systems has recently been approved as an OMG standard. In contrast to the client/server approach, DDS adopts a data-centric publish/subscribe (DCPS) model, grouping data into "topics" (sets of related data-objects with a common data type), and allows the user to specify Quality of Service parameters [27].

The *Jini Lookup Service* (JLS) uses Java RMI (Remote Method Invocation) to allow Java clients to discover services (Java objects or proxies) by specifying an interface. This approach benefits from optimisation (such as bytecode and object caching) available through RMI, but Hoffert et al. [45] note that "it can also have undesirable side effects, such as increased latency and jitter when first transferring the object". Although Jini may superficially appear to be a Java version of CORBA, the differences in approach and implementation are substantial [4, 51].

Low-level protocols are used by networks in support of service discovery. For example, *Simple Service Discovery Protocol* (SSDP) is used by UPnP to allow services (such as external devices and resources) to be identified by clients which use those services. The Bluetooth Service Discovery Protocol (SDP) uses the Logical Link Control and Adaptation Protocol (L2CAP) layer to initialise connections for devices via the Logical Link Control and Adaptation Protocol (L2CAP) layer within the short-range wireless network used by Bluetooth. Service Location Protocol (SLP) is a packet-oriented protocol which allows devices to locate services across a LAN, without prior configuration, and is scalable to large networks. Three agents are employed—a user agent which seeks appropriate services, a service agent which provides information about available services, and an optional directory agent which enhances the performance of the service agents by providing a central repository which stores the locations of the services [45].

JXTA is a collection of open-source XML-based protocols which supports a peer-to-peer communication between networked devices and services via a network overlay. Low-bandwidth devices (edge peers), which may only be connected temporarily, are treated differently to super peers, which co-ordinate other peers and facilitate communication through firewalls and between subnets [52].

UDDI supports service discovery by registering service descriptions in the *UDDI Business Registry* (UBR), which users can query to find either a given provider or the category of service [84].

Peer-to-peer (P2P) architectures—perhaps most commonly used for file-sharing and MP3 downloads rather than for more general resources—can also support distributed service provision. *Gnutella* (and its fork Gnutella2) is a P2P resource sharing network which—like products such as *Bittorrent*—is typically used to exchange files, and uses a network overlay scheme together with a number of optimisation techniques. These include QRP (Query Routing Protocol), which uses a hash table to prevent queries being forwarded to inappropriate network nodes, and DQ (Dynamic Querying) which caps the number of results returned by a search and so reduces network traffic [41]. Napster is an architecture which, unlike Gnutella, uses a centralised registry in addition to using network nodes as resource servers, so that the registry can direct traffic to an appropriate server [57].

2.7 Agents in Service Advertisement and Discovery

The technologies and approaches discussed in this chapter present service advertisement and discovery as typically decentralised and asynchronous activities. The software components which implement and support them have attributes—such as autonomy and adaptivity—which are characteristics of an agent-based approach, suggesting that the incorporation of agent technologies into service oriented architectures may improve the effectiveness of the process [15,65]. Singh [75] notes that:

> "Typical agent architectures have many of the same features as service oriented architectures. Agent architectures provide service directories, where agents advertise their distinct functionalities and where other agents search to locate the agents in order to request those functionalities."

Luck [55] also remarks:

> "It is natural to view large systems in terms of the services they offer, and consequently in terms of the entities or agents providing or consuming services. In this view agents act on behalf of service owners, managing across to services, and ensuring that contracts are fulfilled. They also act on behalf of service consumers, locating services, agreeing contracts, and receiving and presenting results."

2.7.1 Agents in Service Oriented Computing

In service oriented systems, an agent can assume a role such as that of service provider, consumer (user) or broker. The tasks a broker agent would be responsible for might include:

- identifying and locating appropriate service agents;
- implementing directory services;
- managing namespace services;
- storing, forwarding and delivering messages;
- managing communication between the other agents, databases and application programs.

Singh and Huhns [75] advocate a generic agent-based service-oriented system architecture containing agent types, as illustrated in Figure 2.6. Of these, directory and broker agents and resource agents perform the tasks of service advertisement and discovery. They claim that "[b]rokers simplify the configuration of multi-agent systems", and note that a broker's knowledge about other agents within a system allows it to identify and negotiate with potential agents which may be able to offer a desired service. Resource agents provide access to information based services, and user agents can behave as "an intermediary between users and information systems" [12,58,69,75].

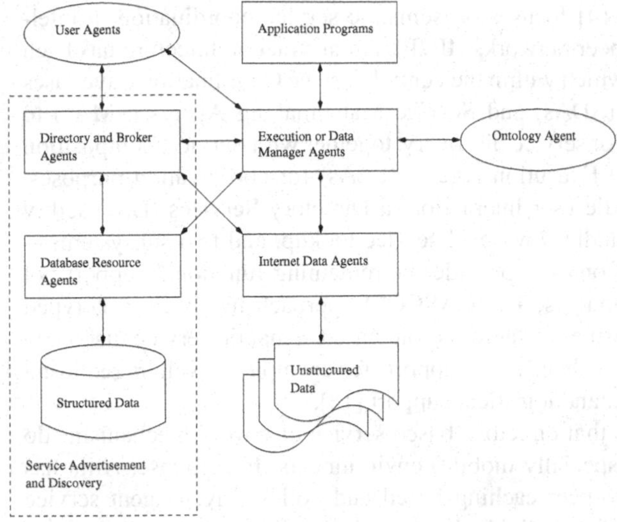

Fig. 2.6 Singh and Huhns' agent based service oriented architecture

2.7.2 *Development of Agents in Service Advertisement and Discovery*

The model offered by Singh and Huhns above is generic, and serves as a useful starting point for exploring other approaches.

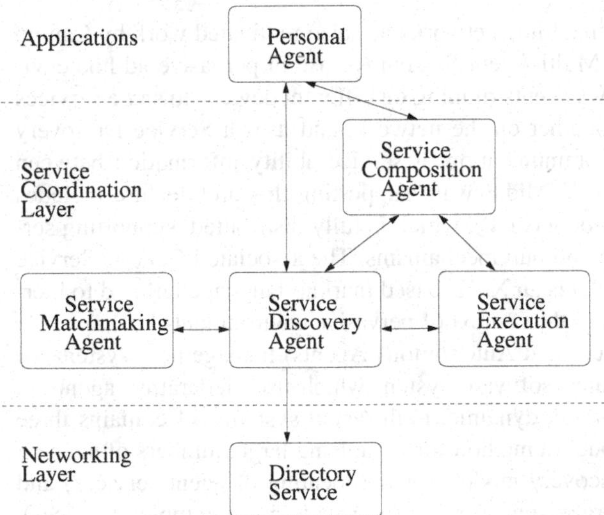

Fig. 2.7 CASCOM: Agent based service oriented architecture

The CASCOM project [14] focuses on semantic service coordination in intelligent agent-based peer-to-peer networks (IP2P). An abstract architecture has been developed (see Figure 2.7) which within the central Service Coordination Layer uses Service Discovery Agents (SDAs) and Service Matchmaking Agents (SMAs) to handle the semantic aspects of service discovery, together with Service Composition Agents (SCAs) and Service Execution Agents (SEAs) for coordination purposes. Personal Agents (PAs) handle user interaction, a Directory Services (DS) facility in the Networking Layer handles low-level service lookup, and two subsystems—Security and Privacy, and Context—provide the remaining functional support not handled by the other components. The CASCOM approach has been prototyped in the field of healthcare business, where its role based semantic service discovery approach provides a novel mechanism to support (for example) travellers requiring complex emergency medical and logistical support [14].

Ratsimor et al. [68] note that directory-based service discovery mechanisms do not work well in ad-hoc (especially mobile) environments. In response, Allia has been developed as a peer-to-peer caching based and policy driven agent service discovery framework, in which individual agents form *alliances*. An alliance (of a node) is a set of local agent nodes in the network whose service information is cached by that node. A member of an alliance is aware of the other agents in that alliance but is not aware of which alliances it is a member of. As the network changes in an ad-hoc manner, so do the alliances which have been set up, based on the local topology in the vicinity of a given node, and on the service advertisements that node has received. The dynamic nature of this approach is claimed to be effective in supporting agent-service discovery in dynamically changing ad-hoc environments. It has been implemented as an extension of the LEAP Agent Platform using Bluetooth as the network communications technology, and its performance has been evaluated in a GlomoSim simulator.

The proximity of agents in ad-hoc networks has also motivated work by Campo et al. [16], who proposed a Multi-Agent System for use in pervasive ad-hoc environments. Their system allows agents running on different devices to share services if those devices are close together on the network, and uses a Service Discovery Agent which supports the communication of service ability information between different agents in the network. Middleware supporting this architecture includes the Pervasive Discovery Protocol (PDP), which is fully distributed, supporting service discovery via both push and pull mechanisms. The associated Generic Service Description Language (GSDL) is an XML-based markup language tailored to hierarchical service descriptions in the context of pervasive environments [16].

The A4 (Agile Architecture and Autonomous Agents) management system for grid computing is a distributed software system which uses federating agents to provide services to a large-scale, dynamic, multi-agent system. A4 contains three models—an hierarchical model (a method for organising large numbers of agents), which is supported by a discovery model (for the locating of agent services) and a coordination model (for organising services to provide more complex services). The hierarchical model is illustrated in Figure 2.8. At the top of the hierarchy is a single broker agent, and each sub-level contains a single coordinator agent together with individual agents and further sub-levels. The topology of the network is dynamic, and each agent can act as a router facilitating communication between agent requesters and service providers. Each agent's service information can be advertised either up or down the hierarchy, and service discovery is likewise facilitated by the topology of the hierarchy. As implemented, agents include the functionality of the PACE performance prediction toolset, allowing efficiency issues for such a system to be investigated [90].

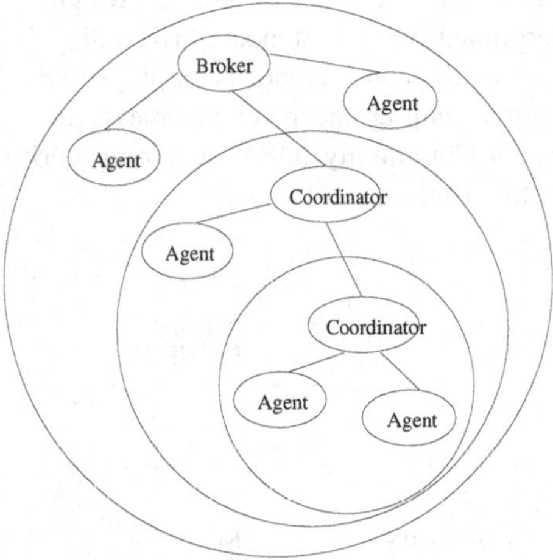

Fig. 2.8 A4: Agent based service oriented architecture

A similar architectural approach has been adopted by the Mobile Service Management Architecture based on Mobile Agent (MA-MSMA), which uses an hierarchical tree-like structure populated by identical mobile agents, each of which can be both a provider and a requester of Grid services. Agents forming internal nodes of the tree adopt the role of broker or lookup agent [43].

The Southampton agent Framework for Agent Research (SoFAR) project shows that the "agent concept can be closely aligned with a web service, in that an agent can be described as a web service and discovered using a standard mechanism UDDI". Using WSDL gives an agent the ability to describe and advertise their capabilities. The use of ontologies as a semantic enhancement to WSDL and UDDI enables services to be discovered and invoked by software through common terminology and shared meanings. Avila-Rosas [5] notes that "this is a vital property in an open system such as the Grid".

The Software Agent-Based Groupware using E-services (SAGE) project "incorporates the use of intelligent agents to integrate human users with web services". The approach taken by SAGE is to identify a (human) user's operational context, and for each agent in the system to learn the rule-based preferences for that user based on that contextual information. This allows for targeting of relevant web services to be identified by the system and presented to the user [12].

Matchmaking and brokering are multi-agent coordination mechanisms for web services. Sycara et al. [81] have used novel extensions to the Web Ontology

Language for Semantic Web Services (OWL-S) and to its process model to implement a broker which both provides discovery services and mediates between agents and web services. They suggest agents might subcontract, by finding and interacting with a provider who can solve a goal. The problems with this approach are similar to those associated with brokering, their current research concerns automatic multi-agent interaction and automatic Web service composition [81].

The Agent Approach for Service Discovery and Utilisation (AASDU) (Figure 2.9) is a flexible and scalable multi-agent system which allows dynamic insertion and deletion of services and lightweight autonomous agents. The approach is underpinned by web standards (including UDDI, SOAP, WSDL and XML), and a communication protocol is employed which does not depend on addresses of the agents sending and receiving messages. An extension to the Oak Ridge Mobile Agent Community (ORMAC) framework is used as the basis of the agent architecture [65].

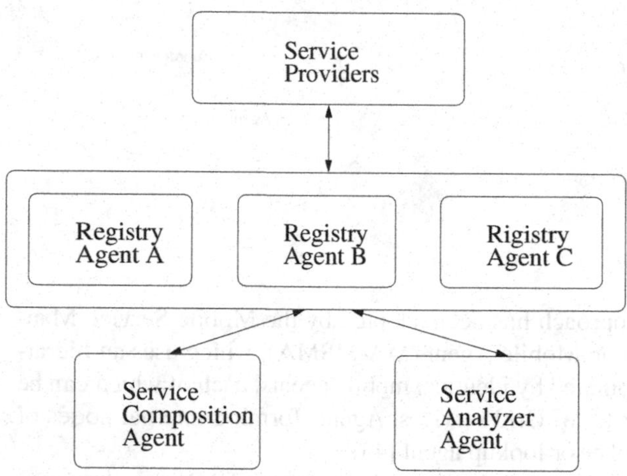

Fig. 2.9 Palathingal and Chandra's agent based service oriented architecture

2.8 Challenges in Service Advertisement and Discovery

Service advertisement and discovery is a focus of active research, and a number of popular areas of investigation and specific challenges have been identified, and can be categorised as for system requirements and for system modelling.

2.8.1 System Requirements

Scalability and adaptability [1,15]: In particular, Wu [93] proposes that efficient mechanisms should be introduced to allow "system function gracefully at very high load of service discovery requests given reasonable resource consumptions".

Security: Different security requirements for different environments, such as in mobile computing, should be identified. Issues might include secure service registration, and deregistration; secure discovery and secure delivery, secure communication protocols and more appropriate trust models and communication paradigms [3,24,26,44,76].

Quality of service: Efficient protocols for the awareness of quality of service should be introduced, as "QoS information is particularly important for real time applications like streaming high quality video over wireless networks" [34].

Interoperability: Interoperability is also important since complex messages exchanged by web services are structurally and semantically heterogeneous [2,56].

2.8.2 System Modelling

Theoretical foundations: Little work has been done on theoretical foundations. No generally accepted principle or procedure for system design and evaluation has been identified so far, although a number of definitions regarding the concepts and principles of service and service oriented architecture have been proposed by different scholars [49,60].

System structures: A number of different styles of system structures have been summarised in Section 2, and it is challenge to design more and moreover to combine these styles of structures together to improve the overall effectiveness of the systems [32].

Agents based service oriented computing: We have introduced the idea of agent based service discovery in Section 7, and it is important to identify and adopt efficient approaches to merge agent technology into service oriented computing, and develop efficient algorithms for agents to search, match and compose services [5,11,76].

Technologies integration: It is also an opportunity and challenge to integrate SOA with other technologies, such as wireless communications and the Grid, in order to provide more powerful advertisement and discovery mechanisms [19,54,96].

2.9 Summary

The Service Broker (or Registry), which is one of the entities in current model of Service Oriented Computing, plays a key role in the process of service advertisement and discovery. Three types of registry architectures have been introduced—*centralised*, *decentralised* and *hybrid*—together with major users' requirements for service advertisement and discovery systems. We have also described a number of *mature* discovery technologies in this area, and explored how agent based technology might improve the effectiveness of this process. This chapter provides a foundation for understanding the rest of the processes in Agent Based Service Oriented Computing.

References

1. Al-Masri, E., Mahnoud, Q.H.: Discovery the Best Web Service. In: WWW Poster Paper, pp. 1257–1258. ACM Press, Canada (2001)
2. Anjum, F.: Chanllenges on Providing Services in a Ubiquitous, Mobile Environment. In: the 3rd International Conference on Mobile and Ubiquitous Systems: Networking and Services, pp. 1–3. IEEE Press, California (2006)
3. Antonopoulos, N., Shafarenko, A.: An Active Organisation System for Customized, Secure Agent Discovery. The Journal of Supercomputing. 20, 5–35 (2001)
4. Arnold, K., Osullivan, B., Scheifler, R.W., Waldo, J., Wollrath, A., O'Osullivan, B.: The Jini Specification. Addison Wesley, Reading (1999)
5. Avila-Rosas, A., Moreau, L., Dianlani, V., Miles, S., Liu, X.: Agents for the Grid: A Comparison with Web Services. In: Workshop on Challenges in Open Agent Systems, PP. 238–244. Bologna (2002)
6. Baresi, L., Miraz, M.: A Distributed Approach for the Federation of Heterogeneous Registries. In: 4th International conference on Service Oriented Computing, pp. 240–251. Chicago (2006)
7. Balken, R., Haukrogh, J., Jensen, J.L., Jensen, M.N., Roost, L.J., Toft, P.N., Olsen, R.L., Schwefel, H.P.: Context Sensitive Service Discovery Experiment Prototype and Evaluation. Wireless Personal Communications. 40, 417–431 (2007)
8. Baresi, L., Nitto, E., Ghezzi, C., Guinea, S.: A Framework for the Deployment of Adaptable Web Service Compositions. SOCA. 1, 75–91 (2007)
9. Bell, D., Ludwig, S.A., Lycett, M.: Enterprise application reuse: Semantic Discovery of Business Grid Services. Information Technology Management. 8, 223–239 (2007)
10. Benbernou, S., Hacid, M., Liris,: Resolution and Constraint Propagation for Semantic Web Services Discovery. Distributed and Parallel Databases. 18, 65–81 (2005)
11. Blake, M., Cheung, W., Jaeger, M.C., Wombacher, A.: WSC-06: the Web Service Challenge. In: the IEEE international Conference on E-Commerce Technology, pp. 62. IEEE Press, New York (2006)
12. Blake, M.B., Kahan, D. R., Nowlan, M. F.: Context-aware Agents for Use r-oriented Web Services Discovery and Execution. Distributed and Parallel Databases. 21, 39–58 (2007)
13. Bucur, D., Bardram, J.E.: Resource Discovery in Activity-Based Sensor Networks. Mobile Networks and Applications. 12, 129–142 (2007)
14. Caceres, C., Fernandez, A., Ossowski, S., Vasirani, M.: Agent-Based Semantic Service Discovery for Healthcare: An Organizational Approach. In: IEEE Intelligent Systems, pp.11–20. IEEE Press, New York (2006)
15. Cao, J., Kerbyson, D.J., Nudd, G.R.: High Performance Service Discovery in Large-Scale Multi-Agent and Mobile-Agnet Systems. International Journal of Software Engineering and Knowledge Engineering. 11, 621–641 (2001)
16. Campo, C.: Service Discovery in Pervasive Multi-agent Systems. In: Workshop on Ubiquitous Agents on embedded, wearable, and mobile devices, pp. 133–146. Bologna (2002)
17. Campo, C., Munoz, M., Perea, J.C., Mann, A., Garcia-Rubio, C.: PDP and GSDL: A New Service Discovery Middleware to Support Spontaneous Interactions in Pervasive Systems. In: 3rd IEEE International Conference on Pervasive Computing and Communications, pp. 178–182. IEEE Press, New York (2005)

18. Caporuscio, M., Carzangiga, A., Wolf, A.L.: Design and Evaluation of a Support Service for Mobile, Wireless Publish/Subscribe Applications. IEEE Transactions on Software Engineering. 29, 1059–1071 (2003)
19. Caron, E., Desprez, F., Tedeschi, C.: Enhancing Computational Grids with Peer-to Peer Technology for Large Scale Service Discovery. Journal of Grid Computing. 5, 337–360 (2007)
20. Chakraborty, D., Joshi, A., Yesha, Y., Finin, T.: Toward Distributed Service Discovery in Pervasive Computing Environments. IEEE Transactions on Mobile Computing. 5, 97–112 (2006)
21. Chappell, D.: Who Cares about UDDI. Addison Wesley, New York (2002)
22. Charlet, D., Issarny, V., Chibout, R.: Service Discovery in Multi-radio Networks: An assessment of Existing Protocols. In: MSWiM'06, pp. 229–238. ACM Press, New York (2006)
23. Chen, H., Joshi, A., Finin, T.: Dynamic Service Discovery for Mobile Computing: Intelligent Agents Meet Jini in the Aether. Cluster Computing. 4, 343–354 (2001)
24. Cotroneo, D., graziano, A., Russo, S.: Security Requirements in Service Oriented Architectures for Ubiquitous Computing. Middleware for Pervasive and Ad-Hoc Computing. In: 2nd Workshop on Middleware for Pervasive and Ad-Hoc Computing, pp.172–177. ACM Press, Canada (2004)
25. Curbera, F., Duftler, M., Khalaf, D., Nagy, W., Mukhi, N., Weerawarana, S.: Unraveling the Web Services Web, An Introduction to SOAP, WSDL, and UDDI. IEEE Internet Computing. 6, 86–93 (2002)
26. Czerwinski, S., Zhao, B., Hodes, T. D., Joseph, vA.D., Katz, R.H.: An Architecture for A Secure Service Discovery Service. In: International Conference on Mobile Computing and Networking, pp. 24–35. Washington (1999)
27. Data Distribution Service, `http://www.omg.org`
28. Degwekar, S., Lam, H., Su, S.Y.W.: Constraint-Based Brokering(CBB) for Publishing and Discovery of Web Services. Electronic Commerce Research. 7, 45–67 (2007)
29. Doulkeridis, C., Vazirgiannis, M.: Querying and Updating a Context-aware Service Directory in Mobile Environments. In: IEEE/WIC/ACM Int. Conference on Web Intelligence (WI'04), pp.562–565, IEEE Press, New York (2004)
30. Doulkeridis, C., Zafeiris, V. N?rv?g, K., Vazirgiannis, M., Giakoumakis, E.A.: Context-Based Caching and Routing for P2P Web Service Discovery. Distrib Parallel Databases. 21, 59–84 (2007)
31. Dustdar, S., Treiber, M.: A View Based Analysis on Web Service Registries. Distributed and Parallel Databases. 18, 147–171 (2005)
32. Dustdar, S., Treiber, M.: View Based Integration of Heterogeneous Web Service Registries—the Case of VISR. World Wide Web. 9, 457–483 (2006)
33. ebXML Project, `http://www.ebxml.org`
34. Fan, Z., Ho, E.G.: Service Discovery in Ad Hoc Networks: Performance Evaluation and QoS Enhancement. Wireless Personal Communications. 40, pp. 215–231 (2007)
35. Flores-Cortés, C.A., Blair, G.S., Grace, P.: A Multi-Protocol Framework for As-hoc Service Discovery. In: MPAC'06, pp.10. ACM Press, New York (2006)
36. Foster, I.: Globus Toolkit Version 4: Software for Service-Oriented Systems. In: the Proedding of the IFIP International Conference on Network and Parallel Computing, pp. 2–13, Springer-Verlag, New York (2006)
37. Friday, A., Davies, N., Wallbank, N., Catterall, E., Pink, S.: Supporting Service Discovery, Querying and Interaction in Ubiquitous Computing Environments. Wireless Networks. 10, 631–641 (2004)
38. Garg, P., Griss, M., Machiraju, V.: Auto-Discovery Configurations for Service Management. Journal of Network and Systems Management. 11, 217–239 (2003)
39. Ghamri-Doudane, S., Agoulmine, N.: Enhanced DHT-Based P2P Architecture for Effective Resource Discovery and Management. Journal of Network and Systems Management. 15, 335–354 (2007)
40. Globus Project, `http://www.globus.org/`
41. Gnutella Project, `http://www.gnutella.com/`
42. Guttman, E.: Service Location Protocol: Automatic Discovery of IP Network Service. IEEE Internet Computing. 3, 71–80 (1999)

43. He, Y., Wen, W., Jin, H., Liu, H.: Agent based Mobile Service Discovery in Grid Computing. In: Proceedings of the Fifth International Conference on Computer and Information Technology, pp. 78–101. IEEE Press, New York (2005)
44. Hodes, T.D., Czerwinski, S.E, Zhao, B.Y., Joseph, A.D., Katz, R.H.: An Architecture for Secure Wide-Area Service Discovery. Wireless Networks. 3, 213–230 (2002)
45. Hoffert, J., Jang, S., Schmidt, D.C.: A Taxonomy of Discovery Services and Gap Analysis for Ultra-Large Scale Systems. In: ACMSE 2007, pp. 355–361. ACM Press, New York (2007)
46. Hoschek, W.: The Web Service Discovery Architecture. In: ACM/IEEE SC Conference (SC'02), pp.38. IEEE Press, New York (2002)
47. Hu, C., Zhu, Y., Huai, H., Liu, Y., Ni, L.M.: S-Club: An Overlay-Based Efficient Service Discovery Mechanism in CROWN Grid. Knowledge and Information Systems. 12, 55–75 (2007)
48. Huang, A. C., Steenkiste, P.: Network-Sensitive Service Discovery. Journal of Grid Computing. 1, 309–326 (2003)
49. Huhns, M., Singh, M.: Service Oriented Computing: Key Concepts and Principles. IEEE Internet Computing. 9, 75–81 (2005)
50. Issarny, V., Caporuscio, M., Georgantas, N: A Perspective on the Future of Middleware-Based Software Engineering. In: Future of Software Engineering, pp. 244–258. IEEE Press, New York (2007)
51. Jini Lookup Service, `http://www.jini.org/`
52. JXTA Project, `https://jxta.dev.java.net/`
53. Kontogiannis, K., Smith, G.A., Litoiu, M., Müller, H., Schuster, S., Stroulia, E.: The Landscape of Service Oriented Systems: A Research Perspective. In: the International Workshop on Systems Development in SOA Environments, pp. 1. IEEE Press, New York (2007)
54. Li, J., Mohapatra, P.: PANDA: A Novel Mechanism for Flooding Based Route Discovery in Ad-hoc Networks. Wireless Netw. 12, 771–787 (2006)
55. Luck, M., McBurney, P., Shehory, O., Willmott, S.: Agent Technology: Computing as Interaction. University of Southampton, Southamptom (2005)
56. Nagarajan, M., Verma, K., Sheth, A.P., Miller, J., Lathem, J.: Semantic Interoperability of Web Services—Challenges and Experiences. In: Proceeding of the IEEE International Conference on Web Services, pp.373–382. IEEE Press, New York (2006)
57. Napster Project, `http://www.napster.co.uk/`
58. Naumenko, A., Nikitin, S., Terziyan, V.: Service Matching in Agent Systems. Applied Intelligence. 25, 223–237 (2006)
59. Nedos, A., Singh, K., Clarke, S: Mobile Ad Hoc Services: Semantic Service Discovery in Mobile Ad Hoc Networks. Springer, Berlin (2006)
60. Newcomer, E., Lomow, G.: Understanding SOA with Web Services. Addison Wesley, London (2005)
61. OASIS Homepage, `http://www.oasis-open.org/home/index.php`
62. O'Brien, L., Merson, P., Bass, L.: Quality Attributes for Service Oriented Architectures. In: Internal Workshop on Systems Development in SOA Environments, pp. 216–122. IEEE Press, New York (2007)
63. Object Management Group, `http://www.omg.org/gettingstarted/`
64. The Open Group Homepage, `http://www.opengroup.org/`
65. Palathingal, P., Chandra, S.: Agent Approach for Service Discovery and Utilization. In: Proceedings of the 37th Hawaii International Conference on System Sciences, pp. 1–9. IEEE Press, New York (2004)
66. Papazoglou, M.P., Krimer, B.J., Yang, J.: Leveraging web services and Peer to Peer Networks. Springer, Berlin (2003)
67. Papazoglou, M., Heuvel, W.: Service Oriented Architectures: Approaches, Technologies and Research Issues. The VLDB Journal. 16, 389–415 (2007)
68. Ratsimor, D. Chakraborty, D., Joshi, A., Finin, T.: Allia: Alliance-Based Service Discovery for Ad-Hoc Environments. In: International Workshop on Mobile Commerce, pp. 1–9. ACM Press, New York (2002)

69. Ratsimor, O. Chakraborty, D. Joshi, A., Finin, T., Yesha, Y.: Service Discovery in Agent-Based Pervasive Computing Environments. Mobile Networks and Applications. 9, 679–692 (2004)
70. Richard III, G.G.: Service Advertisement and Discovery: Enabling Universal Device Cooperation. IEEE Internet Computing. 5, 18–26 (2000)
71. Salutation Architecture Specification, http://www.salutation.org/specordr.htm
72. Scherson, I.D. and Cauich, E., Valencia, D.S.: Service Discovery for GRID Computing Using LCAN-mapped Hierarchical Directories. Journal of Supercomputing. 42, 19–32 (2007)
73. Service Oriented Architecture, http://www.w3.org/TR/ws-arch
74. ShaikhAli, A., Rana, O.F., AI-Ali, R., Walker, D.W. UDDIe: an tetended registry for web services. In: the Proceedings of Application and the Internet Workshops, pp.85–89, IEEE Press, New York (2003)
75. Singh, M.P., Huhns, M.N.: Service Oriented Computing, Semantics, Processes, Agents. John Wiley & Sons, Chichester (2005)
76. Singha, A.: Web Services Security: Chanllenges and Techniques. In: 8th IEEE International Workshop on Policies for Distributed Systems and Networks, pp. 282. IEEE Press, New York (2007)
77. Sivavakeesar, S., Gonzalez, O.F., Pavlou, G.: Service Discovery Strategies in Ubiquitous Communication Environments. IEEE Communications Magazine, 12, 106-113 (2006)
78. SOAP Specification, http://www.w3.org/TR/soap/
79. Soldatos, J., Dimarkis, N., Stamatis. K., Polymenakos, L.: A Breadboard Architecture for Pervasive Context-Aware Services in Smart Spaces: Middleware Components and Prototype Applications. Personal and Ubiquitous Computing. 11, 193–212 (2007)
80. Sreenath, R., Singh, M.: Agent based service selection. Web Semantics: Science, Services and Agents on the World Wide Web. 1, 261–279 (2004)
81. Sycara, K., Paolucci, M., Soudry, J., Srinivasan, N.: Dynamic Discovery and Coordination of Agent Based Semantic Web Services. IEEE Internet Computing, 66–73 (2004)
82. Talwar, B., Venkataram, P., Patnaik, L.M.. A Method for Resource and Service Discovery in MANETs. Wireless Personal Communications. 41: 301–323 (2007)
83. Tyan, J., Mahmoud, Q.H.: A Comprehensive Service Discovery solution for Mobile Ad-Hoc Networks. Mobile Networks and Applications. 10, 423–434 (2005)
84. UDDI Project Version 3.0.2, http://uddi.org/pubs/uddi-v3.0.2-20041019.htm#_Ref8884251
85. Vanthournout, K., Deconinck, G., Belmans, R.: A Taxonomy for Resource Discovery. Personal and Ubiquitous Computing. 9, 81–19 (2005)
86. Verma, K., Sivashanmugam, K., Sheth, A. Patil, A., Oundhakar, S., Miller, J.: METEOR-S WSDI: A Scalable P2P Infrastructure of Registries for Semantic Publication and Discovery of Web Services. Information Technology and Management. 6, 17–39 (2005)
87. Vitvar, T., Mocan, A., Kerrigan, M., Zaremba, M., Zeremba, M., Moran, M., Cimpian, E., Haselwanter, T., Fensel, D.: Semantically-Enable Service Oriented Architecture: Concepts, Technology and Application. In: Service Oriented Computing and Applications. 1, 129–154 (2007)
88. W3C School, http://www.w3schools.com/
89. Wang, H., Huang, J. Z., Qu, Y., Xie, J.:Web Semantics: Science, Services and Agents. World Wide Web. 1, 309–320 (2004)
90. Warwick University Computer Science Department High Performance Systems Research Group, http://www.dcs.warwick.ac.uk/research/hpsg/A4/A4.html
91. Web Services Inspection Language, http://www.ibm.com/developerworks/library/ws/wsilover/
92. WSDL Specification, http://www.w3.org/TR/wsdl
93. Wu, C., Chang, E.: Aligning with the Web: an Atom-based Architecture for Web Service Discovery. SOCA. 1, 97–116 (2007)
94. Yang, Y., Dunlap, R., Rexroad, M, Cooper, B.: Performance of full text search in structured and unstructured peer to peer systems. In: Proceedings of the 5th IPTPS, pp. 27–28. Santa Barbara, USA (2006)

95. Yu, J., Venugopal, S., Buyya, R.: A Market-Oriented Grid Directory Service for Publication and Discovery of Grid Service Providers and their Services. Journal of Supercomputing. 36, 17–31 (2006)
96. Yu, Q., Liu, X., Bouguettaya, A., Medjahed, B.: Deploying and managing Web Services: Issues, Solutions and Directions. The VLDB Journal The International Journal on Very Large Data Bases. 17, 537–572 (2006)

Chapter 3
Multi-Agent Coordination for Service Composition

Junzhou Luo, Wei Li, Bo Liu, Xiao Zheng and Fang Dong

Abstract Service composition is an active ongoing area of research in the field of Service-Oriented Computing. One of the research challenges is to provide a mechanism for the autonomous search and selection of suitable service provid-ers for each service type within service composition while guaranteeing the end-to-end QoS. A multi-agent based QoS-aware Service Composition solution (MQSC) is presented in this chapter. MQSC not only can provide a mechanism for the dynamic service composition but also can ensure the end-to-end QoS of the composite service.

Junzhou Luo
School of Computer Science and Engineering, Southeast University, Nanjing 210096, P.R. China; Key Laboratory of Computer Network and Information Integration, Ministry of Education, Nanjing 210096, P.R. China
e-mail: jluo@seu.edu.cn

Wei Li
School of Computer Science and Engineering, Southeast University, Nanjing 210096, P.R. China; Key Laboratory of Computer Network and Information Integration, Ministry of Education, Nanjing 210096, P.R. China
e-mail: xchlw@seu.edu.cn

Bo Liu
School of Computer Science and Engineering, Southeast University, Nanjing 210096, P.R. China; Key Laboratory of Computer Network and Information Integration, Ministry of Education, Nanjing 210096, P.R. China
e-mail: bliu@seu.edu.cn

Xiao Zheng
School of Computer Science and Engineering, Southeast University, Nanjing 210096, P.R. China; Key Laboratory of Computer Network and Information Integration, Ministry of Education, Nanjing 210096, P.R. China
e-mail: xzheng@seu.edu.cn

Fang Dong
School of Computer Science and Engineering, Southeast University, Nanjing 210096, P.R. China; Key Laboratory of Computer Network and Information Integration, Ministry of Education, Nanjing 210096, P.R. China
e-mail: fdong@seu.edu.cn

N. Griffiths, K.-M. Chao (eds.), *Agent-Based Service-Oriented Computing*, Advanced Information and Knowledge Processing,
DOI 10.1007/978-1-84996-041-0_3,

3.1 Introduction

In Service-Oriented Computing (SOC), a service is the fundamental element of distributed and heterogeneous applications. Service providers and customers can dynamically publish, discover and invoke services. When a requirement from a customer cannot be achieved directly by the existing services, there should be a possibility to combine and compose the functions of several services in order to fulfill the requirement. Service composition offers a way to expand the ability of the single service and implement service reuse [1]. It allows a distributed application to be constructed through the combination of other existing services, and this composition offers an added value to the original services. Service composition accelerates rapid application development, and implements service reuse for the providers and enables seamless access to a variety of complex services for the customers.

The issues related to service composition are being addressed by ongoing work in the area of Semantic Web [15, 23], agent [18, 20] and business process workflow management [24]. Their overall approaches are to define a composition plan for each customers goal involving abstract service descriptions. However, the service discovery and selection mechanisms are static and not flexible in these approaches, and the end-to-end Quality of Service (QoS) of a composite service can also not be ensured. During the course of composing services, different services with the same function may have different QoS, such as performance, cost, availability and so on, and some QoS criteria are dynamic. So the composition plan should be adjusted dynamically in order to satisfy the global QoS requirement of the composition. One of the research challenges is to provide a mechanism for the autonomous search and selection of suitable service providers for each service type within service composition while guaranteeing the end-to-end QoS. Multi-Agent Systems (MAS), which originated from the Distributed Artificial Intelligence field, offers solutions that can benefit the provision and design of a dynamic approach, and is very suitable for dynamic service composition. On the one hand, service composition could be performed dynamically through agent collaboration without predefining abstract plans. On the other hand, the local and reactive processing in MAS can avoid the bottlenecks caused by centralized systems and improve scalability. This chapter puts forward a Multi-agent based QoS-aware Service Composition solution (MQSC). MQSC not only provides a mechanism for the dynamic service composition but also can ensure the end-to-end QoS of the composite service.

Multi-Agent Systems (MAS), which originated from the Distributed Artificial Intelligence field, offers solutions that can benefit the provision and design of a dynamic approach, and is very suitable for dynamic service composition. On the one hand, service composition could be performed dynamically through agent collaboration without predefining abstract plans. On the other hand, the local and reactive processing in MAS can avoid the bottlenecks caused by centralized systems and improve scalability. This chapter puts forward a Multi-agent based QoS-aware Service Composition solution (MQSC). MQSC not only provides a mechanism for the dynamic service composition but also can ensure the end-to-end QoS of the composite service.

The remainder of this chapter is organized as follows. The next section overviews the concepts and definitions of service composition, QoS attributes and user satisfaction degree of service, task graph, service composition graph, and ant algorithm. The related works in the area of multi-agent based service composition is discussed in Section 3.3. Section 3.4 describes the architecture of MQSC and illuminates each component. The mechanism of service search, service selection and service execution is presented in Sections 3.5 and 3.6 respectively. Section 3.7 analyzes a use-case scenario in order to demonstrate MQSC. Finally, we conclude the chapter in Section 3.8 with remarks on future work.

3.2 Preliminaries

In this section, some basic concepts and definitions are explained so that our solution can be understood easily.

3.2.1 Service Composition

Service composition refers to the process of combining several services to provide a value-added service. In SOC, it is impossible for a single service to accomplish a complex task. One solution is to combine many different services and make them collaborate to finish the complex task. Each service can locate in a wide area and the composition relation between them is a loose coupling. The composite service is usually composed according to the requirements of a customer and its deployment is temporal and prompt. The composition relation can be canceled after tasks are finished. Therefore, service composition is an important way of service reuse, the construction and the deployment of a complex application in a SOC environment. In the context of SOC, a service participating in a composition process is called a *component service*. The result of service composition produces a *composite service*. A *service class* is a collection of component services, which have the same functions but different nonfunctional properties (such as QoS). The element in a service class is also called a *candidate service*. An overview of the approaches for implementing service composition is presented as follows.

3.2.1.1 Manual Composition Versus Automatic Composition

The execution process of manual composition is decided in a manual way. Such a method manually chooses services that can participate in the composition, analyzes functions and interface parameters of each service to decide the dependencies of the data flow and the control flow, and uses some modeling languages, such as BPEL4WS [3] and EFLOW [5], to describe services and their dependencies. Figure 3.1 shows an example describing a process for handing a loan application using BPEL4WS, which is derived from a tutorial on BPEL4WS by IBM [11]. In

```
<process name="loanApprovalProcess" ... />
  <partners>
    <partner name="customer" ... />
    <partner name="assessor" ... />
    <partner name="approver" ... />
  </partners>
  <containers>
    <container name="request" messageType="loandef:CreditInformationMessage"/>
    <container name="approvalInfo" messageType="apns:approvalMessage"/>
    <container name="riskAssessment" messageType="asns:AssessMessage"/>
  </containers>
  <sequence>
    <receive name="receive1" partner="customer" portType="apns:loanApprovalPT"
        operation ="approve" container="request" createInstance="yes">
    </receive>
    <invoke name="invokeassessor" partner="assessor" portType="asns:riskAssessmentPT"
        operation ="check" inputContainer="request" outputContainer="riskAssessment">
    </invoke>
    ...
    <invoke name="invokeapprover" partner="approver" portType="apns:loanApprovalPT"
        operation ="approve" inputContainer="request" outputContainer="approvalInfo">
    </invoke>
    <reply name="reply" partner="customer" portType="apns:loanApprovalPT"
        operation ="approve" container="approvalInfo">
    </reply>
  </sequence>
</process>
```

Fig. 3.1 A simplified BPEL4WS document for the loan approval process

this process, the customer and two web services, namely assessor and approver, are all represented as partners. The technical details of each activity are as follows:

- receive: allows the business process to do a blocking wait for a matching message to arrive, e.g., customer.
- invoke: allows the business process to invoke a one-way or request-response operation on a portType offered by a partner, e.g., assessor and approver.
- reply: used to send a response to a previous request accepted through a receive activity.

The disadvantage of manual composition is that the professional persons would be required to finish the service composition, which cannot be finished automatically according to the customers requirements. Thus, the efficiency of the manual way is very low in a complex business process.

Automatic composition is automatically generated based on requirements from customers. To increase the automatic degree of service composition, the machine should understand and deal with the information on services. Semantic Web Services, which is a combination of semantic web techniques and web service techniques, can make use of some existing methods in the field of artificial intelligence or logical inference to generate a new composite service according to the requirements automatically. In general, semantic web enabled automatic approaches consists of three conceptual phases: specification, matchmaking and generation [16]. The specification phase enables high-level and customized descriptions of the desired compositions. The specifications of the composers include constructs for the orchestration and semantic descriptions of composition sub-requests. The matchmaking phase uses the composability model to generate composition plans conforming to requirements from composers. Because services are described semantically, the machine could understand which services could contribute to the composition and how these participant services could interact with each other. A set of algorithms are developed for checking the composability and matching services to generate composition plans automatically. The generation phase returns detailed composite service descriptions. Such descriptions include the orchestration (composer-defined and system-generated) of participant services.

3.2.1.2 Proactive Composition Versus Reactive Composition

Proactive composition is an offline process that gathers available component services to constitute a composite service in advance. The composite service is precompiled and ready to be triggered upon customers requests. In a proactive composition, the component services are usually stable and may be running on the resource-rich platforms. In enterprise computing, the storage resources and the computing resources are sufficient as to guarantee running of participant services. Moreover, enterprise applications are solid. Consequently, such a composition is designed and deployed in advance, and its QoS is stable.

Reactive composition is the process of creating a composite service on-the-fly. A composite service is devised on a request-basis from customers. Because of the on-the-fly property, a component manager is required and ensures the identification and collaboration of component services. Despite a certain complexity of reactive composition, it has several advantages over proactive composition, for instance, the possibility of tracking the status of the composition process to take correct actions promptly and the possibility of optimizing run-time parameters, such as bandwidth use, data transfer routes, and execution charges. This kind of composition is suitable to a dynamic Internet environment.

3.2.1.3 Mandatory Composite Service Versus Optional Composite Service

A mandatory composite service corresponds to the compulsory participation of all the component services in the execution process. Under this situation, the participant has no substitution and no requirements for selecting an appropriate candidate service from a service class. Because it is expected that the component services will be spread over the network, QoS of the execution process of each component service affects the whole QoS of the composite service. Due to no substitution, the QoS of each component service must be guaranteed as much as possible.

An optional composite service does not necessarily involve all of the component services. Some component services can be skipped during the course of execution due to various reasons, such as the possibility of substitution or unavailability. For example, in some high-reliability required situations, such as emergency response applications, some service replicas will be deployed to ensure load balancing, fault-tolerance, etc. A composite service only chooses a “free” and “healthy” replica.

3.2.2 QoS Attributes and User Satisfaction Degree of Service

QoS is a combination of several qualities or properties of a service, which is used to measure a satisfaction degree of the service to customers. This chapter considers multiple QoS attributes consisting of the response time, the service availability and the service cost. The response time is the interval between a customer sending a request to and receiving results from a service provider, which includes the total time for the service and the round-trip communication delay. The service availability is the probability that the service can be used. The service cost is the spending of the customer in acquiring a certain service. In a general way, the range of each QoS criterion value is different and its meaning is also not the same. Some of the criteria such as the response time and the service cost could be negative, e.g., the higher the value is, the lower the quality is. Other criteria are positive, e.g., the higher the value is, the higher the quality is.

In order to measure the overall quality of a service, its QoS attributes should be scaled by a uniform standard and considered in the round. In this chapter, the concepts of user satisfaction degree and user satisfaction function, which are our early work [26] and suit the dynamic environment, are adopted and a utility function is suggested as the objective function of selecting a candidate service during the course of service composition.

Definition 1: User satisfaction degree of a service is a real number $d \in [0,1]$. As its value increases, customers are more satisfied with the service. When the value reaches 1, customers are satisfied perfectly whereas 0 means customer requirements are not satisfied.

Definition 2: User satisfaction function for the i-th service s_{ij} represents the mapping from the j-th QoS criterion of the i-th service to user satisfaction degree.

User satisfaction degree is a subjective concept. It varies with the different customers preference and the application. User satisfaction function describes the relation between a given QoS criterion and user satisfaction degree for the service. It is defined by customers and submitted to a service composition mechanism with the requirements. Figure 3.2 shows examples of user satisfaction function. In Figure 3.2(a), t_1 and t_2 are two thresholds. When the response time is higher than t_2, user satisfaction degree is zero, whereas the value is 1 when the time is less than t_1. The curve of the service cost in Figure 3.2(b) is the same as that of the response time. The curve in Figure 3.2(c) is a function which is $f(x) = x$ where $x \in [0,1]$.

Definition 3: Utility function for the i-th service u_i is:

$$u_i = \sum_j (w_j . s_{ij}) \tag{3.1}$$

where $w_j \in [0,1]$ and $\sum_j w_j = 1$. w_j represents the weight of the criterion j, which is used to reflect customers preferences, and s_{ij} is user satisfaction function depicted in definition 2.

It is well known that the end-to-end QoS of a composite service is dependent on the QoS of each component service. How to calculate the QoS criteria of a com-

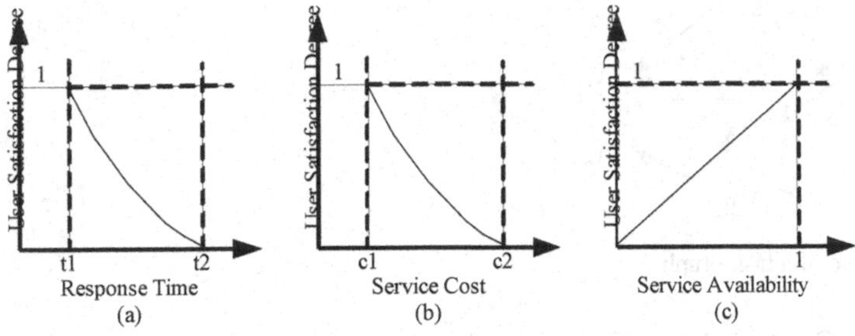

Fig. 3.2 Examples of the user satisfaction function

posite service according to that of component services is introduced in [17]. Once getting the QoS criteria of the composite service, its utility function could be calculated based on formula 3.1. Since customers always want to maximize the benefits received by them, the service composition plan with the maximum value of utility function will be selected.

3.2.3 Task Graph

As introduced above, a composite service is to execute a complex task corresponding with the requirements from a customer, which could be partitioned into several subtasks implemented by single services. These subtasks and their dependencies are represented by a task graph, which is a directed acyclic graph. Each subtask is represented with a rectangle and connected via directed arrows, which represent the control-flow or data-flow dependencies among subtasks. There are three kinds of dependencies among subtasks, namely selection dependency, concurrence dependency and mixture dependency.

- Selection dependency is that only one of the successor subtasks can be selected.
- Concurrence dependency is that all of the successors of a subtask can be executed concurrently.
- Mixture dependency is that there are the two above-mentioned relations simultaneously.

As shown in Figure 3.3, a whole task could be partitioned into nine subtasks, namely st_1, st_2, etc. Subtask "+" denotes the selection dependency and "*" denotes the concurrence dependency. st_4 and st_5 must be executed concurrently whereas one of st_2 and st_3 would be selected to be executed.

This chapter does not consider how to decompose a task and generate a task graph, which is one of our future works. It is assumed that the task has been decomposed to several subtasks, and each subtask could be implemented by any one of a group of candidate services with a same function but different QoS properties.

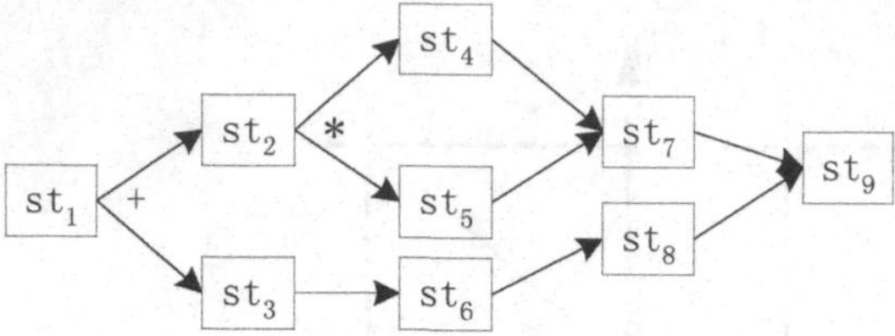

Fig. 3.3 An example of a task graph

3.2.4 Service Composition Graph

In order to research the problem of service composition, how to model service composition should be considered. So the Service Composition Graph (SCG) is presented as a modeling tool.

Definition 4: Formally, a SCG is a triple (V,E,Q), where:

1. $V = V_{or} \cup V_{and} \cup V_{end}$. V is the set of vertexes denoting services. V_{or}, called OR-Vertex, is the set of vertexes which denote the selection dependency, V_{and}, called AND-Vertex, is the set of vertexes which denote the concurrence dependency, and V_{end} is a set of vertexes which have no successors and do not denote any dependency.
2. $E = \{(i,j)|i,j \in V\}$ is the edge set. And if $(i,j) \in E$, then $(j,i) \notin E$.
3. $Q = \{q(i,j)|(i,j) \in E\}$ is the weight set associated with E. $q(i,j) = (t,a,c)$, where $t,a,c \in R^+ \cup \{0\}$ and $a \in [0,1]$.
4. There is no path from r to itself, where $r \in V$.
5. There is a single vertex called the source vertex, which has no predecessors and belongs to V_{or}, and there is a single destination vertex, which has no successors and belongs to V_{end}.

Therefore, the SCG is a kind of the directed acyclic graph, which has a single source vertex and a destination vertex. Except the source vertex and the destination vertex, it contains two types of vertexes, namely OR-Vertex and AND-Vertex, which represent services involved in the composition. An edge represents a dependency, whose weight is a triple (t,a,c), where t is the response time of the invoked service, a is the service availability, and c is the service cost of the invocation. A SCG represents all possible compositions of services.

Definition 5: A service executable plan of a SCG is a sequence of vertexes, namely $[s_1, s_2, \ldots, s_n]$, where s_1 is the source vertex, s_n is the destination vertex, and for every $s_i (1 < i < n)$:

1. s_i is a direct successor of one of the vertexes in $[s_1, \ldots, s_{i-1}]$.
2. s_i is not a direct successor of any of the vertexes in $[s+i+1, \ldots, s_n]$.
3. There is no s_j in $[s_1, \ldots, s_{i-1}]$ such that s_j and s_i belong to two alternative branches of the SCG.
4. If s_i is the AND-Vertex, then all s_i's successors will be include in $[s_1, s_2, \ldots, s_n]$. In other words, if an AND-Vertex is entered, all of its concurrent branches will be executed.

Definition 6: An optimal service executable plan is a service executable plan with the maximum utility.

There are many different service executable plans in a SCG. A service executable plan denotes a composition plan of services and different plans may have different end-to-end QoS. The objective of QoS-aware service composition is to find all the service executable plans from the source vertex to the destination vertex and choose an optimal service executable plan from them.

3.2.5 From Task Graph to Services Composition Graph

In a task graph, each subtask can be mapped to a collection of services with the same function. So a task graph can be translated into a directed acyclic graph only composed of services, namely a SCG. Figure 3.4 illustrates a service composition scenario, which is a part of Figure 3.3 including st_1, st_2 and st_3. Without loss of generality, suppose that each subtask corresponds to two candidate services. In Figure 3.4, each service is represented with an oval and connected via directed arrows. An arrow from service A to service B indicates that A executes before B. The subscript in the label of the oval includes two numbers separated by a comma. The former denotes which subtask the service belongs to, and the latter denotes the index of the service in the same subtask. For example, $S_{1,1}$ and $S_{1,2}$ respectively represent two different services implementing the subtask st_1 in Figure 3.3. The index of $S_{1,1}$ is 1 and that of $S_{1,2}$ is 2.

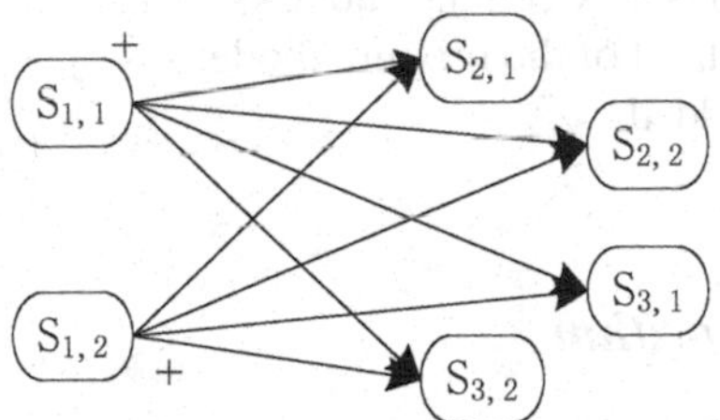

Fig. 3.4 A service composition scenario

There are the same dependencies as subtasks between services. But in Definition 4, there are only two types of vertexes except the source vertex and the destination vertex in a SCG, namely AND-Vertex and OR-Vertex. So, how can we represent the mixture relation? The transition rules from the mixture mode to the other modes are presented as follows. Suppose that s is a service of the mixture mode, and it invokes n groups of concurrent successors.

1. For each group of concurrent successors cs_i, an extra vertex vs_i is added to invoke them, where $i \in [1..n]$.
2. Cancel the original arrows from s to services in cs_i, and add a arrow from s to vs_i, where $i \in [1..n]$.

3. Finally, s invokes vs_i by the selection mode and the latter invokes each service in cs_i by the concurrence mode, where $i \in [1..n]$.

This method reduces the complexity of the graph and makes the graph only include the selection relation and the concurrence relation. Figure 3.5 shows the substitution method. By adding an extra vertex vs, called virtual service, the mixture mode could be expressed by only using the selection mode and the concurrence mode. In addition, a source vertex and a destination vertex are added. The source vertex is connected to every vertex that denotes the services belonging to the initial subtasks by directed arrows. Similarly, all the vertexes that denote the services belonging to the last subtasks are connected to the destination vertex.

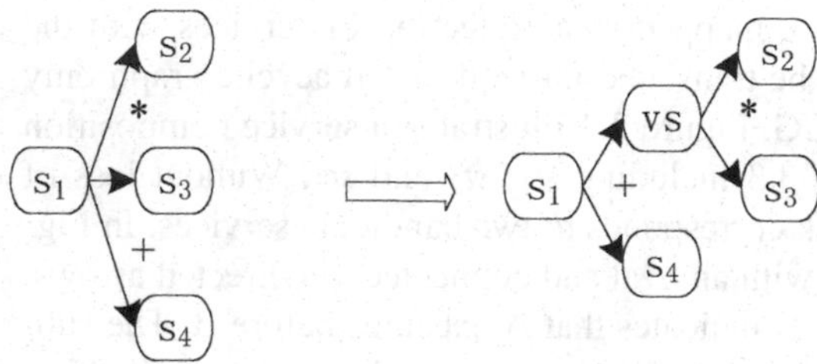

Fig. 3.5 A service composition scenario

In a conclusion, there are three steps from a task graph to a SCG.

1. Every subtask in the task graph is replaced by its candidate services, and then the services are connected according to the relations between the subtasks.
2. The graph is reduced with the substitution method of the mixture mode.
3. A source vertex and a destination vertex are added.

3.2.6 The Fundamentals of the Ant Algorithm

In Section 3.5, the mechanism for the autonomous search and selection of suitable services within service composition is inspired by ant colony intelligence. Therefore, the fundamentals of ant algorithm are introduced in advance below.

In nature, ants always find the shortest path between their nest and the food source. Scientists found a special substance, called the pheromone, which plays a key role in the path selection. While walking, ants always deposit the pheromone on the ground and follow the pheromone previously deposited by other ants probabilistically. The probability of choosing a path is decided by the amount of the pheromone on the path. In other words, ants prefer to visit a path owning the more pheromone. Furthermore, the pheromone can fluctuate over time. This effect can enable ants to find the shortest path.

The Ant System (AS) algorithm, based on the behaviors of the real ants, is first applied to Traveling Salesman Problem (TSP). In the AS, there are some artificial ants deployed on the vertexes in a graph. The artificial ants imitate real ants behaviors to find a shortest path. The algorithm is suitable for small instances of the TSP (up to 30 cities) [7]. The Ant Colony System (ACS)Ant Colony System (ACS) is an algorithm based on the AS. It is feasible for larger problems. The ACS differs from the previous AS because of three main aspects. Firstly, the state transition rule provides a direct way to balance between the exploration of new edges and the exploitation of a prior edge to accumulate knowledge about the problem. Secondly, the global updating rule is only applied to edges that belong to the optimal ant tour. Finally, while ants construct a solution, a local pheromone updating rule is applied.

3.3 Related Work

There are several research initiatives in the field of service composition. This section introduces some representative work in four areas of service composition respectively, which are the framework of service composition, service composition plan generation, service selection and plan optimization, and multi-agent based service composition.

3.3.1 Framework of Service Composition

In survey [10], three approaches of building a composite service are discussed, namely peer-to-peer approach, mediated approach and brokered approach.

Peer-to-peer is the most general situation in which all services are essentially equal and any pair of peers can communicate with each other directly. Mediated approach is based on a "hub-and-spoke" topology, where one service plays a special role called the process mediator and the other services can communicate with the mediator but not with each other in terms of both the control and the data sharing. The mediator coordinates the activities of other services. The widely used languages such as BPEL4WS are designed for specifying the behaviors of the mediator. In the topology of the mediated approach, all "leaves" are atomic services. Some or all of the leaves can be composite services mediated. Assuming that the new mediator is linked to exactly one service from each of the existing composite services, this will lead in most practical cases to a composite service whose topology is a tree. A variation of the mediated approach is the brokered approach, where the process control is centralized but the data can be passed between any pair of the peers directly. QBroker, suggested in [27], is a broker-based architecture, which provides the end-to-end QoS management for distributed services and some functions including service discovery, planning, selection and adaptation.

3.3.2 Service Composition Plan Generation

The service composition plan should include details such as the list of participant services, their execution order, the way they are interconnected and the mappings between their messages. How is a service composition plan generated? There are two types of method [22]: business-flow-based and semantics-based. The first approach is primarily syntactical: web service interfaces are like remote procedure calls and the interaction protocols are manually written. The semantic web community focuses on reasoning about web resources by explicitly declaring their preconditions and effects with terms precisely defined in the ontology. For the composition of web services, they draw on goal-oriented inference from planning. So far, both approaches have been developed rather independently from each other.

Service composition based on the business flow is adopted by industry. This method uses Web Service Definition Language (WSDL) to describe the interface of web service. The interactions and message exchanges between the services are described in a business protocol specification language, which specifies the roles of each of the partners and the logical flow of the message exchanges. The language includes BPEL4WS proposed by IBM and Microsoft. The most difficult task for an IT specialist is to specify the logic of the message flow. For this purpose, BPEL4WS provides programming-language like constructs (sequence, switch, while, pick) as well as graph-based links that represent additional ordering constraints on constructs.

Semantics-based service composition uses the concepts of service ontology to describe the meaning of services and identify the synonyms. For example, the laptop service and the notebook service are of the same semanteme. Consequently, they may provide the same service. Service ontology consists of a common language agreed by a domain. It defines a terminology that is used by all participants in that domain. Within a domain, service providers describe their services using the terms of the domains ontology, while service customers use the terms of the ontology to formulate queries over the registry of the domain. Ontologies described in languages such as OWL [21] and DAML [9] can be completely interpreted by machine. In the condition that the machine can understand services, it can make use of artificial intelligence approaches to compose services in terms of the service composition plan.

3.3.3 Service Selection and Plan Optimization

Requirements for a composite service from customers are important for most practical distributed applications. For example, a customer may need a real-time response while another customer may prefer cost to the execution time. Therefore, besides functional properties, the end-to-end QoS of a composite service should be considered. In general, services with similar and compatible functions may be offered at different QoS levels. Thus, the decision must be made to select component services at appropriate QoS levels in service composition [28] and a QoS-aware algorithm to select services is needed to optimize the service composition plan. A variety of approaches are suggested to solve the problem of service selection. Representative works include using heuristic algorithms [19, 28], integer programming [29] and genetic algorithms [13, 30].

In [28], Yu et al. design a broker-based architecture called Qbroker to facilitate the selection of QoS-based services. The objective of service selection is to maximize an application-specific utility function under the end-to-end QoS constraints. The problem is modeled in two ways: the combinatorial model and the graph model. The combinatorial model defines the problem as a Multi-dimension Multi-choice 0–1 Knapsack Problem (MMKP). The graph model defines the problem as a Multi-Constraint Optimal Path (MCOP) problem. Efficient heuristic algorithms for service processes of different composition structures are presented in this chapter.

In [29], AgFlow is presented as a middleware platform that enables the QoS-driven composition of web services. In AgFlow, the QoS of web services is evaluated by means of an extensible multi-dimensional QoS model, and the selection of component services is performed in such a way as to optimize the QoS of the composite service. Furthermore, AgFlow adapts to changes that occur during the execution of a composite service by revising the execution plan in order to conform to the customers constraints on QoS. The salient features of AgFlow include two alternative QoS-driven service selection approaches for the composite service execution: one is based on the local (task-level) selection of services and the other is based on the global allocation of tasks to services using integer programming.

3.3.4 Multi-Agent Based Service Composition

Up to now, multi-agent based service composition also appears in the literature. Agent based systems facilitate the deployment of a widely distributed architecture, with high capabilities for communication and negotiation among all the components. Because the agent characterizes autonomy, social ability, reactivity, proactiveness and mobility, it has been introduced to build a composite service. During the composition process, agents engage in conversations with their peers to agree on the services that participate in this process. Mobile agents can represent the customer or the main web service, and navigate around the network to contact interesting services.

Maamar et al. [14] put forward an approach for service composition based on agents and context. In their paper, three types of agents have been suggested, namely composite-service-agent associated with composite services, master-service-agent associated with web services and service-agent associated with service instances. The different agents are aware of the context of their respective services in the objective to devise composite services on-the-fly. LEAP is a project supported by European Commission, in which a multi-agent based architecture model for service composition is developed [2]. Its main feature is a set of generic services that are implemented independently of agents and can be installed into agents by the application developer in a flexible way. Therefore, services plugged into agents can be composed on the multi-agent platform. Moreover, two applications using this architecture model are also developed within the LEAP project. Their application domain is the support of mobile, virtual teams for the German automobile club ADAC and for British Telecommunications.

3.4 Architecture of MQSC

The process of service composition can be usually characterized by four phases: task decomposition phase, service search phase, service selection phase and service execution phase. Firstly, the task submitted by a customer can be decomposed into several subtasks, which can be accomplished by each single service. Secondly, it is necessary to search services and gain their information in order to map each subtask to all corresponding candidate services with the same function. Thirdly, a suitable service for each subtask needs be chosen to generate an optimal service executable plan in order to satisfy the customers end-to-end QoS constraints. Finally, a composite service is executed based on the optimal service executable plan. In order to accomplish the service composition life-cycle, MQSC is presented in this chapter. MQSC not only provides a mechanism for the dynamic service composition but also can ensure the end-to-end QoS of the composite service by using a multi-agent system. Figure 3.6 shows the architecture of MQSC. According to the role played in service composition, agents in MQSC are divided into six classes: Portal Agent (PA), Decision Agent (DA), Search Agent (SA), Registry Agent (RA), Management Agent (MA) and Execution Agent (EA). They can work together in order to accomplish a complex task.

3.4.1 Portal Agent

The Portal Agent is the interface to the customers and provides them with the capability of the seamless access to a variety of complex services on the pervasive network. There is one single PA in the whole system, which provides customers with Web-based access. By adopting the Web browser as the Graphic User Interface (GUI), a customer can download the hypertext pages with Java Applets from the PA through HTTP and put forward the requirements (task) and the initial parameters. Then the PA can automatically formalize the task submitted by the customer to generate a Task Graph, in which each node represents a subtask, and then send the Task Graph to the Decision Agent. After the task is accomplished, the PA provides the results from the DA to the customer.

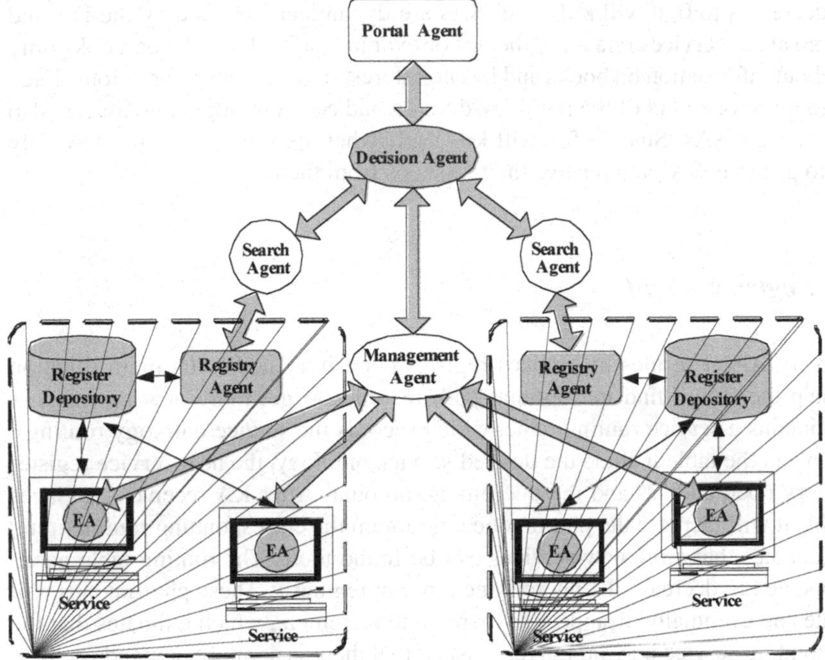

Fig. 3.6 Architecture of MQSC

3.4.2 Decision Agent

There is a single Decision Agent, which is a static intelligent agent. According to the ontology domains of services in the Task Graph submitted by the PA, the DA can dynamically create Search Agents and then send them to service register depository nodes to search the suitable services. After receiving the information on services from the SAs, the DA translates the Task Graph into the SCG and then executes the service selection algorithm depicted in Section 3.5.2 to automatically generate an optimal service executable plan, which satisfies end-to-end QoS constraints of the customer. Finally, the DA creates a Management Agent to implement the optimal service executable plan and sends the executable results to the PA.

3.4.3 Search Agent

A Search Agent is a mobile agent that is responsible for searching for services in service register depositories over the network. The length of its lifecycle is related to its search efficiency. In the normal situation, its life decays as time goes on. However, if the SA keeps on finding new services, its life will increase. When the life value decreases to 0, it will kill itself. SAs are dynamically created by the DA and only care about services related to them. For example, a SA focusing on books only cares about information on books and has no interest in restaurant reservations. Each SA belongs to one kind of the ontology domain and each ontology domain can also generate many SAs. Since a SA will kill itself when its life is over, the DA only needs to generate SAs and receive the messages from them.

3.4.4 Registry Agent

A Registry Agent resides in services register depository nodes. Its main function is to help the SA to find the optimal path in order to get more new services. A RA maintains a service routing table, which records the service ontology routings. The items in the table include the desired service ontology, the next service register depository node address and the pheromone amount. After RA receives messages from SA, it will increase the pheromone amount on the corresponding routing item, which denotes that more new services can be found there. The routing table needs to be updated to decrease the pheromone amount regularly. These pheromones will fluctuate and eventually disappear as there is no increment, which indicates that the corresponding service may no longer exist or that there is no more demand for such a service.

3.4.5 Management Agent

The Management Agent is dynamically created by the DA and is responsible for implementing an optimal service executable plan. According to the optimal service executable plan, the MA can create an EA assembled with the SCG and the specified domain knowledge to implement the composite service. The MA can communicate with the EA by messages. When an EA access to a web service fails, the EA will send a message to the MA, and then the MA will dispatch a replicated EA to retry the prior EAs work so as to make the prior EA to continue its composition plan.

3.4.6 Execution Agent

The Execution Agent is a mobile agent created by the MA dynamically. Compared with the MA, the main function of the EA is to implement the composite service. So EAs behaviors are related with the process of the services. Four basic behaviors are important for the EA: cloning, messaging, service triggering and disposal. During the course of the composite service implementation, one component services output may be the other component services input. Under this condition, an EA can clone a new EA to execute the following services. When an EA has finished its task, it will terminate its execution and die.

3.5 Service Composition Generation

In this chapter, tasks submitted by customers are described by a Task Graph. Assuming that Task Graph is given, the next step is how to get each candidate service to form a SCG and how to get an optimal service executable plan by service selection. A service search algorithm and a service selection algorithm are introduced as below, which are inspired by Ant Colony Systems.

3.5.1 Service Search and Composition Plan Generation

For mapping the subtask to corresponding candidate services, it is necessary to gain information on the services. Services are usually maintained by the creator and information is deployed to a service register depository provided to the service composition organization. The service register depository can be either centralized or distributed. The advantage of the centralized model is that it is easily implemented, but it has a bottleneck. If the centralized register depository is corrupted, the running of the system would be affected. The distributed model has many different service register depositories, which are responsible for service registries in distinct domains. These nodes compose an overlay network. There is a routing table in each service register depository node, which is used to locate other nodes

There are two types of agents incorporated to query services in the register depository network: SA and RA. An algorithm is needed to guide a SA to search services in order to reduce the total search time and improve efficiency. In this chapter, we adopt the mechanism of ant colony algorithm and use a pheromone to label the path to guide the search path of a SA. This is indirect coordination, which needs no direct communication or message passing.

A SA roams in the service register depository network and queries services belonging to its own ontology domain. Its behaviors are shown as follows:

1. If a new service, which the SA never discovered before, is found in the service register depository, a report about this service will be given to the DA. The report contains information on the function, QoS attributes and the physical location of this service. The life of the SA will be increased and it also informs the RA in the last hop register depository node that a new service has been found.
2. If a SA cannot find a new service, its life value will be decreased.
3. If the life value of a SA is 0, it will kill itself.
4. If there is more than one service ontology in the table, an SA compares the amount of pheromones and chooses the path that has the most pheromone.

5. If there is not any related service ontology, an SA will randomly choose any node as next hop.

The RAs mainly maintain the service routing tables. Its behaviors are described as follows:

1. Receive the reports from an SA. If there is no such service that a SA finds in the table, a new item is added. Otherwise, the corresponding pheromone amount is increased.
2. Regularly update the table to decrease the pheromone amount in all items. If an items pheromone amount is 0, it will be discarded.

In the above method, the path that has the highest pheromone amount would be chosen. The drawback of this method is the path which has the least pheromone will never been chosen. So roulette wheel selection can be applied to improve it. Every time, the wheel location is partitioned by the value of the pheromone in the route table. The higher the pheromone is, the bigger the area in the roulette wheel. As the area is bigger, the probability that the corresponding path is chosen is greater. Then a point from roulette wheel is chosen randomly, and the corresponding path is also chosen. After adopting this method, the paths with low pheromones also get the chance to be chosen, even if the probability is smaller.

3.5.2 QoS-Aware Service Selection

Ant system algorithms have been applied to the shortest-path problem [12] and the packet routing problem in communications networks [4] successfully. For these complex combinatorial optimization problems, Ant system algorithms may provide a good solution. The goal of our algorithm is to discover an optimal service executable plan in a SCG. Different from the generic shortest-path problem, the service executable plan includes parallel sub-paths, and the parallel execution part of that is also a critical path problem. The difficulty of our solution is how to process parallel paths.

Informally, the algorithm works as follows. In SCG, *m* ants are initially positioned on the source vertex. The task of each ant is to find a path from the source to the destination. While finding the path, if the ant is in an OR-vertex, it will apply a state transition rule to choose the successor. And if the ant is in an AND-vertex, it will clone several new ants and each ant will choose one of the successors respectively. The ant also modifies the amount of pheromone on the visited edges by applying the local updating rule. Once all ants have terminated their tour, the vertexes visited by all ants, which belong to the same clone matrix, compose a service executable plan. Then the amount of pheromone on edges of the optimal service executable plan are modified by applying the global update rule. In the algorithm, ants should be guided by both heuristic information and pheromones. An edge with a higher amount of pheromone will have more chance to be chosen.

The key to the algorithm is the state transition rule, the ant clone rule, the global updating rule and the local updating rule.

3.5.2.1 State Transition Rule

When an ant is at an OR-Vertex i, it will choose and move to a successor j by applying the rule given by formula 3.2,

$$j = \begin{cases} arg\ max_{u \in J_K(i)} \{[\tau(i,j)][\eta(i,u)]^{\beta}\} & \text{if} q \leq q_0 \\ S & \text{otherwise} \end{cases} \quad (3.2)$$

where q is a random number uniformly distributed in $[0..1]$, q_0 is a parameter $(0 \leq q_0 \leq 1)$, and S is a random variable selected according to the probability distribution given in formula 3.3.

$$p_k(i,j) = \begin{cases} \frac{[\tau(i,j)][\eta(i,j)]^{\beta}}{\Sigma_{u \in J_K(i)}[\tau(i,u)][\eta(i,u)]^{\beta}} & \text{if} j \in J_k(i) \\ 0 & \text{otherwise} \end{cases} \quad (3.3)$$

$p_k(i,j)$ is the probability with which ant k at OR-Vertex i chooses and moves to its successors.

In formulas 3.2 and 3.3, τ is the pheromone, $J_k(i)$ is the successor set of i, and β is a parameter which determines the relative importance of the pheromone versus the heuristic information $(\beta > 0)$. The heuristic function is $\eta = u_j$, where utility function u_j is introduced as the heuristic information.

According to definitions 2 and 3,$u_j = w_c.s_{cost}(j) + w_i.s_{time}(j) + w_a.s_{avai}(j)$ where $s_{cost}(j) = s_{cost}(c(i,j))$, $s_{time}(j) = s_{time}(t(i,j))$ and $s_{avai}(j) = s_{avai}(a(i,j))$.

3.5.2.2 Ant Clone Rule

When an ant is at an AND-Vertex, it will firstly clone $n-1$ ants, where n equals the number of this vertex's successors. Then each ant will choose and move to a successor vertex. The rule is that only one of successor vertexes belonging to the same task will be chosen by each ant respectively according to the state transition rule depicted above. In other words, an ant could only choose one of successor vertexes belonging to the same task, and a different ant does not choose successors from the same task.

3.5.2.3 Global Updating Rule

Just like ACS, this algorithm also has a global pheromone updating rule. It is executed after all ants have arrived at the destination vertex. The amount of pheromone is updated according to:

$$\tau(i,j) = (1-\alpha).\tau(i,j) + \alpha.\Delta\tau(i,j) \tag{3.4}$$

where

$$\Delta\tau(i,j) = \begin{cases} U \text{ if}(i,j) \in \text{owsp} \\ 0 \text{ otherwise} \end{cases}$$

$0 < \alpha < 1$ is the pheromone decay parameter, owsp denotes the optimal service executable plan and $U = w_c.s_{cost}(C) + w_t.s_{time}(T) + w_a.s_{avai}(A)$ is a utility function of owsp. In formula U, $C = \sum_{(i,j)\in \text{owsp}} c(i,j)$, $T = \max(T_k)$, and $A = \prod_{(i,j)\in \text{Path}_k} a(i,j)$ iff $k = \arg\max(T_k)$ where $T_k = \sum_{(i,j)\in \text{Path}_k} t(i,j)$ and Path_k is the path that the k-th ant has passed by, which belongs to a clone group having found owsp.

Formula 3.4 indicates that only pheromones on the edges belonging to the optimal plan will be reinforced.

3.5.2.4 Local Updating Rule

While finding the plan, ants change the pheromone levels on the passing edges using

$$\tau(i,j) = (1-\rho).\tau(i,j) + \rho.\Delta\tau(i,j) \tag{3.5}$$

where $\Delta\tau(i,j) = \tau_0$, τ_0 is the initial pheromone level, and ρ $(0 < \rho < 1)$ is a parameter.

The detailed algorithm is depicted as follows:

1. Set $t = 0$, and randomly set as a positive constant for all edges (i,j);
2. m ants are positioned at the source vertex;
3. If ant k is at an AND-Vertex, it executes the ant clone rule. Otherwise, if ant k is at an OR-Vertex, it will choose a successor according to formulas 3.2 and 3.3;
4. Apply the local updating rule;
5. If ant k arrives at the destination vertex, goto (6), or else goto (3);
6. When all ants arrive at the destination vertex, a group of ants having the same clone matrix will get a service executable plan;
7. Apply the global updating rule;
8. $t = t + 1$;
9. If the optimal service executable plan satisfies the customer's requirements, the process is completed, otherwise goto (2).

3.6 Service Composition Deployment and Execution

There are typically two types of agents incorporated into the service composition deployment. One is the MA, the other is the EA. Every optimal service composition plan is submitted to the MA by the DA. The MA will create and dispatch an EA to execute the plan, and then the EA with the plan information will visit the service nodes according to a certain scheduling algorithm.

3.6.1 How to Manage the EA to Implement the Composite Plan for the MA

The MA is responsible for creating and deploying the EA to implement the composition plan online. The major function of the MA includes:

- Preparing Agent: Because a composite service plan has a unique entry node, the MA only needs to prepare an EA for one plan and the EA with the whole plan will start to migrate from the entry node of the composite plan.
- Dispatching Agent: The entry node of the composite plan is the first site of the EA's migrating itinerary, so the EA is firstly dispatched by the MA to the entry node of the plan.
- Monitoring Agent: If an exception happens during plan execution and the EA is destroyed, it is desired to recover the EA to continue service processing. If the executing time of one plan surpasses the defined threshold, the MA will dispatch a new EA to execute the plan again.

3.6.2 The Plan Scheduling Algorithm of the EA

Every composite service plan transmitted to the EA is a Directed Acyclic Graph (DAG), which has a unique entry node and a unique end node. Every node in the graph corresponds to one service node and the service processing flow is the EA's migrating itinerary from the entry node to the end node.
Definition 7: Given two nodes T_1 and T_2, if there is an edge from T_1 to T_2, then T_1 is the predecessor of T_2 and T_2 is the successor of T_1.
Definition 8: Given two nodes T_1 and T_2, if there is a path from T_1 to T_2, then T_1 is an ancestor of T_2 and T_2 is a descendant of T_1.

3.6.2.1 Basic Execution Patterns

In the DAG of the composite plan, every service node can be executed after all of its predecessors have been finished. As shown in Figure 3.7, there are four basic execution patterns for the EA and any complex execution process can be divided into these patterns.

- Sequential Pattern. If ST_1 is the unique predecessor of ST_2, then one EA is allocated to ST_1 and ST_2 to invoke services on them sequentially.

- Branched Pattern. If ST_1 is a predecessor of ST_2 and ST_3, then one EA is allocated to ST_1. After EA reaches ST_1 and finishes the subtask, it will clone itself to dispatch the new EA to ST_3, and then move to ST_2.
- Joined Pattern. If ST_1 and ST_2 are the predecessors of ST_3, then two EAs are allocated to ST_1 and ST_2 respectively. After the two EAs reach ST_3 and communicate with each other, one of them destroys itself.
- Double Sequential Pattern. If ST_1 and ST_2 are the predecessors of ST_3 and ST_1 is also the predecessor of ST_2, namely there are two paths from ST_1 to ST_3, and then one EA is dispatched to invoke services on ST_1, $ST_2$and ST_3.

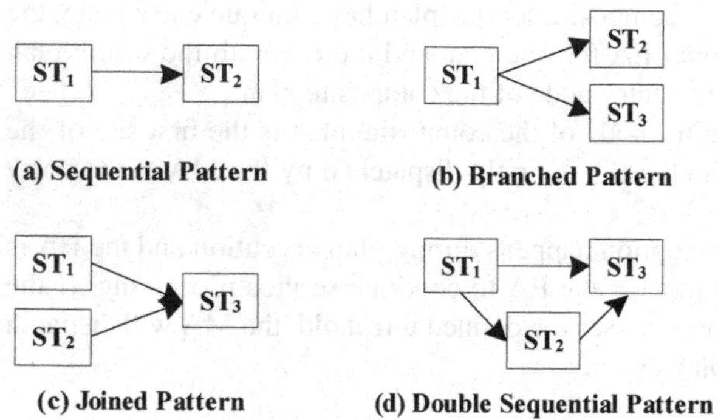

Fig. 3.7 Basic execution patterns for EA

```
Input: DAG of the Composite Plan (G)
Output: The Marked DAG (G')
W: the working queue;
L: integer (layer number);
1. W = null, L = 1;
2. The entry node of G is marked with L and added into W;
3. while W is not empty do
      L := L+1;
      Select the head node P from W;
      for each successor S of P in G do
          if there is only one path from P to S then
              S is marked with L;
              Add S into the tail of W;
          end if
      end for
      Delete P from W;
   end while
```

Algorithm 1: Using Breadth First Search algorithm to traverse the DAG to mark every node with the layer number.

Input: The Marked DAG (G')
Output: Executing Report (Agent Message)
S: the work node;
1. S = the entry node of G'; L = the layer number of S;
2. EA executes **migrate**(S);
3. **function migrate**(S);
    1. EA migrates to S;
    2. **if** S has more than one predecessor in the $(L-1)$ layer **then**
        EA waits for other cloned EAs and gets their outputs;
        Other cloned EAs are destroyed by themselves;
    end if
    3. **if** the service on S is available **then**
        EA invokes the service on S and takes the output of the service;
        else EA sends a fail message to MA and the algorithm is ended;
    end if
    4. U = the successors nodes of S in the $(L+1)$ layer; m=the length of U;
    5. **if** $m = 0$ **then**
        EA sends the final result to MA and the algorithm is ended;
        else $(m-1)$ EAs are cloned;
    end if
    6. **for each** node N **in** U **do**
        One EA executes **migrate**(N);
    end for
  end function

Algorithm 2: The EA will start to work from the entry node of the marked DAG according to the four basic execution patterns mentioned above. Multiple EAs may be created to perform the tasks in parallel during the course of scheduling.

3.6.2.2 Scheduling Algorithm of the EA

Along with the DAG, the EA will execute the task according to the basic execution patterns mentioned above, and the directed edges in the DAG direct the EAs migration. The scheduling algorithm of EA is divided into two parts: Algorithm 1 and Algorithm 2. Algorithm 1 makes the nodes of the DAG with the layer number and Algorithm 2 gives the method of scheduling the EA, such as cloning a new EA, disposing oneself, communicating with each other and so on.

3.6.3 An Example for the Scheduling Algorithm of the EA

To describe the algorithm controlling the behavior of the EA explicitly, an example of the composite plan (shown in Figure 3.8) and its execution process are given respectively.

When the MA receives the composite plan, Algorithm 1 is firstly executed to mark every node in DAG with the layer number. The execution result is shown in Figure 3.9. Then, the MA creates an EA named A_1 with the marked DAG and A_1

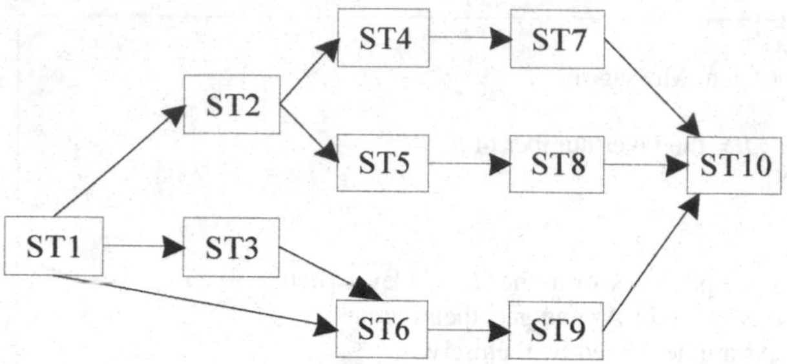

Fig. 3.8 An example of the composite plan

migrates to ST_1 to invoke the service on ST_1. After A_1 finishes the task, it clones itself to dispatch a new EA named A_2 to ST_3, and then itself moves to ST_2. After A_1 reaches ST_2 and finishes the task, it clones itself to dispatch a new EA named A_3 to ST_5 again, and then itself moves to ST_4. When A_1, A_2 and A_3 all reach ST_{10}, A_2 and A_3 transfer their outputs to A_1 and then are destroyed by themselves. Because ST_{10} is the end node, A_1 reports the final result to MA after it invokes the service on ST_{10}.

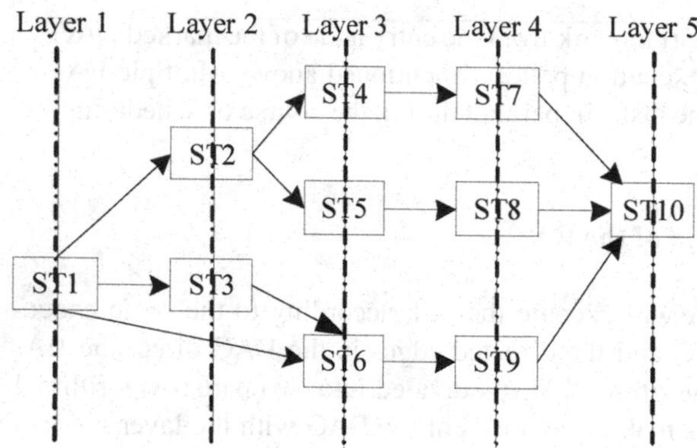

Fig. 3.9 The marked DAG

As shown in Figure 3.10, it is known there are three paths between ST_1 and ST_{10}. They are $(ST_1, ST_2, ST_4, ST_7, ST_{10})$, $(ST_1, ST_2, ST_5, ST_8, ST_{10})$ and $(ST_1, ST_3, ST_6, ST_9, ST_{10})$ respectively. These three paths can be traveled by A_1, A_2 and A_3 in parallel. This menas that the composite service can be implemented with the most flexibility by agents.

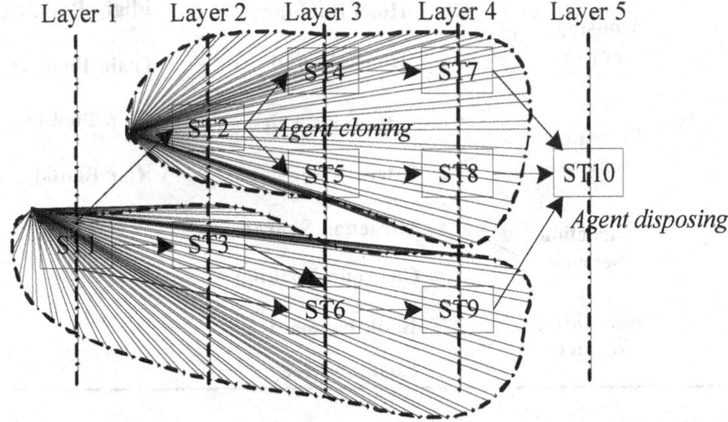

Fig. 3.10 The execution process for EA

3.7 Case Study

While the outcomes of our research are generic enough to be applicable to a wide range of applications, we use the area of e-traveling as a case study to ease the understanding of our solution for service composition.

3.7.1 Case Scenario Description

The major concern of e-traveling is to provide a detailed travel schedule and accomplish the relevant e-business process to customers by using information and communication technologies. With the dev AgFlow elopment of Web Service techniques, travel domain enterprises attempt to encapsulate their application processing into web services. Previously, when establishing a travel schedule, customers may access several different web services provided by the different enterprises; meanwhile the enterprises also need to communicate with each other. It not only reduces the burden on customers and enterprises but also improves the efficiency of travel planning. In the case study, four generic categories of services relevant to e-traveling, which are used in the travel assistant application, are presented, as shown in Figure 3.11.

Housing service

This kind of generic service can provide house rental and hotel booking services according to the users' needs.

- Hotel booking: Aimed at short-term housing. This service provides the relevant hotel booking service and its unit price is higher.

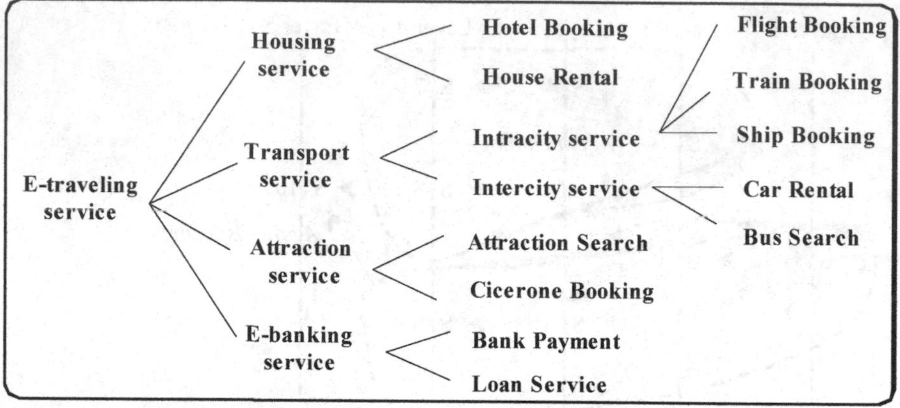

Fig. 3.11 The structure of four generic services

- House rental: Aimed at long-term housing. This service provides the relevant house rental service. Its unit price is lower, but you must rent more than one month.

Transport service
This kind of generic service can provide the transport search, vehicle rental and tickets booking services according to the customers' needs. Furthermore, in terms of the location of departure and destination, it can be divided into intercity transport and intracity transport.

1. Intercity transport. Mainly aimed at the different locations for departure and destination, provides the ticket booking for long-distance transport, including three special services:
   - Flight Booking: Both the departure and the destination must have an airport.
   - Train Booking: Both the departure and the destination must have a railway station.
   - Ship Booking: Needs an accessible sea route between the departure and the destination.
2. Intracity transport. Mainly aimed at the same locations for departure and destination, provides car rental and intracity vehicle search, including:
   - Car rental: Build a connection between users and the automobile leasing company, and provide users the convenient car rental operation.
   - Bus search: According to the departure and the destination, this service provides the bus search operation.

Attraction service
This kind of generic service can provide the attraction search and the cicerone booking services according to the users' need.

- Attraction search: This service provides users an individual attraction search service. It can search and find the recommended attractions in terms of the city and the users' preference.
- Cicerone booking: This service provides the cicerone booking operation to users.

E-banking service

This kind of generic service can provide users the relevant banking functions, including bank payment and loan services.

- Bank payment: Providing users an e-business payment operation using the Internet.
- Loan service: Providing users a loan-relevant operation

Let us consider the following typical scenario to the e-traveling application domain. Assume that John, a travel fan, wants to have a holiday in Beijing with his family. Typically, he would have to communicate with flight or train tickets offices to book and pay for the tickets. Then, he would book a hotel or search for attractions by using Internet. Also, when he arrived at the destination, he would want to rent a car or search for local travel passes. The resulting information is transmitted by different means of communication using different relevant single e-traveling services. John may also have to visit some of the departments. The difficulties in collecting the information and communicating with different services prevent consumers from the convenient e-traveling self-service. To facilitate the use of e-traveling services and expeditiously satisfy consumers' needs, we organize these independent services into a composite service called "Travel Assistant", which can achieve the whole business process, hide the underlying-details and provide a uniform access method to users.

Request:
Departure: *Nanjing*;
Destination:*Beijing*;
Date: 2008-8-8 ~ 2008-8-18;
Expense: no more than $2000;
Payment method: e-banking;
Additional: Need attraction search; Need local traffic.

Fig. 3.12 Example travel request

In this case, John is planning to travel to Beijing from Nanjing, then he sends a travel request to the Travel Assistant service, such as that shown in Figure 3.12

John's travel request can be divided into several sub-requests. Each sub-request would typically be performed by executing one or more web services relevant to e-traveling. The detailed description of the service processing will be described later. Our work is mainly about how these e-traveling services can be used to build up one composite service to achieve users' requirements by using a multi-agent based service composition infrastructure.

3.7.2 Multi-Agent System for Service Composition

As shown in Figure 3.13, there are two service virtual domains denoted respectively by two dashed line frames in the multi-agent system used by this case study. There is one distributed service register depository and three workstations in every virtual domain. In each service register depository, one Registry Agent has been deployed. Also the serviccs rclevant to e-traveling have been deployed on each workstation. Meanwhile, the system has one portal workstation C and there are two agents called Portal Agent and Decision Agent respectively in it. In order to simplify the case description, every kind of service has only two different services provided by different providers. The details of all services relevant to e-traveling, which have been deployed on the workstations, are described as follows in Table 3.1.

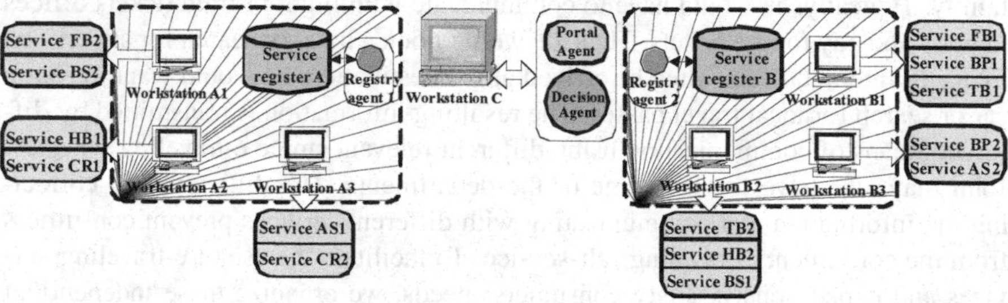

Fig. 3.13 The multi-agent system for service composition

Table 3.1 The services relevant to e-traveling in the system

Service name	Short name	Category	Location
Flight booking 1	FB1	Transport service	Workstation B1
Flight booking 2	FB2	Transport service	Workstation A1
Train booking 1	TB1	Transport service	Workstation B1
Train booking 2	TB2	Transport service	Workstation B2
Bank payment 1	BP1	E-banking service	Workstation B1
Bank payment 2	BP2	E-banking service	Workstation B3
Hotel booking 1	HB1	Housing service	Workstation A2
Hotel booking 2	HB2	Housing service	Workstation B2
Attraction search 1	AS1	Attraction service	Workstation A3
Attraction search 2	AS2	Attraction service	Workstation B3
Car rental 1	CR1	Transport service	Workstation A2
Car rental 2	CR2	Transport service	Workstation A3
Bus search 1	BS1	Transport service	Workstation B2
Bus search 2	BS2	Transport service	Workstation A1

3.7.3 Travel Assistant Service Compositing

According to the multi-agent system and the case study scenario mentioned above, the processing sequences of the service composition for the travel assistant service can be denoted by the sequence numbers in Figure 3.14. The details of the process are as follows.

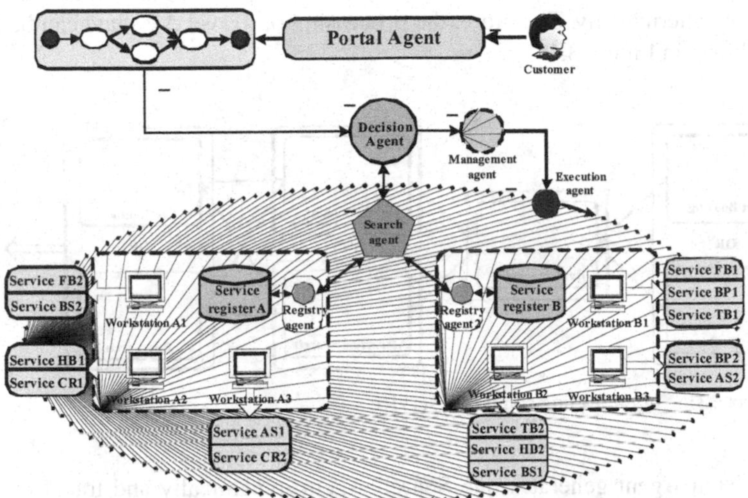

Fig. 3.14 The processing of travel assistant service composing

Step1. The customer (John) submits the request to the Portal Agent. The request can be denoted by XML as shown in Figure 3.15.

```
<Request>
   < Departure>Nanjing<Departure>
   <Destination>Beijing</Destination>
   < Date>
      < Begin>2008-8-8</Begin>
      < End>2008-8-18</End>
   </ Date>
   < Expense><= $2000</Expense>
   < Payment method>e-banking</Payment method>
   < Additional>
      < A>Need attraction search </A>
      < B>Need local traffic</B>
   </ Additional>
</Request>
```

Fig. 3.15 The XML format of John's request

Step2. The Portal Agent decomposes John's request into several subtasks and submits the service composition processing to the Decision Agent. According to the departure and the destination, flight and train are two possible travel methods. So the flight booking service and the train booking service are chosen, but they are alternatives. Whichever ticket booking service is chosen, the e-banking service is necessary. After the payment for the ticket, two kinds of services, hotel booking and attraction search, can be executed synchronously. At last, according to the location of the hotel and the attraction, the car rental service or the bus search service should be chosen alternatively. Therefore, the processing of Travel Assistant can be described as shown in Figure 3.16.

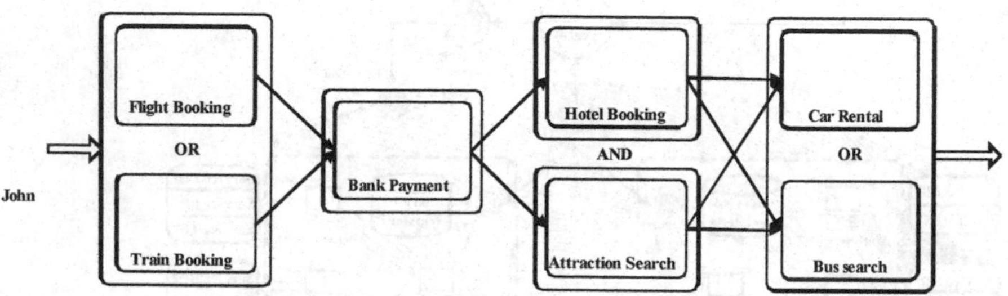

Fig. 3.16 The processing of e-traveling composite service

Step3. Decision Agent generates one Search Agent dynamically and transfers the information about every kind of service in the composition processing to it. Afterwards, the Search Agent makes a conversation with Registry Agents located at domain-A and domain-B respectively in order to discover all available services and get the relevant QoS parameters from them, which are located at every workstation, that satisfy the demands of the travel assistant service. Meanwhile, according to the dynamical change of the network topology, every Registry Agent maintains the position of the neighbor domain's Registry Agent. In this scenario situation, the details and QoS parameters of the services relevant to e-traveling, which are obtained by the Search Agent, are denoted in Table 3.2. In order to simplify the discussion, the QoS of every service is denoted by three parameters described in the third column of Table 3.2, including the response time, the service availability and the service cost. The fourth column of Table 3.2 denotes the QoS benefit value of the service, which can be calculated by user satisfaction function and utility function defined as follows.

$$s_{time} = \begin{cases} 1 & t \in [0,50] \\ 1/(t-50) & t \in (50,150) \\ 0 & t \in [150,+\infty) \end{cases} \tag{3.6}$$

$$s_{expensive} = \begin{cases} 1 & e \in [0,40] \\ 1/(e-40) & e \in (40,120) \\ 0 & e \in [120,+\infty) \end{cases} \tag{3.7}$$

Table 3.2 The details of all the available services

Service name	Location	QoS parameters (Response time/cost/availability)	Benefit value of the service
Flight booking 1	B1	40/60/0.99	0.711
Flight booking 2	A1	50/50/0.94	0.706
Train booking 1	B1	80/100/0.94	0.391
Train booking 2	B2	90/80/0.97	0.403
Bank payment 1	B1	80/140/0.96	0.397
Bank payment 2	B3	100/120/0.98	0.402
Hotel booking 1	A2	70/100/0.98	0.412
Hotel booking 2	B2	80/90/0.97	0.404
Attraction search 1	A3	110/130/0.98	0.400
Attraction search 2	B3	130/100/0.97	0.397
Car rental 1	A2	120/40/0.92	0.672
Car rental 2	A3	90/80/0.97	0.403
Bus search 1	B2	70/50/0.98	0.437
Bus search 2	A1	50/60/0.96	0.699

$$s_{avai} = a \; a \in [0.8, 1] \tag{3.8}$$

$$u = 0.3.s_{time} + 0.3.s_{expensive} + 0.4.s_{avai} \tag{3.9}$$

For example, three QoS parameters of Flight Booking 1 are X, Y and Z respectively. In term of formulas 3.6, 3.7, and 3.8, the benefit value of every QoS parameter is 1, 0.05 and 0.99 respectively. Using formula 3.9, the benefit value of Flight Booking 1 can be calculated as follows: $u = 0.3*1+0.3*0.05+0.4*0.99 = 0.711$.

Step4. According to the scheduling algorithm mentioned above, the Decision Agent accomplishes the service selection of the travel assistant composite service. The final composition plan is denoted in Figure 3.17. The optimal selection of services, which maximized the sum of all service utilities, is {F1, B2, H1, A1, B2} with a total utility of 823, an execution time of 300, an expense of 480 and an availability of 91.28%.

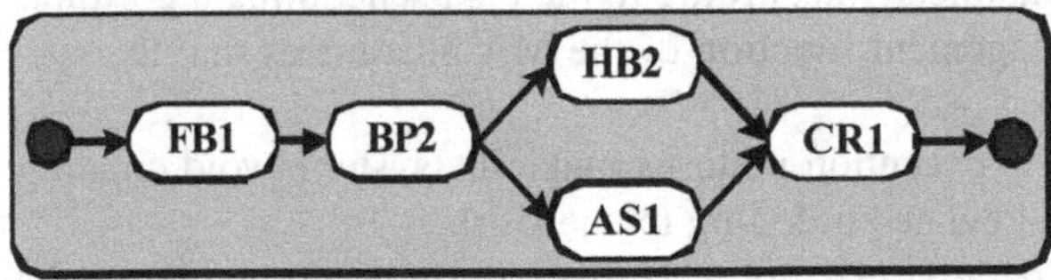

Fig. 3.17 Final composition plan of travel assistant service

Step5. Subsequently, the Decision Agent generates a Management Agent dynamically and transfers the optimal composition plan to the MA.

Step6. Finally, the Management Agent creates an Execution Agent with the optimal composition plan dynamically. Then, the EA should call the services in the proper sequence according to the optimal composition plan. Firstly, the EA moves to the entry service FB1 located at workstation B1 in domain B. After calling FB1 and obtaining its result, EA moves to workstation B3 to call the service BP2. After BP2 is executed, HB2 and AS1 can be executed synchronously. Therefore, EA should be cloned and takes the remnant plan to HB2 and AS1 located at workstation B2 and A3 respectively. When both of them are executed successfully and move to the final service CR1, only one EA is needed and the cloned EA should be destroyed. Finally, after all the services of the travel assistant are executed successfully, the final result of the composite service will be transferred to the MA, and then John will receive all the Nanjing-Beijing travel information about the flight ticket booking, hotel booking, the relevant attractions and car rental.

3.8 Conclusion and Future Work

Service composition offers a way to expand the ability of the single service and implement service reuse. It allows a distributed application to be constructed through the combination of other existing services, and this composition offers added value to the original services. However, the service discovery and selection mechanisms are static and not flexible in existing approaches to service composition, and the end-to-end QoS of a composite service can not always be ensured. This chapter puts forward a Multi-agent based QoS-aware Service Composition solution (MQSC), which not only provides a mechanism for dynamic service composition but also can ensure the end-to-end QoS of the composite service. Compared with the existing methods for using multi-agent systems in service composition [6, 8, 20, 25], our solution has the following characteristics:

1. Executing automatically: Once the task is submitted to the PA, the process of service composition including service search, service selection and service execution will be executed automatically.
2. Deciding dynamically: On the one hand, the DA decides the optimal service composition plan dynamically based on the ACS. On the other hand, the EA decides their behaviors dynamically according to the plan scheduling algorithm.
3. Fault recovering: The management function of the MA guarantees that the system has fault tolerance.
4. Saving resources: The basic execution patterns make the system avoid creating redundant agents so as to alleviate burdening the network.
5. Allowing distributed and parallel execution: If there are multiple parallel paths in the SCG, multiple EAs will travel these paths in parallel without waiting. This avoids the frequent communication between agents presented in [6].

In this chapter, we assume that the Task Graph has been given and focus on service search, service selection and service execution. Thus, how to get the Task Graph from the general requirements submitted by customers is one of our future works.

In addition, heuristic information could improve the performance of the ASC based algorithm, so other heuristic methods would be also considered in our future work.

Acknowledgements

This work is supported by the National Natural Science Foundation of China under Grants No. 90604004 and 90412014, Jiangsu Provincial Natural Science Foundation of China under Grants No. BK2007708 and Jiangsu Provincial Key Laboratory of Network and Information Security under Grants No. BM2003201.

References

1. B. Benatallah, Q. Z. Sheng and M. Dumas. The Self-serve Environment for Web Services Composition. *IEEE Internet Computing*, 1:40–48, 2003.
2. M. Berger, M. Bouzid and M. Buckland. An Approach to Agent-Based Service Composition and Its Application to Mobile Business Processes. *IEEE Transaction on Mobile Computing*, 2(3):197–206, 2003.
3. BPEL4WS Consortium. Business Process Execution Language for Web Services http://www.ibm.com/Developerworks/library/ws-bpel, 2003.
4. G. D. Caro and M. Dorigo. AntNet: Distributed Stigmergetic Control for Communications Networks. *Journal of Artificial Intelligence Research*, 9:317–365, 1998.
5. F. Casati, S. Ilnicki and L. J. Jin. Adaptive and Dynamic Service Composition in eFlow. In *Proceedings of CAiSE00*, pages 13–31, 2000.
6. Y. Charif-Djebbar and N. Sabouret Dynamic Service Composition and Selection through an Agent Interaction Protocol. In *Proceedings of IEEE/WIC/ACM International Conference on Web Intelligence and International Agent Technology Workshops*, pages 105–108, 2006.
7. M. Dorigo, L. M. Gambardella. Ant Colony System: A Cooperative Learning Approach to the Traveling Salesman Problem. *IEEE Transactions on Evolutionary Computation*, 1(1):53–66, 1997.
8. F. Ensan, M. Kahani and E. Bagheri. Web Service Composition based on Agent Societies and Ontological Concepts. In *Proceedings of IEEE International Conference on Computational Cybernetics*, pages 1–10, 2006.
9. J. Hendler and D. McGuinness. The DARPA Agent Markup Language. *IEEE Intelligent Systems*, 15(6):72–73, 2000.
10. R. Hull, M. Benedikt and V. Christophides E-Services: A Look Behind the Curtain. In *Proceedings of the 22nd ACM Symposium on Principles of Database Systems* pages 1–14, 2003.
11. IBM. Business Process with BPEL4WS: Learning BPEL. http://www.128.ibm.com/-developerworks/webservices/library/ws-bpelcol2/.
12. S. Liu, J. Lin and Z. Lin. A Shortest-path Network Problem Using an Annealed Ant System Algorithm. In *Proceedings of the 4th Annual ACIS International Conference on Computer and Information Science*, pages 245–250, 2005.
13. S. Liu, Y. Liu and F. Zhang. A Dynamic Web Services Selection Algorithm with QoS Global Optimal in Web Services Composition. *Journal of Software*, 18(3):646–656, 2007.
14. Z. Maamar, S. K. Mostefaoui and H. Yahyaoui. Toward an Agent-Based and Context-Oriented Approach for Web Services Composition. *IEEE Transaction on Knowledge and Data Engineering*, 17(5):686–697, 2005.
15. S. McIlraith and T. C. Son. Adapting Golog for Composition of Semantic Web Services. In *Proceedings of KR02*, pages 482–496, 2002.

16. B. Medjahed, A. Bouguettaya, and A. K. Elmagarmid. Composing Web services on the Semantic Web. *The International Journal on Very Large Data Bases*, 12(4):333–351, 2003.
17. D. A. Menasce. Composing Web Service: A QoS View. *IEEE Internet Computing*, 8(6):88–90, 2004.
18. I. Muller and R. Kowalczyk. Service Composition through Agent-based Coalition Formation. In *Proceedings of the first workshop on Service Composition with Semantic Web Services*, pages 44–53, 2005.
19. S. C. Oh, B. W. On and E. J. Larson. Web Services Discovery and Composition as Graph Search Problem. In *Proceedings of EEE05*, pages 784–786, 2005.
20. Z. Qian, S. Lu and L. Xie. Mobile-Agent-Based Web Service Composition *LNCS 3795*, pages 35–46, 2005.
21. M. K. Smith, C. Welty and D. McGuinness. Owl Web Ontology Language Guide. http://www.w3.org/TR/owl-guide/, 2003.
22. B. Srivastava and J. Koehler. Web Service Composition—Current Solutions and Open Problems. In *Proceedings of ICAPS03*, pages 28–35, 2003.
23. H. Sun, X. Wang and B. Zhou. Research and Implementation of Dynamic Web Services Composition. In *Proceedings of APPT03*, pages 457–466, 2003.
24. P. Traverso and M. Pistore. Automated Composition of Semantic Web Services into Executable Processes. In *Proceedings of ISWC04*, pages 380–394, 2004.
25. J. R. Velascol and S. F. Castillo. Mobile Agents for Web Service Composition. In *Proceedings of EC-Web03*, pages 135–144, 2003.
26. Z. Wu, J. Luo and A. Song. Qos-Based grid resource management. *Journal of Software*, 17(11):2264–2276, 2006.
27. T. Yu and K. J. Lin. A Broker-Based Framework for QoS-Aware Web Service Composition. In *Proceedings of EEE05*, pages 22–29, 2005.
28. T. Yu, Y. Zhang and K. J. Lin. Efficient Algorithms for Web Services Selection with End-to-End QoS Constrains. *ACM Transactions on the Web*, 1(1), 2007.
29. L. Zeng, B. Benatallah and A. H. H. Ngu. QoS-aware Middleware for Web Services Composition. *IEEE Transaction on Software Engineering*, 30(5):311–327, 2004.
30. L. Zhang, B. Li and T. Chao. On Demand Web Services-based Business Process Composition. In *Proceedings of the IEEE International Conference on System, Man, and Cybernetics*, pages 4057–4064, 2003.

Chapter 4
Flexible Workflow Management in Service Oriented Environments

Birgit Hofreiter and Christian Huemer

Abstract Ever faster changing market conditions require businesses to frequently adapt their business processes and the underlying workflow systems. Service-oriented architectures are said to deliver this flexibility by loose coupling. In this chapter we provide a survey on realizing flexible workflows on top of service oriented architectures. We show how orchestrations and choreographies may be implemented by state-of-the-art web services technology. The role of agents in realizing workflows among services is discussed. Furthermore, we discuss service provision in dynamic environments, when partners are dynamically bound to the workflow and when changes to the workflow schema happen.

4.1 Introduction

In the 1990s the work of Hammer and Champy on business process reengineering [10] attracted a lot of attention and companies started to rethink their business processes. Hammer and Champy define a business process as an organized group of related activities that together create customer value. It is the goal to optimize business processes in a way to meet a company's business goals, such as financial targets. Accordingly, the activities of a business process must be arranged to optimize a company's output. This arrangement defines which activities have to be executed in which order, under which conditions, by whom and by using which resources. The result is described in a business process model. Over the last decade a lot of different approaches to business process modeling have been developed, such

Birgit Hofreiter
Institute of Information Systems, University of Liechtenstein, Vaduz 9490, Liechtenstein
e-mail: Birgit.Hofreiter@hochschule.li

Christian Huemer
Vienna University of Technology, Favoritenstrasse 9-11/188-3, Vienna 1040, Austria
e-mail: huemer@big.tuwien.ac.at

N. Griffiths, K.-M. Chao (eds.), *Agent-Based Service-Oriented Computing*,
Advanced Information and Knowledge Processing,
DOI 10.1007/978-1-84996-041-0_4, © Springer-Verlag London Limited 2010

as [2, 34, 40]. Today, business process modeling is supported by a lot of different analysis, design and implementation tools.

Once the business process has been modeled and optimized, it must be executed as defined. The correct and model-compliant execution is guaranteed by a workflow system [21]. Workflow systems already started in the 1970s to automate office paper processing. However, in the 1990s the focus shifted towards elevating the abstractions of IT to a level that these abstractions are directly understood and manipulated by business users to optimize their business processes and to achieve competitive advantage [14].

In the last decade new business challenges have a significant impact on workflow systems. Shorter life cycles of products and services require faster changing business models and business process models. Information systems must quickly adjust to the adapted business processes. It is necessary that the following changes in a business process are directly reflected in an underlying workflow system [45]: changing the flow of activities of a business process, changing the actors who are performing these activities, changing the tools that support these activities, etc.

The ever increasing speed of changes in business and, consequently, in the IT infrastructure require a very flexible architecture. Service-oriented architectures are the current state-of-the-art providing this flexibility by a loose coupling between a service and the consumer of this service. Loose coupling does not mandate any knowledge about platforms, implementations, format protocols neither on the requester nor on the provider side. Precluding this knowledge facilitates changing services and their providers. Also, services within a composite service may easily be replaced by other ones. Since a workflow may be seen as a composite service defining an orchestrated set of services, it seems to be beneficial to realize a workflow by web services [15]—the current state-of-the-art technology for service oriented architectures.

This chapter provides a survey of realizing workflows in service oriented environments. Conceptually, we distinguish between orchestrated and choreographed flows. Section 4.2 introduces the concepts of orchestration and choreography. Orchestrated workflows are under control of a single workflow engine, whereas choreographed workflows describe how autonomous workflow engines interact with each other in an inter-organizational workflow. Choreographies may be described from the local view of one engine or from a neutral, global view. The concepts of orchestration as well as of local and global choreography are introduced by means of a simple order management example. Furthermore, we refer to approaches realizing transformations between orchestrations and choreographies.

In Section 4.3 we show how workflows are realized in web services. We start with an introduction to web services standards for specifying workflows. From these standards we select the most promising one—the business process execution language (BPEL)—to demonstrate the specification of a workflow among web services. This demonstration uses the same example as in Section 4.2. Additionally, BPEL is checked against the workflow patterns from Aalst et al. [39] to analyze its expressiveness.

Section 4.4 deals with the role of agents in realizing flexible workflows in service oriented environments. We have a look at useful agents in orchestrations, which are search agents, selection agents and composition agents. Furthermore, agents may also be used in establishing choreographies between business partners. Here we discuss the role of agents in two different approaches: a bottom-up approach starting from an existing local choreography of a partner and a top-down approach in which a global choreography is agreed before deriving the local choreographies of each partner.

The service provision in dynamic environments is discussed in Section 4.5. We concentrate on meeting service constraints in environments where the characteristics of the services of a workflow may change. In the beginning, we analyze the requirements of such dynamic workflows. Following these requirements we focus on two major aspects: Firstly, we concentrate on the dynamic selection of services being part of a workflow. Secondly, we focus on unplanned situations that have not been considered in the design of a workflow. Accordingly, the workflow has to undergo modifications leading to a workflow schema evolution which may affect running instances of the workflow. Hereby, we differ between the dynamic evolution of local processes and the one of inter-organizational processes. Again, we will use the order management example of Section 4.2 to demonstrate the dynamic workflows. Finally, a summary and outlook in Section 4.6 concludes this chapter.

4.2 Orchestration and Choreography

4.2.1 Motivation and Definitions

Hammer and Champy's definition of a business process [10] targets at (re-)structuring the business processes from a single company's perspective optimizing its outcome. Over the last few years supply chain management involving multiple parties became more and more popular, leading to an inter-organizational focus of business process management. In this context the above given definition of a business process of Hammer and Champy toward creating customer value does not fit anymore, because a supply chain includes many seller—customer relationships. An inter-organizational business process is an organized group of related activities carried out by multiple organizations to accomplish a common business goal. An inter-organizational business process does not focus on the internal tasks of an individual organization, it rather focuses on the tasks carried out between the actors in the network of organizations.

A service oriented architecture and its realization by web services, may be used to describe and implement the workflow of both kinds of business processes described above. In the area of web services two terms have emerged to distinguish the two kinds of business processes: orchestration and choreography. These terms describe closely related, but well distinguished concepts [28]. Orchestration deals with the sequence and conditions in which one business process calls its components to realize a business goal. Choreography describes business processes in a peer-to-peer collaboration. It describes the flow of interactions between the participating business partners that interlink their individual processes. We distinguish local and global choreographies. A local choreography describes the flow from a participating partner's point of view. It makes the public parts of its local process visible to others. A global choreography defines the inter-organizational process from a neutral perspective. A global choreography has the potential to achieve an agreement between the partners. Local choreographies enable the configuration of each partner's system.

4.2.2 Orchestration

In order to illustrate the differences between orchestration and choreography we use the following example that is used throughout this chapter: we take a detailed look on a simplified order management processes at the sales department of the seller which interfaces with the processes of a buyer and a carrier. Once the seller receives an order from the buyer, the seller checks compliance of the order against an offer he made before. In order to fulfill the order the seller reserves necessary products from the stock as well as the resources of the production line. Once these tasks are accomplished he is able to calculate a delivery date for the order. Knowing the delivery date, the seller reserves transport at the carrier. Now the seller is able to accept (or reject) the order of the buyer. Once the order is accepted, the buyer may (repeatedly) ask for the status of the order. The buyer may cancel the order until the goods are shipped. In this case the seller has to clear the reservation of the stock and the reservation of the production line. If the buyer does not cancel the order and the goods are ready to ship the seller sends a notification of shipment to the buyer—this indicates also that he is not able to cancel the order anymore and that status request is not possible anymore since the "final" status *shipped* is reached. After shipping takes places, the sales department of the seller hands over the case to the accounting department.

A service-oriented model of the example process described above is presented in Figure 4.1. This example process focuses on the orchestration of the seller's tasks in the middle lane of Figure 4.1. We do not detail the orchestrations of the buyer and the carrier, but show their choreographies in the left lane and in the right lane, respectively. Each node in Figure 4.1 represents a service executing a specific task. The abbreviation within the node shows who is offering the service: the seller's sales department (Ss), the seller's production department (Sp), the seller's accounting department (Sa), the buyer (B), or the carrier (C). A new process instance is created when the seller's sales department receives a call of the *order product* service. The fact that this is an asynchronous incoming call is denoted by the little incoming arrow above the node *order product.* Afterwards, the seller's department uses the service *check against offer* from the accounting department which is a synchronous

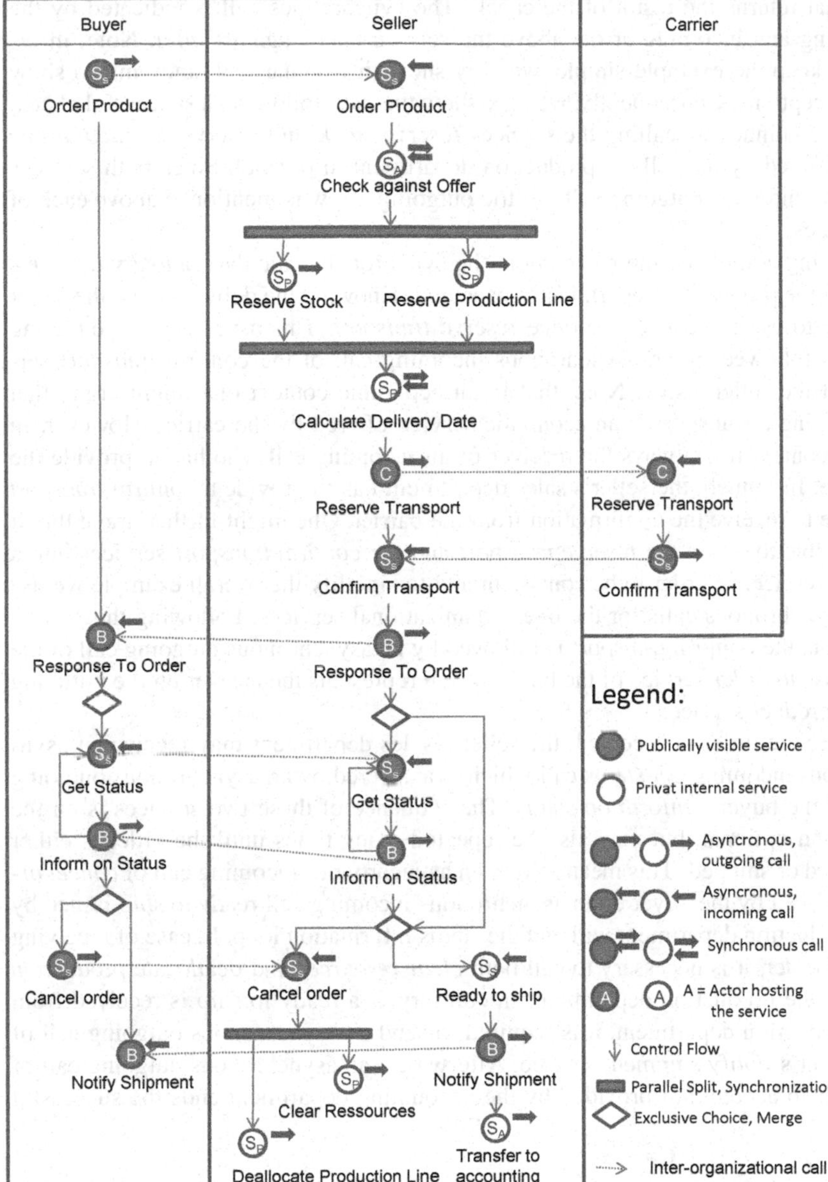

Fig. 4.1 Seller's orchestration of the order management

call that returns the result of the check. The synchronous call is indicated by the outgoing and incoming arrow above the service *check against offer.* Note, in order to keep the example simple, we only show the regular path and omit to show any exceptions. Consequently, we only show the path following a successful check, which continues by calling the services *reserve stock* and *reserve production line* both offered by the seller's production department in parallel. Since both services are asynchronous outgoing calls a little outgoing arrow is mentioned above each of the nodes.

Having completed the reservation, the synchronous *calculate delivery date* service of the production department is executed. Knowing the delivery data, the seller is able to use the carrier's service *reserve transport.* This asynchronous outgoing call, is followed by an asynchronous incoming call of the *confirm transport* service at the seller's side. Note, that in an economic context one might argue that confirming a transport is an economic service offered by the carrier. However, in an IT context it is always the receiver of an incoming call who has to provide the service. Inasmuch, the seller's sales department has to provide a *confirm transport* service to receive the confirmation from the carrier. One might further argue that it is possible to group the *reserve transport* and the *confirm transport* services into a single service. In order to be consistent and to simplify the overall example we use just asynchronous calls for the inter-organizational services. Following this design decision, the *confirm transport* is followed by an asynchronous outgoing call of the *response to order* service of the buyer which represents the answer on the initiating *order product* service.

After the order is accepted, the seller's sales department may receive an asynchronous incoming *get status* call which is answered by an asynchronous outgoing call of the buyer's *inform on status.* The sequence of these two services is on the one hand optional, but may also be repeated many times until the order is either canceled or shipped. This means either an asynchronous incoming call of *cancel order* invoked by the buyer or an asynchronous incoming call *ready to ship* issued by the production department will end the status information loop. In case of receiving *cancel order,* it is necessary to call both *clear resources* and *deallocate production line* of the production department. In contrary, if a *ready to ship* is received from the production department, it is required to send an asynchronous outgoing call of the buyer's *notify shipment* service. Afterwards, an asynchronous outgoing call of *transfer to accounting* provided by the accounting department ends the successful case.

4.2.3 Local Choreography

In Figure 4.2 we show the local choreographies of the seller, the buyer, and the carrier. Since we did not detail the internals of the buyer and the carrier in Figure 4.1, their local choreographies remain unchanged in Figure 4.2. In contrary, Figure 4.1 shows the seller's orchestration. It includes services visible to the outside world,

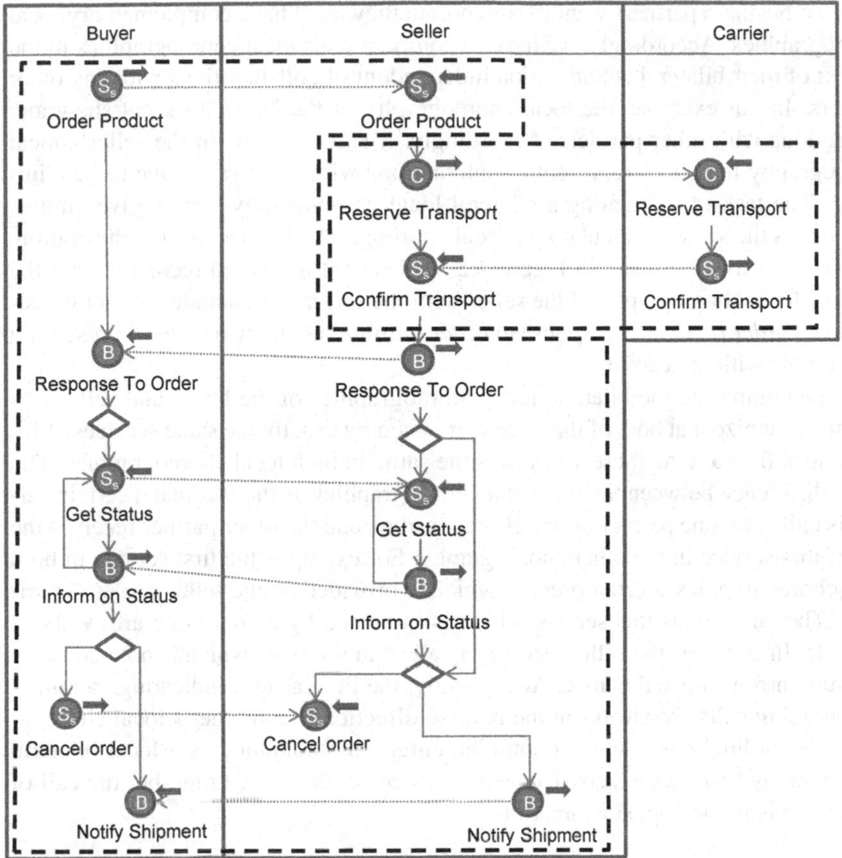

Fig. 4.2 Local choreographies

which are shown as gray nodes, and services visible only within the seller, which are presented as white nodes. By calculating the local orchestration of the seller we have to eliminate the white nodes of the internal services. In other words, we produce a projection of the orchestration including only the gray nodes of the externally visible services. Eliminating some nodes results also in eliminating transitions to/from these nodes. Accordingly, this leads to some tangling nodes that have to be connected in order to complete the graph of a local choreography. Approaches that deal with such transformations are introduced in 4.2.5.

The elimination of the internal white nodes ends up in the local choreography of the seller in the middle lane of Figure 4.2. This local choreography is a multi-party choreography, since it comprises interactions between the seller and the buyer as well as interactions between the seller and the carrier. In Figure 4.2 we have marked the regions of the bilateral interactions by dotted line borders.

If two business partners want to collaborate they must have complementary local choreographies. Accordingly, we have to compare their local choreographies in the context of their bilateral collaboration independent of collaborations with any other partners. In our example, the local choreography of the buyer does not show any interactions with other partners. Accordingly, it stays as it is. In the seller's local choreography the nodes representing interactions with the carrier have to be eliminated. The task of calculating a bilateral local choreography from a given multi-party one is the same as calculating a local choreography from a given orchestration. We omit to show the result in Figure 4.2 , because it is easy to recognize that the bilateral local choreography of the seller with the buyer will include a direct transition from *order product* to *response to order* eliminating the two nodes representing interactions with the carrier.

When comparing the bilateral local choreographies of the buyer and seller it is easy to recognize that both of them are composed by exactly the same services. Also the control flow among these services is the same in both local choreographies. The major difference between the two local choreographies, is the fact that a certain service is called by one partner in one choreography, and the other partner receives the call of this service in the other choreography. For example, the first service in both local choreographies is *order product* which is provided by the seller's sales department. The buyer calls this service which is indicated by an outgoing arrow above the node. In contrary, the seller receives a call of this service which is notated by an incoming arrow above the node. Accordingly, the little arrows indicating incoming and outgoing calls are always in the reverse direction in a partner's local choreography. Accordingly, we define a complementary choreography as a local bilateral choreography that uses exactly the same services in the same order, but the call of the service is in the opposite direction.

4.2.4 Global Choreography

In the previous subsection we learned that each business partner describes its local choreography from its own perspective. This means if two business partners collaborate, there will be two local choreographies—one for each business partner. In order to negotiate the collaboration, the business partners have to adjust their own local choreographies in a way that they are complementary to each other. In order to reach agreement and commitment between the business partners, it is more convenient to discuss the choreography between them from a common neutral perspective. This means that a single global choreography describes the services that are involved in the interaction and the order in which the services are executed. For each of the services being part of the steps of a global choreography it is fixed who calls the service and who receives the call of the service.

Figure 4.3 shows the global choreography between buyer and seller for our example process. The control flow of the services remains the same as in Figure 4.2. However, instead of having two local choreographies assigned to the corresponding

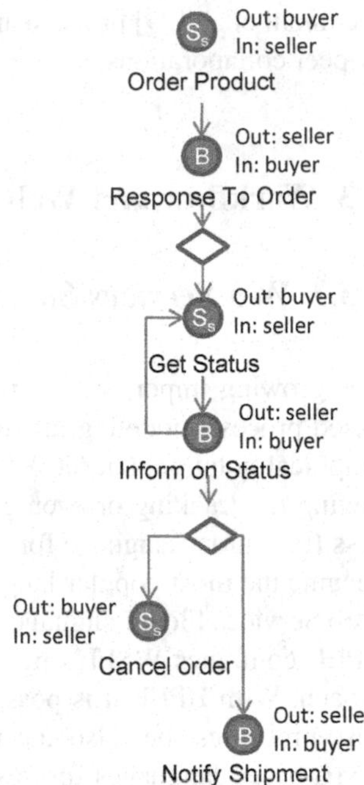

Fig. 4.3 Global choreography between buyer and seller

lanes of the buyer and the seller, respectively, the global choreography uses just a single description of this control flow and mentions for each service the outbound and the inbound role. Having reached an agreement on the global choreography it is an easy task for the buyer and the seller to derive their local choreographies.

4.2.5 Approaches to Transform Between Orchestration and Choreography

There exist some approaches that take care of the relationship between orchestration, local choreography, and global choreography. In particular, the different perspectives can be transformed into each other. The global choreography can be transformed into the local choreography, and the local choreography can be transformed into an orchestration. The basic idea of transforming a global choreography into a local choreography is partitioning the global choreography in a way that the messages used in the resulting local choreographies are matched to the corresponding party. This partitioning is achieved by eliminating messages which are not related to the particular party. Such an approach is described by Aalst in [41]. The transformation of a local choreography into a global choreography can be realized by relating message exchanges of different local choreographies that semantically complement one another. An approach based on workflow nets is proposed by Aalst [36, 37].

Piccinelli et al. [29] propose another transformation approach in particular for peer-to-peer collaborations.

4.3 Workflow and Web Services

4.3.1 Web Services Standards for Business Processes

The growing importance of web services triggered a lot of efforts towards XML-based process modeling languages. These languages usually have no standardized graphical notation, but the XML-based notation may be interpreted by software allowing the tracking or even execution of the business process. The Business Process Execution Language for Web Services (BPEL4WS or BPEL for short) [22, 27] became the most popular language in this area. BPEL is a successor of both IBM's Web Services Flow Language (WSFL) [16] and Microsoft's XLANG [25]. Thereby, BPEL combines WSFL's petri net based approach and XLANG's pi calculus approach. With BPEL it is possible to describe the orchestration of executable business processes, but also the message exchanges in a local choreography. Other XML-based languages for describing orchestrations are the XML Process Definition Language (XPDL) [49] and the Petri Net Markup Language (PNML) [17]. Languages based on XML for describing local choreographies are the Web Services Choreography Interface (WSCI) [42] and the Web Services Conversation Language (WSCL) [43].

With regard to modeling global choreographies, the Web Services Choreography Description Language (WS-CDL) [44] is the choice in the area of web services. However, WS-CDL uses its own set of control flow constructs which are hard to map to those of BPEL. In order to overcome this limitation, BPEL4chor [8] has recently been proposed to extend BPEL for describing global choreographies. Another XML-based language for describing global choreographies is ebXML's Business Process Specification Schema (BPSS) [26].

4.3.2 Specifying a Business Process by Means of BPEL

As mentioned above, the Business Process Execution Language (BPEL) has become the most dominant language for specifying workflows in the area of web services. Thus, we concentrate on BPEL for specifying workflows in a service-oriented environment and do not further detail any of the other orchestration and choreography languages. In this subsection we introduce the main concepts of BPEL. Furthermore, we demonstrate how the examples of Section 4.2 are represented in BPEL.

BPEL specifies a business process among web services. To be more precise, it is a flow among web services operations that are provided by one or more business partners. These operations are defined as part of port types in one or more WSDL files. In order to keep our example simple, we assume that all port types are defined in a single WSDL file shown in lines 001–078. In reality, the port types of different business partners are more likely to be defined in different WSDL files.

In our order management process as depicted in Figure 4.1 five organizations are involved. Accordingly, we define five port types for the following organizations: buyer (B) in lines 003–012, carrier (C) in lines 013–017, seller sales department (Ss) in lines 018–034, seller accounting department (Sa) in lines 035–043, and seller production department (Sp) in lines 044–061. Each of the nodes in Figure 4.1 represent an operation. These nodes are already marked with organization (B, C, Ss, Sa, Sp) or the port type, respectively, which provides the operation. Consequently, we assign these operations to the respective port type in the WSDL file. Most of these operations are asynchronous message exchanges. It follows that most of these services only have an input message. The exceptions are the operations *check against offer* and *calculate delivery date* which are synchronous message exchanges comprising an input and an output message. All the input and output messages refer to messages declared in the same WSDL file. Due to space limitations we have skipped the message definitions and only highlight the need for message declarations in line 002.

```
001 <wsdl:definitions xmlns:wsdl="http://schemas.xmlsoap.org/wsdl/"
      xmlns:tns="http://new.webservice.namespace"
      xmlns:plnk="http://docs.oasis-open.org/wsbpel/2.0/plnktype"
      targetNamespace="http://new.webservice.namespace" ...>

002   <wsdl:message name="..."/>

003   <wsdl:portType name="B">
004     <wsdl:operation name="responseToOrder">
005       <wsdl:input message="tns:OrderResponse"/>
006     </wsdl:operation>
007     <wsdl:operation name="informOnStatus">
008       <wsdl:input message="tns:Status"/>
009     </wsdl:operation>
010     <wsdl:operation name="notifyShipment">
011       <wsdl:input message="tns:NotificationOfShipment"/>
010     </wsdl:operation>
012   </wsdl:portType>

013   <wsdl:portType name="C">
014   <wsdl:operation name="reserveTransport">
015       <wsdl:input message="tns:TransportRequest"/>
016     </wsdl:operation>
017   </wsdl:portType>

018   <wsdl:portType name="Ss">
019     <wsdl:operation name="orderProduct">
020       <wsdl:input message="tns:PurchaseOrder"/>
021     </wsdl:operation>
022     <wsdl:operation name="confirmTransport">
023       <wsdl:input message="tns:TransportConfirmation"/>
024     </wsdl:operation>
025     <wsdl:operation name="getStatus">
026       <wsdl:input message="tns:StatusRequest"/>
027     </wsdl:operation>
028     <wsdl:operation name="cancelOrder">
029       <wsdl:input message="tns:OrderCancellation"/>
030     </wsdl:operation>
```

```
    <wsdl:operation name="readyToShip">
      <wsdl:input message="tns:NotificationOfShipment"/>
    </wsdl:operation>
  </wsdl:portType>
  <wsdl:portType name="Sa">
    <wsdl:operation name="checkAgainstOffer">
      <wsdl:input message="tns:PurchaseOrder"/>
      <wsdl:output message="tns:CheckResult"/>
    </wsdl:operation>
    <wsdl:operation name="transferToAccounting">
      <wsdl:input message="tns:OrderInformation"/>
    </wsdl:operation>
  </wsdl:portType>
  <wsdl:portType name="Sp">
    <wsdl:operation name="reserveStock">
      <wsdl:input message="tns:ListOfProducts"/>
    </wsdl:operation>
    <wsdl:operation name="reserveProductionLine">
      <wsdl:input message="tns:ProductionLineRequest"/>
    </wsdl:operation>
    <wsdl:operation name="calculateDeliveryDate">
      <wsdl:input message="tns:ProductionInformation"/>
      <wsdl:output message="tns:DeliveryDate"/>
    </wsdl:operation>
    <wsdl:operation name="deallocateProductionLine">
      <wsdl:input message="tns:ProductionLineRequest"/>
    </wsdl:operation>
    <wsdl:operation name="clearRessources">
      <wsdl:input message="tns:ListOfProducts"/>
    </wsdl:operation>
  </wsdl:portType>
  <plnk:partnerLinkType name="B2SsLT">
    <plnk:role name="buyer" portType="tns:B"/>
    <plnk:role name="seller" portType="tns:Ss"/>
  </plnk:partnerLinkType>
  <plnk:partnerLinkType name="Ss2CLT">
    <plnk:role name="seller" portType="tns:Ss"/>
    <plnk:role name="carrier" portType="tns:C"/>
  </plnk:partnerLinkType>
  <plnk:partnerLinkType name="Ss2SaLT">
    <plnk:role name="sales" portType="tns:Ss"/>
    <plnk:role name="accounting" portType="tns:Sa"/>
  </plnk:partnerLinkType>
  <plnk:partnerLinkType name="Ss2SpLT">
    <plnk:role name="sales" portType="tns:Ss"/>
    <plnk:role name="production" portType="tns:Sp"/>
  </plnk:partnerLinkType>
</wsdl:definitions>
```

In a BPEL process, partners always interact in a bilateral manner, i.e., one partner invokes an operation and the other partner receives a call of this operation. In order to reflect the bilateral collaborations, the WSDL file is extended by the concept of partner link types. Owing to its bilateral nature, a partner link type always includes two roles representing the two collaborating partners. Each role references the port type that has to be provided by the corresponding role. In our order management example, the seller sales department acts as a hub which has bilateral collaborations with the four other organizations, whereas the other organizations do not directly interact with each other. Accordingly, the WSDL file includes four partner link types representing the interactions of the sellers sales department (i) with the buyer (B2SsLT) in lines 062–065, (ii) with the carrier (Ss2CLT) in lines 066–069, (iii) with the seller accounting department (Ss2SaLT) in lines 070–073, and (iv) with the seller production department (Ss2SpLT) in lines 074–077.

A BPEL process is built by nested scopes, where the outermost scope is the process definition itself. It contains partner links that define the relationships to other business partners, declaration of process data, handlers for various purposes and the activities that are orchestrated/choreographed. We distinguish between basic activities and structured activities. Basic activities are incoming and outgoing operation calls as well as activities for data manipulation. Structured activities cover other activities and define the process logic amongst them.

The most important basic activities are the following: *Invoke* is used to call an operation. *Receive* is an activity that receives an operation call. *Reply* is used to return the response of an operation which was previously called by a *receive* activity. *Pick* waits for the first event of a set of alternative events to happen and executes the activity associated with this event. Each *pick* must include at least one *onMessage* event. The *onMessage* event is semantically equivalent to a *receive* activity. Other basic activities are *empty* rendering of a no-operation, *wait* interrupting the execution of a process for some time, *exit* immediately stopping the process, and *throw* generating a fault. The following structured activities are considered as the most important ones. *Sequence* specifies a sequential execution of activities. *Switch* provides a multi-branch decision construct. *While* allows the definition of loops. *Flow* is in general used for specifying parallel execution. However, conditional control links may be used to define a partial acyclic order of the activities within a *flow*. Most of these activities will be further illustrated in the example below.

In the lines 079–128 we present the BPEL process of the seller sales department as illustrated in Figure 4.1. This BPEL process imports in line 080 the WSDL file as illustrated in the lines 001–078. The partner links in the lines 081–086 define the bilateral collaborations of the seller sales department with the other organizations. At first sight, one may think that this was already done in the partner link types of the WSDL file. However, the partner link types are defined from a somewhat neutral position defining two roles. The BPEL process is always described from the perspective of a specific role—in our case from the perspective of the seller sales department. Consequently, a partner link references a partner link type and defines which role is played by the process owner and which by the collaborating organization. For example, the partner link in line 082 reflects the collaboration between the buyer and the seller sales department (B2Ss). The partnerLinkType attribute references the corresponding partner link type (B2SsLT) as defined in lines 062–065. The myRole attribute is set to *seller*, and the partnerRole attribute to *buyer*—which correspond to the roles defined in the partner link type in lines 063 and 064.

A business process defined in BPEL describes the exchange of messages by means of operations. These messages, or at least some of them are relevant for the correct execution of the business process. Thus, these messages have to be included in the business context of the business process. This is realized by variables that serve as data manipulation containers for incoming and outgoing messages. The declaration of variables is highlighted in lines 087–089. However, we omit to show the declaration of all variables that relate to message exchanges. We just demonstrate the declaration by means of the variable for the purchase order in line 088.

```
079 <bpws:process name="sellersOrderManagement"
      targetNamespace="http://new.process.namespace"
      xmlns:bpws="http://docs.oasis-open.org/wsbpel/2.0/process/executable"
      xmlns:ns="http://new.webservice.namespace"
      xmlns:tns="http://new.process.namespace">

080    <bpws:import importType="http://schemas.xmlsoap.org/wsdl/"
        location="OrderManagement.wsdl"
        namespace="http://new.webservice.namespace" />

081    <bpws:partnerLinks>
082      <bpws:partnerLink myRole="seller" name="B2Ss"
            partnerLinkType="ns:B2SsLT" partnerRole="buyer" />
083      <bpws:partnerLink myRole="sales" name="Ss2Sp"
            partnerLinkType="ns:Ss2SpLT" partnerRole="production" />
084      <bpws:partnerLink myRole="sales" name="Ss2Sa"
            partnerLinkType="ns:Ss2SaLT" partnerRole="accounting" />
085      <bpws:partnerLink myRole="seller" name="Ss2C"
            partnerLinkType="ns:Ss2CLT" partnerRole="carrier" />
086    </bpws:partnerLinks>

087    <bpws:variables>
088    <bpws:variable messageType="ns:PurchaseOrder" name="purchaseOrder" />
...
089    </bpws:variables>

090   <bpws:sequence>
091      <bpws:receive createInstance="yes" operation="orderProduct"
            partnerLink="B2Ss" portType="ns:Ss" variable="purchaseOrder" />
092      <bpws:invoke inputVariable="purchaseOrder"
            operation="checkAgainstOffer" outputVariable="checkResult"
            partnerLink="Ss2Sa" portType="ns:Sa" />
093      <bpws:flow name="Flow">
094        <bpws:invoke inputVariable="listOfProducts"
              operation="reserveStock" partnerLink="Ss2Sp" portType="ns:Sp" />
095        <bpws:invoke inputVariable="productLineRequest"
              operation="reserveProductionLine" partnerLink="Ss2Sp"
              portType="ns:Sp" />
096      </bpws:flow>
097      <bpws:invoke inputVariable="productionInformation"
            operation="calculateDeliveryDate" outputVariable="deliveryDate"
            partnerLink="Ss2Sp" portType="ns:Sp" />
098      <bpws:invoke inputVariable="transportRequest"
            operation="reserveTransport" partnerLink="Ss2C"
            portType="ns:C" />
099      <bpws:receive name="confirmTransport" partnerLink="Ss2C"
            portType="ns:Ss" variable="transportConfirmation" />
100      <bpws:invoke inputVariable="orderResponse"
            operation="responseToOrder" partnerLink="B2Ss" portType="ns:B" />

101      <bpws:while>
102        <bpws:condition><![CDATA[true()]]></bpws:condition>
103        <bpws:pick name="Pick">

104          <bpws:onMessage operation="getStatus" partnerLink="B2Ss"
                portType="ns:Ss" variable="statusRequest">
105            <bpws:sequence name="Sequence">
106              <bpws:invoke inputVariable="status"
                    operation="informOnStatus" partnerLink="B2Ss"
```

```
                portType="ns:B" />
107           </bpws:sequence>
108         </bpws:onMessage>

109         <bpws:onMessage operation="cancelOrder" partnerLink="B2Ss"
               portType="ns:Ss" variable="orderCancellation">
110           <bpws:sequence>
111             <bpws:flow>
112               <bpws:invoke inputVariable="productLineRequest"
                     operation="deallocateProductionLine"
                     partnerLink="Ss2Sp" portType="ns:Sp" />
113               <bpws:invoke inputVariable="listOfProducts"
                     operation="clearRessources" partnerLink="Ss2Sp"
                     portType="ns:Sp" />
114             </bpws:flow>
115             <bpws:exit/>
116           </bpws:sequence>
117         </bpws:onMessage>

118         <bpws:onMessage operation="readyToShip" partnerLink="Ss2Sp"
               portType="ns:Ss" variable="notificationOfShipment">
119           <bpws:sequence>
120             <bpws:invoke inputVariable="notificationOfShipment"
                   operation="notifyShipment" partnerLink="B2Ss"
                   portType="ns:B" />
121             <bpws:invoke inputVariable="orderInformation"
                   operation="transferToAccounting"
                   partnerLink="Ss2Sa" portType="ns:Sa" />
122             <bpws:exit/>
123           </bpws:sequence>
124         </bpws:onMessage>

125       </bpws:pick>
126     </bpws:while>
127   </bpws:sequence>
128 </bpws:process>
```

The definition of the control flow of the seller's order management process is defined in a block structure in lines 090–127. Its outermost scope defines a sequence of basic and structured activities. Before going into the details of the process structure, we describe the basic notation to *invoke/receive* service calls by examples. In line 092 the seller sales department calls the operation *check against offer* from the seller accounting department. This is realized by an *invoke* activity. Its attributes provide the necessary details: The *operation* being called is *check against offer* which belongs to the *partner link* between the seller sales department and its accounting department (*Ss2Sa*) and is part of the *port type* of the seller accounting department (*Sa*). According to the WSDL file this operation defines a synchronous message exchange (lines 036–039), the *input* variable for the call is *purchase order* and the *output variable* is *check result.* In the case of an asynchronous message call that does not get a return, there will be no output variable—such as the invocation of *reserve stock* in line 094.

In line 091 the buyer calls the operation *order product* from the seller sales department. From the seller's perspective it is a *receive* activity. Again the the attributes provide the details: The *operation* called is *order product* which belongs to the *partner link* between the buyer and the seller sales department (*B2Ss*) and is part of the *port type* of the seller sales department (*Sa*). The incoming message is stored in the *variable purchaseOrder*. A variable in a *receive* activity is always an input, because a *receive* activity does not output anything. If the *receive* activity refers to an incoming synchronous operation call, the return of the output message must be defined by a following *reply* activity which uses the same values for *operation*, *partner link* and *port type* as the *receive* activity, but specifies the output to be sent in the attribute *variable*. In our example, there is no reply activity at the seller sales department. The *receive* activity *order product* in 091 is special in the case that it marks the beginning of a new process instance. Therefore, the Boolean value of the attribute *create instance* is set to *yes*.

The second kind of activity that refers to an incoming operation call is the *on message* activity. It is always used in conjunction with a *pick* activity in order to specify that this incoming operation call is one of more alternative events that appear next within a *pick*. The attributes of an *on message* activity are exactly the same as the ones for the *receive* activity. As an example, line 104 shows the *on message* activity that receives a call of the *get status operation* on the seller sales department (*Ss*) *port type* as part of the *partner link* with the buyer (*B2Ss*). The incoming message is captured in the *status request variable*.

The block structure in the lines 090–128 describes the orchestration among the incoming and outgoing operation calls of the seller sales department as depicted in the middle lane of Figure 4.1. The outermost scope of this block structure is a sequence. After the first two activities of this sequence namely *order product* (091) and *check against offer* (092), a *flow* activity follows. The *flow* activity (093–096) is used for parallel execution of the activities *reserve stock* (094) and *reserve production line* (095). After completion of the two activities within the flow, the sequence continues with *calculate delivery date* (097), *reserve transport* (098), *confirm transport* (099), and *response to order* (100).

Looking at the remaining activities in Figure 4.1, it follows that a block of getting status information is optional, but may be repeated until either a block marking the shipment of the goods or a block for canceling of the order starts. This business fact is represented within a *while* loop (101–126), which is the last activity in the overall sequence. The condition of the *while* loop is permanently set to *true* in line 102—it is stopped by an *exit* either in line 115 or in 122, which terminates the overall process. The only activity within the *while* loop is a *pick* activity (103–125). The *pick* activity reacts on one of three possible incoming calls of operations: *get status* (104), *cancel order* (109), or *ready to ship* (118). In case of a call of *get status*, the process continues with a *sequence* (105–107) that consists of an *inform on status* (106) only. Having executed the specified action after picking the *get status* event, the *while* loop restarts again.

If the *cancel order* operation is picked, it results in a *sequence* (110–116) of two activities. The first one is a *flow* (111–114) for the parallel execution of *deallocate product line* (112) and clear resources (113). The second activity of the *sequence* is an *exit* in line 115 which terminates the whole process. Finally, if a *ready to ship* operation is picked, it results in a *sequence* (119–123) of *notify shipment* (120), *transfer to accounting* (121) and again in an *exit* (122) stopping the process.

4.3.3 Analyzing BPEL by Workflow Patterns

Having introduced BPEL as the de-facto language for specify workflows in web services, it is important to illustrate which of the concepts known from workflow products are also supported by BPEL. Aalst et al. [39] propose a pattern based approach for the comparison of the capabilities and limitations of commercial workflow management systems. These patterns are also used in their work on the evaluation of BPEL [46]. In the following we highlight those patterns that are supported by BPEL, but do not concentrate on the other ones.

The first class of patterns covers the basic control-flow patterns. These patterns are *sequence*, *parallel split*, *synchronization*, *exclusive choice*, and *simple merge*. The *sequence* pattern means that an activity starts after the completion of its predecessor. This is the most simple case. The *parallel split* pattern specifies the behavior of an AND-fork. This means a single activity has multiple successors that occur in parallel. The *synchronization* pattern forms an antithesis to the parallel split pattern. A successor starts only if all its predecessors are completed. The *exclusive choice* pattern chooses only one transition from several alternatives based on a decision. The *simple merge* pattern makes an antithesis of the exclusive choice pattern. Multiple branches of which only one can be active due to a previous exclusive choice are merged into a single activity. There is no need for synchronization.

The second category addresses the advanced branching and synchronization patterns. The *multi-choice pattern* allows one or more threads to continue according to given conditions. Conditions must guard the transitions from the fork to a successor. The *structured synchronizing merge* pattern is the antithesis of the multiple choice. Those branches which fulfilled the conditions of the multi choice converge into one continuing activity.

The third class of patterns are the structural patterns. Only one pattern of this class is supported by BPEL: The *implicit termination* pattern implies that no activity is performed anymore, although no deadlock exists and no end state is reached. The forth category addresses the patterns involving multiple instances. BPEL supports only the *multiple instances without synchronization* pattern of this family of patterns. This pattern allows multiple instances to be created and the resulting threads remain independent of each other. As the pattern's name indicates, there is no need to synchronize these threads.

If the execution of one activity depends on the state of another activity, the pattern is categorized into the class of state-based patterns. The BPEL supported patterns include *deferred choice*, and *interleaved parallel routing*. The *deferred choice* pattern selects only one continuing activity from several candidates like exclusive choice, but the decision is implicit. The *interleaved parallel routing* pattern defines the execution of a set of activities in an arbitrary order. Each activity of the set is executed once. At a given point in time only one activity is executed. The execution order is fixed at run time. This pattern is supported by BPEL only for activities within the same scope.

The sixth and final class of patterns are the cancellation patterns. The *cancel activity* pattern disables an enabled activity, whereas the *cancel case* pattern terminates a workflow instance even in the case that parts of the process have been instantiated.

4.4 The Role of Agents in Service-Based Business Processes

In the previous subsections we introduced the concepts of orchestration and choreography as well as their presentation by means of BPEL. We learned that both orchestrations and choreographies may be built by services that are provided by different organizations. A key argument for using a service based approach towards workflow management is its flexibility. Flexibility may be needed for a few reasons in workflow management: Some services within a workflow may be outsourced to a different partner. Furthermore, some services in a workflow may be delivered by different, competing partners and the best service should be selected, possibly on the fly. Changing business needs may require a change in the flow of services. New business requirements may lead to establishing contacts with new business partners, which requires a matching of the choreographies.

These flexible adaptations may be made manually or one may use agents to perform these adaptations. Flexible adaptations to an orchestrated workflow relate very much to the topics of semantic techniques for service description, service selection and composition of services, which are all addressed in separate chapters in this book. On an abstract level one may think of the following kind of agents: search agent, selection agent, and composition agent. A search agent is responsible for finding possible services that are able to fulfill a certain task in a workflow. A selection agent is responsible for selecting the most appropriate service among those found by the search agent. This selection may be performed at design time or at runtime. In case of design time, the service selected by the agent becomes part of the set of orchestrated services, e.g., a call of this service becomes a BPEL activity. If the selection is performed at runtime time, a static binding of an activity to a specific service does not work. In this case the corresponding activity in the workflow may bind to the service that itself performs the search and the selection agent and, further, calls the selected service and returns the result back to the workflow. Another option would be that a call to the workflow only calls the search/selection agent, which returns the parameters of the selected service to the workflow. In a next step the workflow continues with a parameterized service using these parameters to dynamically link to the selected service. It is commonly agreed that the search and selection of web services by agents cannot be limited to a pure syntax based approach, rather it needs an approach that is based on semantic web services [3, 24]. An overview of the major relevant semantic web service frameworks IRS-II, OWL-S and WSFM is provided in [5]. A composition agent may be used to semi-automatically define the control flow between the services based on semantic descriptions. Approaches to the semantically based composition of orchestrations are found in [6, 35]. Due to space limitations we are not able to discuss all the approaches to semantic search, selection and composition of services discussed in the literature, but refer to the more specific chapters of this book on these topics.

In addition to specifying the orchestration of a business process, agents may also be used in the definition of a choreography. In Section 4.2 we defined that a choreography describes the flow of interactions between business partners that interlink their individual processes. It follows that business partners wishing to collaborate must have complimentary local choreographies. In principle, we distinguish a bottom-up approach and a top-down approach in order to come to an agreement on the choreography between business partners.

The bottom-up approach starts off from the local choreography of one of the participating business partners. This business partner announces his local choreography in a registry. Another business partner wants to establish a new business contact. For this purpose he searches for potential business partners in the registry. This search may be supported by a search agent that works similar to one in the orchestration case based on semantic descriptions. However, there is another challenge in the case of choreographies. Not only, the found business partner must provide the business functionality a business partner is requesting, but also the found local choreography of the business partner must be complimentary to one's own local choreography. This means a match making of the local choreographies is required for all potential business partners found. An approach for the comparison of choreographies is described by Wombacher et al. [47] based on annotated deterministic finite state automata [48].

If two local choreographies have been developed in isolation from each other it is rather unlikely that they will be complementary—but this is required to do business with each other. Accordingly, a process must start to align the local choreographies. One option would be that the searching business partner—knowing what the found business partner expects—accommodates its own local choreography. Since the local choreography is nothing else than a projection of the publicly visible services of the orchestration of the business process of this partner, this means rearranging one's own business process. Again, one may think of an agent that semi-automatically supports the adoptions of the local choreography / orchestration according to a given partner's local choreography. Work on such kind of agents is still subject to future research work. If a business partner cannot accept or does not want to accept another partner's choreography, there is no other option than getting to a common agreement on the choreography with the other business partner. This negotiation process may be supported by a negotiation agent. Although this idea is similar to creating an ebXML business collaboration protocol agreement (CPA). (*Cf.* our work in [12], no research papers on the semi-automatic alignment of choreographies exist. Such future work may take advantage of the literature on electronic negotiation [4], which may be adopted to the special goal of negotiating choreographies).

A top-down approach provides an alternative to the previously described scenario for establishing complementary local choreographies. An analysis may start with the economic drivers for the electronic partnerships. This means describing the economic values that are exchanged between the business partners. The e3-value ontology [9] serves this purpose. In order to guarantee that each partner deserves his economic value, the value model must be transformed semi-automatically into a global choreography. This resulting global choreography becomes a kind of contract guiding the business partnership. As project team leads, we have delivered the UN/CEFACT modeling methodology (UMM) [13] for the unambiguous definition of global choreographies. The semi-automatic transformation from business models to choreographies in general, and from e3-value to UMM in particular, is open to future research work. In order to implement the global choreography, it is important to transform it into local choreographies—one for each partner. This is done fully automatically—we provide a mapping from UMM to BPEL [11].

The top-down approach may be used on a bilateral basis to establish a choreography between a specific set of business partners. However, it reaches its full potential when it is used to define popular, commonly supported business scenarios. In this case a business partner has to adapt his approach to bind the orchestration of his own business process only once to the choreography, in order to collaborate with many business partners. Also the effort for searching for potential business partners is considerably reduced. We assume that the global choreography is stored in a registry. Furthermore, business partners not only register their local choreography, but also reference the public choreography and declare the role which they support in the choreography. Accordingly, a search agent is much simpler to realize. Firstly, the search agent searches for a public choreography that fulfills the expected business functionality. Having found an appropriate public choreography, the search agent queries the registry for business partners that have established a link to the public choreography and have declared that their local choreography supports the complementary role in the choreography. Using this approach, the complex and time-consuming match making of local choreographies is eliminated.

4.5 Dynamic Workflows

In this section we focus on service workflows in a dynamic environment, where changes to the workflow happen. We mainly concentrate on two different kinds of dynamic aspects. The first is about dynamically selecting a provider for a specific task within the workflow. The second is about changing the schema of the workflow and the consequences on running instances of this workflow.

4.5.1 Dynamic Selection of Best Service Providers

In a web services environment a workflow specifies a control flow among services. These services may be provided by different providers—in-house and by different partners. By looking at our order management example of Section 4.2 and its BPEL representation in Section 4.3 it becomes evident that all these services are bound statically. This means that each service is called from a fixed provider. There is no dynamic selection of the best provider. However, there may be the desire to bind the services or at least some of them to the best provider. In our example, we assume that all the services provided in-house, i.e., the services of the different departments of the seller, remain fixed. However, there may be different partners providing the transport. In the example, the booking of transport is defined as shown in Figure 4.4 and the following BPEL code:

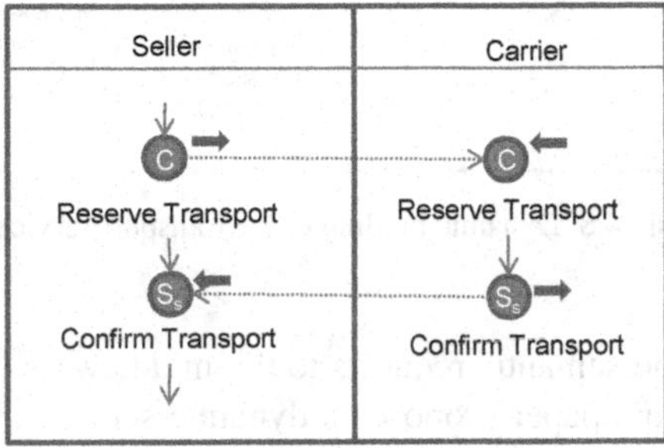

Fig. 4.4 Static binding of the transport service

```
<bpws:invoke inputVariable="transportRequest"
    operation="reserveTransport" partnerLink="Ss2C" portType="ns:C" />
<bpws:receive name="confirmTransport" partnerLink="Ss2C"
    portType="ns:Ss" variable="transportConfirmation" />
```

One option to overcome the current limitations in BPEL is to indirectly call the dynamic services by a special dynamic invocation service. As a result, all activities that are currently static bound must be replaced by a call to the dynamic invocation service. This dynamic invocation service acts as a search and selection agent, as described in Section 4.4. This means, the dynamic selection service dynamically discovers potential providers of the service and selects the best one. Furthermore, the dynamic invocation service has to bind to the selected service, issue the corresponding call, and receive a potential result. The result received from the dynamically invoked service is then returned to the main workflow. Figure 4.5 presents this scenario for dynamically selecting the transport in our order management example. In this case we assume that a dynamic invocation service offers an operation *dynamically invoke transport* on its port type *D*. Note, another option would be that the dynamic invocation service offers just one general operation and the kind of service to be dynamically invoked is semantically described in the parameters. Once the dynamic invocation service has received the call of *dynamically invoke transport*, it searches the registry for potential providers. In our case it finds services of carrier 1 and carrier 2. From these services it selects the best one—lets say the one of carrier 2. Next, it calls the synchronous operation *enquire transport* from carrier 2 that returns a *confirmation of booking*. Having received this confirmation the dynamic invocation service is able to *confirm the transport* to the seller.

Kuestner et al. [19] propose the Diane middleware to dynamically bind services to BPEL activities. The Diane middleware uses predefined templates to is-

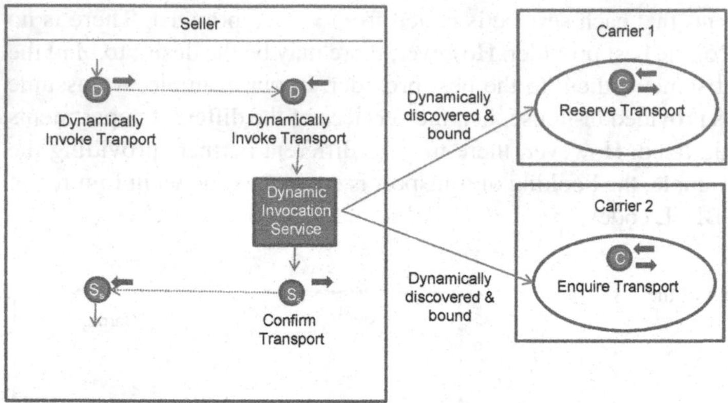

Fig. 4.5 Dynamic binding of the transport service

sue semantic requests to the middleware. A similar approach is described by [23]. This paper proposes a dynamic service discovery and its binding into BPEL process. The discovery and matchmaking is performed by querying a knowledge base of DAML-S service profiles with requests expressed in DAML Query Language. In the METEOR-S project [1] developers create abstract processes that contain service templates as semantic requests. At runtime a configuration module binds these to concrete services using semantic discovery. Furthermore, an execution environment is introduced that handles their invocation. Lemcke and Drumm [20] create a single business process for each of a set of alternative service providers. At runtime they use semantic technology to pick and instantiate the most appropriate process.

All the above mentioned approaches take BPEL as it is. They just bind some BPEL activities to some kind of dynamic invocation service. Karastoyanova et al. present an approach [18] to extend BPEL by concepts allowing dynamic invocations. They suggest so-called parameterized BPEL processes which eliminate the dependency of invocations of operation names, port types, and partner links. The idea is that processes are executable if all partner endpoints are known at runtime. However, this information is not necessarily needed at design time, if it can be calculated. Since this information is required in BPEL at design time, it is proposed to add another element to BPEL that allows substituting the port types and operations. This element is called *evaluate*. Its syntax is defined as follows:

```
<invoke name=" " ...>
    <evaluate activated="yes|no" changeType =
            "static|prompt|query|fromVariable" substitute="value"/>
</invoke>
```

The *evaluate* element is nested into an *invoke* element, if the operations and port types of this invoke statement are subject to substitution. The Boolean activated attribute is used to turn on/off the substitution. The change type attribute allows for four different kinds of substitution: (1) static: substitution by another static service, (2) prompt: substitution according to user input, (3) query: substitution by a result of an issued query, and (4) from variable: substitution by information stored in a variable. The input for the parameter evaluation strategy is a proper value of the substitute attribute. The solution proposed by the evaluate element is independent of any semantic web services technology.

4.5.2 Changes to the Workflow Schema

Businesses must react quickly on changing market conditions. This means that they have to change their business processes to meet changing business requirements. Changing business processes must be reflected in the underlying workflow systems. New activities may be added, old activities may be removed, the control flow (i.e., order and conditions) of the activities may change, and the data dependencies between the activities due to changing input and output of activities may change. In summary, this means changing the workflow structure or, in other words, changing the workflow schema.

Changing the workflow schema requires operations for inserting and deleting activities as well as control/data dependencies between them [31]. The characteristic of completeness refers to the provision of such operations to transform a workflow schema into another one without restricting the user to specify the required changes [7, 31]. It is the goal to provide completeness by a minimal set of operations.

Once a workflow schema is changed it must be guaranteed that the changes do not result in compile-time and run-time errors. The correctness of changes concerns both the workflow schema and the workflow instances. According to these two levels, Casati et al. [7] distinguish between structural consistency and behavioral consistency. Structural consistency refers to the schema level changes. It implies that after modifications to a schema the resulting schema is valid. Behavioral consistency refers to the instance level changes. This addresses the problem of changing a schema at a point in time when instances of that schema are still running. Behavioral consistency implies that applying a set of operations to a running instance of the old schema results in a valid execution of this instance under the new schema. This means the instance evolves without causing run-time errors. Different approaches to reach behavioral consistency have been developed that sometimes differ significantly in their principal approach and solution. A survey of the different approaches towards consistency of workflow evolutions ensuring its correctness is provided by Rinderle et al. [31].

If a change to the workflow schema of an orchestration O happens resulting in the new workflow schema O' the following principle approaches may be taken.

- All running instances of O are aborted, and all new instances are started following the schema O'.
- All running instances of O have to terminate following the schema O. No new instances are started until all the running instances of O are completed. Once they are completed, new instances are able to start following the schema O'.

- Running instances of O will complete following the schema O, new instances will start immediately following the schema O'. This requires that both schema versions O and O' must be supported by the workflow engine at the same time.
- Running instances of the workflow O are transformed according to correctness criteria to become valid instances of O' and continue running following schema O'.

In the above mentioned case 4, an instance I of schema O must correctly be transformed into an instance I of schema O'. An instance of schema O is also a valid instance of O' if its resulting state could also have been produced by following schema O'. This is always the case when the running instance of O is still in a phase that was not affected by the change to O'. In other words, the running instance has only passed activities where O and O' are identical. In case that the running instance has already passed the position of the change, it is necessary to check the execution history of the running instance. If the execution history describes a flow that is a valid flow instance of schema O', then the instance is compliant and is migrated. In [30] Rinderle et al. this approach is described—also using a reduced execution history—in more detail.

The previously described situation—where a running instance I of schema O is also a valid instance of O'—is preferred, but not always given. If the instance of I is not a valid instance of O', the running instance must not be migrated in its current state to the new schema O'. The running instance must first undergo some modifications that guarantee that the instance is compliant to schema O' [7, 33]. In general, it is necessary to undo some activities that have already been executed by the instance I. The undo may or may not require compensation. Following the reverse execution history one activity is undone after the other until the instance is compliant to schema O'. In the worst case scenario all activities must be undone and the instance starts from the beginning following schema O'.

In order to demonstrate the dynamic schema evolution we assume the following change to the order management example: Given the fact that the seller experiences the fact that some of the buyers get bankrupt, the seller decides to perform a credibility check with a financial institution (F) for purchase orders that exceed an amount of 10,000 Euro. Figure 4.6 displays the change in the order management process. In the seller's orchestration a change is made after *check against offer*. A decision checks whether the amount of the purchase order is above 10,000 by an XPath expression on the variable *purchase order* (which was instantiated by the previous received call of *order product*). If so, the sequence of invoking *check credibility* and receiving *get credit check* is executed. If not, no new activities are executed. After merging the two alternative paths again, the orchestration continues like in the old schema with the parallel execution of *reserve stock* and *reserve production line*.

In the following we are going to exemplify the different cases of running instances of the purchase order management process at the seller:

- All running instances that are in a state up to *check against offer* and have not started *reserve stock* or *reserve production line* are transformed into the new

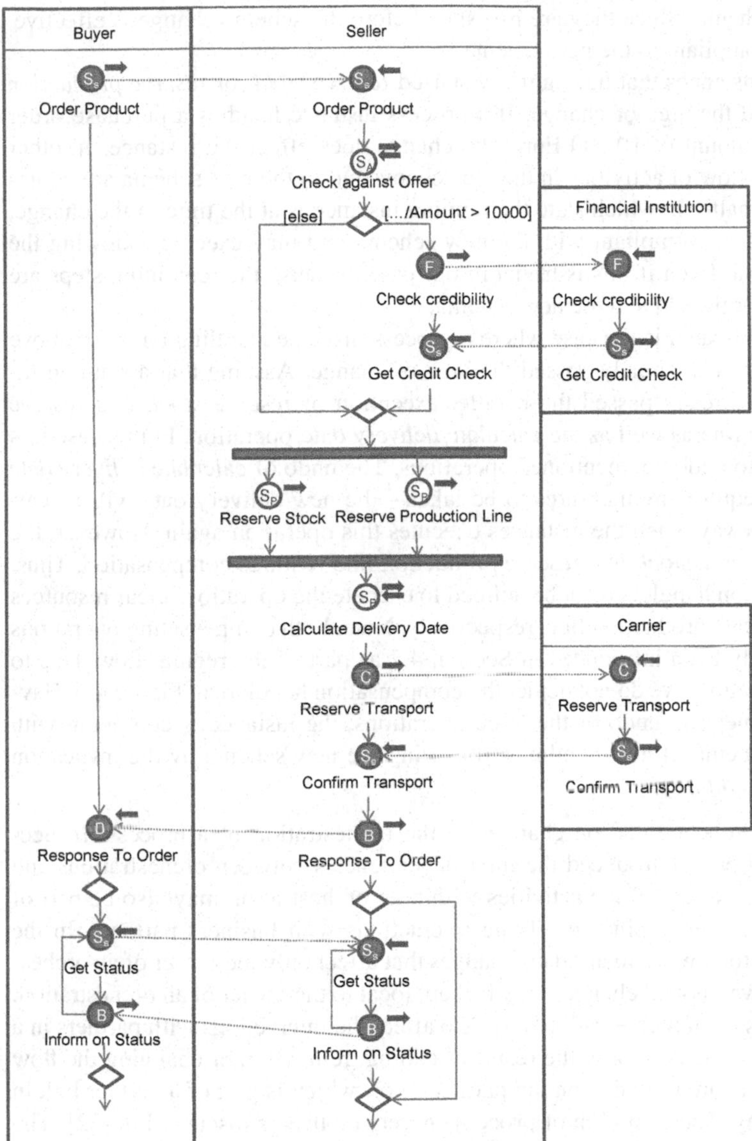

Fig. 4.6 Changing the order management process

process schema. Since they are in a state before the schema change is effective, they are compliant to the new schema.

- Running instances that have already started *reserve stock* or *reserve production line* passed the area of change. If a process instance handles a purchase order up to an amount of 10,000 Euro, the change does effect the instance. In other words, the flow of activities in the old schema and in the new schema are equivalent. No matter in which state the running instance is at the time of the change, the instance is compliant with the new schema and may execute following the new schema. Even if this is trivial in our case, because the remaining steps are identical for the old and the new schema.
- More complicated is the case where a process instance handling an order above 10,000 Euro has already passed the area of change. Assume that a running instance has already passed the parallel execution of *reserve stock* and *reserve production line* as well as the *calculate delivery date* operation. In this case it is necessary to undo the mentioned operations. The undo of *calculate delivery date* does not require any measures to be taken—the new delivery date will be calculated anyway when the instances executes this operation again. However, the undo of *reserve stock* and *reserve production line* requires compensation. Thus, compensation handlers must be defined to execute the operations clear resources and deallocate production line, respectively. Note, both compensating operations have already been introduced in Section 4.2 as part of the regular flow. Due to space limitations we do not depict the compensation handlers in Figure 4.6. Having performed the undo of the three operations, the instance is compliant with the new schema. It now continues following the new schema by the invocation of *check credibility*.

So far we concentrated on changes to the orchestration of a process. In Section 4.2 we already introduced the inter-dependencies between orchestrations and choreographies. Some of the activities within an orchestration may also be part of one or more choreographies involving interactions with business partners. In the discussion up to now we focused on changes that affect only the owner of an orchestration. However, not all changes may be kept local to the owner of an orchestration. Some changes in an orchestration may also affect the interactions with partners in a choreography. This is usually the result of adding, removing, or changing the flow of activities that are provided on the partner's port which is part of a partner link in a choreography. The evolution of process choreographies is discussed in [32]. The paper provides an approach to calculate the consistency of two local choreographies once one of them is changed. In case of inconsistency the second local choreography must be changed as well. Since business partners interacting in a choreography must be considered as autonomous, an automatic adaptation of the second local choreography is not envisioned. Nevertheless, the adaptation may be assisted by suggesting respective adaptations—but this is not detailed in the paper.

Furthermore, we see problems in the case of undoing operations in an orchestration that are part of a choreography. Undoing such operations may require compensations that are not part of the agreed choreography with a business partner. In the schema evolution example of our order management process we have stated that all running instances for purchase orders above 10,000 Euro must be undone to get to an state of *check against offer* to be able to continue with *check credibility*. Assume that a running instance has already past the *response to order* operation. From a business point of view, this means that the order has been accepted and that a contract has been established. Also a transport for delivering the order has already been reserved. In this case an undo is rather problematic, it requires interactions with the buyer and the carrier. However, these interactions have not been defined in the choreography with the buyer nor with the carrier. Accordingly, there is no cancellation of an order possible from the seller's side once the order is accepted by *response to order*. Only the buyer may cancel the order. Also the cancellation of a transport reservation is not detailed with the carrier.

Unless the choreography agreement with the buyer and the carrier, respectively, is changed, the instances of the seller's orchestration must not undo the the *response to order* and *reserve transport* operation. Otherwise the changes to running instances will violate contracts with business partners. So far there does not exist any work that elaborates on the undos of orchestrations and its effects on choreographies. In order to avoid contractual conflicts, we propose to mark those operations which result in contractual obligations and must not be undone without changing the choreography as well. We have developed the UN/CEFACT modeling methodology (UMM) [13] that uses six business transaction patterns classifying the basic interactions between business partners. Among these the one-way *notification* pattern, and the two-way patterns *commercial business transaction* and *request/confirm* have contractual consequences. Following the definition of the three mentioned patters, undo operations must never cross the boundaries of these business transactions.

4.6 Summary and Outlook

In this chapter we provided a survey of the most important topics regarding flexible workflow management in service-oriented environments. Flexibility in workflow management becomes more and more important due to shorter product life-cycles. Companies are required to adapt their business processes in shorter time cycles. This implies that the supporting IT-infrastructure must quickly adapt itself to changing business processes. The concept of loose coupling in service-oriented architectures provides a means to cope with the required flexibility to adapt to changing business requirements.

Flexible business process support is required for both internal processes delivering customer value and inter-organizational processes co-ordinating the interactions with business partners. These two views on business processes are addressed in service-oriented environments by the concepts of orchestration and choreography. Accordingly, we demonstrated how orchestration and choreography are supported in service-oriented architectures. Furthermore, we explicitly show the interdependencies between orchestrated and choreographed processes.

Orchestration and Choreography are abstract concepts to describe business processes. These concepts are independent of the underlying IT-systems. We briefly discussed relevant standard languages in the web services world used to describe orchestrations and choreographies in a machine-readable way to be processed by workflow systems. Currently, the business process execution language (BPEL) is the most commonly supported language by tools and workflow systems. Accordingly, we used BPEL to show how orchestrations and choreographies are presented in a language that is compatible to the web services approach.

Today, orchestrations and choreographies are specified at design time and instances at run time have to follow the specifications made at design time. In order to increase the flexibility in web services-based workflows agents may assist in the construction of workflows at design time and to cope with dynamic adjustments at run time. We discussed agent-based approaches to search and select services being part of an orchestration as well as to construct the execution order within the orchestration. Furthermore, we highlighted agent-based approaches to establish choreographies between business partners that have not conducted electronic business processes before.

We elaborated on the need to dynamically support the execution of web services workflows. Since the current approach taken by BPEL describes a static binding to operations, port types, and partner links, dynamically bindings to the best service provider are not supported. We introduced two major approaches found in the literature overcoming this problem. One is based on redirecting the call of services requiring these dynamics to a special service that performs the dynamic binding. The other one is based on extensions to BPEL allowing dynamic bindings.

Frequently adapting business processes to changing requirements results in multiple schema versions of a workflow. Accordingly, we discussed approaches to schema evolution. This covers solutions to dynamically adapting running instances of an orchestration to an updated schema version. In addition, we focused on the effect of schema evolution in orchestrations of private processes on the choreography of dependent inter-organizational processes.

This survey highlights the different aspects to be considered in flexible workflow management. However, solutions for the different aspects have been developed in isolation from each other. Consequently, these solutions are not well aligned to each other. This requires a fine tuning of the referenced approaches to become complementary to each other. Thus, this survey may serve as a starting point to deliver a well-aligned framework to implement a flexible workflow management by means of web services.

References

1. Rohit Aggarwal, Kunal Verma, John A. Miller, and William Milnor. Constraint driven web service composition in meteor-s. In *IEEE SCC*, pages 23–30. IEEE Computer Society, 2004.
2. Jörg Becker, Michael Rosemann, and Christoph von Uthmann. Guidelines of business process modeling. In van der Aalst et al. [38], pages 30–49.

3. Christoph Bussler, Dieter Fensel, and Alexander Maedche. A conceptual architecture for semantic web enabled web services. *SIGMOD Record*, 31(4):24–29, 2002.
4. Ricardo Büttner. The state of the art in automated negotiation models of the behavior and information perspective. *International Transactions on Systems Science and Applications (ITSSA)*, 1(4):351–356, 2006.
5. Liliana Cabral, John Domingue, Enrico Motta, Terry R. Payne, and Farshad Hakimpour. Approaches to semantic web services: an overview and comparisons. In Christoph Bussler, John Davies, Dieter Fensel, and Rudi Studer, editors, *ESWS*, volume 3053 of *Lecture Notes in Computer Science*, pages 225–239. Springer, 2004.
6. Jorge Cardoso and Amit P. Sheth. Semantic e-workflow composition. *Journal of Intelligence and Information Systems*, 21(3):191–225, 2003.
7. Fabio Casati, Stefano Ceri, Barbara Pernici, and Giuseppe Pozzi. Workflow evolution. In Bernhard Thalheim, editor, *ER*, volume 1157 of *Lecture Notes in Computer Science*, pages 438–455. Springer, 1996.
8. Gero Decker, Oliver Kopp, Frank Leymann, and Mathias Weske. Bpel4chor: Extending bpel for modeling choreographies. In *ICWS*, pages 296–303. IEEE Computer Society, 2007.
9. Jaap Gordijn and Hans Akkermans. Designing and evaluating e-business models. *IEEE Intelligent Systems*, 16(4):11–17, 2001.
10. Michael Hammer and James Champy. *Reengineering the Corporation: A Manifesto for Business Revolution*. Harper Business, 1993.
11. Birgit Hofreiter and Christian Huemer. Transforming umm business collaboration models to bpel. In Robert Meersman, Zahir Tari, and Angelo Corsaro, editors, *OTM Workshops*, volume 3292 of *Lecture Notes in Computer Science*, pages 507–519. Springer, 2004.
12. Birgit Hofreiter, Christian Huemer, and Wolfgang Klas. ebxml: Status, research issues, and obstacles. In *RIDE*, pages 7–16, 2002.
13. Birgit Hofreiter, Christian Huemer, Philipp Liegl, Rainer Schuster, and Marco Zapletal. Un/cefact's modeling methodology (umm): A uml profile for b2b e-commerce. In John F. Roddick, V. Richard Benjamins, Samira Si-Said Cherfi, Roger H. L. Chiang, Christophe Claramunt, Ramez Elmasri, Fabio Grandi, Hyoil Han, Martin Hepp, Miltiadis D. Lytras, Vojislav B. Misic, Geert Poels, Il-Yeol Song, Juan Trujillo, and Christelle Vangenot, editors, *ER (Workshops)*, volume 4231 of *Lecture Notes in Computer Science*, pages 19–31. Springer, 2006.
14. Meichun Hsu. Letter from the special issue editor on workflow and extended transaction systems. *IEEE Data Engineering Bulletim*, 16(2):3, 1993.
15. Patrick C. K. Hung and Dickson K. W. Chiu. Workflow-based information integration in a web services environment. In Liang-Jie Zhang, editor, *ICWS*, pages 10–16. CSREA Press, 2003.
16. IBM. *Web Services Flow Language*, May 2001. http://xml.coverpages.org/XLANG-C-200106.html.
17. ISO/IEC. *Software and Systems Engineering – High-level Petri Nets, Part 2: Transfer Format*, June 2005. ISO/IEC 15909-2 Working Draft Version 0.9, http://wwwcs.uni-paderborn.de/cs/kindler/publications/copies/ISO-IEC15909-2.WD.V0.9.0.pdf.
18. Dimka Karastoyanova, Frank Leymann, Jörg Nitzsche, Branimir Wetzstein, and Daniel Wutke. Parameterized bpel processes: Concepts and implementation. In Schahram Dustdar, José Luiz Fiadeiro, and Amit P. Sheth, editors, *Business Process Management*, volume 4102 of *Lecture Notes in Computer Science*, pages 471–476. Springer, 2006.
19. Ulrich Küster and Birgitta König-Ries. Dynamic binding for bpel processes—a lightweight approach to integrate semantics into web services. In Dimitrios Georgakopoulos, Norbert Ritter, Boualem Benatallah, Christian Zirpins, George Feuerlicht, Marten Schönherr, and Hamid R. Motahari Nezhad, editors, *ICSOC Workshops*, volume 4652 of *Lecture Notes in Computer Science*, pages 116–127. Springer, 2006.
20. Jens Lemcke and Christian Drumm. Semantic business automation. In *3rd European Semantic Web Conference*, 2006.
21. Frank Leymann and Dieter Roller. *Production Workflow: Concepts and Techniques*. Prentice Hall, 2000.

22. Frank Leymann, Dieter Roller, and Marc-Thomas Schmidt. Web services and business process management. *IBM Systems Journal*, 41(2):198–211, 2002.
23. Daniel J. Mandell and Sheila A. McIlraith. Adapting bpel4ws for the semantic web: The bottom-up approach to web service interoperation. In Dieter Fensel, Katia P. Sycara, and John Mylopoulos, editors, *International Semantic Web Conference*, volume 2870 of *Lecture Notes in Computer Science*, pages 227–241. Springer, 2003.
24. Sheila A. McIlraith and David L. Martin. Bringing semantics to web services. *IEEE Intelligent Systems*, 18(1):90–93, 2003.
25. Microsoft. *XLANG—Web Services for Business Process Design*, June 2001. Version 1.0, http://xml.coverpages.org/WSFL-Guide-200110.pdf.
26. OASIS. *ebXML Business Process Specification Schema Technical Specification*, December 2006. Version 2.0.4, http://docs.oasis-open.org/ebxml-bp/2.0.4/OS/spec/ebxmlbp-v2.0.4-Spec-os-en.pdf.
27. OASIS. *Web Services Business Process Execution Language*, April 2007. Version 2.0, http://docs.oasis-open.org/wsbpel/2.0/OS/wsbpel-v2.0-OS.html.
28. Chris Peltz. Web services orchestration and choreography. *IEEE Computer*, 36(10):46–52, 2003.
29. Giacomo Piccinelli, Wolfgang Emmerich, Christian Zirpins, and Kevin Schütt. Web service interfaces for inter-organisational business processes: An infrastructure for automated reconciliation. In *EDOC*, pages 285–292. IEEE Computer Society, 2002.
30. Manfred Reichert and Stefanie Rinderle. On design principles for realizing adaptive service flows with bpel. In Mathias Weske and Markus Nüttgens, editors, *EMISA*, volume 95 of *LNI*, pages 133–146. GI, 2006.
31. Stefanie Rinderle, Manfred Reichert, and Peter Dadam. Correctness criteria for dynamic changes in workflow systems—a survey. *Data and Knowledge Engineering*, 50(1):9–34, 2004.
32. Stefanie Rinderle, Andreas Wombacher, and Manfred Reichert. On the controlled evolution of process choreographies. In Ling Liu, Andreas Reuter, Kyu-Young Whang, and Jianjun Zhang, editors, *ICDE*, page 124. IEEE Computer Society, 2006.
33. Wasim Sadiq, Olivera Marjanovic, and Maria E. Orlowska. Managing change and time in dynamic workflow processes. *International Journal of Cooperative Information Systems*, 9(1–2):93–116, 2000.
34. August-Wilhelm Scheer and Markus Nüttgens. Aris architecture and reference models for business process management. In van der Aalst et al. [38], pages 376–389.
35. Evren Sirin, James A. Hendler, and Bijan Parsia. Semi-automatic composition ofweb services using semantic descriptions. In Jean Bézivin, Jiankun Hu, and Zahir Tari, editors, *WSMAI*, pages 17–24. ICEIS Press, 2003.
36. W. M. P. van der Aalst. Interorganizational workflows: An approach based on message sequence charts and petri nets. *Systems Analysis—Modelling—Simulation*, 34(3):335–367, 1999.
37. Wil M. P. van der Aalst. Inheritance of interorganizational workflows to enable business-to-business. *Electronic Commerce Research*, 2(3):195–231, 2002.
38. Wil M. P. van der Aalst, Jörg Desel, and Andreas Oberweis, editors. *Business Process Management, Models, Techniques, and Empirical Studies*, volume 1806 of *Lecture Notes in Computer Science*. Springer, 2000.
39. Wil M. P. van der Aalst, Arthur H. M. ter Hofstede, Bartek Kiepuszewski, and Alistair P. Barros. Workflow patterns. *Distributed and Parallel Databases*, 14(1):5–51, 2003.
40. Wil M. P. van der Aalst and Kees M. van Hee. Framework for business process redesign. In *WETICE*, pages 36–45. IEEE Computer Society, 1995.
41. Wil M. P. van der Aalst and Mathias Weske. The p2p approach to interorganizational workflows. In Klaus R. Dittrich, Andreas Geppert, and Moira C. Norrie, editors, *CAiSE*, volume 2068 of *Lecture Notes in Computer Science*, pages 140–156. Springer, 2001.
42. W3C. *Web Service Choreography Interface (WSCI)*, August 2002. Version 1.0, http://www.w3.org/TR/wsci/.
43. W3C. *Web Services Conversation Language (WSCL)*, March 2002. Version 1.0, http://www.w3.org/TR/wscl10/.

44. W3C. *Web Services Choreography Description Language*, November 2005. Version 1.0, http://www.w3.org/TR/ws-cdl-10/.
45. Sanjiva Weerawarana, Francisco Curbera, Frank Leymann, Tony Storey, and Donald F. Ferguson. *Production Workflow: Concepts and Techniques*. Prentice Hall, 2000.
46. Petia Wohed, Wil M. P. van der Aalst, Marlon Dumas, and Arthur H. M. ter Hofstede. Analysis of web services composition languages: The case of bpel4ws. In Il-Yeol Song, Stephen W. Liddle, Tok Wang Ling, and Peter Scheuermann, editors, *ER*, volume 2813 of *Lecture Notes in Computer Science*, pages 200–215. Springer, 2003.
47. Andreas Wombacher, Peter Fankhauser, Bendick Mahleko, and Erich J. Neuhold. Matchmaking for business processes based on choreographies. In *EEE*, pages 359–368. IEEE Computer Society, 2004.
48. Andreas Wombacher, Peter Fankhauser, and Erich J. Neuhold. Transforming bpel into annotated deterministic finite state automata for service discovery. In *ICWS*, pages 316–323. IEEE Computer Society, 2004.
49. Workflow Management Coalition. *Process Definition Interface—XML Process Definition Language*, October 2005. Version 2.0, http://www.wfmc.org/standards/docs/TC-1025_xpdl_2_2005-10-03.pdf.

Chapter 5
Semantics for Service-Oriented Architectures

Michael Stollberg and Dieter Fensel

Abstract The concept of Service-Oriented Architectures (SOA) is the latest design paradigm for IT systems. The aim is to use Web services as the basic building blocks, which provide reusable functionalities that are invokable over the Internet. The initial Web service technology stack around WSDL, SOAP, and UDDI enables the technical provision and usage of Web services. However, the support for the detection of the suitable Web services for a specific client application is limited to manual inspection. To better support this for SOA applications with the larger numbers of available Web services that can be expected in real-world scenarios, the emerging concept of Semantic Web services (SWS) develops inference-based techniques for the automated discovery, composition, and execution of Web services. This chapter provides an overview on the SWS approach as well as the latest technology developments.

5.1 Introduction

The concept of Web services as been invented by a consortium of leading IT vendors in the late 1990s. Essentially, a Web service is a program that can be invoked over the Internet. It is accessible via an interface that specifies the physical address as well as the messages via which a client can consume the Web service. The actual consumption is realized by the exchange of XML data over the Web via SOAP. Remaining independent of the actual implementation, this technology facilitates computing

Michael Stollberg
SAP Research CEC Dresden, SAP AG, Dresden D-01187, Germany
e-mail: michael.stollberg@sap.com

Dieter Fensel
Semantic Technology Institute (STI), University of Innsbruck, Innsbruck Austria
e-mail: dieter.fensel@sti2.at

N. Griffiths, K.-M. Chao (eds.), *Agent-Based Service-Oriented Computing*,
Advanced Information and Knowledge Processing,
DOI 10.1007/978-1-84996-041-0_5,

over the Web as well as seamless information exchange and reuse functionalities within and between organizations.

Because of this, Web services have been proclaimed as the core technology for Service-Oriented Architectures (SOA). In the future, IT systems shall be composed of Web services as the basic building blocks instead of proprietary solutions. The aim is to exploit the potential of the World Wide Web (WWW) as an infrastructure for computation, and also to reduce the development and maintenance costs for IT systems. The adaptation of Web services and the SOA paradigm within industry as well as by non-profit software developers has been facilitated by the early standardization of the necessary technologies. Commonly referred to as the initial Web service technology stack, these are (1) the *Web Service Description Language* (WSDL) for specifying the technical information, as well as the messages for invoking and consuming a Web service, (2) SOAP as a messaging technology for exchanging XML data over the Web, and (3) the *Universal Description, Discovery and Integration Protocol* (UDDI) which provides a registry technology for Web services.

This allows service providers to offer functionalities as Web services, and also supports the technical usage of Web services by clients. However, the descriptions remain on a syntactic level which limits the Web service usage to manual inspection: the developer of a client application needs to search for a suitable Web service within a UDDI repository, then inspect the WSDL description in order to determine how and in which order the necessary messages shall be exchanged, and finally integrate the Web service invocation into the application.

In order to overcome these deficiencies, the emerging concept of Semantic Web services (SWS) develops techniques for better supporting the detection and usage of Web services on the basis of semantic descriptions. The aim is to better support and eventually automate the Web service usage process, and to facilitate the dynamic detection and execution of the necessary Web services for solving a particular client request within SOA systems. For this, inference-based techniques for automated *discovery* as the detection of suitable candidates out of the available Web services, *composition* as the automated combination of several Web services, and the *automated execution* of Web services are developed. The SWS approach uses ontologies as the underlying data model, which are formally specified knowledge models propagated as the base technology for the Semantic Web—another prominent amendment of the existing Web.

This chapter provides an overview of the SWS approach as well as the latest technology developments for this. Firstly, Section 5.2 recalls the initial Web service technologies and the vision of Service-Oriented Architectures. Then, Section 5.3 introduces the concept and the most prominent frameworks for Semantic Web services, and Section 5.4 presents recent developments on SWS techniques for automating the detection, usability analysis, and execution of Web services. Finally, Section 5.5 summarizes the chapter and outlines perspectives for the future development and standardization of semantic SOA technologies.

5.2 Web Services and SOA

The following recalls the concept of Web services and the basic technologies, and depicts the intended usage of Web services as the base technology for Service-Oriented Architectures (SOA). We also identify the deficiencies for supporting Web service usage in SOA environments in order to motivate the need for semantic technologies to enhance the quality of SOA systems.

5.2.1 Web Services

The concept of Web services has been invented in the late 1990s by a mostly industry-driven initiative. The aim was to define a new technology that on the one hand makes use of the WWW as an infrastructure for computation, and, on the other hand, allows to effectively tackle the intra- and inter-organizational integration of information and services. For this, three contiguous technologies have been specified which are commonly referred to as the initial *Web service technology stack*: WSDL as the language for describing the interface of a Web service, SOAP as a messaging protocol for exchanging XML data over the Web, and UDDI as a registry technology for Web services. These have been published by the World Wide Web Consortium W3C (`www.w3.org`), and respectively by OASIS as a mostly industry-driven standardization body (`www.oasis-open.org`). The standardized specifications have been first released in the years 2000–2002; the latest versions have been published in 2007.

The following explains the basics of the central Web service technologies. We refer to the technical specifications as well as to extensive secondary literature for details, e.g., [5, 25, 45].

5.2.1.1 Web Service Description Language (WSDL)

As the heart of Web service technology, this is an XML-based language for describing the interface of a Web service [11]. Essentially, a WSDL description specifies the supported operations for invoking and consuming the Web service, its physical location, and it supports bindings to several transport protocols and formats for the actual information exchange between the Web service and the requester.

The WSDL description of a Web service is defined as an XML document that consists of the following elements: the *service* element describes the name and the physical location of the Web service, mostly in form of a URI. A Web service can have several physical endpoints. These are called *ports*, for which a *binding* defines the supported transport protocols and formats. While this specifies how to carry out the actual information exchange, the *port type* element specifies the set of operations that are supported by the Web service. An *operation* consists of a set of messages and their direction (i.e., in- or out-going). A *message* describes the data being communicated between the requester and the provider. The message content is described in terms of XML Schemas; the *type* element allows the specification of the complex data types used in the WSDL description.

The main merit is that WSDL is independent of the technologies used for the actual implementation of a Web service. Thus, in principle any program can be provided as a Web service by defining a WSDL description. This is supported by existing development environments, e.g., the Java2WSDL tool from the Apache Axis tool kit which allows the automatic generation of the WSDL description for a Java program (see `http://ws.apache.org/axis/`).

5.2.1.2 SOAP

Formerly the abbreviation for *Simple Object Access Protocol*, this is a messaging technology for exchanging XML data over the Web [52]. Although SOAP is not restricted to the context of Web services, it has become the standard communication protocol for consuming Web services by the exchange of messages over the Internet.

Every operation in a WSDL description is associated with one or more messages. To consume a Web service, these need to be instantiated with concrete values and then are exchanged between the endpoints via a specific transport protocol. A SOAP message is a XML document which consists of a *header* with technical information, and a *body* that carries the actual content in the form of XML data. This is wrapped into an envelope, which then can be bound to a transport protocol for conducting the actual information exchange. In the context of Web services, SOAP is mostly bound to HTTP in order to enable document exchange over the WWW; however, it can also be bound to other transport protocols.

5.2.1.3 Universal Description Discovery and Integration Protocol (UDDI)

This is a registry technology intended to support the publishing, management, and discovery of Web services. It defines a generic data model for describing Web services with respect to the providing business entity, the technical access information, a natural language description, and a keyword-based classification scheme [18]. In addition, the detailed specification of Web services can be bundled in so-called technical models. The specification comes along with an API in order to support programmatic access to UDDI registries.

The purpose of a UDDI registry is to allow service providers to publish and advertise their Web services, and also to facilitate the search and inspection of suitable Web services by clients. Initially, big vendors such as Microsoft, SAP, and IBM maintained the UDDI Business Registry (UBR) as a single repository for publicly available Web services. However, this effort has been abandoned because the categorization scheme used as well as the UDDI support for publishing and searching Web services proved to be insufficient. Nowadays, most SOA systems employ registry techniques that are specialized for the specific application scenario. Nevertheless, these proprietary registries follow the principles of UDDI—i.e., describing and organizing Web services in a classification scheme to support clients in the detection of the suitable Web services.

Concluding, the initial Web service technology stack is comprised of three cohesive technologies standardized by the W3C, and respectively by OASIS:

1. WSDL as the standardized description language for Web services
2. SOAP as the communication protocol for executing Web services
3. UDDI as a registry technology for publishing and searching Web services.

In addition, several accessory technology standards have been specified, which are concerned with usage policies, addressing schemes, security, and other aspects that occur to be relevant for real-world applications [72]. A reliable indicator for the thorough adaptation and success of Web services is that essentially all big software vendors are committed to this technology.

5.2.2 Service-Oriented Architectures

The invention of Web services and the standardization of necessary technologies has initiated the concept of Service-Oriented Architectures (SOA) as a new IT system design paradigm [25]. The idea is to use Web services as the basic building blocks of software systems in order to exploit the potential of this new technology. The motivation for this is twofold:

- Software fragments from distributed locations that are offered as Web services can be seamlessly integrated, which eases the aggregation of services from different providers [5].
- Web services can help to reduce the development and maintenance costs of IT systems by reuse of existing services and by flexible replacement [45].
- Web services allow us to tackle the integration problem, i.e., the exchange of data and services between business partners that use different technologies: if two businesses agree on a common data model and provide their public processes as Web services, then the relevant information can be interchanged while the internal processes remain unchanged [13].

The initial Web service technology stack as explained above provides the technical basis for realizing the SOA vision, and the standardization has triggered major research and development efforts in industry as well as in academia. Existing SOA technologies range from freely available tools (e.g., the Methods Web service browser) and open source development kits (e.g., AXIS from Apache) to exhaustive development and management environments from the major software vendors, e.g., the Microsoft's .NET framework, IBM's WebSphere, Oracle's SOA Suite, NetWeaver (SAP), or Crossvision (Software AG). Moreover, the rising interest in Web services and SOA has led to further developments such as the integration into business process management technology (e.g., BPEL4WS, [6]) as well as to service orientation as a new business model [4].

However, the development of sophisticated SOA technologies is an immense challenge. A central challenge is the adequate support for the detection of suitable Web services for a concrete client application. This requires an appropriate description that allows clients to determine whether a Web service is actually suitable for the given problem, and SOA systems should support this in an adequate manner. We discuss the deficiencies of the basic Web service technologies for the usability analysis in more detail, which will reveal the motivation for Semantic Web services that we shall discuss in the next section.

Figure 5.1 illustrates the procedure of Web service usage by clients on the basis of WSDL, SOAP, and a registry technology like UDDI. The client—which in most cases is the developer of an application wherein Web services shall be used—wants to find a suitable Web service for a certain problem setting. As the first step, the client searches the UDDI registry of the available Web services. When a candidate has been found, its actual usability must be determined. This means that the client needs to figure out in what order which messages with what content and under which transport binding must be exchanged with the Web service in order to consume the desired functionality. The relevant information for this is available in the WSDL description of a Web service. However, the client needs to manually analyze the supported operations as well as the required data in order to determine how to invoke the Web service in a way such that it will solve the given task. This problem remains when using automatically generated client stubs for WSDL descriptions, because the generated code merely reflects the description in a programmatic environment. Once the usability analysis is completed successfully, the Web service can be invoked and consumed over the specified binding (which usually is SOAP as explained above).

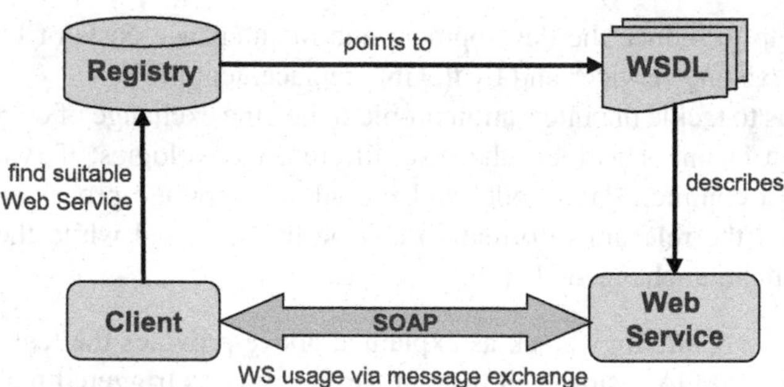

Fig. 5.1 Web service usage procedure

Obviously, the outlined procedure can not be considered to provide sophisticated support for the detection of suitable Web services, because most of the usability analysis tasks are left to manual analysis by the client. Moreover, several problems may occur during the analysis, e.g., that the classification scheme in the repository is too inexpressive so that the candidate search result is imprecise, or that the data of the client and the Web service are incompatible. Thus, more appropriate technologies are needed for supporting Web service detection and the usability analysis, which is at least as important for realizing the SOA vision as the technical infrastructure for the publication and consumption of Web services. One prominent approach that addresses this problem is the emerging concept of Semantic Web services that we will explain in the following.

5.3 Semantic Web Services

The aim of Semantic Web services (SWS) is to overcome the deficiencies of the initial Web service technologies, especially for the service detection and usability analysis as discussed above. The approach is to extended Web service descriptions with sufficiently rich semantic annotations and, upon these, provide inference-based techniques for automating the detection and usage of Web services [28,50]. Several research and development efforts work on SWS technologies, and there is a wealth of work on this. We here provide a concise overview, referring to more exhaustive literature for further details (e.g., [15,29,66]).

Essentially, SWS technologies apply reasoning techniques on formalized descriptions in order to better support the usability analysis of Web services and also to handle the integration problem on a semantic level. The primary tasks that can beneficially be supported by SWS technologies are *discovery* as the detection of suitable Web services for a given task, *composition* as the combination of several Web services to solve a more complex task, and *mediation* as the handling of heterogeneities that may occur between the requester and the provider. For this, the SWS approach extends Web service descriptions as follows (Figure 5.2).

1. Instead of XML, *ontologies are used as the data model* for describing Web services. These provide formalized knowledge models of a domain that allow advanced information processing. Moreover, this pursues the alignment of Web service technology with the Semantic Web for which ontologies are considered as the base technology (see below).
2. Apart from *non-functional aspects* such as the owner, usage rights, quality-of-service and financial information, also the *provided functionality* of a Web service is formally described. The primary purpose is to support semantic matchmaking techniques for more precise Web service discovery.
3. The *Web service interface for consumption*, i.e., the WSDL description, is formally described in order to support automated compatibility analysis of the communication behavior supported by the client and the Web service.
4. In addition, the *aggregation of Web services* describes how a complex Web service achieves its functionality by combining several other Web services. This aims at automated techniques for analyzing the executability of Web service aggregations in more complex SOA applications.

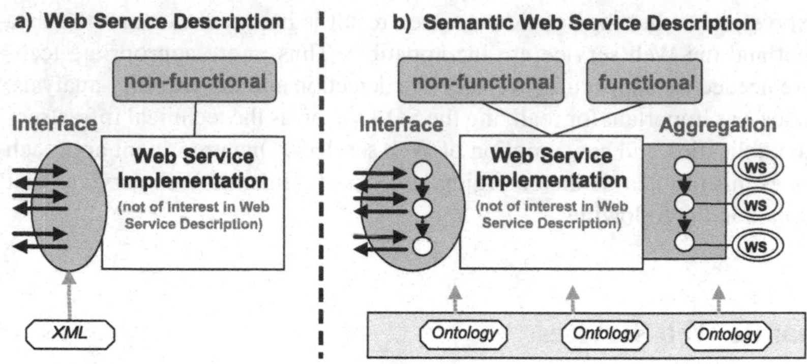

Fig. 5.2 From web services to semantic web services

The following explains the foundations of the SWS approach in more detail. We commence with the Semantic Web and ontologies, and then present the most prominent SWS frameworks that have been developed in the last years. We shall discuss the state-of-the-art in the development of SWS techniques for automating the detection and execution of Web services in the next section.

5.3.1 Ontologies and the Semantic Web

Ontologies are a modern AI knowledge representation technique. They have been identified as the base technology for the Semantic Web—the grand vision for the further evolution of the WWW [9]—and they are used as the formalized domain knowledge specifications for SWS descriptions. The following explains the definition and the benefits of ontologies as formalized knowledge models, and depicts the status of Semantic Web technology developments.

Adopting the denotation from the philosophical study of being and existence, an ontology is defined as a "formal, explicit specification of a shared conceptualization" [31]. This means that an ontology defines a conceptual model of a domain that ideally represents an agreed consensus among involved parties. The conceptual model is defined in terms of *concepts* that denote the entities in the domain of discourse. These are associated with *attributes* that describe specific properties, and *relations* that specify the relationships among the concepts. The subsumption and membership relations define the taxonomic backbone of the ontology. In addition, further knowledge on the domain can be specified in terms of logical statements referred to as *axioms*. Individuals in the domain are represented as *instances* of a concept. The conceptual model is then represented in a formal, machine-processable language upon which reasoning techniques can be employed for advanced information processing. The major merit is that ontologies provide a technology independent model of the domain of discourse, which allows us to better bridge the gap between the real world and IT systems [27]. Furthermore, ontologies allow us to integrate heterogeneous data on the semantic level by defining mappings between ontologies [3].

The Semantic Web envisions that Web resources are described on the basis of ontologies, so that their potential for advanced and meaning-preserving information processing can be exploited for processing Web-content. Proposed by Tim Berners-Lee—inventor of the WWW and director of the W3C—this is embedded in a larger vision for subsequently augmenting the current WWW with additional languages and technologies that shall be standardized by the W3C. Figure 5.3 shows the so-called *Semantic Web Layer Cake* that illustrates the overall vision: the bottom layers are the already existing WWW technologies (URI, XML, Namespaces). Upon this, several ontology languages are defined that are the current focus of standardization work. On top of this, languages for proof and trust on the Web are targeted as future work.[1]

The Semantic Web has received high interest in academia and industry, resulting in a steadily growing, international research community. This has produced a wealth of work that mainly covers the following areas.

1. Formal ontology languages [21] and efficient reasoning techniques (e.g., [54]).
2. Ontology management technologies [35], i.e., methodologies and tools for ontology engineering [30], scalable ontology repositories (e.g., [34]), and ontology evolution support (e.g., [23]).
3. Ontology-based data integration techniques (e.g., [57]).
4. Applications that demonstrate the benefits of Semantic Web technologies [20].

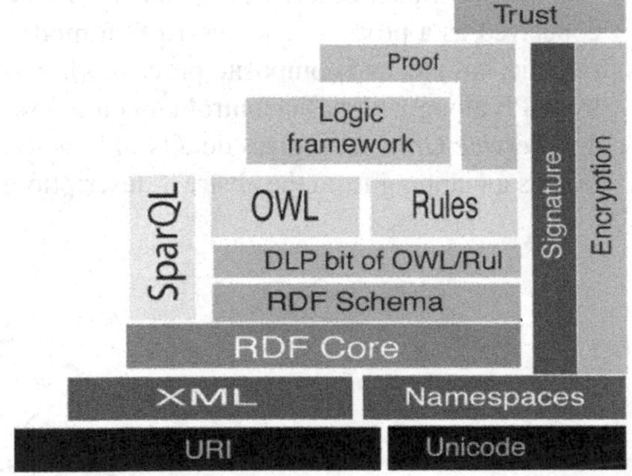

Fig. 5.3 The semantic web layer cake (revised version, 2005)

[1] Figure 5.3 is taken from a keynote talk by Tim Berners-Lee, see `http://www.w3.org/2005/Talks/0511-keynote-tbl/`. At the time of writing, W3C standard recommendations exist for the Resource Description Framework RDF (see `www.w3.org/RDF/`), the Web Ontology Language OWL [49], and the RDF query language SPARQL [44]; standardization work on a rule language is ongoing, e.g., in the RIF working group (see `http://www.w3.org/2005/rules/wg`).

5.3.2 SWS Frameworks

We now present SWS frameworks that define comprehensive specifications for semantically describing Web services, in general following the approach as outlined above. The following provides an overview of the conceptual frameworks that most of the research on Semantic Web services is based upon. As the most relevant ones, we here depict the approaches that have been submitted to or published by acknowledged standardization bodies.

5.3.2.1 OWL-S

As the chronologically first approach for SWS, OWL-S defines an upper ontology for semantically annotating Web services [47]. This has been developed in the years 2003–2005, driven by a mostly US-based consortium under the DAML programme (see `www.daml.org`).

The OWL-S model defines three elements for describing Web services as shown in Figure 5.4 (taken from [47]). Every description element is defined on the basis of domain ontologies, and OWL as the standard ontology language currently recommended by the W3C is used as the specification language.

1. The *Service Profile* holds information for Web service advertisement, containing the name of the service, its provider, a natural language description, and a formal functional description defined in terms of the inputs and outputs, preconditions and effects (short: IOPE).
2. The *Service Model* describes how the Web service works whereby the service is conceived as a process. The description model defines three types of processes (atomic, simple, and composite processes), in which each construct is described by IOPE along with basic control and data flow constructs.
3. The *Service Grounding* gives details of how to access the service, which is realized as a mapping from the abstract descriptions to WSDL.

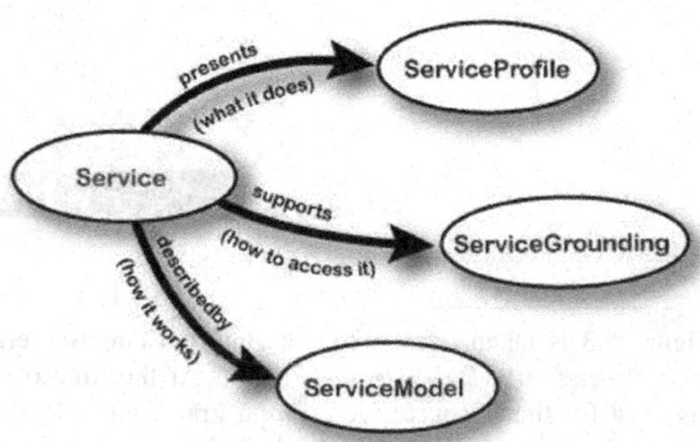

Fig. 5.4 Overview OWL-S

The intended usage of an OWL-S description is as follows. The service profile relates to the information stored in UDDI repositories. While the natural language descriptions are for human consumption, the formal functional description is used for automated Web service discovery by semantic matchmaking (see Section 5.4 below). The service model formally describes the external visible behavior of a Web service, i.e., how to invoke and consume the service and what happens when it is executed. This is used to determine whether the communication between a client and the Web service as well as with other aggregated Web services can be carried out successfully. Finally, the service grounding maps the abstract, semantic descriptions to conventional Web service technologies in order to conduct the actual message exchange for execution. Although being criticized especially on the inadequacy of the process description language [41], OWL-S has served as the basis for various SWS research and development activities.

5.3.2.2 WSMO

The Web Service Modeling Ontology WSMO is developed by a European initiative since 2004 (see `www.wsmo.org`) [42]. It takes a broader approach than OWL-S, aiming at a comprehensive framework for semantically enabled SOA technologies [12]. For this, it defines four top-level notions: *ontologies* that define formalized domain knowledge, *goals* that describe objectives that clients want to achieve by using Web services, semantically described *Web services*, and *mediators* for handling potentially occurring heterogeneities (see Figure 5.5).

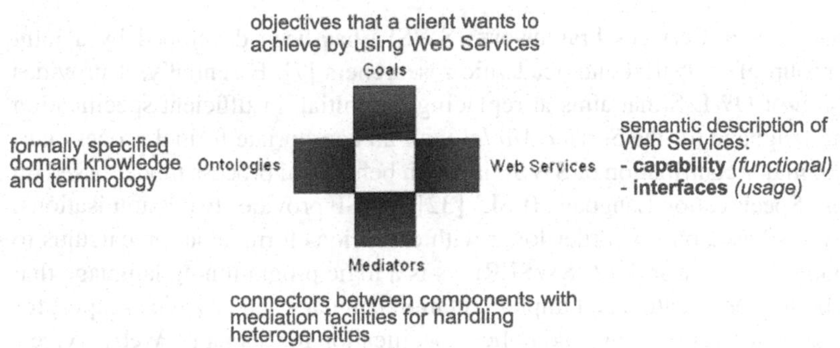

Fig. 5.5 WSMO top level notions

In contrast to the other frameworks, WSMO does not only cover the semantic annotation of Web services but propagates a goal-based approach for Semantic Web services along with mediation as an integral part. The idea is that a client formulates requests in terms of a goal, which formally describes the objective to be achieved while abstracting from technical details; the system then automatically detects and executes the suitable Web services in order to solve the goal [65]. The notion of goals provides an explicit element for the client side of SOA applications that facilitates the lifting of Web service usage by clients to the level of problems that can be solved. In addition, integrated mediators allow us to handle and resolve potentially occurring heterogeneities that can be expected in open and decentralized environments like the Web and may hamper the successful interaction between clients and Web services [17].

The WSMO framework defines description models for all four elements along with an own specification language. Analogous to Figure 5.2 above, Web services in WSMO are described by non-functional properties, a capability that specifies the provided functionality in terms of preconditions, assumptions, postconditions and effects, a choreography interface that describes how a client can invoke and consume a Web service, and an orchestration interface that describes how the Web service interacts with other Web services to achieve its functionality. WSMO provides an own specification language called WSML [22], which is a conceptual language for the WSMO elements along with five variants of logical languages that corresponds to the ontology languages developed for the Semantic Web (*cf.* Figure 5.3). Several tools are provided for WSMO, including a suite of reasoners for the different variants and an API for the programmatic management of WSMO elements and definitions. Moreover, there are implementations of execution environments for Semantic Web services, namely WSMX as the WSMO reference implementation (see `www.wsmx.org`) and the IRS system that provides a broker for Semantic Web services [14].

5.3.2.3 SWSF

The Semantic Web Services Framework (SWSF) has been developed by a joint working group of industrial and academic researchers [7]. Essentially, it provides an extension of OWL-S that aims at replacing the initial, insufficient specification model and language for the *Service Model* with an appropriate formal process language. The major contribution of SWSF is a rich behavioral process model based on the Process Specification Language (PSL) [32]. SWSF provides two axiomisations: (1) FLOWS is based on first-order logic with extensions form situation calculus to model changes of the world; (2) SWSLRules is a logic programming language that serves as both a specification and implementation language and provides support for tasks like discovery, contacting, and policy specification for Semantic Web services.

5.3.2.4 WSDL-S

The WSDL-S approach has been defined in a joint effort by IBM and the University of Georgia [1]. Instead of a comprehensive framework for semantically describing Web services, WSDL-S defines extensions to WSDL in order to semantically annotate the XML data types as well as the messages and operations in a WSDL description. For this, a WSDL document is augmented with additional tags that refer to an external domain ontology. While not fixing the ontology language, WSDL-S proposes three types of annotations:

1. WSDL types (i.e., XML data elements) are referenced to concepts in the domain ontology,
2. WSDL operations can be described by preconditions and effects that refer to respective axioms, and
3. a categorization of Web services can be defined on the basis of the ontology taxonomy.

5.3.2.5 SAWSDL

While the previous approaches are merely W3C member submissions, *Semantic Annotations for WSDL and XML Schema* (short: SAWSDL) is the only official W3C technology recommendation for Semantic Web services existing at this point in time [26]. It essentially follows the idea of WSDL-S, i.e., the annotation of WSDL documents with additional tags that reference a domain ontology. SAWSDL consists of two parts as illustrated in Figure 5.6 (taken from [40]): (1) mappings of XML schema definitions to ontology concepts which allow the definition of the correspondence of SOAP message contents to ontology data, and (2) the semantic annotation of WSDL operations. For the latter, SAWSDL limits the annotation by referring to ontology concepts but does not support the definition of preconditions and effects, which limits the annotations to merely consists of keywords associated with a domain ontology.

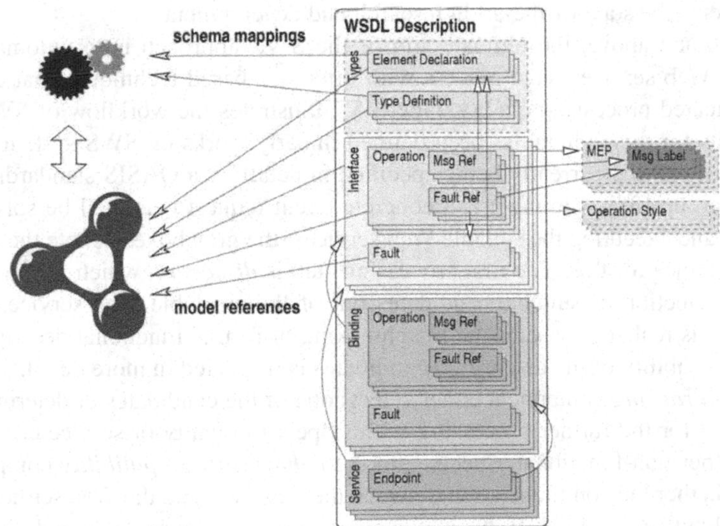

Fig. 5.6 SAWSDL overview

A comparison of the SWS frameworks reveals the following commonalities and differences. OWL-S as the first approach defines a description model for Web services that covers all aspects of the SWS approach as described above, i.e., non-functional aspects, a formal functional description, and formal descriptions of the interfaces for consumption and aggregation of Web services. It uses OWL as the specification language, thus is compliant with the W3C standards for the Semantic Web. SWSF extends this model with a more sophisticated process description language. WSMO is a more exhaustive framework that propagates a goal-driven approach along with integrated mediation facilities. Going beyond the idea of merely annotating Web services, this aims at an all-embracing framework for semantically enabled SOA technology. WSMO defines its own specification language that covers all ontology languages that are considered for the Semantic Web, and provides reasoners for this along with a set of development tools as well as reference implementations. WSDL-S only partially realizes the SWS approach, and therefore can be considered a light-weight framework. However, it follows the W3C tradition of extending existing standards, and it has served as the conceptual basis for SAWSDL as the only approach for the semantic annotation of Web services that is recommended by a standardization body as of today. Recent works take over this approach, e.g., [48].

5.4 Semantic Techniques for Automating SOA

After explaining the motivation and prominent approaches for Semantic Web services, we now turn towards the techniques for automated support of Web service detection and execution. The following first identifies the central techniques, and then presents the state-of-the-art in research and development.

As outlined above, the ultimate aim of the SWS approach is to automate the complete Web service usage process with inference-based techniques that expose a sophisticated processing quality. Figure 5.7 illustrates the workflow of SWS environments for this, which has been defined in early works on SWS system architectures [61] and is currently being specified in detail by a OASIS standardization working group [56]. The input is a concrete client request that shall be solved by detecting and executing the suitable Web services; the gray boxes denote the necessary techniques for this. The first processing step is *discovery*, which is concerned with the detection of suitable candidates out of the available Web services. This commonly is realized by semantic matchmaking of formal functional descriptions. Then, the usability of the discovered candidates is inspected in more detail. The *selection and ranking* component either selects one of the candidates or determines a priority list for the further processing with respect to quality-of-service criteria as well as other non-functional aspects, and the *behavioral compatibility* component checks whether the communication between the requester and the Web services can be carried out successfully. If this is given, then the *executor* automatically invokes the Web service in order to solve the client request. If a single suitable Web service does not exist, then the *composer* is invoked which tries to construct a combination of several Web services for solving the request; this utilizes the previously mentioned components. In addition, *mediation* facilities can be employed in order to handle potentially occurring mismatches that hamper the successful interaction between the requester and the provider. In the following, we explain each of the techniques in more detail and depict the latest research works on this.

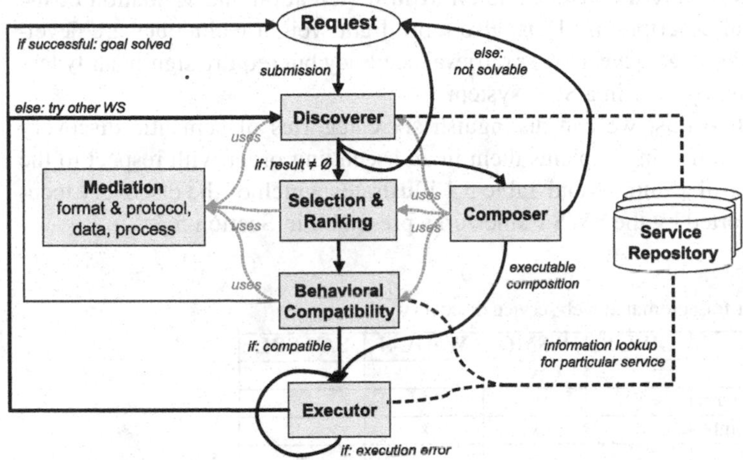

Fig. 5.7 SWS techniques for automated web service usage

5.4.1 Discovery

Web service discovery is concerned with the detection of the suitable Web services for a given request out of the available ones. This is a central operation in SOA systems for which a significant quality increase can be achieved by SWS techniques: on the basis of more precise Web service descriptions, discovery techniques can be developed that expose a higher precision and recall than the syntactic keyword-based search supported by UDDI.

A wealth of work exists on semantically enabled Web service discovery. Most approaches address this by semantic matchmaking of formally described requested and provided functionalities, i.e., OWL-S service profiles or WSMO capabilities as explained above. This is commonly referred to as *functional discovery* that determines whether a Web service can solve the given request with respect to the preconditions and effects. Prominent works for this are [37, 43, 60]. In addition to the basic matchmaking, techniques have been developed for handling cases where a match is not given but can be established by relaxing requirements in the request (e.g., [19]), and also approaches that integrate other techniques for the discovery task (e.g., [38, 55]).

In principle, semantically enabled Web service discovery techniques can achieve a very high retrieval accuracy. On the basis of sufficiently rich functional descriptions with expedient formal semantics and an exhaustive domain ontology, one can specify semantic matchmaking techniques that allow us to very precisely determine whether a Web service can be used for the given client request or not. This appears to be desirable in comprehensive SWS environments as outlined above. However, such techniques require a considerable effort in the creation and validation of the necessary formal descriptions. Thus, also more light-weight techniques are developed that can merely achieve a lower retrieval accuracy but require significantly less effort for the employment in a SOA system.

With respect to this, we can distinguish six categories of semantic discovery techniques. The following explains them in an ascending order with respect to the achievable retrieval accuracy, and Table 5.1 illustrates which of the discovery techniques are supported by the SWS frameworks presented in Section 5.3.

Table 5.1 Support for automated web service discovery

	OWL-S	WSMO	WSDL-S	SAWSDL
Goal-based		x		
Precond. / effect heavy	x	x		
Precond. / effect light	x	x	x	
Input / output	x	x	x	x
Categorization	x	x	x	x
Keyword-based	x	x	x	x

1. *Keyword-based:* the simplest techniques perform discovery on the basis of keywords. For example, the flight booking Web service from United Airlines is annotated with the keyword "flight, booking, UA". Usually, the keywords are based on a domain ontology, e.g., by the referencing mechanism defined in WSDL-S and SAWSDL. This is relatively easy to realize, but only a very low retrieval accuracy can be achieved.
2. *Categorization:* this refers to techniques that perform discovery on the basis of a categorization. Mostly, the Web services are annotated with concepts of a domain ontology, and the taxonomic structure of the ontology serves as the categorization scheme—e.g., all the Web services annotated with the concepts `car`, `train`, and `plane` are organized in the category `vehicle` as the common super-concept in the ontology. Although the actual retrieval accuracy is similar to the keyword-based techniques, the categorization allows us to browse and pre-filter potential candidates for a more detailed inspection. A SWS system that realizes this approach is presented in [68].
3. *Matchmaking input/output:* this refers to techniques that consider the compatibility of the inputs and outputs. In principle, a Web service is considered to be usable if (1) the requester can provide all required inputs, and (2) if the outputs of the Web service satisfy those expected by the requester. This can achieve a

significantly higher retrieval accuracy than the above approaches, and thus is the most commonly used discovery technique in SWS systems.

4. *Matchmaking precondition/effect:* the next group of discovery techniques does not only consider the inputs and outputs but also further conditions that are defined in terms of preconditions and effects. We here need to further distinguish *light-weight* techniques wherein the pre- and post-execution constraints are considered as isolated logical formulae, and *heavy-weight* techniques wherein the functional descriptions are considered as a coherent formal specification. Naturally, the latter can achieve a higher retrieval accuracy because the relationship between preconditions and effects is considered as well. An exhaustive discussion on this is provided in [37].
5. *Goal-based:* the last group of automated Web service discovery techniques follows the goal-based approach promoted by the WSMO framework (see above). Therein, client requests are associated to generic goal descriptions. Apart from a high retrieval accuracy, this allows the development of efficient and scalable discovery techniques by separating design-time and runtime operations [64].

5.4.2 Selection and Ranking

This encompasses semantically enabled techniques for determining the usability of Web services with respect to non-functional aspects, which includes quality-of-service information, and in particular data security and usage rights. The benefit of semantic techniques for this is that—on the basis of respective ontologies—a more precise and serviceable processing of quality requirements and usage policies can be achieved than with conventional techniques.

While Web service discovery as discussed above is concerned with *what* a Web service does, the techniques that we consider here are concerned with quality and usage conditions. The former aspect relates to the operational reliability of a Web service as a software artifact (i.e., regarding the availability, robustness, and execution performance) as well as the quality of the provided business service. These parameters are usually described in terms of respective time and quality measurements. The latter aspect is concerned with access rights and data security, which becomes particularly relevant when Web services are applied in IT systems for intra- and inter-organizational communication.

The approach for handling both quality-of-service as well as usage rights of Web services by semantic techniques is to reason upon *policies* that are defined on the basis of respective domain ontologies [58]. For example, if the access to an electronic journal might only be granted for members of a specific department of a university, this can be checked by the user profile of a requester; moreover, the specification of such conditions in an ontology makes the usage rights more transparent for the involved parties. Upon this, techniques are developed for automatically selecting a Web services which conforms with the relevant policies, or to determine a priority list of the usable candidates with respect to the client requirements (e.g., [70, 71]).

5.4.3 Behavioral Compatibility

The third group of SWS techniques is concerned with determining whether the communication between the requester and the provider can be conducted successfully. This is necessary in order to ensure that the actual consumption of the Web service can be carried out successfully.

This problem does not occur within conventional Web service technologies, because the client needs to explicitly trigger every outgoing SOAP message. However, in order to do this the developer of a client application must manually implement the correct communication behavior before the Web service can be used. In the context of Semantic Web services, the aim is to automatically execute the suitable Web services after they have been detected. For this, the communication behavior expected by the client and the one supported by the Web service must be compatible.

This can be checked automatically on the basis of the formally described interfaces, i.e., the OWL-S service model or the choreography and orchestration interfaces in WSMO (see above). Although this problem has only received little attention in the research community so far, existing approaches apply *conformance testing* techniques from the field of formal process management (e.g., [46, 69]). In a nutshell, the behavioral compatibility is considered to be given if (1) the incoming and outgoing messages of the requester and the provider are compatible, and (2) there exists at least one possible sequence of message exchange that can be carried out between the involved parties.

5.4.4 Composition

The aim of Web service composition is to automatically combine several Web services in order to obtain a more complex functionality. The surplus value of semantically enabled composition techniques is that new functionalities can be created that are not provided by the actually existing Web services, which is hardly achievable without any automation support.

The overall task for Web service composition is as follows: given a client request that can not be solved by a single Web services, an executable combination of several Web services that can solve the client request shall be constructed. A lot of research works address this challenge, applying different techniques for the composition problem. In general, we can distinguish composition techniques on two levels. The first one considers the functionalities of the Web services for determining a suitable execution order, hence referred to as *functional composition*. The respective techniques work on the formal functional descriptions—i.e., OWL-S service profiles or WSMO capabilities—and mostly apply AI planning techniques for the composition task (e.g., [36, 51, 73]). The second level is concerned with the communication behavior in a composition of Web services. The aim is to ensure that the interaction between the client and the composed Web services can be conducted successfully, i.e., the problem of behavioral compatibility as discussed above for a composition of Web services. This is commonly referred to as *behavioral composition*, and most approaches apply formal workflow or process management techniques for this (e.g., [2, 8]).

To leverage automated Web service composition within SWS environments, both types of composition techniques need to be integrated in order to attain executable compositions of Web services for solving a given client request. For this, [67] presents an approach wherein at first functional composition is applied to create a skeleton of a composition that is suitable for solving the client request, and in the second step its executability is verified by behavioral composition techniques. Besides, recent approaches consider Web service discovery and composition as interleaved operations: composition is only needed if a directly usable Web service cannot be discovered, and discovery techniques are used to find the candidates during the composition procedure (e.g., [10]).

5.4.5 Mediation

In the context of Semantic Web services, mediation refers to handling and resolving potentially occurring heterogeneities which may hamper the interoperability between a requester and a provider. This becomes particularly important within open and distributed environments like the Web where requesters and providers can be expected to use different data representation formats, incompatible terminologies, or expose business processes that are not compatible a priori. The main merit of SWS technologies is that such heterogeneities can be handled on the semantic level, i.e., by domain independent mediation techniques that allow us to properly resolve and handle the mismatches [28].

WSMO is the only SWS framework that encompasses mediation as an integral part. It defines specific mediators for handling different types of heterogeneities, provides respective mediation techniques, and defines an integrated architecture for the specification and usage of mediators within SWS environments [63]. The most relevant mediation techniques are (1) *data level mediation* that is concerned with mismatch handling on terminologies, domain knowledge, and representation formats [53], and (2) *process level mediation* that is concerned with handling incompatible communication behaviors and business processes of requesters and providers [16]. The other SWS frameworks presented in Section 5.3 do not consider mediation; in fact, they are merely concerned with the semantic description of Web services while remaining orthogonal to all other aspects that occur to be relevant for the employment of semantic technology in SOA systems. However, existing techniques for heterogeneity handling can be employed, e.g., ontology-based data integration techniques that have been developed for the Semantic Web in order to handle data-level mismatches [57].

5.4.6 Automated Execution

The final aspect of SWS technology is the automated execution of Web services. Once the suitable Web services for solving a given request have been detected and all other relevant aspects have been checked, they should be executed automatically in order to minimize the need for human intervention.

For this, the semantic descriptions of the Web services need to be mapped to technologies that support the actual information interchange. Commonly, this is achieved by mapping the semantic annotations to a WSDL description, upon which the Web services can actually be invoked and consumed by exchanging SOAP messages as explained in Section 5.2. This usually also includes an explicit mapping between the XML data types used within SOAP messages and domain ontologies used for the semantic descriptions in order to facilitate the processing of the interchanged data on the semantic level.

This is supported by all SWS frameworks presented above. OWL-S and SWSF define the mappings in the service grounding element, which specifies the mapping of the domain ontology to an XML Schema definition and maps the service model definitions to WSDL operations. This can be processed by the OWL-S Virtual Machine for automated execution [59]. The same approach is realized in WSMO: the mappings from the ontology definitions to XML as well as the mapping to WSDL operations is defined within the WSMO choreography interface description, and the WSMX execution component invokes the Web services via WSDL [39]. Within WSDL-S and SAWSDL, the mappings are defined explicitly by the references to a domain ontology within additional tags in the WSDL document, which can be processed by respective execution environments.

Summarizing, we have shown that there is a wealth of work on SWS techniques for the automated detection, usability analysis, composition, and execution of Web services. The individual solutions vary in the achievable quality and the necessary efforts for their employment. Next to the theoretic foundations, several open-source tools and even comprehensive development and execution environments are provided for Semantic Web services. The most prominent are the OWL-S IDE [62], the WSMX system as the reference implementation of the WSMO framework [33], and the IRS system that provides a broker for Semantic Web services [24]. However, most of the currently existing SWS technologies have been developed in the course of academic research, and their employment in real-world applications requires additional software development.

5.5 Conclusions and Outlook

This chapter has provided an overview of the emerging concept of Semantic Web services (SWS) and the state-of-the-art in respective technology developments. The following summarizes the chapter, and discusses the potential as well as the challenges for the future developments of semantic SOA technologies.

5.5.1 Summary

The idea of Service-Oriented Architectures (SOA) is to employ Web services as the basic building blocks of future IT systems. For this, the initial Web service technology provides a standardized description language for the technical accessibility and the interfaces of Web services (WSDL), a communication protocol for the consumption of Web services by exchanging messages over the Web (SOAP), and a registry technology that allows us to publish and search Web services (UDDI).

Although this allows the technical use of Web services, the detection and usability analysis of suitable Web services for a specific client application is limited to manual inspection. To overcome this, the SWS approach develops techniques for the automated discovery, usability analysis, composition, mediation, and execution of Web services. These techniques work on rich formal descriptions of Web services that are defined on the basis of domain ontologies, i.e., formal knowledge models which are propagated as the base technology for the Semantic Web.

We have explained the most prominent frameworks for Semantic Web services that have been submitted to, and respectively published as recommendations by the W3C. The chronologically first approach is OWL-S, which semantically describes Web services by a service profile (the "who" and "what"), a service model (the "how"), and a grounding to WSDL for the execution. This has later been extended by the SWSF initiative wherein a more sophisticated formal process language for describing Web services has been developed. The second important framework is the Web Service Modeling Ontology WSMO that defines a comprehensive framework for semantically enabled SOA technology. Going beyond the semantic annotation of Web services, WSMO propagates a goal-driven approach for Semantic Web services wherein clients request and consume Web services on the basis of goals that abstract from technical details, and it considers mediation facilitates for the handling and resolving potentially occurring mismatches as an integral part. The third approach is the WSDL-S model which—in contrast to the other frameworks—defines the semantic annotation of Web services by extending WSDL descriptions with references to a domain ontology. A light-weight version of this approach is SAWSDL which supports the annotation of XML Schemas and WSDL descriptions with ontology concepts. Although the obtainable support for the automated detection and usability analysis is fairly limited, SAWSDL is the only existing W3C technology recommendation for Semantic Web services at this point in time.

We then considered the central SWS techniques for automating the Web service usage process by clients. The usual first processing step is *discovery*, i.e., the detection of the suitable Web services for a given client's requests. This is commonly performed by matchmaking of the requested and the provided functionalities, and we have depicted several techniques for this. Next, the usability of the discovered candidates is inspected with respect to non-functional aspects such as quality-of-service criteria, data security, and usage rights, and finally the behavioral compatibility is tested in order to ensure the successful interaction between the client and the Web service. Techniques for automated composition allow the combination of several Web services into more complex functionalities, and mediation techniques can be employed as auxiliary facilities to handle possibly occurring mismatches that may hamper thc successful interaction. When the Web services for solving a client request have been detected, they are executed automatically by lowering the semantic descriptions to WSDL and XML.

5.5.2 Future Challenges

So far, we have explained the motivation and state-of-the-art in SWS technologies. We also have shown that significant improvements for both the quality of the usability analysis and the degree of automation can be achieved. However, the existing SWS technologies are mostly academic developments. With respect to this, the following discusses challenges for future developments in order to make SWS techniques employable in real-world SOA applications.

The pre-requisite for SWS techniques is the existence of appropriate semantic descriptions for the available Web services and all other related resources. Most of the existing SWS techniques focus on new functionalities and the achievable benefits under the assumption that the necessary resource descriptions are given. However, this may not be the case, in particular when SWS technology shall be applied within existing systems. Thus, techniques for the semantic annotation of legacy systems appear to be essential in order to assure the applicability of SWS technologies in real-world settings. This challenge has only received very little attention in the research community so far. It seems to be possible to adopt techniques for the ontology-based annotation of natural language texts for this; however, in general this can only be supported in a semi-automated manner due to the gap between syntactic and adequate semantic descriptions, and also the annotation of Web services is expectably much more complex.

Another concern related to the general applicability of SWS techniques is the extent to which they shall be employed such that a substantial benefit can be achieved while the effort and costs remain moderate. The initial Web service technologies are not sufficient because they limit the Web service usage to manual inspection. The SAWSDL approach seems to be only a little bit better: the semantic annotation by additional tags in WSDL documents is relatively easy to realize, but on the other hand the obtainable benefits are only marginal. The OWL-S approach requires exhaustive descriptions of Web services on which significant quality improvements can be achieved; however, the employment an existing system is very expensive. The WSMO approach can achieve the highest benefits because it encompasses the goal-based approach and integrated integrated mediation facilities, but its employment requires a comprehensive re-design of a SOA system. With respect to this, the aim for future research should be to identify the degree of employment for which the cost-benefit relation is optimal and then initiate respective technology standardisations.

A further aspect for the employment of SWS technology in real-world applications is the provision of adequate tooling support. Although a remarkable number of graphical editors, APIs, and execution environments already exist, they are still not sufficient in order to properly support users in real SOA applications. In particular, expedient graphical user interfaces for managing Web services and their semantic descriptions, as well as sophisticated validation services for the formal specifications, are desirable in order to better support end-users and system administrators. However, this can be considered as supplementary development efforts once the underlying technologies exist.

To conclude, semantic techniques for the automated detection and usage of Web services, as explained in this chapter, are capable and eligible to effectively support the idea of Service-Oriented Architectures. In fact, some "intelligence" seems to be necessary in order to prosperously realize the SOA vision, and the employment of semantic technologies seems to be a suitable promising approach for this. However, in order to leverage a successful deployment of such techniques within future SOA technology, it appears to be evident to properly address the mentioned challenges.

Acknowledgements

The presented work has been supported by the European Commission under the projects SUPER (FP6-026850) and by the Austrian BMVIT/FFG under the FIT-IT project myOntology (Grant no. 812515/9284).

References

1. R. Akkiraju, J. Farrell, J. Miller, M. Nagarajan, M.-T. Schmidt, A. Sheth, and K. Verma. Web Service Semantics—WSDL-S. W3C Member Submission 7 November 2005, 2005.
2. P. Albert, L. Henocque, and M. Kleiner. Configuration-Based Workflow Composition. In *Proc of 3rd International Conference on Web Services (ICWS-05), Orlando, Florida*, 2005.
3. V. Alexiev, M. Breu, J. de Bruijn, D. Fensel, R. Lara, and H. Lausen. *Information Integration with Ontologies*. Wiley, West Sussex, UK, 2005.
4. P. Allen. *Service Orientation: Winning Strategies and Best Practices*. Cambridge University Press, 2006.
5. G. Alonso, F. Casati, H. Kuno, and V. Machiraju. *Web Services: Concepts, Architectures and Applications*. Data-Centric Systems and Applications. Springer, Berlin, Heidelberg, 2004.
6. T. Andrews, F. Curbera, H. Dholakia, Y. Goland, J. Klein, F. Leymann, K. Liu, D. Roller, D. Smith, S. Thatte, I. Trickovic, and S. Weerawarana. Business Process Execution Language for Web Services version 1.1. Specification, IBM, BEA Systems, Microsoft, SAP AG, Siebel Systems, May 2003.
7. S. Battle, A. Bernstein, H. Boley, B. Grosof, M. Gruninger, R. Hull, M. Kifer, Martin. D., McIlraith. S., D. McGuinness, J. Su, and S. Tabet. Semantic Web Services Framework (SWSF). W3C Member Submission 9 September 2005, 2005.

8. D. Berardi, D. Calvanese, G. De Giacomo, M. Lenzerini, and M. Mecella. Automatic Composition of e-Services that Export their Behavior. In *Proc. of First Int. Conference on Service Oriented Computing (ICSOC)*, 2003.
9. T. Berners-Lee, J. Hendler, and O. Lassila. The Semantic Web. A new form of Web content that is meaningful to computers will uleash a revolution of new possibilities. *Scientific American*, 284(5):34–43, May 2001.
10. P. Bertoli, J. Hoffmann, F. Lecue, and M. Pistore. Integrating Discovery and Automated Composition: from Semantic Requirements to Executable Code. In *Proc. of the IEEE 2007 International Conference on Web Services (ICWS'07), Salt Lake City, USA*, 2007.
11. D. Booth and C. K. Liu. Web Services Description Language (WSDL) Version 2.0 Part 0: Primer. Recommendation 26 June 2007, W3C, 2007.
12. M. Brodie, C. Bussler, J. de Brujin, T. Fahringer, D. Fensel, M. Hepp, H. Lausen, D. Roman, T. Strang, H. Werthner, and M. Zaremba. Semantically Enabled ServiceOriented Architectures: A Manifesto and a Paradigm Shift in Computer Science. Technical Report TR-2005-12-26, DERI, 2005.
13. C. Bussler. *B2B Integration: Concepts and Architecture*. Springer, Berlin, Heidelberg, 2003.
14. L. Cabral, J. Domingue, S. Galizia, A. Gugliotta, B. Norton, V. Tanasescu, and C. Pedrinaci. IRS-III—A Broker for Semantic Web Services based Applications. In *Proc. of the 5th International Semantic Web Conference (ISWC 2006), Athens(GA), USA*, 2006.
15. J. Cardoso and A. Sheth. *Semantic Web Services, Processes and Applications*. Semantic Web and Beyond. Springer, 2006.
16. E. Cimpian and A. Mocan. WSMX Process Mediation Based on Choreographies. In *Proceedings of the 1st International Workshop on Web Service Choreography and Orchestration for Business Process Management at the BPM 2005, Nancy, France*, 2005.
17. E. Cimpian, A. Mocan, and M. Stollberg. Mediation Enabled SemanticWeb Services Usage. In *Proc. of the 1st Asian Semantic Web Conference (ASWC 2006), Beijing, China*, 2006.
18. L. Clement, A. Hately, C. von Riegen, and T. (eds) Rogers. UDDI Version 3.0.2. UDDI Spec Technical Committee Draft, OASIS, 2004.
19. S. Colucci, T. Di Noia, E. Di Sciascio, F. M. Donini, and M. Mongiello. Concept abduction and contraction for semantic-based discovery of matches and negotiation spaces in an e-marketplace. *Electronic Commerce Research and Applications*, 4:345–361, 2005.
20. J. Davis, R. Studer, and P. Warren. *Semantic Web Technology. Trends and Research in Ontology-based System*. Wiley & Sons, 2006.
21. J. de Bruijn. Logics for the Semantic Web. In J. Cardoses, editor, *Semantic Web: Theory, Tools and Applications*. Idea Publishing Group, 2006.
22. J. de Bruijn, H. Lausen, R. Krummenacher, A. Polleres, L. Predoiu, M. Kifer, and D. Fensel. The Web Service Modeling Language WSML. Deliverable D16.1 final draft 05 Oct 2005, WSML Working Group, 2005.
23. P. de Leenheer and T. Mens. Ontology Evolution: State of the Art and Future Directions. In M. Hepp, P. De Leenheer, A. de Moor, and Y. Sure, editors, *Ontology Management*. Springer, 2006.
24. J. Domingue, L. Cabral, S. Galizia, V. Tanasescu, A. Gugliotta, B. Norton, and C. Pedrinaci. IRS-III: A Broker-based Approach to Semantic Web Services. *Journal of Web Semantics*, 2008.
25. T. Erl. *Service-Oriented Architecture (SOA). Concepts, Technology, and Design*. Prentice Hall PTR, 2005.
26. J. Farrell and H. Lausen. Semantic Annotations for WSDL and XML Schema. W3C Recommendation 28 August 2007, 2007.
27. D. Fensel. *Ontologies: A Silver Bullet for Knowledge Management and E-Commerce*. Springer, Berlin, Heidelberg, 2 edition, 2003.
28. D. Fensel and C. Bussler. The Web Service Modeling Framework WSMF. *Electronic Commerce Research and Applications*, 1(2), 2002.
29. D. Fensel, H. Lausen, A. Polleres, J. de Bruijn, M. Stollberg, D. Roman, and J. Domigue. *Enabling Semantic Web Services. The Web Service Modeling Ontology*. Springer, Berlin, Heidelberg, 2006.

30. A. Goméz-Peréz, O. Corcho, and M. Fernandez-Lopez. *Ontological Engineering. With Examples from the Areas of Knowledge Management, E-Commerce and Semantic Web*. Series of Advanced Information and Knowledge Processing. Springer, Berlin, Heidelberg, 2003.
31. Thomas R. Gruber. A Translation Approach to Portable Ontology Specifications. *Knowledge Acquisition*, 5:199–220, 1993.
32. M. Gruninger and C. Menzel. The Process Specification Language (PSL) Theory and Applications. *AI Magazine*, 24(3):63–74, 2003.
33. A. Haller, E. Cimpian, A. Mocan, E. Oren, and C. Bussler. WSMX—A Semantic Service-Oriented Architecture. In *Proceedings of the International Conference on Web Service (ICWS 2005), Orlando, Florida*, 2005.
34. A. Harth and S. Decker. Optimized Index Structures for Querying RDF from the Web. In *Proc. of 3rd Latin American Web Congress, Buenos Aires, Argentina, Oct 31–Nov*, 2005.
35. M. Hepp, P. de Leenheer, A. de Moor, and Y. Sure. *Ontology Management. Semantic Web, Semantic Web Services, and Business Applications*. Semantic Web and Beyond. Springer, 2007.
36. J. Hoffmann, P. Bertoli, and M. Pistore. Service Composition as Planning, Revisited: In Between Background Theories and Initial State Uncertainty. In *Proc. of the 22nd National Conference of the American Association for Artificial Intelligence (AAAI'07), Vancouver, Canada*, 2007.
37. U. Keller, R. Lara, H. Lausen, and D. Fensel. Semantic Web Service Discovery in the WSMO Framework. In J. Cardoses, editor, *Semantic Web: Theory, Tools and Applications*. Idea Publishing Group, 2006.
38. M. Klusch, B. Fries, and K. Sycara. Automated Semantic Web Service Discovery with OWLS-MX. In *Proc. of the 5th International Joint Conference on Autonomous Agents and Multiagent Systems (AAMAS 2006), Hakodate, Japan, May 8–12*, 2006.
39. J. Kopecký, D. Roman, M. Moran, and D. Fensel. Semantic Web Services Grounding. In *Proc. of the International Conference on Internet and Web Applications and Services (ICIW'06), Guadeloupe, French Caribbean*, 2006.
40. Jacek Kopecky. Semantic Annotations for WSDL and XML Schema. Talk at W3C track in the WWW 2007 Conference, Banff, Canada, 2007.
41. L. Lara, D. Roman, A. Polleres, and D. Fensel. A Conceptual Comparison of WSMO and OWL-S. In *Proc. of the European Conference on Web Services (ECOWS 2004), Erfurt, Germany*, 2004.
42. H. Lausen, A. Polleres, and D. Roman (eds.). Web Service Modeling Ontology (WSMO). W3C Member Submission 3 June 2005.
43. L. Li and I. Horrocks. A Software Fframework for Matchmaking based on Semantic Web Technology. In *Proceedings of the 12th International Conference on the World Wide Web, Budapest, Hungary*, 2003.
44. F. Manola and E. Miller. SPARQL Query Language for RDF. W3C Candidate Recommendation 14 June 2007.
45. E. A. Marks and M. Bell. *Service-Oriented Architecture (SOA): A Planning and Implementation Guide for Business and Technology*. Wiley, 2006.
46. A. Martens. On Compatibility of Web Services. *Petri Net Newletter*, 65:12–20, 2003.
47. D. Martin. OWL-S: Semantic Markup for Web Services. W3C Member Submission 22 November 2004.
48. D. Martin, M. Paolucci, and M. Wagner. Towards Semantic Annotations of Web Services: OWL-S from the SAWSDL Perspective. In *Proc. of the ESWC 2007 workshop OWL-S: Experiences and Directions, Innsbruck, Austria*, 2007.
49. D. McGuinness and F. van Harmelen. OWL Web Ontology Language—Overview. W3C Recommendation 10 February 2004.
50. S. McIlraith, T. Cao Son, and H. Zeng. Semantic Web Services. *IEEE Intelligent Systems, Special Issue on the Semantic Web*, 16(2):46–53, 2001.
51. S. McIlraith and T. C. Son. Adapting Golog for Composition of Semantic Web Services. In *roc. of the 8th International Conference on Knowledge Representation and Reasoning (KR '02), Toulouse, France*, 2002.

52. N. Mitra and Y. Lafon. SOAP Version 1.2 Part 0: Primer (Second Edition). Recommendation 27 April 2007, W3C, 2007.
53. A. Mocan and E. Cimpian. An Ontology-based Data Mediation Framework for Semantic Environments. *International Journal on Semantic Web and Information Systems (IJSWIS)*, 3(2):66–95, April–June 2007.
54. B. Motik, R. Shearer, and I. Horrocks. Optimized Reasoning in Description Logics using Hypertableaux. In *Proc. of the 21st Conference on Automated Deduction (CADE-21), Bremen, Germany, July 17–20*, 2007.
55. T. Di Noia, E. Di Sciascio, F. Donini, and M. Mongiello. A System for Principled Matchmaking in an Electronic Marketplace. In *Proc. of the 12th International Conference on the World Wide Web (WWW'03), Budapest, Hungary*, 2003.
56. B. Norton and A. Mocan. Reference Model for Semantic Service Oriented Architecture. Working Draft, 21 March 2007, OASIS, 2007.
57. N. Noy. Semantic Integration: a Survey of Ontology-based Approaches. *ACM SIGMOD Record*, 33(4):65–70, 2004.
58. D. Olmedilla, R. Lara, A. Polleres, and H. Lausen. Trust Negotiation for Semantic Web Services. In *Proc. of the 1st International Workshop on Semantic Web Services and Web Process Composition at the ICWS 2004, SanDiego, California (USA)*, 2004.
59. M. Paolucci, A. Ankolekar, N. Srinivasan, and K. Sycara. The DAML-S Virtual Machine. In *Proc. of the 2nd International Semantic Web Conference (ISWC),Sandial Island, Florida*, 2003.
60. M. Paolucci, T. Kawamura, T. Payne, and K. Sycara. Semantic Matching of Web Services Capabilities. In *Proc. of the 1st International Semantic Web Conference, Sardinia, Italy*, 2002.
61. C. Preist. A Conceptual Architecture for Semantic Web Services. In *Proc. of the 2nd International Semantic Web Conference (ISWC 2004)*, 2004.
62. N. Srinivasan, M. Paolucci, and K. Sycara. CODE: A Development Environment for OWL-S Web services. In *Demonstration at 3rd International Semantic Web Conference (ISWC 2004), Hiroshima, Japan.*, 2004.
63. M. Stollberg, E. Cimpian, A. Mocan, and D. Fensel. A Semantic Web Mediation Architecture. In *Proceedings of the 1st Canadian Semantic Web Working Symposium (CSWWS 2006), Quebec, Canada*, 2006.
64. M. Stollberg, M. Hepp, and J. Hoffmann. A Caching Mechanism for Semantic Web Service Discovery. In *Proc. of the 6th International Semantic Web Conference (ISWC 2007), Busan, South Korea*, 2007.
65. M. Stollberg and B. Norton. A Refined Goal Model for Semantic Web Services. In *Proc. of the 2nd International Conference on Internet and Web Applications and Services (ICIW 2007), Mauritius*, 2007.
66. R. Studer, S. Grimm, and A. Abecker. *Semantic Web Services. Concepts, Technologies, and Applications*. Springer, 2007.
67. P. Traverso and M. Pistore. Automatic Composition of Semantic Web Services into Executable Processes. In *Proc. of the 3rd International Semantic Web Conference (ISWC 2004), Hiroshima, Japan*, 2004.
68. K. Verma, K. Sivashanmugam, A. Sheth, A. Patil, S. Oundhakar, and J. Miller. METEOR-S WSDI: A Scalable P2P Infrastructure of Registries for Semantic Publication and Discovery of Web Services. *Journal of Information Technology and Management*, 6(1):17–39, 2005.
69. T. Vitvar, M. Zaremba, and M. Moran. Dynamic Service Discovery through Meta-Interactions with Service Providers. In *Proc. of the 4th European Semantic Web Conference (ESWC 2007), Innsbruck, Austria*, 2007.
70. L.-H. Vu, M. Hauswirth, and K. Aberer. QoS-Based Service Selection and Ranking with Trust and Reputation Management. In *Proc. of the OTM Confederated International Conferences CoopIS, DOA, and ODBASE 2005, Cyprus*, pages 466–483, 2005.
71. X. Wang, T. Vitvar, M. Kerrigan, and I. Toma. A QoS-aware Selection Model for Semantic Web Services. In *Proc. of the 4th International Conference on Service Oriented Computing (ICSOC), December, 2006, Chicago, USA*, 2006.

72. S. Weerawarana, F. Curbera, F. Leymann, T. Storey, and D. F. Ferguson. *Web Services Platform Architecture: SOAP, WSDL, WS-Policy, WS-Addressing, WS-BPEL, WS-Reliable Messaging, and More*. Prentice Hall PTR, 2005.
73. D. Wu, B. Parsia, Sirin E., J. Hendler, and D. Nau. Automating DAML-S Web Services Composition Using SHOP2. In *Proceedings of 2nd International Semantic Web Conference (ISWC 2003), Sanibel Island, Florida*, 2003.

Chapter 6
Dependability in Service-Oriented Computing

Arshad Jhumka

Abstract Service-oriented computing (SOC) is emerging as a new approach to developing extensible computing systems, including distributed systems. This new paradigm is based on the interoperability and the loose coupling among the computing elements involved. The loose coupling property among the computing elements allows for the development of adaptive systems, however, it also introduces the possibilities for failures to occur at various levels. In this chapter, we investigate the various dependability issues involved in service-oriented computing. Specifically, we look at the various faults that can occur in the system. We then look at various dependability approaches to handle the faults identified. We further propose how to estimate the dependability of an application. We conclude by providing two case studies to highlight aspects of dependability in service-oriented computing.

6.1 Introduction

The design and implementation of computer systems are becoming increasingly complex and error-prone. In turn, these systems are becoming increasingly hard to maintain. Issues such as reliability, performance, and security only exacerbate the design problem. One potential solution that has been advocated to conquer the complexity of designing such systems is the use (or reuse) of components that provide services. In fact, the areas of *component-based software engineering* and *service-oriented computing* are rapidly growing. Both advocate the use of artefacts (software, hardware, middleware) that provide services to others. Both areas are similar, however, for service-oriented computing an additional requirement tends to be that parts of the process need to be automated. Henceforth, we will use the terms components and services interchangeably, depending on the context. In component-based

---

Arshad Jhumka
Department of Computer Science, University of Warwick, Coventry, CV4 7AL, UK
e-mail: `H.A.Jhumka@warwick.ac.uk`

N. Griffiths, K.-M. Chao (eds.), *Agent-Based Service-Oriented Computing*, Advanced Information and Knowledge Processing,
DOI 10.1007/978-1-84996-041-0_6,

software engineering and service-oriented computing, two components may provide the same functionality, but each component can have different resource requirements and also they can guarantee different non-functional properties. A component A may provide a functionality F using a set of resources R, whereas component B provides the same functionality F but using resources R'. For example, consider a sorting procedure. The component A may provide a sorting procedure through *insertion sort*, whereas component B sorts a list according to *quicksort*, and thus components A and B give different performance guarantees.

To enable the component-based approach, a new design methodology needs to be adopted. The methodology needs to be able to allow the design of systems based on smaller subsystems that are composed together. In other words, it should be possible to realize a system based on the behaviour of smaller subsystems. For this methodology to work, two important constraints need to be satisfied: (i) components need to be able to work with each other, i.e., they are *interoperable*, and (ii) the working of one component should not be based on the implementation details of another component, i.e., the components need to be *loosely coupled*. The interoperability property ensures that when a component A makes a request to another component B, then component B is able to interpret A's request, and that component A is also able to interpret B's response. Further, the loose coupling property ensures that, even if B's implementation is changed, the change will not impact on A's functionality. For example, using the sorting procedure example, the behaviour of a component should be the same irrespective of whether quicksort or insertion sort is used, excluding non-functional properties.

In such a scenario, we say that a component provides *services* to another component. In the sorting example, component provides a *sorting* service. As such, services can be search, mathematical operations, IO operations etc. Once the notion of a component providing some services is reached, a service-oriented architecture becomes important. An *architecture* [19] is a formal description of a system, defining its purpose, functions, externally visible properties, and interfaces. It also includes the descriptions of the system's internal components, and their relationships, along with the principles governing its design, operation and evolutions. In brief, the architecture contains all the artefacts, and rules that will enable the development of software systems. A service-oriented architecture is, thus, an architecture that has services at its core. A service-oriented architecture will have a set of components that provide services, and will also contain rules that govern how these components will relate to each other. For example, there will be rules that govern the syntactic compatibility of some components, whereas others may govern their semantic capability, yet another rule can refer to dependability properties and so on.

Unfortunately, the flexibility of being able to build systems out of services brings about several problems. For example, incomplete interface descriptions may result in one component requesting a service from the wrong service provider. Another problem can be that a service provider is not able to process a request because the request has been wrongly formatted. Thus, the design flexibility afforded by service-oriented architectures introduces several dependability problems. It becomes important therefore to be able to firstly analyse and understand the various dependability threats, and then to assess the overall dependability of the system.

6.2 Service-Oriented Architecture

As previously argued, components and services (component-based software engineering and service-oriented computing) are being viewed as potential solutions in conquering the complexity of developing reliable computing systems, including distributed systems. Component-based designs are centred around individual components exposing their interfaces (and associated meta-data) via which they interact. A component A can only request a service from component B via B's interface, while B responds via its own interface.

In its broadest interpretation, a service-oriented architecure is an architectural style that has services as first class citizens. It refers to the design of a system, rather than its implementation [19]. The design consists of a set of components linked together via their interfaces. Sometimes, incompatibilities may exist between the components' interfaces, and *connectors* are needed to connect these components [8, 19]. The linking up process is done according to some specific rules. Sometimes, a syntactic link-up is sufficient, while at other times, semantic information is needed before the linking-up process is performed. This linking-up process is what is generally known as *composition*. A service oriented architecture emphasises the development of a system in a modular fashion, i.e., a component A implements a service S_A, and can be composed with a component B that implements a service S_B to provide an overall service S_{AB}. In other words, in service-oriented computing, an application is built as a composition of components and services.

To enable the composition process, a component needs to export (or publish) a description of the services it provides. The services that it exports can be viewed as its *export interface*. Further, a component needs to also publish its *import interface*, i.e., the set of services that it requires from other components. Other information that a component needs to provide is any resource requirement or other constraints that can prevent it from providing its exported services. All of this information is needed for a correct matching between offered and provided services. For example, consider a component that provides the following two services. (i) multiplication, and (ii) division. The component's export interface is: (i) multiply(a:int, b:int), and (ii) div(a:int, b:int). However, for the *div* service, the component has to mention that the parameter b needs to be non-zero (a constraint that needs to be satisfied whenever the service is used). If the constraints defined by the component are satisfied, then the component will provide the required service, i.e., if the service is used appropriately, then the component will provide correctness guarantees as to the service it is providing. This resembles the *design-by-contract* paradigm [13, 14], where the client request satisfies the preconditions specified for the service and, in turn, the component guarantees the correctness condition, i.e., the service's output will satisfy a specified postcondition.

In general, these components (and services) need to be discovered, i.e., when a service is needed, the client requesting the service has to determine a potential service provider. In domain areas where automation is required, such as in service-oriented computing, these services are published at a service registry, residing at a service broker. Figure 6.1 shows the process of service discovery and binding in a distributed system. The registry is located on a dedicated server (service broker), which can be possibly replicated, to handle crashes. The client requests a service from the service broker, which in turn returns the identity of a known provider of the service [3]. The client then agrees on the semantics with the provider. The client then binds itself to the provider, and uses the service. In other areas, where automation is not important, these services still need to be published and discovered. However, there are no dedicated service registry available. On the other hand, these services are possibly kept in a centralised service library. However, the architecture is similar to that of Figure 6.1. In an adaptive distributed system that supports web-based applications, these services can be discovered at run-time, whilst in single process-based applications, these services can be discovered at design and/or compile-time.

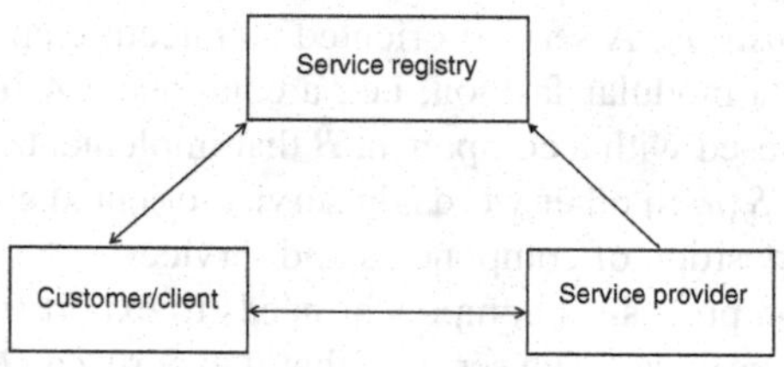

Fig. 6.1 Service interaction in a service-oriented distributed system

There are five basic steps required in a service-oriented architecture [3]. These are:

- publishing,
- discovery,
- composition,
- binding, and
- execution.

Publishing.

Service providers offer services and, in order for these to be used, their descriptions need to be provided. All services descriptions are kept in a service registry, whereas the actual services reside on different servers. All services have to be self-descriptive. The service description needs to be complete, i.e., the description needs to include the service being provided itself, its semantics, the constraints, and the resources needed for successful execution. Very often, this description will be done in a given language, e.g., logic, so that it can be easily understood. For example, web services are described using WSDL documents [18]. However, for web services, WSDL cannot be adequately used to describe non-functional properties.

Discovery.

When a client needs a desired service to perform a given task, it will have to discover the required service. To do so, the client has to have a clear understanding of the service that is required in the form of a description as offered by service providers. Once an offered service has been identified that matches the required service, we have a successful discovery.

Composition.

It may be the case when there is no successful discovery of a service. In this instance, smaller services may be composed together to provide a more complex service, which hopefully will match the service that is required. When doing so, both functional and non-functional properties need to be taken into consideration. If there is a mismatch, connectors may be used to link the two services. Two techniques are usually used, namely, service choreography [3] and service orchestration [3].

Both techniques yield the same result, however the approaches are different.

Binding.

Once an appropriate service has been discovered that offers the required functionality, the client binds itself to the service for execution. At this point, side aspects of the service can be set, such as security, authentication and so on. In service-oriented architectures such as web services, the binding takes place late in the process, allowing for dynamic adaptation when needed.

Execution.

Once the service is bound to the client, the service (single or composed) can be executed. The input parameters to the service are transmitted to the service provider which, upon receipt, executes the service. At the end of the execution, the result is returned to the client.

6.2.1 Dependability Issues in Service-Oriented Architectures

However, several problems can occur in a service-oriented architecture. For example, a given service may be requested with the wrong number of parameters during the execution phase. Another problem can be that the service is no longer available during the binding phase. Overall, this indicates that faults can occur at every step in the system. Before the development of a dependable system, it is of utmost importance to be able to predict the nature of the faults [17] that can affect the system. Once the possible faults are identified, remedial actions can be identified that will correct any problem in the system. Further, depending of the type of application and the service requested (whether it is stateful or stateless), the type of dependability mechanisms used will be different.

Overall, dependability can be addressed in four main ways, namely:

- fault avoidance,
- fault removal,
- fault forecasting, and
- fault tolerance.

Fault avoidance approaches are those that minimise the chance of faults occurring in the system. Fault removal approaches, on the other hand, look at removing faults that occur in the system. Fault forecasting approaches try to predict the number and impact of any residual faults on the system. Lastly, fault tolerance approaches work on the basis that faults are inevitable, and work by detecting and correcting the faults. We will look at each approach in more detail in Section 4.

The chapter is structured as follows. In Section 2, we provide an overview of the main steps involved in the setting up of a service-oriented architecture. In Section 3, we develop the system model, as well as the fault model. The fault model is developed by closely looking at the main steps in the service-oriented architecture, and looking at possible failure modes. In Section 4, we analyse the different ways of imparting dependability to a system, and then provide an overview of several possible approaches in each category. In Section 5, we discuss dependability metrics, and dependability evaluation. We explain the various concepts in two case studies developed in Section 6, and summarise and conclude the chapter in Section 7.

6.3 Models

In this section, we explain the various models that are relevant. We will first discuss system models, followed by fault models.

6.3.1 System Models

Using a software architecture approach, an application can be seen as a collection of components that offer and require services [19]. A component is an artefact (software, hardware, middleware) that implements a set of services. A service is an abstraction of a given functionality. It can be regarded as a unit of work. The set of services is partitioned between exported and imported services. A service exported by a component is one that is provided by the component to other components, while a service imported by a component is one that is used by the component and is provided by another component. Some components do not need to import other services to provide their own services, e.g., a time server/clock. Figure 6.2 represents a component. In general, a component publishes both its imported and exported services.

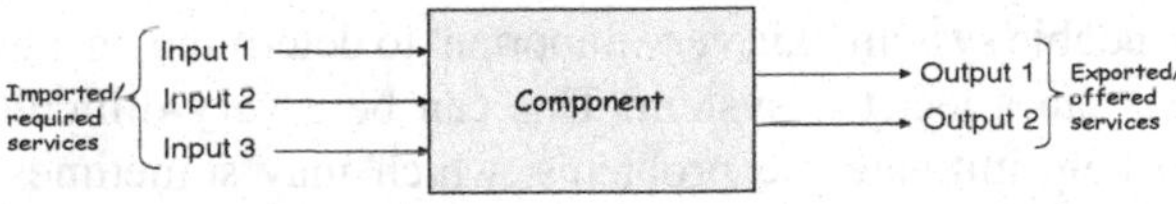

Fig. 6.2 A component with three imported services and two exported services. The imported services can be provided by different components. Similarly, the two exported services can be to different components

There exists a special class of components, called *connectors*, that enable the interconnection of non-connector components. Specifically, the tasks of the connectors can range from basic information transmission between components to providing the necessary security and fault tolerance guarantees necessary during data transmission. Owing to the fact that services can be provided by different third parties, incompatibilities between offered and required services will exist. To redress this problem, connectors are used to bridge the gap. At its simplest, i.e., where services match, a connector can just relay information from one component to another. However, when incompatibilities exist, connectors are used to provide the required functionality to enable the *composition* of the two non-connector components. For example, if a component makes a service request without any security guarantee, which is in turn required by the service provider, a connector can be used to provide the necessary security clearance before relaying the request to the provider. The modularisation of a system into components and services provides a very elegant approach to system design.

Although it can be beneficial to access a given service through a semantically well-defined interface, a greater value is obtained when higher-level services are provided, made up from lower-level services. This can be achieved through the composition of components, possibly via the use of connectors. Composition (of services or components) then means that the output of a service is fed into the input of another component, which in turn may need input from services from more than one component. In a distributed system, such as the Web, a component can use different connectors as appropriate for the network conditions and requirements of the end-user. For dependability purposes, the separation of concern between components/services and connectors allows failures due to the network to be handled cleanly and differently from failures due to computational (component/service) errors.

6.3.2 Fault Models

When developing a dependable system, it is very important to determine, in advance, the classes of faults that can affect the system. This can be a very difficult, and error-prone process. To help mitigate the problems, which may sometimes have catastrophic consequences, associated with an incomplete fault model, the concept of multitolerance has been advocated [1, 16]. However, to help ease the development of a fault model, it becomes important to adopt a systematic approach to determine the various faults that can occur at various levels.

From Figure 6.1, there are several levels at which faults can occur. For example, faults can occur during the service publishing phase. Faults can also occur during service discovery. Overall, in a service-oriented architecture, any of the following service-oriented architecture-specific faults can occur [3]:

- publishing fault,
- discovery fault,
- composition fault,
- binding fault, and
- execution fault.

In addition to these faults, a number of other failures can occur in a system, including distributed systems. These can be network failures, hardware crashes, or middleware (such as OS) failures. However, we will focus on the failures specific to service-oriented architectures.

Publishing faults.

During the publishing phase, the service is deployed on a server so it can be executed, and the service description is made public. Faults that can occur at this level are service description faults and service deployment faults.

A service description fault occurs when problems arise when describing the service. Either the service is not completely described, or the service is wrongly described. These faults can lead to problems during the discovery phase, or during the execution phase, which we will detail in later sections. On the other hand, service deployment faults occur when any aspect during the deployment is incorrect. For example, a service deployment fault can occur when the service is deployed without the required resources.

Discovery faults.

In the discovery phase, three possible failures can occur, namely:

- the service is not found,
- wrong service is found, and
- timed out, in a distributed setting.

However, these failures can be brought about by problems occurring in other parts of the system or process. To be able to identify the potential sources of these problems, we build a *fault tree* [21]. A fault tree analysis is a logical, structured process that can help in identifying potential causes of system failure before the actual failure occurs. It is performed using a top-down approach, i.e., starting from a top-level system failure, fault tree analysis is performed by working down to evaluate all contributing events that may ultimately cause the top-level system failure. Fault tree analysis helps determine the possible combinations of software and hardware failures that can lead to the overall system failure. At the core of fault tree analysis is a structure called the fault tree. The root of the tree is a top-level system failure, for which we want to determine its possible sources. Nodes in the tree represent intermediate component failures. Basic failure events are the leaves of the tree. One additional component in the structure is the use of boolean connectives to connect lower-level failure events into a higher-level failure event. For example, a fully functional CD-player will not work (top-level failure) if there is no battery (1st lower level failure) AND the player is not connected to the mains (2nd lower level failure).

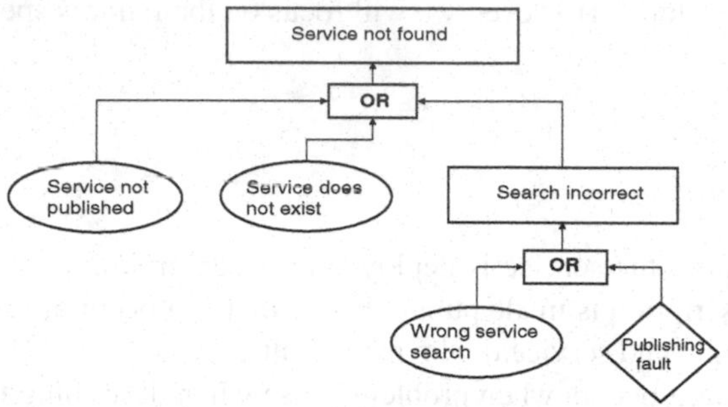

Fig. 6.3 A fault tree showing the possible failure sources for "Service not found" system failure

Figure 6.3 depicts a fault tree for the system failure "Service not found". Events leading to such a failure can be one of the following.

1. *No such service exists.* If no such service exists, then the system will always fail whenever the service is required.
2. *Service not published in registry.* It can be the case that a service exists within the system, but has not yet been published. In such cases, until the service appears in the registry, the system will fail.
3. *Incorrect search has been performed.* It can be the case that a service search is performed with the wrong number of parameters, or with the wrong functional or non-functional requirements, leading to a failure in discovering the correct service. Or still, the correct search has been performed, however, because of publishing faults, no service is found.

The events in ovals represent basic events, while events in diamonds represent undeveloped events. Undeveloped failure events are those whose sources are not further investigated, i.e., the failure in itself is more important than its sources (for the given system failure). However, for another system failure, it may be possible to investigate the failure sources further. In Figure 6.3, an incorrect search can occur if either (i) a wrong service search has been performed, or (ii) a seemingly correct search has been performed, however, publishing faults exist.

Further, it can be argued that, if a service does not exist or has not yet been published, several services can be composed to obtain the required one. However, problems can still occur during the composition phase. Problems occurring at that level will be classified under composition failures. Unless compatible services are found, a failure will occur.

Composition faults.

When an exact service match cannot be found, it is possible to compose different services so as to provide the required functionality. However, failures can occur in this phase too. Three types of failures can occur. These are:

- timed out, in a distributed system environment,
- no valid composition, and
- composition faults.

When a composition fault occurs, this indicates that contracts between components are not being respected. On the other hand, if there exists no compatible service, then a "no valid composition" fault occurs.

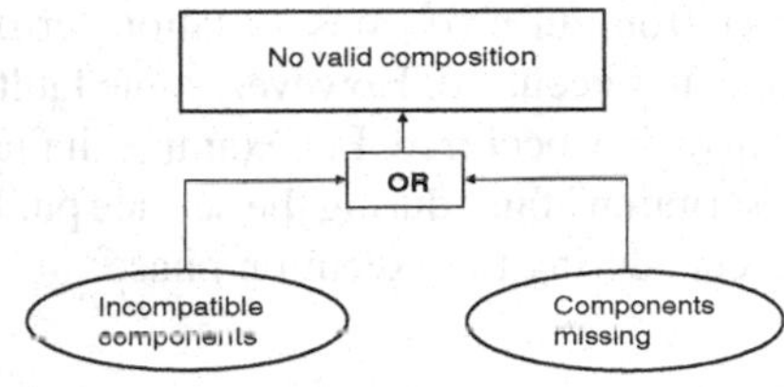

Fig. 6.4 A fault tree showing the possible failure sources for "No valid composition" system failure

In Figure 6.4, when either of the two faults (incompatible components, or components missing) occurs, a "no valid composition" fault occurs during the composition phase.

Binding faults.

During binding, the client and the service provider negotiate conditions to execute the service. The following binding failures can occur:

- timed out, in a distributed system environment,
- bound to the wrong service, and
- binding denied.

During binding, one fault that can occur is “bound to wrong service”. This can occur when there has been a “service description” fault during the publishing phase. A “binding denied” fault occurs when some authorisation has not been granted by the authorisation component.

Execution faults.

Execution faults occur when the outcome of a service does not match the result expected by the client. The following failures can occur:

- timed out, in distributed systems,
- service crashed, in distributed systems, and
- incorrect result.

An incorrect result can occur if the wrong service has been selected. It can also occur if a transient fault occurs in the service provider. On the other hand, a service provider can crash, causing the service to be unavailable.

However, to be able to recover from an erroneous situation (error state), one needs to be able to detect that a fault has occurred. However, some faults may not be detected during the same phase where they occurred. For example, it may not always be possible to detect a “service description” fault during the service publishing phase until an “incorrect result” fault occurs during the execution phase.

6.4 Dependability Enhancement in a Service Oriented Architecture

When developing a dependable system, there are a number of ways by which dependability can be imparted. These are:

- fault prevention,
- fault tolerance,
- fault removal, and
- fault forecasting.

Not every method is applicable in every stage in a service-oriented architecture. For example, during service discovery, a “time-out” cannot be guaranteed using fault removal techniques, since the fault is brought about at runtime.

6.4.1 Fault Prevention

Fault prevention is the process of preventing faults from occurring in the first instance. In other words, fault prevention represents the set of actions that can be taken to minimise the number of bugs that are inserted in a given application. One popular fault prevention technique is the use of high-level programming languages such as Java [11]. Another important fault prevention technique is the use of formal methods [4] to ascertain certain guarantees provided by a system. In a service-oriented architecture, formal methods can be used in different ways. For example, formal methods can be used for the specification and verification of service description and discovery [22]. The mathematical notation employed, together with verification can enable the detection of mismatching assumptions between service provider and clients. Another important line of work in formal specification and verification in service-oriented computing is the verification of service composition [20].

6.4.2 Fault Tolerance

Fault tolerance is the ability of a system to satisfy its specification, in spite of faults that can perturb its execution. When designing a fault-tolerant system, the functionality of the fault tolerance mechanisms needed can be factored along two dimensions [2], namely detection, and correction.

Detection is needed before triggering the correction part. Detection is achieved using predicates, called *detection predicates*. A detection predicate captures the conditions that indicates failures in some part of the system. For example, a well-known predicate is the timeout predicate. When a timeout expires, it indicates that a message had not been reliably delivered. On the other hand, correction mechanisms attempt to impose a given predicate on the system. A popular correction mechanism is message retransmission, whereby a lost message is retransmitted so as the predicate (that captures correct system operation) can be reinstated. The use of detection and/or correction mechanisms gives rise to different levels of fault tolerance. Specifically, the levels of fault tolerance are.

- Fail-safe fault tolerance [2]. It is necessary and sufficient to add detectors to ensure fail-safe fault tolerance. A fail-safe fault-tolerant system is one where the safety of the system is more important than liveness. Several web applications adopt a fail-safe approach in their design.
- Non-masking fault tolerance [2]. It is necessary and sufficient to use correctors to ensure non-masking fault tolerance. A non-masking fault-tolerant system is one where liveness is more important than safety.
- Masking fault tolerance [2]. It is necessary and sufficient to use both detectors and correctors to ensure masking fault tolerance. In masking fault tolerance, both safety and liveness are important. In the domain of web services, masking fault tolerance is important especially if some services become unavailable. Specifically, when a service discovery process times out (detector), another service discovery process can be initiated (corrector). The number of possible retries can be specified as a service parameter.

Detectors and correctors can be implemented through connector components. Given that a connector component can be viewed as a service provider, it needs to export the detection or correction predicate it is implementing. The connector components can be published in a similar way to normal services, and the connectors can be discovered likewise.

6.4.3 Fault Removal

During the development process, design faults (also known as bugs) could have been inserted into the system. These bugs, when activated, can cause the system to violate its specification. Thus, it becomes imperative to remove these faults. Fault removal is the process through which these faults are removed. The most popular fault removal technique is testing. During testing, the system is subjected to a range of test cases. Each test case is designed such that it helps to uncover some bug. The test cases, in general, need to help achieve some test coverage [7]. However, for a carefully-developed system, the number of bugs may be very small, making it very difficult to uncover the bugs, even though the system may have been rigorously tested. In other words, it means that the mean time to failure (MTTF) of such a system is high. The high MTTF then translates into an inability to guarantee a certain level of dependability of the system. What is then needed is to be able to reduce the MTTF of the system by artificially introducing faults in the system. This is achieved through a process called *fault injection* [15], which we will discuss in the next section. Fault injection introduces artificial faults in the system with the intention of mimicking software bugs. If the program cannot handle the effect of the artificial bug, then it means, if the bug does exist, the program will not be able to handle its effect. Hence, it is important to be able to introduce faults that are representative of bugs in the system under test.

6.4.4 Fault Forecasting: Fault Injection

Fault forecasting is the process during which (i) the number of any residual faults in the system is estimated, and (ii) their impact is analysed. However, in systems where the runtime execution can be affected by perturbations in the environment, such as embedded systems, the impact of environmental problems needs to be also assessed. However, because the Mean Time to Failure (MTTF) of a system may be very long, it becomes very difficult to have a statistically significant confidence in the ability of the system to deliver the required services. Hence, faults have to be artificially introduced to lower the MTTF of the system, which in turn will allow us to assess the impact of bugs on the system. Various fault injection techniques and tools have been introduced over the years, and the techniques can generally be divided into three categories:

- simulation-based fault injection,
- physical fault injection, and
- software implemented fault injection (SWIFI).

In this chapter, we will focus on software implemented fault injection. We refer the interested reader to [15] for an in-depth discussion about fault injection.

6.4.4.1 Software-Implemented Fault Injection (SWIFI)

Software-implemented fault injection (SWIFI) is by far the most versatile, and possibly the most popular form of fault injection. The approach uses software to inject faults into physical, and sometimes simulated, systems. Further, it can also be the case that errors (a runtime consequence of a fault execution) can be injected, in which the state of the system is perturbed at runtime. However, for historical reasons, the process is called fault injection (rather than error injection). There are both advantages and disadvantages of using SWIFI for system validation. In order to generate readouts, and inject faults and errors, a target system has to be instrumented. The instrumentation process consists of inserting probes for logging variables and events, as well as inserting injection locations for faults and errors. Once faults or errors are injected, data is collected, and later analysed and interpreted for dependability analysis of the system.

In the context of service-oriented architectures, faults can occur at several levels, as discussed in Section 6.3.2. Thus, during fault injection, faults that are injected need to mimic problems that will lead to failures such as "wrong service called" and "incorrect results". During the fault injection process, in a distributed system, not only are faults injected to corrupt variables, but faults need to be injected at the network level too. For example, faults can be injected by corrupting, dropping or reordering the network packets at the network interface [18]. One way of injecting faults is to instrument the network protocol stack, however the problem is that the receiver's network stack may detect this and then reject the packet. Another way is to inject faults at the application level [9, 10], where the types of faults being injected are corruption of packet header information, injecting random byte errors into packet payloads.

6.5 Dependability Evaluation

When developing a service-oriented application, it becomes important that the service selection is based not only on functional requirements, but also on non-functional requirements such as performance, dependability and real-time properties. Thus, the service discovery and composition aspects need to pay particular attention to such non-functional properties. For example, in the service discovery part, a required service can be specified in terms of its functionality, as well as its dependability, where it can be specified that the service has a dependability factor of say 0.95. Thus, it becomes important to have a way to specify the various dependability aspects that are important in a given application. Since several services may be reused across different applications, it becomes even more important to capture several dependability aspects that may be important in various applications.

For example, two important attributes that are commonly used to capture dependability properties are coverage [6] and latency [6].

Coverage relates to the proportion of faults that a service can successfully handle. Given that detection is an important step in the design of dependable systems, the term detection coverage is often used. The higher the detection coverage, the higher the chance of successful recovery. On the other hand, the latency metric relates to the time taken to detect an error. A low detection latency is preferable since error propagation is limited. This means that only a small number of components, and services will be affected, hence increasing the chance of a successful recovery. Therefore, it becomes important to annotate services with dependability information such as coverage and latency. Specifically, when a service is being published, it needs to be published together with its dependability attributes such as coverage, latency and so on. The service search is then performed on both the functionality of the services and on their dependability attributes.

Evaluation of the dependability attributes of a service is usually achieved by performing fault injection experiments (see Section 6.4.4). Because it is impossible to obtain the absolute value for these attributes, for a given service, the value of these attributes only represents an average. For example, to evaluate the detection coverage of a given service, a certain number of faults, say n, will be injected in the service, at its interface. Assume further that the service fails on f of these injections. This means that, on $n-f$ injections, the service was able to handle the faults. Thus, the coverage of the service is $\frac{n-f}{n}$. Similarly, the latency for a given fault model can be averaged out. However, it can also be the case that the fault model is broken down into smaller fault classes, and a coverage or latency value associated with each fault class. This will allow for finer-grained composition.

There are several other dependability metrics that can be used to capture various properties. For example, one such metric, error permeability [9], captures the case where an error can propagate from an input to an output, i.e., if the parameters passed to a service provider are corrupted, then the results passed back to the client are incorrect. Thus, during service composition, it becomes more beneficial to look for services with a low error propagation. Services with low error permeability have better dependability properties.

Further, if failure rates of the various services are known, then it becomes possible to predict the reliability of services, both basic and composite [8]. A basic service is one that does not need other services to function. A composite service is one that depends on other services to work properly. Service composition can be performed using some reliability equation for overall service reliability.

6.6 Case Studies

In this section, we will develop two examples. The idea is to show that service-oriented computing does not lend itself exclusively to web services, but to other applications too. On the other hand, it is safe to say that web services are very-well suited for service-oriented architectures.

6.6.1 A Web-Based Application

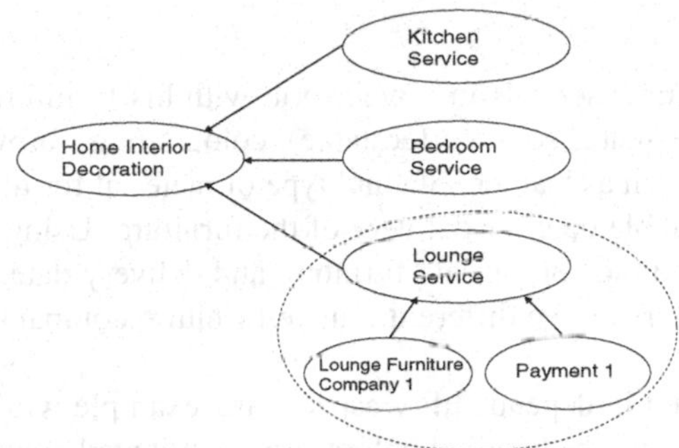

Fig. 6.5 Example of a home interior decoration agency

The first example is a web-based application, based on a home interior decoration agency (see Figure 6.5), similar to the one developed by Brüning et al in [3]. It is a typical example of a home interior decoration agency, where a customer chooses furniture and accessories for his home and then purchases them. This home interior decoration agency service will make use of three different services, namely a kitchen service, a bedroom furniture service service and lounge furniture service (see Figure 6.6). In this section, we will focus on a customer who wants to purchase only some lounge furniture, such as sofas, coffee tables etc. However, the same will apply for customers who want to purchase kitchen or bedroom furniture and accessories. Suppose a customer wants to purchase a three-seater and a two-scater sofa. He first has to find the appropriate sofas, specify a suitable delivery date, and then has to pay for the article(s). He inputs the required description of the sofas, such as colour, size etc.), and the lounge service will then try different companies specialising in sofas until it finds a sofa that matches the description which can be delivered on the specified date. Then, a payment service will be called once the correct article(s) and the delivery date have been agreed upon.

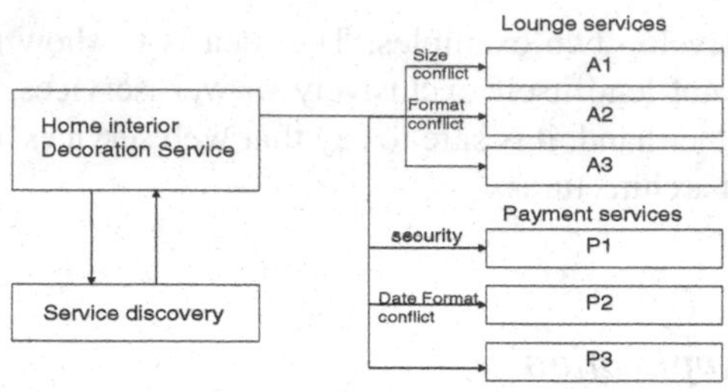

Fig. 6.6 Lounge furniture and accessories services

To start the process, the user fills in a web form with his furniture details, viz. type of furniture (e.g., 2-seater sofa, coffee table), colours (e.g., brown, oak etc.), sizes, and other details such as leather sofa and type of material for the coffee table etc. He also enters a suitable date for delivery of the furniture. Using this data, the lounge service has to find the appropriate furniture and delivery date. Assume that the discovery service returns three different lounge furniture companies A_1,A_2 and A_3.

Since we are interested in dependability aspects, the example will highlight the type of problems that need to be handled before service-oriented computing can be successfully deployed. From Figure 6.6, the first service A_1 seems to have been executed correctly but, unfortunately, does not return any furniture, though A_1 seems to have the specified furniture and can also be delivered on the requested date. Since A_1 can satisfy the customer's requirements (both furniture and date), it means that services supplied by A_1 has failed, for some reason. Closer inspection may reveal some potential problem. For example, as seen in Figure 6.6, the problem was due to a size conflict. This fault was caused by an incorrect unit being used to specify the size of the sofa. This could have occurred due to the fact that the service specified the size in millimetres, whereas the implementation required the format as inches. This corresponds to a service/description mismatch fault. If a fault injection experiment had been performed before deploying these services, such a problem would have been detected. This shows that validation (using fault injection) should be an important part of the validation process before services are being deployed.

For the second company A_2, the problem is a formatting problem, arising possibly due to a date conflict. The problem may arise as follows: the user, when specifying the delivery date, provides the date in a DDMMYY format. whereas the service expects a DD/MM/YY date format. This problem is again due to a service description fault. This problem would also have been detected during fault injection experiments.

On the other hand, there was no problem with the third company A_3, which promised to deliver the ordered furniture on the specified date. Now, the furniture need to be paid for. Again, three services are returned, namely P_1, P_2 and P_3. As shown in Figure 6.6, there are problems occurring with some of the payment services. For example, there are security problems, preventing the binding phase to complete with payment service P_1, and a date format problem arising when the user enters his credit card expiry date in the wrong format with service P_2.

6.6.2 Service-Oriented Computing in Ubiquitous Systems

In the previous case study, we provided an example of a web-based application. In fact, web services tend to be the most popular implementation of service-oriented architectures. To illustrate the fact that service-oriented computing is not exclusively used in web-based systems, we present a case study for service-oriented computing in ubiquitous systems. This example is similar to the one provided in [5].

In a ubiquitous system, a client device needs to connect to a server device for some service. First, the client needs to discover the infrastructure using, say, Bluetooth [12], by identifying the available entry points to the service provision infrastructure. Once the infrastructure has been discovered, there is a need for the client to authenticate himself to the system. He needs to log in for registration. He may do so by providing a description of his own characteristics. Once the client has been authenticated, he looks up the services registry for the appropriate service. Once the right service, satisfying both functional and non-functional requirements, has been chosen, the server proceeds to deliver the service. Once the service has been delivered, the client may request for more services.

Similar to the case of web services, failures in a ubiquitous system can occur at various levels. For example, faults can occur at the infrastructure discovery phase (system may time out), at the client registration phase (thus, the binding phase fails), or at the service look up phase etc. Similarly, faults can occur in specific service parameters that identify the state of the particular service involved in the failure. For example, the state can be one of correct, degraded or incorrect. Different domains will have different failure models.

6.7 Conclusions

In this chapter, we have provided an overview of the issues to be addressed when integrating dependability with service-oriented computing. We introduced a selection of the different types of faults that can affect a service-oriented application

References

1. Anish Arora and Sandeep S. Kulkarni. Component based design of multitolerant systems. *IEEE Transactions on Software Engineering*, 24(1):63–78, January 1998.
2. Anish Arora and Sandeep S. Kulkarni. Detectors and correctors: A theory of fault-tolerance components. In *Proceedings International Conference on Distributed Computing Systems*, May 1998.
3. S. Brüning, S. Weissleder, and M. Malek. A fault taxonomy for service-oriented architecture. In *Proceedings of the IEEE High Assurance Systems Engineering*, 2007.
4. E. Clarke and J. Wing. Formal methods: State of the art and future directions. *ACM Computing Surveys*, 28(4):626–643, 1996.
5. D. Cotroneo, C. Di Flora, and S. Russo. Improving dependability of service-oriented architectures for pervasive computing. In *Proceedings Workshop on Object-Oriented Real-time and Dependable Systems (WORDS)*, 2003.
6. D.Powell, E.Martins, J.Arlat, and Y.Crouzet. Estimators for fault tolerance coverage evaluation. In *Proceedings of the 23rd International Symposium on Fault-Tolerant Computing*, 1993.
7. M. C. Gaudel. Formal methods and testing: Hypotheses and correctness approximation. In *Proceedings of Formal Methods (FM)*, pages 2–8, 2005.
8. V. Grassi. Architecture-based dependability prediction for service-oriented computing. In *DSN 2004 Workshop on Architecting Dependable Systems*, 2005.
9. M. Hiller, A. Jhumka, and N. Suri. An approach for analysing the propagation of data errors in software. In *Proceedings International Conference on Dependable Software and Networks (DSN)*, pages 161–170, 2001.
10. M. Hiller, A. Jhumka, and N. Suri. Propone: An environment for examining the propagation of errors in software. In *Proceedings International Symposium on Software Testing and Analysis (ISSTA)*, pages 81–85, 2002.
11. @http://java.sun.com.
12. @http://www.bluetooth.com.
13. @http://www.eiffel.com.
14. @http://www.javaworld.com.
15. R.K. Iyer and D. Tang. *Experimental Analysis of Computer System Dependability*, Chapter 5. Prentice Hall, 1996.
16. A. Jhumka and N.Suri. Design of efficient fail-safe multitolerance. In *Proceedings Formal Techniques in Networked and Distributed Systems (FORTE)*, 2005.
17. J. C. Laprie. Dependable computing and fault tolerance: concepts and terminology. In *Fault-Tolerant Computing*, pages 2–11, June 1985.
18. N. Looker, B. Gwynne, J. Xu, and M. Munro. An ontology-based approach for determining the dependability of service-oriented architectures. In *Proceedings Workshop on Object-Oriented Real-Time Dependable Systems (WORDS)*, 2005.
19. Z. Mao, E. Brewer, and R. Katz. Fault-tolerant, scalable, wide-area internet service composition. Technical Report UCB/CSD-1-1129, CS Division, UC Berkeley, 2001.
20. S. Pokraev, D. Quartel, M. W. A. Steen, and M. Reichert. A method for formal verificatipn of service interoperability. In *Proceedings International Conference on Web Services (ICWS)*, pages 895–900, 2006.
21. D. K. Pradhan, editor. *Fault-Tolerant Computer System Design*. Prentice Hall, 1996.
22. M. Rouached, O. Perrin, and C. Godart. Towards formal verification of web service composition. In *Proceedings International Conference on Business Process Management*, pages 257–273, 2006.

Chapter 7
Consensus Issues for Service Advertisement and Selection

Ping Wang, Chi-Chun Lo and Leon Smalov

Abstract Several commercial service providers are offering analogous functional features in the advertisements of their services which lead to the problem of efficient selection for the potential service consumers. Generally, the service consumers and providers would have different views on the content of the services. How to reach consensus between the service consumers and providers is an interesting practical aspect of web service selection. This chapter proposes a Quality of Services (QoS) aware web service selection model based on fuzzy linear programming (FLP) technologies, in order to identify their differences on service alternatives, assist service providers and consumers in selecting the most suitable services with consideration of their expectations and preferences. By extending the LINMAP method (LINear programming techniques for Multidimensional Analysis of Preferences), developed by Srinivasan and Shocker, we can offer the optimal solution of consensual weight of QoS attribute and fuzzy positive ideal solution. Finally, two numerical examples are provided to illustrate the solution process.

7.1 Introduction

With the increasing acceptance of e-commerce, various applications over the Internet are becoming part of everyday life. For example, Google research applications

---

Ping Wang
Department of MIS, Kun Shan University, Yung-Kang, Taiwan
e-mail: `pingwang@mail.ksu.edu.tw`

Chi-Chun Lo
Institute of Information Management, National Chiao Tung University, Hsinchu, Taiwan
e-mail: `cclo@faculty.nctu.edu.tw`

Leon Smalov
Faculty of Engineering and Computing, Coventry University, Coventry, CV1 5FB, UK
e-mail: `csx211@coventry.ac.uk`

N. Griffiths, K.-M. Chao (eds.), *Agent-Based Service-Oriented Computing*,
Advanced Information and Knowledge Processing,
DOI 10.1007/978-1-84996-041-0_7,

are accepted as web services and integrated with other services, such as Gmail, to provide an integrated environment for service consumers. Tim Berners-Lee, inventor of the World Wide Web, offered insights to understand the potential impact of web technologies, which change the way people do business, entertain themselves, exchange ideas, and socialize with one another [4]. Two "futuristic" dreams have been depicted by Berners-Lee: one was everyone receiving and sharing the information through the Internet; the other was people communicating with computers in natural language through the Internet. The former became a norm in every-day life; the latter is being partially enabled by Semantics Web Services (SWS). SWS technology aims to add enough semantics to the specifications and implementations of Web Services (WS) to make possible the automatic integration of distributed autonomous systems, with independently designed data and behavior models [19].

An efficient web service can bring a serious competitive advantage to service providers as well as giving social welfare to the consumers. An application assisting in service selection based on certified QoS can bring essential benefits to the service consumers along with reducing the search redundancy. It will also generate advantages for service providers who deliver valuable services. Practically, the service providers are supposed to guarantee QoS of WS, which are advertised on the Internet for service consumers. When service providers announce their available services, current advertising approaches of web services create a WSDL or OWL-S document to subscribe the web service profile and service grounding, and then promote it through UDDI registration, or other web services registries such as ebXML [45]. However, many available web services exhibit overlapping or identical services in terms of functionality, e.g. flight booking and digital music download, but they exhibit divergent Quality of Services (QoS). This multiplicity can lead to a complex problem of service selection. It is inevitable that a suitable mechanism for service selection is needed. As the similar functions in service-oriented applications expand, service selection becomes a crucial issue for both service consumers and providers. Two important issues of service discovery and selection of available web services, namely (i) the semantic confusion problem [6] and (ii) reaching a consensus in web service selection process [16] have been widely discussed as described below.

7.1.1 Semantic Confusion

The semantic confusion problem could be effectively solved by semantic registration and discovery by defining the appropriate meaning of the service's functionality using an ontology. An ontology is a representation of resources on the web by a set of well-defined classes to describe a data model which can be specified using toolkits such as Resource Description Framework (RDF), DAML+OIL or Web Ontology Language (OWL) [34]. OWL, proposed by the World Wide Web Consortium (W3C), is not only for representing information on the web, but also improves the capability of processing information, and increases the interoperability among software agents [30]. A number of works [2, 6, 12, 14, 22, 28, 29, 31, 35, 36, 44, 45] on semantic service discovery and selection have been carried out via SWS technologies to locate the required services and compose them to meet requirements. The "Semantic Web" approach advocates the vision that will bring structure to the meaningful content of web pages, creating an environment where software agents roaming from page to page can readily carry out sophisticated tasks for users. The Semantic Web makes it possible to automatically locate, discover, compose, and execute services [5]. The aim of the Semantic Web initiative is to provide technologies that will enable heterogeneous systems to collaborate in the execution of an activity. For web services description, the introduction of OWL-S is a significant factor in matching service providers and service consumers [31]. OWL-S is an ontology of services for providing richer web service description, and has the following three components.

1. ServiceProfile: describes what the service does, its inputs and outputs and its preconditions and effects, or IOPE. (This is equivalent to UDDI content.)
2. ServiceModel: describes how the service works, its control and dataflow in use. (This is similar to BPEL4WS [1].)
3. ServiceGrounding: describes how the service is implemented and provides a mapping from OWL-S to WSDL.

Using semantic web techniques, can help customers to judge distinct Web Service Levels (WSL) on available services with QoS reports using ontologies, as illustrated in Figure 7.1.

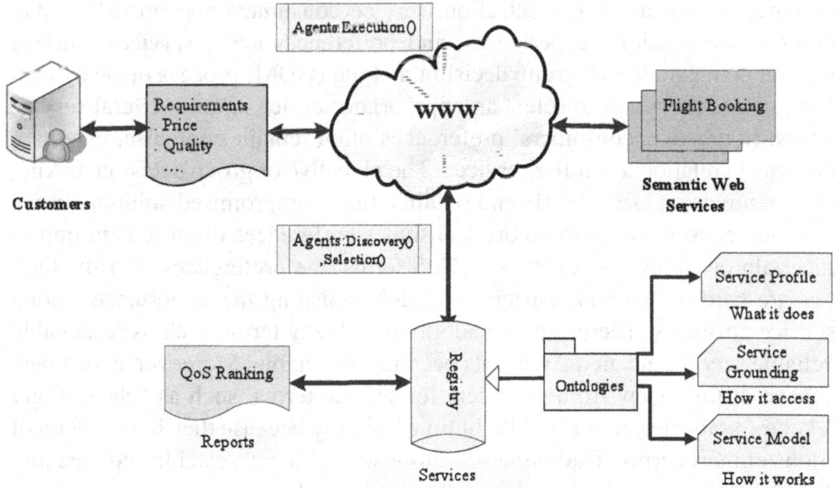

Fig. 7.1 Semantic service discovery, selection and execution using ontology

An agent is a goal-oriented software entity. It possesses a number of properties such as pro-activeness, sociability, autonomy, and reactivity to collaborate with other agents in order to achieve their common goals. There is a gap between software agents and web service technologies, since web services lack semantic descriptions to the interfaces. The semantic gap between XML-based constructs and agents can be bridged by use of Semantic Web technologies, such as OWL-S. Agents have mental states that are often expressed using the notions of BDI (Beliefs, Desires, and Intentions). Agents are suitable for highly dynamic environments and operate at a conceptual level, since they adopt partial planning to reason over their knowledge (or beliefs) and are able to perceive and respond to the environment in which they are situated. So, agents can be designed as delegates to web service consumers and providers to form a community for service discovery and selection. Agents can automatically select services if they are assigned to collect and aggregate the rank information based QoS assessed by consumers as shown in Figure 7.1 above.

After defining the semantics about service specifications, fuzzy matchmaking techniques can be employed to match the requirements between customers and providers. The fuzzy matchmaking scheme uses fuzzy semantics on terms and handles the problem via fuzzy theory. For example, the moderated fuzzy discovery method [15], measures the similarity between services in terms of capabilities, syntax and semantics through a moderator to minimize the differences among service consumers and providers.

7.1.2 Reaching Consensus

For consumer consensus of WS selection, service consumers and providers may have different expectations, experiences, and preferences about services. Service selection can be regarded as a group decision making (GDM) process made by customer's cognitive processes to select an appropriate service among several service alternatives. In practice, consumers' preferences often remain imprecise, uncertain or ambiguous in relation to similar services. The objective of group decision making is to solve conflicts on QoS criteria and obtain a final compromised solution on the basis of group consensus. Furthermore, consumer preferences often remain imprecise, uncertain or ambiguous on service QoS terms; the preferences over the QoS attributes are hard to quantify, especially in distinguishing the importance among these service attributes. Therefore, the adoption of fuzzy terms such as reasonable price, reliable service, etc. in the requests becomes inevitable. Moreover, consumers usually have distinct view from providers for service terms, such as "cheap flight ticket", "comfortable leg-room" or "flight time", simply because they have divergent perceptions of these terms. Traditionally, consensus has a well-established meaning of a full and unanimous agreement. During the process of service selection, reaching a full and unanimous agreement in a large group is often not easy task. Since a unanimous agreement in a large group is rarely reached, soft consensus method [20] is developed for solving partial agreements among customers on service alternatives.

From the consumers' point of view WS providers usually advertise on the Internet the features of web services that appeal to customers, which might lead to misunderstanding or confusion about the service terms for WS consumers. In addition, providers prefer to advertise their services to customers in subjective terms, which might be short of considering the consumers' expectations and preferences. Examples of some dissimilar views of related issues between service consumers and providers are shown in Table 7.1.

Table 7.1 Respective views between service consumers and providers on web service advertisements

Web service issues	Service consumers	Service providers
Price	Affordable price	Low cost
Quality	More stable functions	Service level refer to price
Information disclosure	Sufficient right Information	Exaggeration of the features

Hence, it is imperative to reach consensus for service consumers on the specific specification terms (i.e., QoS), when they find and search WSDL documents in the service discovery process. Based on these requirements, the W3C working group has defined various QoS attributes for WS [20]. These comprise a number of generic and specific items for cross-referencing between the possible needs of service consumers and the functions supported by web services [23].

Although regular QoS attributes have been listed, some unclear problems are yet to be clarified in the selection of WS process. For example, the perception of QoS attributes importance is generally different from consumers and providers preferences. It is widely accepted that consumers have been taking an active role in the expansion of e-commerce. Hence this leads to a need to develop a consensus-centric approach to investigate QoS attribute preferences. Furthermore, obtaining a consensus-based ranking order of alternatives in the services selection process is critically important. In this chapter, we propose a fuzzy linear programming (FLP) model based on consistence and inconsistence measurement of group preferences on service alternatives to obtain consensus-based weights of QoS attributes, and determine the ranking order of service alternatives according to the distance from the positive ideal solution under group consensus. Consequently, a service consumer is able to reduce redundancy in search, and the service provider can improve the quality of services.

The remainder of the chapter is organized as follows. Section 7.2 describes the existing QoS-aware methods for the selection of web services. Section 7.3 describes proposed method. Section 7.4 reports on two illustrational examples of selection of service alternatives. Finally, Section 7.5 contains the concluding remarks and proposes future work.

7.2 Existing Solutions for Web Service Selection

A number of studies for web service selection have been carried out. One of the most well known techniques is "matchmaking". It is employed in the situation where services with semantic descriptions for their functional attributes are available from an

Internet search. Several service matchmaking techniques [7,15,42] have been developed to meet the needs of both consumers and providers as illustrated in Figure 7.2.

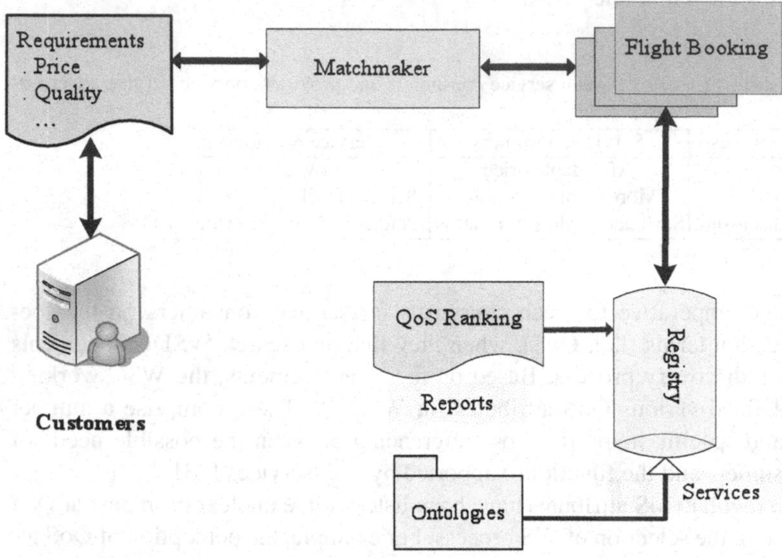

Fig. 7.2 Requirements matchmaking between service customer and service provider

Ran [33] proposed a new QoS-based service registration and discovery model via exchanging SOAP messages [37] to explore the possibility of QoS being involved in UDDI registry information [39]. In this model, service providers have to send QoS claims to QoS certifiers, responding to third party or forum web services, for certification. The service customer is responsible for verifying QoS claims. The QoS information finally will be registered in the UDDI registry associated with the function description, once QoS claims have passed QoS certifier verification. However, QoS of certified services generally are dynamic in nature on the Internet. This might be taken into account through continuous monitoring and checking. Hence we involve adding two checking items, QoS monitoring and opinions feedback from customers into Ran's model, and the original model is modified as shown in Figure 7.3.

The new UDDI registration mechanisms help customers to discover and locate the required service by looking up a WSDL document as well as certified QoS [32]. Moreover, consensus of service consumers on QoS attributes has to be considered for the web service QoS certifier in the QoS computation process. Balke and Wagner [3] introduced the "cooperative discovery" concept for evaluating web services in detail which comprises three phases of interaction with services, namely, (i) service discovery, (ii) service selection, and (iii) service execution. Based on Figure 7.1, we reorganized the three phases as shown in Table 7.2, which specifies the extensive definition for selection of QoS-aware web services provisioning.

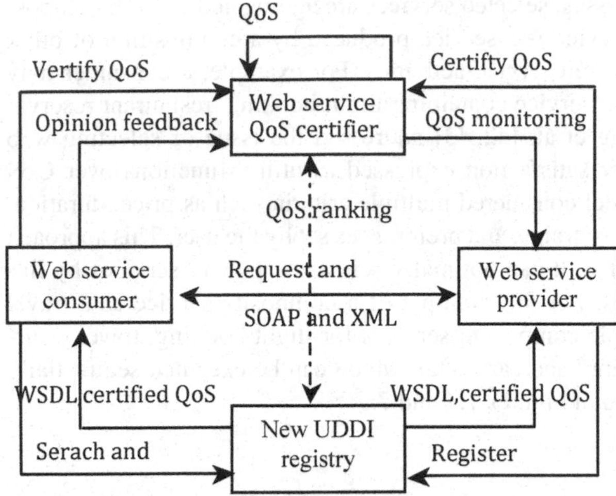

Fig. 7.3 QoS-centric web registration and discovery model

Table 7.2 QoS-aware web services discovery and selection

Phases	Tasks	Task description	Support tools	Dealer
Service registry	Function definition	Specify the terms of WS functionalities using ontology language or WSDL	WSDL, OWL-S	WS provider
	Service registry	Register and receive a official ID for applied service to publish to the Internet	UDDI database	WS provider
Service discovery	QoS certification	Accept and certify the application of service QoS attributes	QoS assessment model	QoS certifier
	Service advertisement	Announce the features of WS	Business portal	WS provider
	Service discovery	Perform and find the related services based on a user's request	Browser	WS consumer
	Service selection	Select one of the desired service	Browser	WS consumer
Service execution	Service execution	Carry out service binding and execution	Browser and service	WS consumer, WS provider
	QoS monitoring	Collect customer opinions to QoS certifier for reflecting user expectation	Browser and QoS opinion database	WS consumer

For emerging B2B businesses, selected services are aggregated to form composite services. A composite service is a service produced by a composition of other services to complete the desired service activities. For example, a consumer may wish to discover a composite service containing flight booking, restaurant reservation, and renting a car. Zeng et al. [42, 43] addressed the issue of selecting web services by maximizing user satisfaction expressed as utility functions over QoS attributes; this selection model considered multiple criteria such as price, duration, reliability in which budget constraints and preferences set by the user. This approach is a global planning method so it can optimally select component services by linear programming techniques. For the example of a composite service as a travel planner, it aggregates multiple component services for flight booking, travel insurance, accommodation booking, and car rental, which can be executed sequentially or concurrently, as illustrated in Figures 7.4 and 7.5.

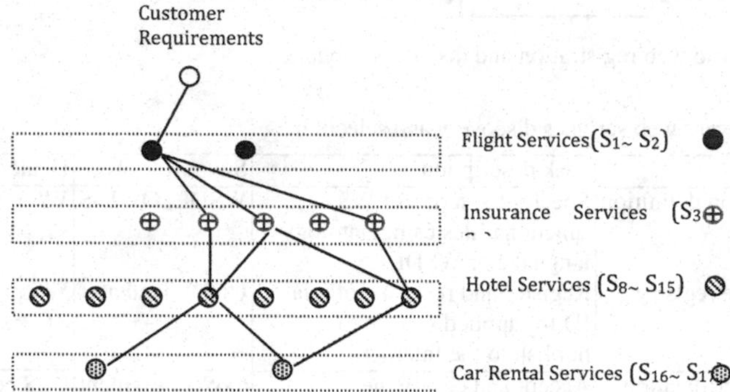

Fig. 7.4 The discovery and selection of composite services

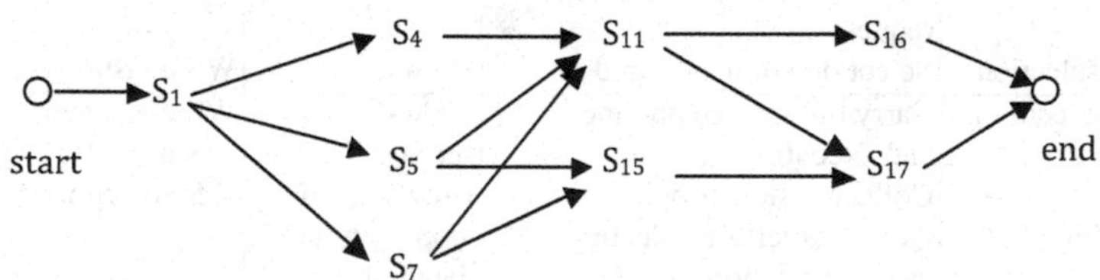

Fig. 7.5 A possible plan of selected composite services

Sirin et al. [36] developed a goal-oriented and interactive composition approach that uses matchmaking algorithms to help users filter and select services while building their composition service. The matches are filtered using ontological reasoning on the semantic descriptions of the services. They developed a prototype on the basis of these ideas to test the system by generating OWL-S descriptions for some of the common web services. Each composition the user generates via the existing prototype will be realized as an OWL-S Composite Process, meaning that it can also be advertised, discovered, and composed with other services. They adopted a quality model considering five generic quality criteria for elementary services: (1) execution price, (2) execution duration, (3) reputation, (4) reliability, and (5) availability. The global service selection is executed with a set of execution plans, $P = (p_1, p_2, \ldots, p_n)$, where n is the number of plans. After a set of execution plans is generated, the scheme selects an optimal execution plan using Simple Additive Weighting (SAW). This work pointed out that the accuracy of the matches found by the inference engine depends on how detailed the ontologies are. Richer ontologies with more specific descriptions for sensors and their nonfunctional properties will help the engine find better answers to the queries.

Zhou et al. [45] discriminated between functional and non-functional QoS properties of web services, where functional properties can be measured in terms of throughput, latency, response time; non-functional properties address of various issues including integrity, reliability, availability and security of web services. Well-defined metrics are utilized by measurement organizations to monitor and evaluate the promised service level objectives. A match-making prototype is designed to prove the feasibility of the approach. For the match between request and advertisement, there are five types of match possibilities: subsume, exact, plugin, intersection, and disjoint ranging from the best matching degree to the worst matching degree, respectively. When the service provider publishes their service QoS profile through the publish interface, the ontology will be parsed. If the parsing process ends successfully, the ontology is stored in the server's repository and then is rendered into a description kept in the knowledge base. By classifying on its knowledge base, the Racer engine organizes the ontologies' taxonomy. When the service requester submits an inquiry, the matchmaker will return the subsume, exact, plugin, and intersection matching list respectively. The prototype demonstrated that the matchmaking is suitable for small or middle sized advertisement repositories.

Lin et al. [25] and Liu et al. [27] treated the selection of QoS-driven web services with dynamic composition as a fuzzy constraint satisfaction problem and applied an optimal search approach with adjustments to service composition. They consider three generic quality criteria which can be measured objectively for elementary services: (i) execution price, (ii) execution duration, and (iii) reputation. Compared to Sirin et al.'s approach [36], criteria such as availability and reliability are not included in the model, due to the use of active user feedback and execution monitoring. The reputation of a service is a measure of its trustworthiness. It mainly depends on end user's experiences of using the service. To demonstrate the proposed QoS model, they implemented a QoS registry within a hypothetical phone service (UPS) provisioning market place that is implemented using BEA Weblogic Workshop toolkit. It consists of various service providers who can register to provide various types of phone services such as long distance and local phone services, wireless and broadband. The UPS marketplace has web interfaces which allow a customer to login and search for phone services based on his/her preferences. For example, the customer can specify whether the search for a particular type of service should be price or service sensitive.

In summary, service selection approaches [15, 27, 36, 43, 45] can be mainly divided into two categories: Multiple Attribute Decision Making (MADM) [8, 41] and mathematical programming. MADM methods [15, 27, 45] concentrate on that QoS attributes can be collected and enforced objectively, then the traditional MADM theory can be applied to obtain a consistent ranking of service alternatives. Mathematical programming methods [36, 43] comprise linear programming (a single objective function) and multiple goal programming. It concerns about interactive composition selection that uses preset planning to optimally select component services during the execution of a composite service.

The "matchmaking" approach, however, relies on the advertisements from service providers' subjective views that could lead to divergent perception between consumers and providers. Consumer expectations and their common preferences (i.e., consensus) on QoS should be considered in the process of service selection. To ensure the consensus between consumers and providers, Lin et al. [26] proposed a QoS Consensus Moderation Approach (QCMA) in order to perform QoS ratings based on [13, 21] in order to alleviate the differences in QoS characteristics.

The aforementioned methods advanced knowledge in QoS-aware service discovery and selection, but nevertheless, there remains the following significant issues for debate: (i) the perception of QoS attributes needs to adjust according to consumers' preferences, (ii) how to determine weights (importance) of QoS attributes, and (iii) the ranking order of service alternatives should be decided on the basis of group consensus. To enable effective QoS-aware service selection, a new web service selection model is proposed, which includes the following important aspects.

- Imprecise preference: this model should be able to handle vague preferences or linguistic opinions for QoS attributes expressed by service consumers in the process of selecting web services.
- Be able to explore the optimal solution weighting of QoS attributes.
- Consensus-centric service ranking: the approach should be capable of realistically gaining a consensual ranking on web service alternatives according to consistence and inconsistence measurements of performance ratings.
- Inspired by Li and Yang's work [24], we extend our previous work [40], to select QoS-aware web services using fuzzy linear programming techniques by minimizing the inconsistency measurement. More detailed information about this model is described in the next section.

7.3 The Proposed QoS-Aware Services Selection Model

In this section, we introduce a new fuzzy group consensus-aware service selection model, which extends the LINMAP (LINear programming techniques for Multidimensional Analysis of Preferences) method [38], developed by Srinivasan and

Shocker (1973). In LINMAP, the decision maker gives the performance ratings matrix of alternatives with a pair wise comparison to obtain the best solution that has the shortest distance to the positive ideal solution (PIS). The aim of the model is to find the optimal weighting of QoS attributes for a set of web services and locate the fuzzy positive ideal solution (FIPS) considering group consensus, and determine a rational ranking order of web service alternatives.

7.3.1 Basic Definitions and Notations

In this section, we review some arithmetic operations on fuzzy numbers for the purpose of representing the proposed algorithm in Section 7.3.2.

Definition 1: Triangular fuzzy number (TFN). A triangular fuzzy number $\tilde{A}$ can be defined by $(a.b.c)$. The membership function is defined as follows.

$$u_A(x) = \begin{cases} 0 & for\, x > a \\ \frac{x-a}{b-a} & for\, a \leq x < b \\ \frac{c-x}{c-b} & for\, b < x \leq c \\ 0 & for\, x < c \end{cases} \tag{7.1}$$

Definition 2: Fuzzy arithmetic operations. The arithmetic operations on the positive fuzzy numbers described by the interval of confidence are expressed below.

$$\begin{aligned} Addition \oplus &: (a_1,b_1,c_1) \oplus (a_2,b_2,c_2) = (a_1+a_2, b_1+b_2, c_1+c_2) \quad (7.2)\\ Subtraction - &: (a_1,b_1,c_1) - (a_2,b_2,c_2) = (a_1-a_2, b_1-b_2, c_1-c_2)\\ Multiplication \otimes &: \tilde{A} \otimes \tilde{B} = (a_1,b_1,c_1) \otimes (a_2,b_2,c_2) = (a_1a_2, b_1b_2, c_1c_2)\\ Multiplication \otimes &: k \otimes \tilde{A} = k \otimes (a_1,b_1,c_1) = (ka_1, kb_1, kc_1), \forall k \in R\\ Division\, / &: \tilde{A}/\tilde{B} = (a_1,b_1,c_1)/(a_2,b_2,c_2) = (a_1/a_2, b_1/b_2, c_1/c_2) \end{aligned}$$

Definition 3: The *normalized Euclidean distance between two triangular fuzzy numbers*. If $\tilde{A}$ and $\tilde{B}$ are two TFNs, then the normalized Euclidean distance between $\tilde{A}$ and $\tilde{B}$ can be calculated as follows.

$$e(\tilde{A},\tilde{B}) = (1/3[(a_1-b_1)^2 + (a_2-b_2)^2 + (a_3-b_3)^2])^{1/2} \tag{7.3}$$

7.3.2 Consistence and Inconsistence Measurements

Consider the problem of ranking WS alternatives $a_i(i = 1,\ldots,m)$. A group of decision makers $(d_p, p = 1,\ldots,q)$ is formed to identify n QoS attributes, say $c_j(j = 1,\ldots,n$. Each decision maker has to assign a performance rating $\tilde{x}_{ij}(d_p)$ to service alternatives, $\tilde{x}_{ij}(d_p)$ represents the rating of web service s_i with respect to criterion

c_j evaluated by d_p. If $\tilde{x}_{ij}(d_p)$ is a fuzzy data item expressed by linguistic terms, then it must be converted to a triangular fuzzy number (TFN) of the form (a_{ij}, b_{ij}, c_{ij}) defined in Definition 1, where a_{ij}, b_{ij}, c_{ij} are real numbers and $a_{ij} \leq b_{ij} \leq c_{ij}$. The performance rating matrix $\tilde{X}$ assessed by decision maker d_p is shown in Equation 7.4.

$$\tilde{X}(d_p) = [\tilde{x}_{ij}(d_p)] = \begin{matrix} \\ s_1 \\ s_2 \\ \dots \\ s_m \end{matrix} \begin{matrix} c_1 \ \ c_2 \ \dots \ c_3 \\ \begin{bmatrix} \tilde{x}_{11} \ \tilde{x}_{12} \ \dots \ \tilde{x}_{1n} \\ \tilde{x}_{21} \ \tilde{x}_{22} \ \dots \ \tilde{x}_{2n} \\ \dots \\ \tilde{x}_{m1} \ \tilde{x}_{m2} \ \dots \ \tilde{x}_{mn} \end{bmatrix} \end{matrix} \tag{7.4}$$

where $\oplus$ and $\otimes$ represent fuzzy additive and multiplication operations as defined in Definition 2, respectively. $\tilde{x}_{ij}(d_p)$ might be in crisp (nonfuzzy) or fuzzy form depending on the nature of the QoS attributes. When $\tilde{x}_{ij}(d_p)$ is a nonfuzzy datum, it should be converted from the distinct scales of ratings to a numerically comparable scale. In contrast, if $\tilde{x}_{ij}(d_p)$ is in fuzzy form then it has to be normalized by using Equation 7.7 to rank the web services compatibly between evaluation of QoS attributes. For QoS attributes, two types simultaneously exist : benefit- oriented and cost-oriented. These are sometimes mutually conflict and are inconsistent so there exists a trade-off. To avoid generating an outbound condition, when $\tilde{r}_{ij}$ exceeds the value 1, it needs to be constrainted by upper bound 1. The linear scale transformation is used for forming the normalized fuzzy matrix $\tilde{R}$ as [9]:

$$\tilde{R} = [\tilde{r}_{ij}]_{mxn} \tag{7.5}$$

$$\tilde{r}_{ij} = \frac{\tilde{x}_{ij}}{\tilde{x}_j^*} = \left(\frac{a_{ij}}{c_j^*}, \frac{b_{ij}}{c_j^*}, \frac{c_{ij}}{c_j^*} \wedge 1 \right), \forall j, \tilde{x}_j \in B$$

$$\tilde{r}_{ij} = \frac{\tilde{x}_{\bar{i}}}{\tilde{x}_{ij}^*} = \left(\frac{a_{\bar{j}}}{c_{ij}^*}, \frac{b_{\bar{j}}}{c_{ij}^*}, \frac{c_{\bar{j}}}{c_{ij}^*} \wedge 1 \right), \forall j, \tilde{x}_j \in C$$

where $a_j^* = max_i \ a_{ij}, b_j^* = max_i \ b_{ij}, c_j^* = max_i \ c_{ij}$ if $j \in B$, $a_{\bar{j}} = min_i \ a_{ij}, b_{\bar{j}} = min_i \ b_{ij}, c_{\bar{j}} = min_i \ c_{ij}$ if $j \in C$, and where B, C represent a set of benefit-based and cost-based QoS attributes, respectively.

Studies regarding distance-based consensus methods have been carried out by Cook and Seiford [10, 11], with focus on solving nonfuzzy ranking order problems. Cook and Seiford [10] investigated two specific cases (i.e., $s = 1; s = 2$) to solve the consensus degree of a group on ordinal rankings. The general form of consensus measurement function is constructed by minimizing a normalized weighted metric distance, D_i, that is:

$$MinD_i = \sum_{j=1}^{n} (w_j |r_{ij} - r_j^*|^s)^{1/s}, i = 1, 2, \dots, m \tag{7.6}$$

where w_j is the weighting of QoS attribute j, $(|r_{ij}-r_j^*|^s)^{1/s}$ is the Minkowski metric, s is the metric number. For example, if $s=2$ then D_i becomes as:

$$d_i=\sum_{j=1}^{n}(w_j|r_{ij}-r_j^*|^2)^{1/2} \tag{7.7}$$

In this chapter, we address the consistence measurement of service customers by aggregated difference between fuzzy performance ratings of each alternative and the fuzzy positive ideal solution (FPIS). Then the square distance, s_i, defined in LINMAP, is used for assessing the weights of QoS attributes, that is:

$$s_i=\sum_{j=1}^{n}w_j(\tilde{r}_{ij}-\tilde{r}_j^*)^2, i=1,2,\dots,m \tag{7.8}$$

Suppose $\Omega=\{(k,l)|a_kPa_l,k,l=1,\dots,m\}$ denotes a set of preference relations which is composed of the ordered pairs (k,l) for service alternatives, where P represents a preference relation given by decision maker. There are $n(n-1)/2$ elements in Ω. Member a_kPa_l represents that decision maker prefers a_k to a_l . Furthermore, analogous to s_i, the fuzzy form of square distance between a pair of alternative (k,l), S_k and S_i, is defined by square distance using the normalized Euclidean distance, defined in Defination 7.3, as follows.

$$S_k=\sum_{j=1}^{n}w_j[e(\tilde{r}_{kj},\tilde{r}_j^*)]^2 \tag{7.9}$$

$$S_l=\sum_{j=1}^{n}w_j[e(\tilde{r}_{lj},\tilde{r}_j^*)]^2$$

By definition of inconsistence measurement in [38], inconsistence index, $(S_l=S_k)^-$, measuring the discrepancy between S_l and S_k, is given by:

$$(S_l-S_k)^-=\begin{cases}0, & if(S_l\geq S_k)\\ S_k-S_l, & if(S_l<S_k)\end{cases}=max\{0,(S_k-S_l)\} \tag{7.10}$$

Then, the inconsistence measurement for all the ordered pairs (k,l) for all service alternatives in Ω can be computed by:

$$B=\sum_{(k,l)\in\Omega}(S_l-S_k)^-=\sum_{(k,l)\in\Omega}max\{0,(S_k-S_k)\} \tag{7.11}$$

Similar to Equation 7.10, the consistence measurement between S_l and S_k, $(S_l-S_k)^+$, is given by:

$$(S_l-S_k)^+=\begin{cases}S_l-S_k, & if(S_l\geq S_k)\\ 0, & if(S_l<S_k)\end{cases} \tag{7.12}$$

The consistence measurement for all the ordered pairs (k,l) in Ω is given by:

$$G = \sum_{(k,l)\in\Omega} (S_l - S_k)^+ \tag{7.13}$$

7.3.3 Problem Formulation

To avoid obtaining a trivial solution with $w_j = 0$, we add two additional constraints, $G - B = h$, where h is also an arbitary positive number, and $w_j \geq \delta$, where δ may be zero or a sufficient positive number. Our goal is to obtain the optimal soloution of weight of QoS attribute and fuzzy positive ideal solution (FIPS), $(w, \tilde{r}^*)$, in terms of mimimizing the inconsistence measurement B. The constraint, $G - B = h$, is needed to ensure the tolerance (h) between G and B. The problem of finding the optimal consensual weights and positive ideal values of the solution can be formulated as a linear programming model as follows.

$$Min \;\; B \tag{7.14}$$
$$s.t. \;\; \begin{cases} G - B = h, \\ w_j \geq \delta, \quad\quad j = 1, \ldots, n \end{cases}$$

By the definition of the Equations 7.11 and 7.13, we have:

$$(S_l - S_k)^+ - (S_l - S_k)^- = S_l - S_k \tag{7.15}$$

Substituting Equation 7.15 into Equation 7.14, then it can be rewritten as:

$$G - B = \sum_{(k,l)\in\Omega} (S_l - S_k) = h \tag{7.16}$$

Therefore, the optimal soloution $(w, \tilde{r}^*)$ can be obtained by solving the constrained optimized problem of:

$$Min \sum_{(k,l)\in\Omega} max\{0, (S_k - S_l)\} \tag{7.17}$$
$$s.t. \;\; \begin{cases} \sum_{(k,l)\in\Omega}(S_l - S_k) = h \\ w_j \geq \delta, \quad\quad\quad j = 1, \ldots, n \end{cases}$$

Let $z_{kl} = max\{0, (S_k - S_l)\}$, we have $z_{kl} \geq 0$ and $z_{kl} \geq (S_k - S_l)$, then the third and the fourth constraints are obtained. $z_{kl} \geq (S_k - S_l)$ can be rewritten as:

$$z_{kl} + (S_k - S_l) \geq 0 \tag{7.18}$$

Adding two constraints, then we get:

$$Min \sum_{(k,l)\in\Omega} z_{kl} \tag{7.19}$$

$$s.t. \begin{cases} \sum_{(k,l)\in\Omega}(S_l - S_k) = h, for(k,l) \in \Omega \\ z_{kl} + (S_l - S_k) \geq 0, \quad for(k,l) \in \Omega \\ z_{kl} \geq 0, \quad for(k,l) \in \Omega \\ w_j \geq \delta, \quad j = 1,\ldots,n \end{cases}$$

In the following, substituting Equations 7.9, 7.10, 7.11, 7.12, 7.13, 7.14, 7.15, 7.16, 7.17, 7.18, and 7.19, then we have:

$$Min \sum_{(k,l)\in\Omega} z_{kl} \tag{7.20}$$

$$s.t. \begin{cases} \sum_{(k,l)\in\Omega}\sum_{j=l}^{n} w_j[e(\tilde{r}_{lj},\tilde{r}_j^*) - e(\tilde{r}_{kj},\tilde{r}_j^*)] = h, for(k,l) \in \Omega \\ z_{kl} + \sum_{j=l}^{n} w_j[e(\tilde{r}_{lj},\tilde{r}_j^*) - e(\tilde{r}_{kj},\tilde{r}_j^*)] \geq 0, \quad for(k,l) \in \Omega \\ z_{kl} \geq 0, \quad for(k,l) \in \Omega \\ w_j \geq \delta, \quad j = 1,\ldots,n \end{cases}$$

Obviously, item $\tilde{r}_j^{*2}$ will be omitted in the computation process of the first constraint. Hence a new variable $\tilde{v}_j$ is introduced to replace $w_j\tilde{r}_j$ for the simplification of computation, that is:

$$\tilde{v}_j = w_j\tilde{r}_j = [a_{vj}, b_{vj}, c_{vj}] \tag{7.21}$$

By using Definitions 1 and 2, Equation 7.20 can be transformed into the following form:

$$Min \sum_{(k,l)\in\Omega} z_{kl} \tag{7.22}$$

$$s.t. \begin{cases} \frac{1}{3}\sum_{(k,l)\in\Omega}\sum_{j=l}^{n} w_j[(a_{r_{lj}}^2 - a_{r_{kj}}^2) + (b_{r_{lj}}^2 - b_{r_{kj}}^2) + (c_{r_{lj}}^2 - c_{r_{kj}}^2)] \\ \quad -\frac{2}{3}\sum_{(k,l)\in\Omega}\sum_{j=l}^{n} w_j[a_{v_j}(a_{r_{lj}} - a_{r_{kj}}) + b_{v_j}(b_{r_{lj}} - b_{r_{kj}}) \\ \quad +c_{v_j}(c_{r_{lj}} - c_{r_{kj}})] = h, \quad for(k,l) \in \Omega \\ z_{kl} + \frac{1}{3}\sum_{(k,l)\in\Omega}\sum_{j=l}^{n} w_j[(a_{r_{lj}}^2 - a_{r_{kj}}^2) + (b_{r_{lj}}^2 - b_{r_{kj}}^2) + (c_{r_{lj}}^2 - c_{r_{kj}}^2)] \\ \quad -\frac{2}{3}\sum_{(k,l)\in\Omega}\sum_{j=l}^{n} w_j[a_{v_j}(a_{r_{lj}} - a_{r_{kj}}) + b_{v_j}(b_{r_{lj}} - b_{r_{kj}}) \\ \quad +c_{v_j}(c_{r_{lj}} - c_{r_{kj}})] \geq 0, \quad for(k,l) \in \Omega \\ z_{kl} \geq 0, \quad for(k,l) \in \Omega \\ w_j \geq \delta, \quad j = 1,\ldots,n \\ 0 \leq a_{v_j} \leq b_{v_j} \leq_{v_j} \leq 1, \quad j = 1,\ldots,n \end{cases}$$

We solve the linear programming using Simplex method, and then the optimal solution of $(w, \tilde{r}^*)$ using linear programming is provided. Once the optimal weights of QoS attributes $(w_j, j = 1,\ldots,n)$ and fuzzy positive ideal solution (FPIS) of web service i are obtained, one can easily decide a ranking order by distance from FPIS. It means that the shortest distance from FPIS is the best solution. From Figure 7.2, we can judge the ranking order of service alternatives by the square distance of service alternatives from FPIS ($\tilde{a}^*$), that is, $\tilde{a}_3$ is the best solution (Figure 7.6).

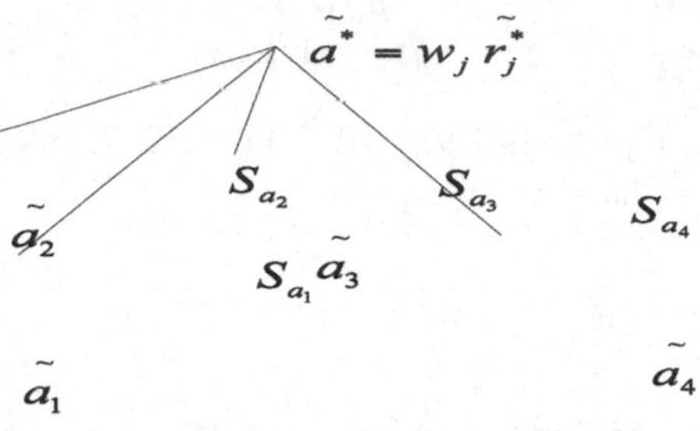

Fig. 7.6 The square distance of all service alternatives from FPIS $\tilde{a}^*$

7.4 Two Numerical Cases

In this section, two examples for selecting an appropriate web service are used as an illustration of the application of the proposed model. To illustrate the process of solutions, the first example is a case which emphases the selection of service alternatives using the traditional LINMAP method, in which QoS attributes are crisp data decided by a single decision maker. The second example is regarded as a group decision problem (GDP) where the rating format is a fuzzy form given by a set of decision makers.

7.4.1 Numerical Case I

Four service alternatives, $a_i (i = 1,\ldots,4)$, are assessed by decision makers d_p based on QoS attributes $c_j (j = 1,\ldots,6)$—maximum baggage allowance (c_1), seat size (c_2), multimedia (c_3), payment when package lost (c_4), satisfaction on ticket price (c_5), and food rating (c_6). The seat size is a scale for the available space of the seat. For the rating of multimedia, we use basic addition to count the following items:

(1) video (2) music (3) games (4) shopping information (5) flight information, to decide the availability of multimedia. Each item is assigned one point. As ticket price is a cost-based attribute, has to take the negative value with respect to benefit attribute. The decision makers assign the performance ratings to all service candidates and determine the ranking order of four candidates. The proposed model is applied to solve this problem according to the following procedures.

Step 1: Three decision makers assess the performance rating of each service candidate and generate the individual performance rating matrix as shown in Table 7.3. In addition, service consumer gives the ranking order between service candidates as follows:

$$\Omega(d) = \{(1,2),(1,3),(4,1),(3,2),(2,4),(3,4)\}$$

Table 7.3 Performance ratings of service alternatives

Airline	QoS attributes					
	c_1(lb)	c_2(cm)	c_3(items)	c_4($)	c_5($)	c_6(1–5)
a_1	40	110	3	120	−400	4.0
a_2	55	125	5	150	−450	5.0
a_3	85	90	4	100	−350	2.0
a_4	35	105	3	90	−300	4.0

Step 2: The performance ratings matrix is converted from the distinct scales of ratings into a numerically comparable scale in $[10,-10]$ as:

$$R(d) = [r_{ij}] = \begin{bmatrix} 4.00 & 1.10 & 3.00 & 1.20 & -4.00 & 4.00 \\ 5.50 & 1.25 & 5.00 & 1.50 & -4.50 & 5.00 \\ 8.50 & 0.90 & 4.00 & 1.00 & -3.50 & 2.00 \\ 3.50 & 1.05 & 3.00 & 0.90 & -3.00 & 4.00 \end{bmatrix}$$

Step 3: Let $h = 1$, and $\delta = 0.0$. We can model the linear programming problem using the crisp form v_j to replace $\tilde{v}_j = [a_{v_j}, b_{v_j}, c_{v_j}]$ and substituting r_{ij} to $\tilde{r}_{ij}$ in Equation 7.22, as follows:

$$Min \ \{z_{12}+z_{13}+z_{41}+z_{32}+z_{24}+z_{34}\}$$

$$s.t. \begin{cases} -53.25w_1+0.43w_2+9.0w_3-0.64w_4-13.0w_5+21.0w_6 \\ \quad +9.0v_1-0.40v_2-2.0v_3+0.8v_4-4.0v_5-6.0v_6=1, \\ z_{12}+14.25w_1+0.353w_2+16.0w_3+0.81w_4+4.25w_5+9.0w_6 \\ \quad -3.0v_1-0.3v_2-4.0v_3-0.6v_4+1.0v_5-2.0v_6 \geq 0, \\ z_{13}+56.25w_1-0.4w_2+7.0w_3-0.44w_4-3.75w_5-12.0w_6 \\ \quad -9.0v_1+0.4v_2-2.0v_3+0.4v_4-1.0v_5+4.0v_6 \geq 0, \\ z_{41}-3.75w_1-0.108w_2-0.63w_4-7w_5 \\ \quad 1.0v_1+0.10v_2+0.60v_4-2.0v_5 \geq 0, \\ z_{32}-42.0w_1+0.750w_2+9.0w_3+1.25w_4+8.0w_5+21.0w_6 \\ \quad +6.0v_1-0.70v_2-2.0v_3-1.0v_4+2.0v_5-6.0v_6 \geq 0, \\ z_{24}-18.0w_1-0.46w_2-16.0w_3-1.44w_4-11.25w_5-9.0w_6 \\ \quad +4.0v_1+0.4v_2+4.0v_3+1.2v_4-3.0v_5+2.0v_6 \geq 0, \\ z_{34}-60.0w_1+0.294w_2-7.0w_3-0.19w_4-3.25w_5+12.0w_6 \\ \quad +10.0v_1-0.30v_2+2.0v_3+0.2v_4-1.0v_5-4.0v_6 \geq 0, \\ z_{12} \geq, z_{13} \geq 0, z_{41} \geq 0, z_{32} \geq 0, z_{24} \geq 0, z_{34} \geq 0, \\ w_j \geq 0, j=1,\ldots,6 \end{cases}$$

Step 4: Solve the optimal solution using the Simplex method. This step produces $(w, \tilde{v}^*)$ as follows:

$$\begin{aligned} z^* &= (z_{12},z_{13},z_{41},z_{32},z_{24},z_{34}) = (0.0,0.0,0.0,0.0,0.0,0.0) \\ w^* &= (w_1,\ldots,w_6) = (0.086,0.0,0.046,0.0,0.0,0.0)^T \\ v^* &= (v_1,\ldots,v_6) = (0.571,0.0,0.0,0.0,0.0,0.0) \end{aligned}$$

The fuzzy positive ideal solution (FIPS) is located using Equation 7.21 as follows:

$$r^* = \frac{v^*}{w} = (r_1,\ldots,r_6) = (6.64,0.0,0.0,0.0,0.0,0.0)$$

Step 5: Outrank the ranking of web services The square distance of service alternatives from FPIS can be calculated using Equation 7.9:

$$\begin{aligned} s_i &= w_1^*(r_i1 - r_1^*)^2, i=1,\ldots,4, j=1 \\ s1 &= 0.599, s2 = 0.112, s3 = 0.298, s4 = 0.848 \end{aligned}$$

So the ranking order of service alternatives is generated as following:

$$a_2 > a_3 > a_1 > a_4$$

7.4.2 Numerical Case II

The second example exhibits the selection of service alternatives for GDPs where the rating format is in a fuzzy form. The problem is described as follows: a set of decision makers $d_p(p = 1,\ldots,3)$ have to assess service alternatives based on QoS attributes $c_j(j = 1,\ldots,3)$ acceptable price of ticket (c_1), taste of food (c_2), service of crew (c_3). The service customers have their different subjective preferences on the definition of the index of satisfaction.

Step 1: We define the QoS term, *satisfaction*, to illustrate the preferences of a consumer. It is assumed that the QoS term: satisfaction denoted as ($\tilde{Q}$) is combined from the following three primitive fuzzy terms, (i) acceptable price: as the ticket price always varies in different seasons, an acceptable price range is judged by the perception of the customer, denoted as $\tilde{A}$ for short, (ii) service of crew: is the satisfaction degree of flight service crew represented as $\tilde{S}$ for short, (iii) service of food: is the satisfaction degree of food taste, quality and diversity denoted as $\tilde{F}$ for short. So, the degree of satisfaction can be formulated by a simple fuzzy additive weighting rule, i.e. $\tilde{Q} = (w_1 \otimes \tilde{A}) \oplus (w_2 \otimes \tilde{S}) \oplus (w_3 \otimes \tilde{F})$. The weightings will be evolved to reflect the situation after a number of consumers' preferences. Then, acceptable price, expressed by $\tilde{x}_{ij} = (a_i, b_i, c_i), j = 1$, can be represented as Figure 7.7. Decision makers assign acceptable price to five service candidates as the first column of Table 7.5.

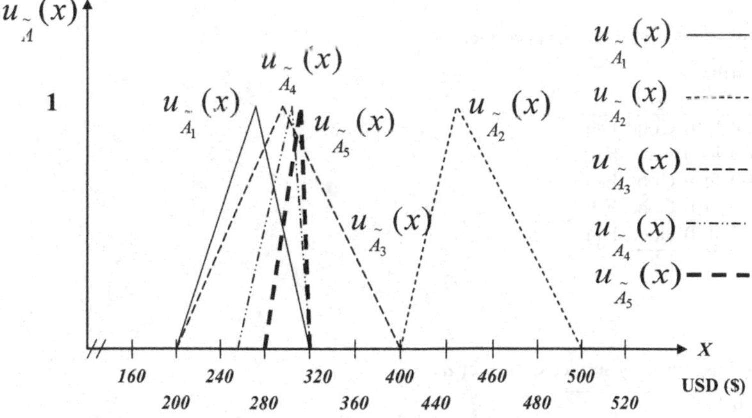

Fig. 7.7 Five different fuzzy sets for acceptable price

Step 2: In the following, each decision maker has to assign a performance rating $\tilde{x}_{ij}(d_p)$ on service of crew and service of food with linguistic terms, defined in Table 7.4, to service alternatives. In Table 7.4, the membership function of linguistic terms for the rating of each service alternative is given by $(x-2,x,x+2)$ for $\tilde{x}_{ij} = (3,5,7)$ except $(0,1,3)$ for $\tilde{x}_{ij}$ is "very poor" and $(7,9,10)$ for $\tilde{x}_{ij}$ is "very good". The decision makers assign acceptable prices to five service candidates as the first column of Tables 7.5, 7.6, and 7.7. The individual fuzzy performance rating matrix is shown in Tables 7.5, 7.6, and 7.7.

Table 7.4 Linguistic terms for the rating of service alternatives

Linguistic terms	Triangular fuzzy number
Very poor (VP)	(0,1,3)
Poor (P)	(1,3,5)
Fair (F)	(3,5,7)
Good (G)	(5,7,9)
Very good (VG)	(7,9,10)

Table 7.5 Ratings assigned by service customer d_1

Airliner	QoS Attributes		
	c_1($)	c_2	c_3
a_1	(200,280,320)	Poor	Good
a_2	(400,450,500)	Good	Very good
a_3	(200,300,400)	Very good	Poor
a_4	(260,300,320)	Good	Fair
a_5	(280,300,320)	Fair	Good

Table 7.6 Ratings assigned by service customer d_2

Airliner	QoS Attributes		
	c_1($)	c_2	c_3
a_1	(280,320,380)	Good	Fair
a_2	(300,360,440)	Fair	Fair
a_3	(300,400,440)	Good	Fair
a_4	(280,300,340)	Good	Fair
a_5	(320,340,380)	Good	Fair

Table 7.7 Ratings assigned by service customer d_3

Airliner	QoS Attributes		
	c_1($)	c_2	c_3
a_1	(200,220,240)	Good	Fair
a_2	(220,240,280)	Good	Good
a_3	(300,340,360)	Poor	Good
a_4	(280,320,400)	Good	Poor
a_5	(260,300,320)	Fair	Good

In addition, three service consumers give their ranking order among six service candidates as follows:

$$\Omega(d_1) = \{(1,2),(2,3),(2,4),(2,5),(3,1),(3,5),(4,1),(4,3),(4,5),(5,1)\}$$
$$\Omega(d_2) = \{(1,5),(2,1),(3,1),(2,3),(2,4),(2,5),(4,3),(5,3),(5,4)\}$$
$$\Omega(d_3) = \{(1,2),(1,3),(1,5),(2,3),(2,4),(2,5),(3,5),(3,4),(5,4)\}$$

Step 3: By applying Equation 7.7, the normalized performance ratings matrix assessed by decision maker d_1 is formed as:

$$\tilde{R}(d_1) = [\tilde{r}_{ij}] = \begin{bmatrix} (0.40,0.62,0.80) & (0.10,0.30,0.50) & (0.50,0.70,0.90) \\ (0.52,0.71,0.95) & (0.50,0.70,0.90) & (0.70,0.90,1.00) \\ (0.80,1.00,1.00) & (0.70,0.90,1.00) & (0.10,0.30,0.50) \\ (0.40,0.67,1.00) & (0.50,0.70,0.90) & (0.30,0.70,0.70) \\ (0.52,0.67,0.80) & (0.30,0.50,0.70) & (0.50,0.70,0.90) \end{bmatrix}$$

Similarly, the normalized performance ratings matrix assessed by decision makers d_2 and d_3 can be obtained, respectively.
Step 4: Let $h = 1$, and $\delta = 0.0$. Using Equation 7.22, we can formulate the linear programming problem as follows:

$$Min \;\; \{z_{12}+z_{31}+z_{41}+z_{51}+z_{23}+z_{24}+z_{25}+z_{35}+z_{45}+z_{43}\}$$

$$s.t. \begin{cases} -0.49w_1-1.28w_2-0.02w_3+(0.119b_{v1}+0.467c_{v1}) \\ \quad +(0.80a_{v2}+0.80b_{v2}+0.80c_{v2})-(0.1333c_{v3})=1 \\ z_{12}+0.164w_1+0.4w_2+0.25w_3-(0.008a_{v1}+0.059b_{v1}+0.10v_1) \\ \quad -(0.267a_{v2}+0.267b_{v2}+0.267c_{v2}) \\ \quad -(0.133a_{v3}+0.133b_{v3}+0.067c_{v3})\geq 0, \\ z_{31}-0.483w_1-0.65w_2+0.4w_3-(0.267a_{v1}+0.252b_{v1}+0.133c_{v1}) \\ \quad +(0.4a_{v2}+0.4b_{v2}+0.333c_{v2}) \\ \quad -(0.267a_{v3}+0.267b_{v3}+0.267c_{v3})\geq 0, \\ z_{41}-0.139w_1-0.4w_2+0.24w_3+(0.0296b_{v1}+0.133c_{v1}) \\ \quad +(0.267a_{v2}+0.267b_{v2}+0.267c_{v2}) \\ \quad -(0.1333a_{v3}+0.1333b_{v3}+0.1333c_{v3})\geq 0, \\ z_{51}-0.0559w_1-0.16w_2+(0.08a_{v1}+0.0296b_{v1}) \\ \quad +(0.133a_{v2}+0.133b_{v2}+0.133c_{v2})\geq 0, \\ z_{23}+0.3205w_1+0.25w_2-0.65w_3-(0.187a_{v1}+0.193b_{v1}+0.033c_{v1}) \\ \quad -(0.133a_{v2}+0.133b_{v2}+0.067c_{v2}) \\ \quad +(0.4a_{v3}+0.4b_{v3}+0.333c_{v3})\geq 0 \\ z_{24}-0.0247w_1-0.49w_3+(0.08a_{v1}+0.0296bv1-0.033c_{v1}) \\ \quad +(0.2667a_{v3}+0.2667b_{v3}+0.2c_{v3})\geq 0, \\ z_{25}-0.1079w_1-0.24w_2-0.25w_3+(0.0296b_{v2}+0.1c_{v2}) \\ \quad +(0.133a_{v3}+0.133b_{v3}+0.133c_{v3}) \\ \quad +(0.133a_{v4}+0.133b_{v4}+0.0667c_{v4})\geq 0, \\ z_{35}-0.428w_1-0.49w_2+0.34w_3+(0.187a_{v1}+0.222b_{v1}+0.133c_{v1}) \\ \quad +(0.267a_{v2}+0.267b_{v2}+0.2c_{v2}) \\ \quad -(0.267a_{v3}+0.267b_{v3}+0.267c_{v3})\geq 0, \\ z_{45}-0.0832w_1-0.24w_2+0.24w_3-(0.08a_{v1}+0.133c_{v1}) \\ \quad +(0.133a_{v2}+0.133b_{v2}+0.133c_{v2}) \\ \quad -(0.133a_{v3}+0.133b_{v3}+0.133c_{v3})\geq 0, \\ z_{43}+0.345w_1+0.25w_2-0.16w_3-(0.267a_{v1}+0.222b_{v1}) \\ \quad -(0.133a_{v2}+0.133b_{v2}+0.067c_{v2}) \\ \quad +(0.133a_{v3}+0.133b_{v3}+0.133c_{v3})\geq 0, \\ z_{12}\geq 0, z_{31}\geq 0, z_{41}\geq 0, z_{51}\geq 0, z_{23}\geq 0, \\ z_{24}\geq 0, z_{25}\geq 0, z_{35}\geq 0, z_{45}\geq 0, z_{43}\geq 0, \\ w_j\geq 0.0, j=1,\ldots,3 \\ a_{vj}, b_{vj}, c_{vj}\geq 0, j=1,\ldots,3 \end{cases}$$

Step 5: Solve the optimal solution using Mathematica software. This step produces $(w,\tilde{v}^*)$ as follows:

$$\begin{aligned} z^* &= (z_{12}, z_{31}, z_{14}, z_{51}, z_{23}, z_{24}, z_{25}, z_{43}, z_{35}, z_{45}) \\ &= (0.41, 0.0, 0.0, 0.0, 0.0, 0.0, 0.0, 0.0, 0.0, 0.0) \\ w^* &= (w_1, w_2, w_3)^T = (0.0, 0.0, 1.0) \\ v^* &= (v_1, v_2, v_3) = ((0.0, 0.0, 0.0), (0.0, 0.0, 0.0), (0.95, 0.95, 0.95)) \end{aligned}$$

The fuzzy positive ideal solution (FIPS) is located using Equation 7.21:

$$\tilde{r}^*(d_1) = \tilde{v}^*/w^* = (\tilde{r}_1,\ldots,\tilde{r}_3)^T = ((0.0,0.0,0.0),(0.0,0.0,0.0),(0.95,0.95,0.95))$$

Step 6: Outrank the ranking of WS. The square distance of service alternatives from FPIS can be computed by using Equation 7.9:

$$S_1(d_1) = 0.386, S_2(d_1) = 0.136, S_3(d_1) = 0.786, S_4(d_1) = 0.626, S_5(d_1) = 0.386$$

So the ranking order of service alternatives is generated as follows

$$a_2 > a_1 > a_5 > a_4 > a_3$$

Similarly, the optimal solution of $(w, \tilde{v}^*)$ is obtained using Steps 1–5 for decision makers d_2 and d_3.

$$\begin{aligned}
z^* &= (z_{15}, z_{21}, z_{31}, z_{23}, z_{24}, z_{25}, z_{43}, z_{53}) \\
&= (0.333, 0.0, 0.0, 0.0, 0.0, 0.0, 0.0, 0.0) \\
w(d_2) &= (w_1, w_2, w_3)^T = (0.0, 1.0, 0.0) \\
\tilde{v}^*(d_2) &= (\tilde{v}_1, \tilde{v}_2, \tilde{v}_3) \\
&= ((0.0,0.0,0.0),(0.21,0.21,0.21),(0.0,0.0,0.0)) \\
\tilde{r}^*(d_2) &= (\tilde{r}_1, \tilde{r}_2, \tilde{r}_3)^T \\
&= ((0.0,0.0,0.0),(0.21,0.21,0.21),(0.0,0.0,0.0)) \\
z^* &= (z_{21}, z_{15}, z_{13}, z_{23}, z_{24}, z_{35}, z_{43}, z_{54}) \\
&= (0.0, 0.0, 0.0, 0.0, 0.0, 0.0, 0.0, 0.0) \\
w(d_3) &= (w_1, w_2, w_3)^T = (0.187, 0.813, 0.0) \\
\tilde{v}^*(d_3) &= (\tilde{v}_1, \tilde{v}_2, \tilde{v}_3) \\
&= ((0.0,0.0,0.9),(0.016,0.016,0.016),(0.0,0.0,0.0)) \\
\tilde{r}^*(d_3) &= (\tilde{r}_1, \tilde{r}_2, \tilde{r}_3)^T \\
&= ((0.0,0.0,0.48),(0.20,0.20,0.20),(0.0,0.0,0.0))
\end{aligned}$$

The square distance of service alternatives from FPIS for decision makers d_2 and d_3 can be calculated:

$$S_1(d_2) = 0.520, S_2(d_2) = 0.328, S_3(d_2) = 0.507, S_4(d_2) = 0.525, S_5(d_2) = 0.514$$

$$S_1(d_3) = 0.064, S_2(d_3) = 0.179, S_3(d_3) = 0.179 S_4(d_3) = 0.224, S_5(d_2) = 0.179$$

Comparing the distance from FPIS using Equation 7.9, the ranking order of five service alternatives for the three decision makers is shown as, respectively.

$$a_2 > a_1 > a_5 > a_4 > a_3$$

$$a_2 > a_3 > a_1 > a_5 > a_4$$

$$a_1 > a_2 \cong a_5 \cong a_3 > a_4$$

Step 7. Using the Borda function [18], the scores of all service alternatives assessed by the three decision makers are listed in Table 7.8.

Table 7.8 Synthetic judgment matrix

Airliner	Service customers			
	d_1	d_2	d_3	Borda's scores
a_1	2	2	2	6
a_2	3	4	1	8
a_3	0	3	1	4
a_4	1	0	0	1
a_5	2	1	1	4

From Table 7.8, the final ranking order of service alternatives is decided as:

$$a_2 > a_1 > a_5 \cong a_3 > a_4$$

7.5 Discussion

Although the optimal solution is obtained, two significant issues for debate remain. First, the normalization process. A normalization of the attributes is not always necessary for solving MADM problems, but it may be essential for some methods, like Maxmin, simple additive weighting (SAW), ELECTRE, etc., to facilitate the computational problems inherent in the presence of the distinct scales of the performance rating matrix [17]. The aim of normalization is to obtain a comparable scale. Obviously, normalization is necessary in the processing of fuzzy data, to rank the web services compatibily, whose performance rating needs to be located in the interval $[0,1]$. In the traditional LINMAP method, users constantly convert from the distinct scales of ratings to a numerically comparable scale only, where the data of decision matrix is in nonfuzzy form. For instance, we translate all the ratings into the interval $[-10,10]$ as in case I for benefit and cost attributes.

Second, a reliable solution. From the solution process of the two cases, one could note that when the number of attributes exceeds the number of service alternatives, then it is not easy to yield a reliable solution of weight by the LIMAP. For example, in case II, three attributes are used for assessing five alternatives that is, $i = 5$ and $j = 3$, then the proposed model can gain a consistent solution when i>j according to suggestions in [17].

Moreover, it may set w_j, δ, intending to stimulate the feasible solutions for obtaining a non-trivial solution of the weight of QoS attributes by adjusting δ. The target of consensus-based weighting is to obtain a compromise solution of weight vectors among items of QoS attributes in the LINMAP method. From the two distinct cases and trial and error examples, we knew that the optimal solution sometimes tends towards converging to a single item of weight of QoS attributes, except that the value of specific attributes are distributed equally or scattered in an average way.

7.6 Conclusion

This work presents a new approach to obtaining a consensual weight of QoS attributes using a fuzzy linear program for QoS-aware service selection, which allows service consumers to reach consensus on the contents of services, even though they have different opinions and preferences. In addition, it can effectively alleviate the differences of QoS characteristics by minimizing the inconsistence measurement in the WS selection, find the optimal solution of weights of QoS attribute alternatives as well as the fuzzy positive ideal solution. Future work will focus on the investigation of other intelligent approaches such as genetic algorithms, simulated annealing and evolutionary computation in order to seek an efficient solution by improving the search effectiveness of feasible solutions.

References

1. R. Anane, K.-M. Chao, and Y. Li Hybrid Composition of Web Services and Grid Services. In *Proceedings of 2005 IEEE International Conference on e-Technology, e-Commerce and e-Service (EEE-05)*, pages 426–431, 2005.
2. A. Ankolenkar, M Burstein, J. Hobbs, et al. DAMLS: Web Service Description for the Semantic Web. In *Proceedings of the International Semantic Web Conference (ISWC02)*, LNCS 2342, Springer, (2002).
3. W.-T. Balke and M. Wagner. *Cooperative Discovery for User-centered Web Service Provisioning*, 2002.
4. T. Berners-Lee. *Weaving the Web*. Harper San Francisco, 1999.
5. T. Berners-Lee, J. Hendler, and O. Lassila. The Semantic Web. *Scientific American*, 2001
6. J. Borenstein and J. Fox. Semantic Discovery for Web Services. *Web Services Journal*, 3(4), 2003.
7. K.-M. Chao, M. Younas, C.-C. Lo, and T.-H. Tan. Fuzzy Matchmaking for Web Services. In *Proceedings of the 19th IEEE Conference on Advanced Networks and Information Applications*, IEEE CS, pages 721–726, 2005.
8. S.-H. Chen and C. L. Hwang. Fuzzy Multiple Attribute Decision Making Methods and Applications. Springer-Verlag, pages 90, 292–323, 1992.
9. C.T. Chen. Extensions of the TOPSIS for Group Decision-Making under Fuzzy Environment. *Fuzzy set and Systems* 114:1–9, 2000.
10. W. D. Cook, M. Kress, and L. M. Seiford. A General Framework for Distance-based Consensus in Ordinal Ranking Models. *European Journal of Operational Research*, 96(2):392–397, 1997.
11. W. D. Cook. Distance-based Consensus Models in Ordinal Preference Ranking. *European Journal of Operational Research* 172:369–385, 2006.
12. A. Dan et al. Web Services on Demand: WSLA Driven Automated Management. *IBM Systems Journal*, 43:136–158, 2004.
13. E. Herrera-Viedma, F. Herrera, and F. Chiclana. A Consensus Model for Multiperson Decision Making With Different Preference Structures *IEEE Transactions on Systems, Man and Cybernetics* 32:394–402, 2002.

14. K. Hogg, P. Chilcott, M. Nolan, and B. Srinivasan. An Evaluation of Web Services in the Design of a B2B Application. In *Proceedings of the 27th Conference on Australasian Computer Science*, pages 331–340, 2004.
15. C.-L. Huang, K.-M. Chao, and C.-C. Lo. A Moderated Fuzzy Matchmaking for Web Services. 2 In *Proceedings of the Fifth International Conference on Computer and Information Technology (CIT05)*, IEEE CS, pages 1116–1122, 2005.
16. C.-L. Huang, C.-C. Lo, and K.-M. Chao. Service Discovery through Multi-agent Consensus. In *Proceedings of IEEE International Workshop on Service-Oriented System Engineering (SOSE 2005)*, pages 37–44, 2005.
17. C.L. Hwang and K. Yoon. Multiple Attribute Decision Making: Methods and Applications In *Lecture Notes in Economics and Mathematical Systems*, Springer-Verlag, 1981.
18. C.-J. Hwang and M.J. Lin. Group Decision Making under Multiple Criteria: Methods & Applications. In *Lectures notes in economics & mathematical systems*, 281:36–45, 1987.
19. C. Jorge and S. Amit P. (Eds.). Semantic Web Services, In *Processes and Applications*, Springer, 2006.
20. J. Kacprzyk and M. Fedrizzi. A "soft" measurement of consensus in the setting of partial (fuzzy) preference. *European Journal of Operational Research* 34:316–326, 1988.
21. A. Kaufmann and M. M. Gupta. Introduction to Fuzzy Arithmetic Theory and Application Van Nostrand Reinhold, New York, pages 2–35, 69–72, 1991.
22. M.-R. Koivunen and E. Miller. W3C Semantic Web Activity. In *Proceedings of the Semantic Web*, 2001.
23. K. C. Lee and J. H. Jeon, et al. QoS for Web Services: Requirements and Possible Approaches. W3C Working Group Note, http://www.w3c.or.kr/kr-office/TR/2003/ws-qos/, 2003
24. D. F. Li and J. B. Yang. Fuzzy Linear Programming Technique for Multiattribute Group Decision Making in Fuzzy Environments. *Information Sciences*, 158:263–275, 2004.
25. M. Lin, J. Xie, and H. Guo. Solving QoS-Driven Web Service Dynamic Composition as Fuzzy Constraint Satisfaction. In *Proceedings of 2005 IEEE International Conference on e-Technology, e-Commerce and e-Service (EEE-05)*, IEEE CS, pages 9–14, 2005.
26. W.-L. Lin, C.-C. Lo, K.-M. Chao, and M. Younas. Fuzzy Consensus on QoS in Web Services Discovery. In *Proceedsings of the 20th International Conference on Advanced Information Networking and Applications (AINA 2006)*, pages 791–798, 2006.
27. Y. Liu, H. H. Ngu and L. Zeng. QoS Computation and Policing in Dynamic Web Service Selection. In *Proceedings of 13th Int Conference World Wide Web 2004* pages 65–73, 2004.
28. H. Ludwig, A. Keller, et al. Web Service Level Agreement (WSLA) Language Specification v1.0. http://www.research.ibm.com/wsla/ WSLASpecV1-20030128.pdf, 2003.
29. A. Mani and A. Nagarajan. Understanding Quality of Service for Web Services. *IBM Developer works*, http://www-128.ibm.com/library/ developerworks/ws-quality.html, 2002.
30. D. L. McGuinness and F. Van Harmelen. OWL Web Ontology Language Overview. W3C World Wide Web Consortium, from http://www.w3.org/TR/2OO3/PR-owl-features-20031215/, 2003.
31. OWL Services Coalition. OWL-S: Semantic Markup for Web Services, OWL-S v. 1.1. White Paper. http://www.daml.org/services/owl-s/1.1/, 2004.
32. M. Paolucci, T. Kawamura, T. R. Payne, and K. Sycara. Importing the Semantic Web in UDDI. In *Proceedings of the International Workshop on Web Services, E-Business, and the Semantic Web*, LNCS Vol. 2512, pages 225–236, 2002.
33. S. Ran A Model for Web Services Discovery with QoS. *ACM SIGecom Exchanges* 4:1–10, 2003.
34. M. Reformat, D.-M. Li, and C. Ly. Approximate reasoning and Semantic Web Services. In *Proceedings of the IEEE Annual Meeting of the Fuzzy Information (NAFIPS'04)*, pages 413–418, 2004.
35. A. Sahai, A. Durante, and V. Machiraju. Towards Automated SLA Management for Web Services. http://www.hpl.hp.com/techreports/2001/HPL-2001-310 R1.pdf, 2001.
36. E. Sirin, B. Parsia, and J. Hendler. Filtering and Selecting Semantic Web Services with Interactive Composition Techniques. *IEEE Intelligent Systems*, 42–49, 2004.

37. SOAP Protocol. http://www.w3.org/2000/xp/Group.
38. V. Srinivasan and A. D. Shocker. Linear Programming Techniques for Multidimensional Analysis of Preference. *Psychometrika*, 38:337–369, 1973.
39. UDDI. The UDDI Technical White Paper. http://www.uddi.org, 2002.
40. P. Wang, K.-M. Chao, C.-C. Lo, C.-L. Huang, and Y. Li. A Fuzzy Model for Selection of QoS-Aware Web Services. In *Proceedings of ICEBE 2006*, pages 585–593, 2006.
41. M. Zeleny. Multiple Attributes Decision Making Mcgraw-Hill, 1982.
42. L. Zeng, B. Benatallah, M. Dumas, J. Kalagnanam, and Q. Z. Sheng. Quality Driven Web Service Composition. In *Proceedings of WWW2003*, pages 411–421, 2003.
43. L. Zeng, B. Benatallah, A. H. H Ngu, M. Dumas, J. Kalagnanam, and H Chang. Qos-Aware Middleware for Web Service Composition. *IEEE Transactions on Software Engineering* 30:311–327, 2004.
44. C. Zhou, L.T. Chin, and B.S. Lee. DAML-QoS Ontology for Web Services. In *International Conference on Web Services (ICWS 2004)*, pages 472–479, 2004.
45. C. Zhou, L.-T. Chia, and B-S Lee. Semantics in Service Discovery and QoS measurement. *IT Professional*, 7: 29–34, 2005.

Chapter 8
Trust and Reputation

Sarah N. Lim Choi Keung and Nathan Griffiths

Abstract Trust and reputation have become standard approaches for supporting the management of interactions in distributed environments. Several alternative approaches have been proposed that take a wide range of approaches, including socio-cognitive, computational, and reputational mechanisms. In this chapter we introduce the various approaches to trust and reputation, and discuss how they relate to agents in a service-oriented computing context.

8.1 Introduction

In this chapter we consider service-oriented computing (SOC) from an agent perspective. Service advertisement, discovery and selection can be seen as processes carried out by agents. The agent view of SOC holds for the various settings in which SOC is used, including peer-to-peer systems, Grid computing and e-commerce. Trust and reputation are useful in all these settings. As we progress from simple to complex settings the issues change, and we need more complex trust and reputation mechanisms.

Sarah N. Lim Choi Keung
Department of Computer Science, University of Warwick, Coventry, CV4 7AL, UK
e-mail: S.N.Lim.Choi.Keung@dcs.warwick.ac.uk

Nathan Griffiths
Department of Computer Science, University of Warwick, Coventry, CV4 7AL, UK
e-mail: nathan@dcs.warwick.ac.uk

N. Griffiths, K.-M. Chao (eds.), *Agent-Based Service-Oriented Computing*, Advanced Information and Knowledge Processing,
DOI 10.1007/978-1-84996-041-0_8, © Springer-Verlag London Limited 2010

8.2 Trust and Reputation

Trust has gained interest with the development of Internet and electronic commerce, due to its importance for security, privacy and also in maintaining customer loyalty [18]. The notion of trust has then been explored in other areas, including multi-agent systems (MAS). In open distributed MAS, autonomous agents want to achieve their own goals, but they often need to interact with other agents in their environment to succeed. For agents to conduct successful interactions and behave optimally over the long term, they require information about important aspects of agent behaviour relevant to decision making. An agent needs to know which interaction partners to trust and how to select them. Additionally, during interactions, an agent wants to be able to control its own behaviour, in deciding whether to provide reputation information to others, making inferences from the information obtained from others, and from the outcomes of previous interactions with those interaction partners. Consequently, the adoption of the concept of trust to support cooperation in MAS has led to an increasing amount of research in the area of trust and reputation models. These models take into consideration many different characteristics of the agents themselves and the environment in which they evolve.

8.2.1 Trust

The concept of trust is defined as a measurable level of risk, through which an agent X assesses the likelihood that another agent Y will successfully perform a particular action, both before X can monitor such action and in a context in which it affects its own actions [27]. We view the notion of trust to represent the assessment of risk when an agent directly interacts with another agent and thus trust is based on its own experience. Research in trust has long been focused on the positive side of trust. However, as indicated by Marsh [49], negative trust, *distrust* is also a motivational force which needs to be considered. Similarly, Marsh introduces the concepts of *untrust* and *mistrust* that lie within the continuum between trust and distrust. Untrust is a measure of how little an agent is trusted; it is a positive value but insufficient for cooperation to take place between two agents. Next, distrust is regarded as negative trust and it is a measure of how much an agent believes another agent will work against its interests in a given situation. Finally, mistrust is defined as misplaced trust, a former trust that has been betrayed or healed.

Research in trust in the agents field has brought about many different approaches. Castelfranchi and Falcone [16, 24] view trust as composed of beliefs, such as competence, disposition, dependence and fulfilment. The approach by Marsh [47] looks at basic, general and situational trust, which considers trust with regards to the agent itself, other agents and particular contexts respectively. Griffiths [29] introduces the multi-dimensional trust (MDT) approach, which allows agents to model the trustworthiness of others according to various criteria. The approach decomposes beliefs about trust, as viewed by Castelfranchi and Falcone, according to the different dimensions of an interaction. Agents can model trust along any number of dimensions, according to their preferences and motivations. For the purposes of illustrating MDT, the author uses four dimensions of success, cost, timeliness and quality.

8.2.2 Reputation

Reputation, a closely related notion to trust, is defined as the information received from third parties by agents about the behaviour of their partners, and this can be used to decide how they are going to behave themselves [14]. Due to its importance in social and commercial relations, the study and modelling of reputation has attracted a lot of interest from researchers in different fields: sociology, economics [42], psychology and computer science, particularly, the areas of multi-agent systems and online communities. We consider reputation to include recommendations from agents who have directly interacted with the agents we are interested in, as well as indirect recommendations, based on the propagation of reputation among agents.

8.2.3 The Multiple Approaches to Trust and Reputation Models

The interest in trust and reputation has resulted in many models being developed for the implementation and management of these notions in multi-agent systems. Researchers have adopted approaches from different disciplines to support the development of their models. The notions of trust and reputation have their roots in sociology, economics and biology and have been applied in domains as diverse as Game Theory, business ethics and politics. Hence, to model them in agent-based systems, techniques from many of the mentioned fields have been used. The main approaches are socio-cognitive, numerical and reputational views.

8.2.3.1 Socio-Cognitive View

The term *cognitive* is defined in the Cambridge Dictionaries Online as "connected with thinking or conscious mental processes" [15]. Thus, models following the socio-cognitive approach are based on underlying beliefs about a society and its members and trust is a function of these beliefs [22]. Additionally, this approach involves the mental states of an agent in relying on another agent and also the consequences of the actual decision of reliance [24]. It is important to understand the mental ingredients of trust in order to explain and predict the perception and decision about an agent's risk. A cognitive analysis of trust also forms the base to the notions of reputation, deception, persuasion and trust signs [17].

In the literature, only a few trust and reputation models are based on the socio-cognitive view. The main model dealing with cognitive approach to trust is that of Castelfranchi and Falcone [16, 24], in which they define the different beliefs that an agent must hold to build up trust. The beliefs are the properties that an agent expects another agent to have in order to be suitable to be relied on. Other models use the social aspect of MAS to closely represent interactions in real situations. Mezzetti [50] stresses the ideas of trust variation with time and context and the modelling of the properties that cause a reputation value to be low or high.

8.2.3.2 Computational View

In this view, trust and reputation are not reflective of the mental state of an agent, but use numbers and mathematical techniques to represent the trust value, in the form of probabilities and numerical aggregations and strategies. Within this view, models can be roughly categorised as decision-theoretical or game-theoretical.

Decision-Theoretical View

Classical decision theory consists of a set of mathematical techniques for making decisions about which action to take when the outcomes of various actions are not known. *Probability theory* is a subset of these techniques, where some aspect of the current state of the environment is captured as a probability. Marsh [47] represents trust as a probability between -1 and $+1$. All the three aspects of trust: basic, general and situational lie within this range and he proposes a formula to calculate the situational trust. Mui et al. [51] also propose a mathematical model based on probability to show the link between trust, reputation and reciprocation. Models by Witkowski et al. [75, 76] and Sen et al. [65, 66] also fall into this category.

Other models place trust values and agent behaviour into categories to make them more meaningful in their utilisation. *Fuzzy set theory* is a means of specifying how well an object satisfies a vague description [57]. Zadeh [81] defines a fuzzy set to be a class of objects with a continuum of grades of membership. Many objects in the real world do not have precisely defined criteria for membership and although they are ambiguous, they are important in human thinking, pattern recognition, communication and abstraction. Fuzzy logic has emerged from fuzzy sets and is a method for reasoning with logical expressions describing membership in fuzzy sets. It allows intermediate values to be defined between conventional evaluations, such as yes or no, late or on time, in terms of the degree of truth. Notions like rather warm or slightly late can be formulated mathematically and processed by computers in an attempt to more accurately represent the way systems behave in the real world.

Wu and Sun [77] classifies a seller's behaviour in a bidding environment as Random, Nice, Tit-for-Tat and Nasty, where each strategy outlines the way the seller behaves in an interaction. Abdul-Rahman and Hailes [1] also use classification in the case of trust and for the adjustment of experiences. Trustworthiness is categorised into four categories, from Very Untrustworthy to Very Trustworthy, while experiences also exist in four types, from Very Bad to very Good.

The fuzzy approach is also adopted by Falcone et al. [25] for an implementation of the socio-cognitive model of trust they have developed [16, 24]. Fuzzy logic has been chosen for their model because trust is a graded phenomenon that can be difficult to estimate experimentally. The implementation is based on Fuzzy Cognitive Maps (FCM) [41], that allow the value of truthfulness to be computed from the belief sources. An FCM is well suited for representing a dynamic system with cause-effect relations, where nodes represent the causal concepts of belief sources for instance, and edges represent the causal power of one node over another. Other work using fuzzy logic includes that of Griffiths et al. [31], used in the context of Peer-to-Peer (P2P) systems to select interaction partners.

Game-Theoretical View

Within the computational or numerical models, there is a sub-category of models and mechanisms which are based on Game Theory, thus making use of utility functions and strategies. Game theory originated with the work of John von Newmann and Oscar Morgenstern [71], where they define a game as any interaction between agents that is governed by a set of rules specifying the possible moves for each participant and a set of outcomes for each possible combination of moves. A theory of games promises to apply to almost any social interaction where individuals have some understanding of how the outcome for one is affected not only by its own actions but also by the actions of others [34].

The Prisoners' Dilemma (PD) problem in game theory was described by Albert Tucker while addressing an audience of psychologists, to explain the puzzles devised by Merrill Flood and Melvin Dresher in 1950, as part of the Rand Corporation's investigations into game theory due to its possible applications to global nuclear strategy [43]. As illustrated by Tucker, two prisoners are held for the robbery of a bank. They are placed in separate cells and the prosecutor makes an offer to each of them while explaining what is likely to happen. Table 8.1 summarises the options and payoffs proposed to the prisoners, where the number pair represents the number of years in prison for prisoners A and B respectively. Cooperation means staying quiet and not giving the prosecution information, i.e. cooperating with the other prisoner. Defection means assisting the prosecution with information thus defecting with respect to the other prisoner.

Table 8.1 Options and payoffs

	Prisoner A cooperates	Prisoner A defects
Prisoner B cooperates	1,1	0,5
Prisoner B defects	5,0	3,3

There is enough evidence to convict each of a minor offence, but there is not enough evidence to convict either of them of a major crime unless one of them defects, and thus acts as an informer. If both defect (i.e., confess), they will each be given three years in prison, due to their being no doubt over their guilt. If only one of them confesses, that prisoner will be freed and used as a witness against the other, who will spend five years in prison. If both cooperate and stay quiet, each will be convicted of the minor offence and spend one year in prison. Given the assumption that each prisoner cares only to avoid spending time in prison, the dominant strategy of each will be to defect. Yet, it yields a paradoxical result of making each worse off than they might have been had they each chosen to cooperate and stay quiet and so to spend only one year in prison [34].

Tit-for-Tat is a fairly efficient and very simple strategy in Game Theory for the iterated Prisoners' Dilemma. The strategy is one of cooperating on the first move and then doing whatever the other agent did on the preceding move. It is thus a strategy of cooperation based on reciprocity [9].

TrustNet [62, 63] uses an extension to the Prisoner's Dilemma for the selection of interaction partners. Wu and Sun's [77] technique makes use of the Tit-for-Tat strategy for the behaviour of its seller agent.

8.2.3.3 Reputational View

In the evaluation of trustworthiness, many models make use of reputation, in the form of recommendations from other agents. Direct interactions with the agents of interest are not always available as sources of information, especially when there have been no previous interactions or past interactions have occurred a long time ago. Many models take into account reputation as a complement of trust in evaluating trustworthiness. Models by Abdul-Rahman and Hailes [1], Regret [60], TrustNet [62, 63], FIRE [35] and TRAVOS [70] all make use of reputation.

The reputation mechanism by Braynov and Sandholm [12, 13] and FIRE use a form of reputation mechanism used by an agent for itself. It consists of revealing their reputation value to other agents with whom they want to interact. Most of the models mentioned use direct recommendations, that is, an agent requests the opinion of other agents who have interacted with the agent of interest. Indirect recommendations, that is the opinions of other agents about an agent of interest even if they have not themselves interacted with it, are used by Regret and FIRE. The trust-based recommendation system proposed by Water et al. [73] also makes use of direct and indirect recommendations from the agents' neighbours in decision making.

8.2.4 Review of Trust and Reputation Models

A selection of trust and reputation models from the different approaches mentioned are reviewed in this section.

8.2.4.1 Castelfranchi and Falcone

The model proposed by Castelfranchi and Falcone [16, 24] is general and domain-independent, and is based on the mental state of trust. It suggests that an agent can trust another if it has a suitable set of goals and beliefs. Trust is defined as comprising of three elements: "core trust", which is a simple evaluation of the trustee, "reliance", the decision to rely on the trustee and "delegation", the actual action of trusting the trustee. To build trust in another agent Y, an agent X requires to have certain beliefs corresponding to these three components of trust. The cognitive analysis of trust is fundamental in the distinction between the internal and external attribution, which predicts different strategies for building trust. Internal attribution concerns the characteristics of willingness, persistence, engagement and competence, while external attribution involves the conditions of the environment, such as opportunities, resources and interference.

The trusting agent X with core trust must have two basic beliefs:

- Competence belief is a positive evaluation of agent Y's usefulness in producing the expected result.
- Disposition belief, when X believes that Y will do the task that is required.

For core trust and reliance to exist, agent X must have an additional belief to support the previous two:

- Dependence belief is necessary for the X to rely on Y to do a task, out of lack of alternatives or as the more advantageous option in comparison to not relying on Y.

Supported by the previous beliefs, another important belief arises:

- Fulfilment belief drives agent X to think that the goal will be pursued and achieved.

Delegation, the last element of trust, can occur in two ways: weak or strong delegation. In weak delegation, there is no agreement and no bilateral awareness of the delegation, while in strong delegation, the trustee Y is aware of the truster X's intention to exploit its action.

The following beliefs apply in weak delegation, in addition to the other beliefs previously mentioned:

- Willingness belief models Y's mind in its intention to work towards a certain goal.
- Persistence belief where X believes that Y is serious in its intention in doing a task.
- Self-confidence belief that Y knows that it can do the task.

In addition to the beliefs in weak delegation, strong delegation requires one more belief:

- Motivation belief; X believes that Y has some motives to help adopt its goal.

The authors present the concept of *reciprocal trust* [23], which is a mutual understanding and communication between two agents that they will help each other, at different points in time. They claim that the reciprocal trust is different to bilateral trust, which occurs between two agents at the same time, but the agents are not explicitly aware of this. They argue that the opposite is also true: agent X's distrust in agent Y induces distrust in Y towards X. Another concept touched upon is that of the diffusion of trust. The authors suggest that the trust agent X has in agent Y can influence agent Z to trust Y. The mechanisms suggested for this diffusion are pseudo-transitivity and conformism. Pseudo-transitivity depends on the cognitive conditions that are present and diffusion of trust will most likely occur if the agent whose trust decisions are followed is a figure of authority in the domain. Conformism, on the other hand, is not based on any special expertise and is based on copying another agent's actions or decisions.

In their socio-cognitive model, the authors do not make any reference to the possibility of having dishonest agents (with respect to their provision of recommendations) or the potential problem of collusion in the system. An overall framework of trust using the various concepts introduced has also not been fully defined.

8.2.4.2 SIR (Socially-Inspired Reputation Model)

Mezzetti [50] proposes a reputation model with a social nature. The model introduces a jurisdiction sub-context, implying that an agent having authority in a particular context or situation, can be trusted in providing reliable recommendations about other agents within that context. The strength of the trust binding between two agents is represented as real value from 0 to 1, where 0 means the absence of trust, while 1 means full trust. These trust degrees serve several functions, namely in deciding whether or not to interact with another agent, and to determine the security mechanisms that are required for the interaction to take place.

Trust is taken to be dynamic in both time and interaction, and this can impact on the trust degree. Moreover, the model considers only the more recent information. This is incorporated into the model as a decay rate for the trust degrees, with the rate varying depending on the level of risk associated with the context. The social reputation model updates trust and reputation values dynamically as a result of the interaction outcomes. Both direct and indirect trust through recommendations are expressed in the model. The model also utilises an attribute to incorporate the property that is relevant within the context. For instance, a low reputation value of 0.2 does not allow an agent to know the cause of unreliability. Hence, with an attribute representing the property of low availability of service, for example, the cause of unreliability is more comprehensible.

SIR takes into account the social characteristics in a multi-agent system. It incorporates different attributes to improve the expressiveness of the model. For example, an attribute for defining the effective property in a particular context helps to understand the reputation value of an agent. The model however, does not handle the possibility of having dishonest agents and ways to deal with them.

8.2.4.3 Marsh's Formalism

In the trust model proposed by Marsh [47], trust is viewed as three different aspects, as a result of direct interactions with other agents:

- *Basic trust*, which is derived from all the past experiences of an agent. This represents the trusting disposition of the agent itself. The basic trust of an agent x is denoted as T_x. This value is in the range $[-1,1)$, that is, $-1 \leq T_x < +1$, where good experiences increase the disposition of the agent to trust.
- *General trust* is the trust an agent has in another agent, irrespective of the situation in which they are found. This is denoted as $T_x(y)$ and the range of general trust values is $[-1,1)$, that is, $-1 \leq T_x(y) < +1$, where -1 is negative trust or complete distrust and $+1$ is complete trust, while 0 means no trust.
- *Situational trust* is the amount of trust an agent has in another agent in a specific situation. Thus, the notation for "x trusts y in situation α" is $T_x(y,\alpha)$. The importance and utility of the situation, together with the general trust value, all determine the situational trust value, which is also in the interval $[-1,1)$.

The understanding of trust and the trust values obtained allows agents to make more informed decisions about which agents are trustworthy and who to cooperate with. Based on the situation, its importance and risk involved, the competence of the potential interaction partner is thus assessed. The basic formula to calculate situational trust is

$$T_x(y,\alpha)^t = U_x(\alpha)^t \times I_x(\alpha)^t \times \widehat{T_x(y)}^t$$

where $U_x(\alpha)^t$ represents the utility x gains from the situation α, $I_x(\alpha)^t$ is the importance of the situation α for agent x and $\widehat{T_x(y)}^t$ is an estimate of the general trust after taking into account all the relevant data with respect to situational trust in past interactions. In order to calculate this estimate, the author proposes three statistical methods: the mean, the maximum and the minimum. These are translated into realism, optimism and pessimism respectively.

These notions of agent dispositions [47,48] give an indication of how agents will act in a given situation. Along a continuum, agents can range from optimists to pessimists. Optimists are those agents who look for the best in those with whom they interact, they are forgiving and their trust in another does not decrease by much, even after being exploited by another agent. On the other extreme, pessimists see the worst in the agents they interact with and are always in doubt of the resulting situation. Even a small exploitation will result in drastic loss in trust, while continued cooperative behaviour will not greatly increase trust. In between these two extremes lie the realists, acting as a control point in studying the agent behaviours.

The formalism proposed also takes into account the notion of reciprocation, where favours are returned to those who offered them. Reciprocation is used to modify trust; if an agent x accepts help from another agent y, x's trust in y is likely to increase, while if y defects, x's trust in y is likely to decrease.

Marsh's formalism does not model reputation and thus does not consider third party recommendations in the evaluation of an agent's trustworthiness. This may limit the amount of information for trust evaluation in cases where there is insufficient or no direct interactions with the agents of interest. The author also does not specifically cater for the trust evaluation of new entrants who have have not interacted before.

Abdul-Rahman and Hailes [1] observe that Marsh's model incorporates too many aspects of social trust and the large number of variables considered make the model large and complex. Furthermore, they consider the notions of risk and competence to be abstract and thus difficult to represent as numbers, especially continuous values.

8.2.4.4 Ntropi

Abdul-Rahman and Hailes [1] propose a trust and reputation model, which is applicable to virtual communities. It is a numerical model with degrees of trust and is based on social characteristics and reputation. Both direct experiences and recommendations are used to form a trust opinion. Many properties of social trust are supported, as follows.

- Positive and negative degrees of belief are supported through a four-value scale.
- Prior experiences are taken into account so that agents can identify similar experiences.
- Reputational information is exchanged among agents though recommendations.
- Non-transitivity of trust is considered and all the evaluations of recommendations take into account their source.
- Subjectivity of trust represents the varying perceptions of different observers with regard to the same agent's trustworthiness.
- Dynamism allows the level of trust in another agent to increase or decrease, according to the experiences and recommendations obtained by the trusting agent.
- Support for *Interpersonal Trust*, which is the direct and contextual trust an agent has for another agent.
- Context dependence of trust is not clearly described by the authors.

The term "belief" is used in a different sense to that of Castelfranchi [16]. The model deals with beliefs about trustworthiness, without considering the risk, utility, and beliefs about motivation. Here, the belief that an agent is trustworthy in giving a recommendation is taken into account. Four degrees of direct trust are used: "Very Trustworthy", "Trustworthy", "Untrustworthy" and "Very Untrustworthy". A similar rating is used for experience adjustments: "Very Good", "Good", "Bad" and "Very Bad". Using evaluations of direct trust, recommender trust, semantic distance and the update of experiences, all these contribute to computing the final trust degree. Semantic distance is used as a similarity measure between an agent X's perception and another agent Y's recommendation. If there are differences, X will adjust future recommendations from Y accordingly. The model is thus intended to obtain trust on the information given by recommenders. Direct experiences are used for comparison and adjustment [61].

The authors recognise that the model is not recommended for agents without any prior experience nor trusted recommenders. This is due to the high level of uncertainty faced by new entrants who do not know whom to trust or distrust and they can thus become the victims of malevolent agents. With this bootstrapping limitation, the model also does not address the situations when agents lie or collude. It is also not possible to differentiate between truthful and lying agents on the basis that they have different reasoning mechanisms [61].

In addition, the authors concede that some aspects of their models, notably the trust degrees and the weightings used are of ad hoc nature and do not represent these metrics concretely.

8.2.4.5 Regret

The Regret system proposed by Sabater and Sierra [58–60] is a trust and reputation mechanism based on the following three dimensions of reputation.

- *Individual dimension* models the direct interactions between two agents. It is considered to be the most reliable dimension of reputation. From an interaction between two agents, the outcome consists of an initial contract of a course of action and the result of the actions taken, and of an initial contract to fix the terms and conditions of the transaction and the values of these terms. The set of outcomes stored in a database is used together with a selection of issues to choose the right subset of outcomes when calculating an *outcome reputation*. In this calculation, a weighted mean of the outcomes is used while giving more relevance to more recent outcomes.
- *Social dimension* looks at indirect interactions, especially when information from direct interaction is not available. Three types of social reputation are used in the regret system.
  - Witness reputation is based on information gathered from other agents who have interacted with the agent of interest. There is the risk of false information being provided in this case.
  - Neighbourhood reputation considers links that are created through interactions, as the behaviour of neighbours can give some indication about the possible behaviour of the target agent.
  - System reputation makes use of common knowledge about the role played by the target agent in society.
- *Ontological dimension* models a combination of reputational aspects relevant to a particular situation. The properties give more information into the reasons why a reputation is high or low. For example, the calculation of reputation using the ontological dimension can consider two dimensions:the reputation of an agent in delivering late, as well as that in over-pricing.

Regret also consists of a credibility module to evaluate the truthfulness of information received from third party agents. It also makes use of social network analysis to improve the knowledge about the surrounding society, especially in the absence of direct experiences. Social network analysis is described by Scott [64] as having emerged as a set of methods for the analysis of social structures, methods that specifically allow an investigation of the relational aspects of these structures. Moreover, the Regret system provides a degree of reliability for the trust, reputation and credibility values, that help an agent to decide whether it is sensible or not to use them in its decision-making process. This model is based on the agent group to which an individual belongs. In looking at agent groups, the model implies that information comes from trustful agents, who would not deliberately manipulate information. However, the model does not consider agents that can belong to more than one group at a time, where there may be potential issues of conflict of group association and competition.

The authors also do not specifically describe how to bootstrap the model and how to deal with new agents who have never interacted before. The Regret system makes use of up to three dimensions in calculating the reputation of agents. The authors however do not specify how the different reputation evaluations from the different dimensions can be used together.

8.2.4.6 TrustNet

Schillo et al. [63] present a mechanism for trust evaluation that will allow an agent to cope in environments where both selfish and cooperative agents evolve. The approach makes use of information from direct interactions, as well as from third party observations. In relying on recommendations, there is the possibility of noise in the information obtained, due to lying and biased agents. In their approach, the authors deal with unreliable witnesses, by making an estimation of how often witnesses have lied.

In order to evaluate trust, the model uses an extension of the Prisoner's Dilemma game, enhanced with a partner selection phase [62]. The disclosed prisoner's dilemma with partner selection consists of the following five steps.

- Each player agent pays a stake out of the limited amount of points it has.
- Pairs of agents are determined by negotiation and they declare their intentions. Agents have the possibility to deceive others.
- The prisoner's dilemma game is played while considering the previously declared intentions.
- The results are published, each agent receives only the results of the players in its neighbourhood.
- Agents receive prizes for their moves.

With this technique, an agent which chooses to diverge from its announced move will be noticed by other agents in its neighbourhood. Even though this agent may seem to gain from abusing the other agents, after a number of interactions, this agent will no longer be trusted and will be excluded from the game.

The model is, however, designed for specific simulation settings. Moreover, it fails to frame direct interactions within the social setting [56].

8.2.4.7 Mui et al.

The model proposed by Mui et al. [51] has four main characteristics. Firstly, the difference between trust and reputation is explicitly made. Secondly, reputation is a quantity relative to the particular social network of the evaluating agent and its encounter history. Thus, reputation is defined as a "perception that an agent creates through past actions about its intentions and norms". The next characteristic concerns trust, defined as "a subjective expectation an agent has about another's future behaviour based on the history of their encounters". Trust is a dyadic quantity between the truster and the trustee which can be inferred from the reputation data of the trustee. Lastly, a probabilistic mechanism is proposed for inference among trust, reputation and the level of reciprocity, to identify a threshold for the number of encounters needed by an agent to achieve a reliable measure of another's trustworthiness.

Reciprocity is closely linked to trust and reputation and suggests a mutual exchange of deeds. An increase in reputation expects an increase in trust. An increase in trust in turn expects an increase in reciprocation, and an increase in reciprocation expects an increase in reputation. The model handles the case of when two agents have no previous encounters by introducing an ignorance assumption called the Complete Stranger Prior Assumption.

The model models only dyadic encounters, those involving only two agents. Other choices made in the model include the assumption that the environment in which agents evolve is static, where no new agents join or leave. Moreover, the binary actions of cooperation or defection restrict the action space of the agents.

8.2.4.8 Braynov and Sandholm

The approach adopted by Braynov and Sandholm [12] targets the context of non-enforceable contracts between two agents, a buyer and a seller. They show that to maximise gains, the seller should make a precise estimation of the trustworthiness of the buyer. Underestimation of the buyer's trustworthiness leads to an insufficient allocation of resources and thus causes losses to both agents. To solve this problem, the authors demonstrate that it is better for the buyer to reveal its actual level of trustworthiness to the seller.

In their later work [13], the authors propose trust revelation as the solution to the problem of learning and estimating trustworthiness. Trust assessment encounters many obstacles, as follows.

- Trust learning requires long-term interactions and is costly for the learning agent who risks being abused, in terms of information search costs and the costs of obtaining guarantees from trusted third parties, for example.

- Trust learning is typically gradual but can be destroyed instantly by misfortune or a mistake. Since trust-destroying events tend to be more noticeable, it can be quite difficult and lengthy for trust to be re-built.
- Trust learning seldom produces complete and accurate trustworthiness value estimates. This can be a result of inaccurate beliefs which cause an agent not to interact with another agent which is completely trustworthy.
- The trust learning mechanism can fail, as it is very likely that a learning agent will encounter a run of bad encounters. This will lower the estimates made by the agent and can discourage it from making any more encounters for learning.
- Trust leaning may be impossible in many cases, for example Internet transactions with total strangers, for whom there is no history of past interactions.

The trust revelation mechanism involves the agents revealing their true level of trustworthiness at the beginning of a transaction, even if they are untrustworthy. This mechanism works on the assumption that the trustee depends on the truster by a parameter, which will make it reveal its trustworthiness. It is suggested that honest reporting informs the other agents about the risks involved so that they can form realistic expectations of the outcomes. Moreover, the mechanism solves the problem of inaccuracies of estimates as the actual values are used, thereby possibly reducing the cost of trust management.

This approach is similar to the concept of certified reputation in FIRE [35], where the agent reveals its trustworthiness as viewed by other agents who have interacted with it. However, the model only uses this mechanism before interaction, which can be problematic for new agents who have not interacted before.

8.2.4.9 Wu and Sun

Wu and Sun [77] propose a computational approach to explore the emergence of trust between agents in a multi-agent bidding setting. In their work, a seller can use four strategies: Random, Nice, Tit-for-Tat and Nasty. Each of these strategies have been defined to reflect the type of behaviour adopted. The findings suggest that interactions in a friendly climate do not necessarily ensure cooperation. Here, a friendly climate is taken to mean where the sellers are using the Nice strategy. This approach strictly deals with cooperation between self-interested parties and has also not considered the utility loss during cooperation, which occurs in the short run [56].

The authors adopt the use of the four strategies: Random, Nice, Tit-for-Tat and Nasty to describe the behaviour of the seller. However, these strategies are only described using an example of price bidding with numbers and equations and have not been explained in a more generalised terms to clearly convey the boundaries of the different strategies.

8.2.4.10 Witkowski et al.

In their approach, Witkowski et al. [75, 76] focus on direct experiences between agents for obtaining information on trust, called "objective trust" by the authors. They use a trading scenario to test and evaluate the objective trust-based agents. The calculation of trust is simplified through equations that deal with measurable quantities of bandwidth allocation and bandwidth use. The trust functions are different for two types of agents, that is, consumers and suppliers. From the experiments carried out, it is shown that the objective trust-based agents tend to form strong partnerships rapidly and these partnerships become more important as the demand and supply for the commodity becomes mismatched. When demand exceeds supply, only the more successful partnerships are sustained, with some customers failing to develop relationships with a sufficient number of suppliers to meet their needs. When supply exceeds demand, less trusted supplier agents are discarded by trusted customers first.

The evaluation of trust in this approach is only based on an agent's direct perception of its opponent's reliability. Thus, problems arise for first time interactions where there is no history to analyse. In this sense, the opinions of third parties can be useful in helping to reinforce the objective trust obtained by the agent.

The approach does not take into account the time dimension when working with the trust value. Therefore, there seems to be no indication of the use of the history of interactions in terms of whether more recent interactions have more weight than older ones, for example.

8.2.4.11 Sen et al.

Sen [65] proposes a probabilistic reciprocal mechanism to generate cooperative behaviour among self-interested agents. Reciprocity involves a predictive mechanism, such that an agent who helps another agent will expect to get benefit from the latter in the future. The probabilistic scheme used is different from a simple deterministic Tit-for-Tat strategy in that an agent may decide to help another agent even if the latter has refused to help it previously. The reciprocative agent uses the balance of costs and savings to stochastically decide to accept a given request for cooperation. From the experiments conducted, it has been shown that agents can use reciprocal behaviour to adapt to the environment and improve their individual performance. In the long run, it is better for agents to be reciprocative as their performance is better than that of selfish agents.

The line of work described above, however, assumes that agents have fixed behaviours. More realistically, agents should be able to change their behaviours as appropriate, based on observed performance. Research by Sen and Dutta [66] explores this. Instead of working in groups of agents having up to two behaviour types, the authors experimented with mixed groups of selfish, reciprocative and philanthropic agents (who always help when asked). Different variants of these behaviours have been used, as follows.

- Believing reciprocative agents use the balances reported by other agents, together with their own when deciding on whether to help or not. Agents of this variant can quickly identify and shun exploitative agents.
- Earned-trust based reciprocative agents consider only the balances of those agents with whom they themselves have favourable balances, when they evaluate a request to help.
- Individual lying selfish agents reveal false impressions about other helpful agents to ruin their reputation.
- Collaborative lying selfish agents tarnish the reputation of helpful agents and also collaboratively boost that of other selfish agents.

Experimental results show that this work corroborates with Sen's previous work and improves it further by making the behaviour of the agents adaptive to more closely represent a more realistic model.

This model does not, however, capture the dynamics of the evolution of an agent population and the authors plan to incorporate a method to predict the behavioural composition of the agent population over time.

8.2.4.12 SPORAS and HISTOS

Zacharia et al. [79, 80] believe that online communities have specific problems which must be addressed by reputation mechanisms for these domains. In online communities, it is relatively easy for agents to change their identity.

SPORAS is a reputation mechanism for loosely connected online communities. In this system the trusting agent bases its opinion of the reputation of its interaction partner on the feedback the latter gives on the trustworthiness of their latest transaction. Only the most recent ratings are stored for agents who have repeated interactions. A new user will have the minimum reputation which is gradually built up as the agent interacts with others. However unreliable an agent may be, its reputation value will nevertheless be higher than that of a new agent. With this strategy, a user is always worse off when it switches identities.

While SPORAS provides a global reputation value to each agent in the online community, HISTOS is a more sophisticated approach which takes into consideration information about its peers when available. Agents in this system rely more on recommendations given by agents they trust than those given by agents that they have never interacted with previously. HISTOS builds a social network from the pairwise ratings it has previously obtained. This is represented as a directed graph with the nodes representing the agents and the weighted edges representing the most recent reputation rating given by one agent to another. The transitive trust relationships are thus applied where there are directed paths between two agents.

8.2.4.13 Griffiths and Luck

Griffiths and Luck [32] consider an extension to a BDI agent architecture, particularly to enhance the process of plan selection. BDI agents are based around their beliefs, about themselves and others in their environment, their desires of what they want to achieve, and their intentions, made up of actions and subgoals which are represented as adopted plans. Cooperation among agents takes the form of interactions with others and a plan can consist of the following three types of actions.

- Individual actions are those performed by an agent, without the help of any other agent. They can be performed by the owner of the plan or by another agent on its behalf.
- Joint actions are made up of individual actions that must be performed together by a group of agents, such that each individual action contributes to the joint action.
- Concurrent actions are parallel actions performed by different agents, where no synchronisation is required.

Plan selection involves choosing the best plan, that is, the plan that is most likely to succeed in terms of least cost of time and resources and least risk. The element of risk is increased in the situation where there are other agents involved in an agent's plans. Besides assessing the likely cost of a plan, an agent also needs to assess the likelihood of finding the agents for the actions that are required to execute the plan, the likelihood that those agents, once found, are likely to cooperate and, once committed, that those agents will actually fulfil their commitments. Four factors have been identified for comparing plans with respect to risk.

- Agent capabilities: Knowing the capabilities of other agents helps to identify which agents can perform the actions required. Even though this knowledge may not not be fully representative, it is assumed to be stable enough to assess plans.
- Risk from others: The risks involved in interacting with the identified potential partners are evaluated so that those who are more likely to be successful are chosen to execute the plans.
- Risk from the view of self: The knowledge of how other agents view oneself is a good measure of the likelihood that they will be likely to cooperate.
- Agent preferences: Plans can also be assessed in terms of the level of motivation of the agents to cooperate.

In this approach, trust is used as a means for an agent to estimate the risks involved in cooperating with others. The model of trust used is based on Marsh's model [47] and the work by Gambetta [27]. The authors utilise Marsh's general trust notion, which looks at the trust one agent has in another, without considering the situation. They do not consider the details of how agents update their trust in others.

When assessing a plan, an agent can use two types of ratings: standard and cooperative. The standard rating is based on standard domain-independent heuristics to evaluate plans, with heuristics including the number of actions in a plan and the cost of the actions it contains. However, the estimates of the risk linked with each action of the plan that requires cooperation, need to be taken into account. A *cooperative rating* is thus determined by summing the risk associated with each action in the plan. Both the standard and cooperative ratings are then combined to form an overall measure of plan quality to enable the selection between alternative applicable plans.

8.2.4.14 MDT-R

MDT-R [30] is a mechanism of Multi-Dimensional Trust and Recommendations. Agents model the trustworthiness of others according to various criteria, such as cost, timeliness or success, depending on which criteria the agent considers important. Agents use their own direct experience of interacting with others, as well as recommendations. Distinguishing trust and recommendations for individual characteristics is valuable in identifying the service characteristics in which the providing agents perform well, or less well. Trust information in multiple dimensions helps to maintain the original interaction data. Trust values are represented numerically in this approach due to the benefits of accuracy and the ease of comparison and update of values. However, MDT-R stratifies trust into levels (*à la* Ntropi) for ease of comparison. The sharing of information among agents often suffers from subjectivity, due to differences in interpretation. MDT-R deals with this by sharing summaries of relevant past interactions, instead of explicit values for trust.

8.2.4.15 FIRE

Huynh et al. [35] propose FIRE, a trust and reputation model that integrates many different information sources to produce a comprehensive assessment of an agent's likely performance. FIRE is designed for open multi-agent systems (MAS), where agents can be owned by several stakeholders and can join and leave the system at at time. Other characteristics of open MAS agents include the assumption that they are unreliable and self-interested. The agents also know a limited amount about their environment and there is no central authority that controls all the agents. Due to the incomplete knowledge about their environment and other agents, trust can facilitate the interactions between agents.

In order to meet the requirements of open MAS, the authors believe that a trust model should possess the following properties.

- The model should take into account a variety of sources of trust information so that the trust measure can be more precise, and to cater for cases when not all sources are available.
- Every agent should be able to evaluate trust for itself.
- The model should be robust against possible lying agents.

FIRE makes use of four different types of trust and reputation sources: interaction trust, role-based trust, witness reputation and certified reputation. These various sources are important in the model as they ensure a combination of available information sources and that a trust measure is obtained whenever it is needed for interaction.

Interaction trust models the trust that occurs as a result of direct interactions between two agents. The individual dimension of the Regret system [60] is adopted as it meets all the requirements for handling direct experiences. Role-based trust models the role-based relationships between two agents and rules are used to assign values to this particular type of trust. One benefit of using rules is that users can add new rules to customise their applications. The witness reputation of an agent X is built on the observations of its behaviour by other agents, acting as witnesses. For an agent Y to evaluate the witness reputation of agent X, Y must find witnesses that have interacted with X. Agents keep a list of acquaintances and query a number of them when a query needs to be made. If the acquaintances cannot answer, they will send referrals pointing to other agents that they think will know the answer. The last kind of information source is certified reputation, where ratings are presented by the rated agent about itself which have been obtained from its partners in previous interactions. An agent is allowed to choose which ratings to show and because rational agents will always present their best ratings, it should be assumed that certified reputation information is an over-estimate of the agent's actual performance. This type of information source is valuable due to its high availability and can hence be used, even when the other three sources cannot provide a trust measure.

The four trust and reputation measures are combined to generate a single composite value, representing an overall picture of an agent's likely performance. Using the weighted mean method, a composite trust value and its reliability are calculated. Through empirical evaluation, the authors show how FIRE helps agents to select more reliable partners for interaction. In a simulated open MAS, FIRE helps agents to obtain better utility and to quickly adapt to a changing environment while maintaining a high performance.

FIRE, however assumes that agents report their trust and reputation information truthfully, thus the model does not yet deal with lying agents. This model is deemed to be ad hoc due to the hand-crafted formulae used to calculate trust [70].

Even though the model differentiates between the concepts of trust and reputation, it does not consider the further notions of untrust, distrust and mistrust, as used by Marsh [49]. The authors are also not clear about how the different trust and reputation measures are updated in the light of new information obtained.

8.2.4.16 TRAVOS

The Trust and Reputation model for Agent-based Virtual OrganisationS (TRAVOS) models an agent's trust in an interaction partner [70]. The model uses probability theory to calculate trust from information about the past interactions between agents. In addition, the model makes use of reputation information from third parties when a lack of personal experience makes direct interaction information unavailable. Dealing with third party information has the risk of inaccuracy and the model handles this aspect.

The model aims to meet the following three requirements.

- A trust metric should be provided to represent the level of trust in an agent, both in the presence or absence of personal experience. It will also be used to compare the trustworthiness of different agents.
- An agent's confidence in its level of trust in another agent should be reflected in the model.
- The model should be able to cope with inaccurate information from other agents, by discounting those opinions in the calculation of reputation.

For any two interacting agents, a history of interactions is recorded as the number of successful and unsuccessful interactions. From this, the variable $B_{a_{tr},a_{te}}$ is obtained, which is the probability that the trustee a_{te} will fulfil its obligations during an interaction with the truster a_{tr}. Thus, using the history of past interactions, the expected value of $B_{a_{tr},a_{te}}$ at a particular time t is calculated using a probability distribution, and is defined as $\tau_{a_{tr},a_{te}}$. If the truster has a low confidence level in its assessment of the trustworthiness of a partner, it can seek the opinions of third party agents. Reputation is modelled as a combination of the true and reported opinions of a source a_{op} about a trustee a_{te}. The authors claim that two conditions must hold for the trust and confidence levels from third party observations to be the same as they would be if all observations had been observed by the truster itself. The first condition states that the behaviour of the trustee must be independent of the identity of the truster with which it is interacting. Secondly, the reputation provider must report its observations accurately and truthfully. However, in a range of situations, these conditions cannot be expected to hold.

When either of the two conditions are broken, inaccurate reputation reports are obtained, due to malicious agents or to inconsistent behaviour towards different agents. In the literature, endogenous and exogenous techniques [37] have been used to assess the reliability of reports. Endogenous methods attempt to identify unreliable reputation information by considering the statistical properties of the reported opinions alone. Meanwhile, exogenous methods rely on other information to make a judgement, for example using the reputation of the source or its relationship with the trustee. TRAVOS proposes an exogenous method to filter out inaccurate reputation, where a reputation provider is judged on the perceived accuracy of its past opinions. In the first step, the probability that an agent will provide an accurate opinion is calculated, given its past opinions and later observed interactions with the trustees for which opinions were given. Secondly, based on this value, the distance is reduced between a rater's opinion and the prior belief that all the possible values for an agent's behaviour are equally probable. In having all the opinions adjusted in this way, the opinion provider's influence on a truster's assessment of a trustee is reduced.

Empirical experiments demonstrate that TRAVOS allows reputation to significantly improve performance despite the negative effects of inaccurate opinions.

However, the model assumes that the behaviour of agents does not change over time, but in many cases this is not a suitable assumption. The representation of the interaction ratings is considered to be oversimplified and limited for this model to be suitable for a wide variety of applications in open MAS [36].

The model makes use of a truster a_{tr}'s estimate that a trustee a_{te} will fulfil its obligations and the confidence a_{tr} has in this value. The authors calculate the confidence metric as the proportion of the probability distribution for the trust metric that lies within the bounds of an error value estimate ε, that is, between $(\tau_{a_{tr},a_{te}} - \varepsilon)$ and $(\tau_{a_{tr},a_{te}} + \varepsilon)$. It is however unclear how this error ε is determined and what is considered to be an acceptable error margin.

Third party recommendations are obtained from those agents who have directly interacted with the agent of interest. TRAVOS does not consider indirect recommendations where an agent obtains the opinion of another agent, who has obtained it from some other agent. This source of information could be useful when not enough information is obtained from agents who have directly interacted with the target agents.

8.2.4.17 Walter et al.

Walter et al. [73] propose a recommendation system on a social network, based on trust. In their model, agents use their social network to gather information and they use trust relationships to filter information they require. Agents get recommendations from neighbours, which are agents directly or indirectly connected in the network. Neighbours pass on queries to their own neighbours when they cannot provide a recommendation themselves. Agents use trust in their decision making, to choose the most appropriate recommendation from a set of recommendations obtained from a query.

Agents are connected in a social network and each agent is linked to a set of neighbours. For example, a group of people recommending books form such a network. Objects are the subject of recommendations, and in the example books are objects. Objects can belong to one or more categories, for instance, books can be in the categories "Computer Science" or "History". Agents are also associated with a preference profile, which maps a rating to an object. Trust relationships exist among agents when they keep trust values of their neighbours. The model considers that trust is transitive and propagates along a path in the network, with the appropriate discounting. The trust value along a path is the product of the trust values of the links on that path. When an agent makes a query, it receives a set of responses back from its neighbours. The agent must then choose the best recommendation for its purposes from the set. The trust values provide a ranking of the recommendations, and the selection mechanism in the model is random selection among all the recommendations with probabilities assigned by a logic function. The higher the trust of recommendations along a path, the higher its probability of being chosen. Once the recommendation is chosen and an interaction occurs as a result of this recommendation, the agent feeds the experience back into the trust relationship with the recommender.

The authors claim that the system self-organises in a state with performance near to optimum. Despite the fact that agents only consider their own utility function and without explicit coordination, long paths of high trust develop in the network, allowing agents to rely on recommendations from agents with similar preferences, even when these are far away in the network.

8.2.5 Summary of Views of Trust and Reputation Models

The trust and reputation models discussed all attempt to provide solutions to accurately represent these notions in cooperation among agents. Nevertheless, they are limited and deal with only some of the important considerations necessary when looking at open and distributed multi-agent systems.

8.2.5.1 Socio-Cognitive Models

The models based on the cognitive and social nature of trust among agents detail the important aspects to consider, such as competence, willingness and motivation of the agent in trust-building. However, they do not explicitly define how these aspects are to be represented and used. Moreover, both models reviewed [16, 50] do not model dishonest agents and ways to deal with lying or collusion.

8.2.5.2 Numerical Models

Numerical models allow trust and reputation to be explicitly represented as values, which can be used for further analysis and decision-making. However, one concern is that they tend to over-simplify those notions and the important considerations in obtaining those values tend to be blurred and are no longer readily available once the trust value has been calculated. The values used in the calculations and the formulae also tend to be ad hoc in nature and there is often a lack of justification for the choice of calculation methods. Furthermore, with information being increasingly shared among agents, the trust values and their meanings can prove to be an obstacle to the efficient propagation of trust and reputation for other agents to use. While a particular number and formula can be perfectly satisfactory for an agent's sole use, their value on sharing can be very much reduced.

8.2.5.3 Reputational Models

Most reputational models have used reputation as the complement of trust. In doing so, they have reinforced the information from direct interaction with information from third-party agents. Models like TRAVOS do not make use of indirect recommendations. This could be a problem when direct recommendations and direct interactions are rare and the agent needs to get information about the trustworthiness of another. Moreover, many reputational models do not handle lying and dishonest agents or differentiate between mistakes in opinion and malevolent behaviour.

8.3 Agents and Service-Oriented Computing

Trust and reputation can be very useful concepts in establishing, managing and maintaining cooperation, along with providing a mechanism to minimise the risk associated with interacting with others. In this section we discuss how trust and reputation can be integrated with two alternative views of SOC, namely peer-to-peer and Grid computing.

8.3.1 Peer-to-Peer Architectures

A Peer-to-Peer (P2P) system can be defined as a self-organising system of equal, autonomous entities, which aim for the shared usage of distributed resources in a networked environment, avoiding central services [52,68]. Self-organisation expresses properties, including the distribution of control, the locality of processing, and the emergence of global structures from local interactions [3]. P2P systems are generally classified into two categories: structured and unstructured overlay networks. Overlay networks construct a logical network on top of the physical network, to help in application-specific organisation in P2P systems. Unstructured P2P systems, such as Gnutella [7] use flooding techniques to discover other peers in the network, as peers are randomly connected. Look-up queries are forwarded to all the neighbouring peers and results are sent back until the required item or peer is found. In contrast, structured P2P systems, such as Chord [69], use structures such as Distributed Hash Tables (DHTs) to achieve scalability, reliability and fault tolerance. Structured systems organise peers in a clear logical way, which allows them to be located and identified.

The issue of trust arises from the decentralisation characteristic of P2P systems. In some dynamic environments, repeated interactions with the same peers might be few and this makes the evaluation of risk associated with the transaction difficult. Some other P2P applications, such as those involving file sharing, might involve the peers needing to also evaluate the credibility of other peers to avoid interacting with malicious ones. In the absence of a central point of control, trust needs to be built into the P2P system to ensure that peers are treated fairly. However, information about peer interactions is dispersed throughout the network and peers can only build a partial view. Moreover, the trust information stored by peers cannot be considered as entirely trustworthy. Several trust and reputation mechanisms have been proposed in that respect and these are described below.

8.3.1.1 PeerTrust

PeerTrust [78] is a reputation-based trust supporting framework that consists of an adaptive trust model for quantifying and comparing the trustworthiness of peers based on a transaction-based feedback system, as well as a decentralised implementation of the model over a structured P2P network. The model uses five parameters to evaluate the trustworthiness of a peer. The three basic trust parameters are the feedback from other peers, the total number of transactions performed by a peer and the credibility of the feedback sources. PeerTrust also uses two adaptive factors: a transaction context factor and a community context factor. The model also defines a general trust metric to combine all these parameters. Two basic trust parameters (feedback and the number of transactions) can be collected automatically. The third parameter—the credibility of feedback—needs to be computed from the past behaviour of the peers who give feedback and the authors propose two credibility measures to determine the credibility factor and compute the credible amount of satisfaction. The first measure is based on a function of the trust value of a peer as its credibility factor. Therefore, feedback from more trustworthy peers are considered more credible. This is based on the assumptions that: (i) untrustworthy peers are more likely to submit false feedback to hide their malicious behaviour, and (ii) trustworthy peers are more likely to be honest about the feedback they provide. The authors, however, argue that the second assumption may not hold in some cases, for instance, when a peer maintains good reputation by providing a high quality of service, but sends malicious feedback about its competitors. For such cases, a second credibility measure is proposed and a peer uses a personalised similarity measure to rate the credibility of another peer through its experience of the feedback given.

Srivatsa et al. propose TrustGuard [67] as an extension to PeerTrust. TrustGuard is a framework for building dependable distributed reputation management systems and proposes countermeasures against three vulnerabilities: strategic oscillation, fake transaction and dishonest feedback.

8.3.1.2 Personalised Trust Model (PET)

PET [45] is a personalised trust model for P2P resource sharing, which aims to build good cooperation among peers. It is an intermediate trust model and lies between the central and transitive models of trust. The central model has a central trust point and every entity in the system uses that same trust opinion, such as in eBay. This class of trust model works well when the central point is reliable and trustworthy and provides only one type of service. The other class of trust model, the transitive model has a transitive trust chain where recommendations are used. In PET, recommendation plays a moderate role and is only one of many factors used to derive local trustworthiness values. PET models reputation as the accumulative assessment of the long-term behaviour (reputation evaluation) and the opinion of the short-term behaviour (risk evaluation). The model quantifies these two behaviours and the weights of reputation and risk are adjustable, according to different environments and requirements.

PET is combined with M-CUBE, a multiple-currency based economic model, to enable resource sharing in untrusted P2P environments [44]. The M-CUBE model provides the infrastructure for building high-level resource management related services and is made up of four main modules: (i) the Price Regulator, which decides the price of the resources, (ii) the Ratio Regulator determines the exchange ratio of the currency, based on the trustworthiness value computed by the PET model, (iii) Service Discovery finds the resources provided by remote peers, and (iv) the Currency Exchange module enables bargaining among peers until an agreed currency exchange is reached.

8.3.1.3 P2PRep and XRep

P2PRep [19] is an approach that allows a servent (a peer acting as both server and client) in a P2P network to enquire about the reputation of providers before deciding from where to download a resource, by polling its peers. After receiving responses to its query when looking for a resource, the servent selects a provider or a set of providers based on the quality of the offer and on its own past experience. It then polls its peers asking for their opinion about the reputation of each of the selected providers. The servent can then make a decision by using the opinions obtained from the voters.

There are two approaches to P2PRep: the first one is called *basic polling* and involves the servents responding to a poll to not provide their servent identity. The second approach called *enhanced polling*, requires the voters to declare their servent identity. This can be used by the servent, which is selecting a provider, to weigh the votes it has received according to the level of credibility of the voters.

XRep [21] is a protocol for maintaining and exchanging reputations that can be instantiated on existing P2P protocols. The aim is to provide a self-regulating system that implements a robust reputation mechanism in the P2P network, to solve the problem of user anonymity and the subsequent misuses and abuses of the network. Compared to related work (e.g., [4, 19]), which associate reputation to the servents, XRep combines resource-based and servent-based reputation to bring together advantages from both approaches. This approach thus provides more informative polling and also overcomes the limitations of servent-based only solutions. Servent reputations are associated with the servent identity, which must be resistant against tampering. Meanwhile, resource reputations are closely linked to the content of the resources, via a digest, and this prevents forging from malicious peers.

Resource-based reputation has the benefit of having votes that express the property of the resource rather than the provider, making it more reliable. However, resource-based reputation can only be applied when resources have a history and are known to several servents. Thus, by using both reputations, XRep can efficiently protect P2P networks against attacks such as self-replication, pseudospoofing and shilling.

X^2Rep [20] is presented as an enhanced trust semantics algorithm that extends the XRep protocol, to address the weaknesses of XRep in producing the correct trust values when used against a range of strategies that can be employed by malicious agents. The algorithm gives additional expressiveness to peers when giving their opinions about resources and other peers. Whereas XRep uses a series of challenge and response messages to ensure that a vote is provided by a genuine peers, X^2Rep eliminates this complex process by using voter credibility information, which helps to assess the trustworthiness of a voter's vote.

8.3.1.4 P-Grid

Aberer et al. [2,4] proposed a decentralised trust management model, called P-Grid, that they implemented on a P2P system. Their aim was to find a solution to the problems of search efficiency and resource allocation optimisation, by using a self-organisation process to construct an overlay network that uses a DHT-like routing infrastructure. P-Grid is a P2P look-up system, based on a virtual distributed search tree, which is similar in structure to a standard DHT [2].

The model analyses past interactions among peers to make a probabilistic assessment of whether any peer has cheated. It integrates trust management as well as a scalable data management scheme, suitable for decentralised networks. The trust management method models global trust as a binary value, that is whether an agent is trustworthy or not. The reputations in this system arise from the dissemination of information by peers about the malicious behaviour of others. Only malicious behaviour is considered as relevant and this is expressed as complaints; the more complaints a peer gets, the less trustworthy it could be. The reputation of an agent p is calculated as the number of complaints p stored, multiplied by the number of complaints about p stored by other agents. Higher values of this reputation indicate that agent p is not trustworthy. The downside to this model is that since only complaints are recorded, new peers are considered to be as trustworthy as peers who have had many successful interactions.

8.3.1.5 Other P2P Applications of Trust and Reputation for Service-Oriented Agents

Jurca and Faltings [38] propose a reputation-based mechanism that allows a P2P service-oriented market to function efficiently, with the aim of maintaining a cooperative equilibrium. The mechanism is based on averaging feedback and repeated failures influence the price that the provider can charge in the future. This is different to other mechanisms, such as eBay, where repeated failures lead to the exclusion of the provider from the market. Thus, the proposed reputation-based mechanism works through flexible service level agreements (SLAs) in the form of incentives, rather than social exclusion.

Gupta et al. [33] propose a reputation system for decentralised unstructured P2P networks like Gnutella. The system comprises two schemes: *debit-credit reputation computation* (DCRC), and *credit-only reputation computation* (CORC), that utilise objective criteria for updating peer reputations. DCRC updates the reputation scores based on the average query-response message size, the upload credit, the download debit and the sharing credit. CORC differs from DCRC by not using the download debit component, implying that the peer reputation scores only increase.

Farenholtz and Lamersdorf [26] propose a reputation management system, which uses context-dependent feedback gathered in questionnaires and provides security for peer transactions to ensure integrity, confidentiality and privacy.

Liau et al. [46] propose a completely decentralised reputation scheme for P2P networks, based on the concept of Public Key Infrastructure (PKI). It is based on a certificate *RCert*, which is a tamper resistant document that resides on a P2P node. RCert contains the information ratings collected from past interactions with other peers and simplifies the reputation request process, as the reputation is stored by the owner. To ensure that the owner does not change any information, every update to the certificate is digitally signed by the rating peer. The authors also present the protocols *RCertP* and *RCertPX* to facilitate the updating of the *RCert* certificates.

Credence [72] is a decentralised object reputation and ranking system for large-scale P2P filesharing networks. It allows honest peers to assess the authenticity of online content through secure tabulation and management of endorsements from other peers. Credence also enables peers to learn relationships even in the absence of direct observations or interactions through a flow-based trust computation to discover trustworthy peers.

8.3.2 Grid Computing

A Grid can be considered to be a decentralised system that spans multiple administrative domains and provides a nontrivial quality of service where both the set of users and the total set of resources can (and do) vary dynamically and continuously [74]. It handles large numbers of hardware and software systems to perform functions and computations on large volumes of data. Uniform and transparent access to heterogeneous systems (again hardware and software) is provided to both end users and their applications. In a grid computing system, autonomous domains share resources among themselves. One primary goal of the grid environment is to encourage domain-to-domain interactions and increase the confidence of domains to use or share resources. One way to achieve this is to address the notion of trust, to make the geographically distributed systems more attractive and reliable. Trust is used to firstly verify the identity of an entity and what that entity is authorised to do and secondly, to monitor and manage the behaviour of the entity and building a trust level based on the behaviour.

8.3.2.1 Trust-Aware Resource Management System

Azzedin and Maheswaran [10, 11] present a trust-aware resource management system, which includes a model of behaviour trust, based on trust from direct interactions, as well as reputation. In this model, the Grid is viewed as a set of grid domains and there are two virtual domains associated with each grid domain: resource domain and client domain. Behaviour trust consists of 6 trust levels and these trust levels are built on past experiences and are context-specific and time-specific. Each domain maintains trust level tables about its trust relationships with other domains. The authors suggest that the efficient creation and maintenance of the trust level tables is made possible due to three reasons. First, the division of the grid into grid domains increases scalability as resources and clients inherit parameters of the resource and client domains. Second, trust is considered to vary slowly, thereby making the update overhead insignificant. Finally, the model limits the number of contexts to only the primary service types and this reduces the fragmentation of the trust management space. This reduction of the number of contexts is seen by Alunkal et al. [8] to be a limitation of this model as the Grid environment involves many more contexts and the model should be able to include all the essential features of a Grid infrastructure.

8.3.2.2 CONOISE-G

The CONOISE-G system [55] provides mechanisms to assure the effective operation of agent-based virtual organisations (VOs) in the face of disruptive and potentially malicious entities in dynamic, open and competitive environments, such as the Grid environment. The system uses three key technologies for the formation of virtual organisations, namely agent decision-making, auctions for the allocation of contracts and service discovery that includes the assessment of quality of service. The issues of trust and reputation are important especially during the formation of a virtual organisation, when there is a choice of various service providers to whom tasks may be delegated. In such cases, trust serves as an indicator of which of the possible partners are likely to carry out the task specified. The probabilistic view of trust is considered and in the absence of a direct interaction history, reputation information is used to establish the level of trust to place in another entity. CONOISE-G makes use of the TRAVOS trust and reputation model [54, 70] to establish trust and reputation in the system.

8.3.2.3 GridEigenTrust

The GridEigenTrust framework [8] is used to manage reputation for Grid-based systems, to facilitate a distributed and efficient mechanism for resource selection. The framework's reputation management service includes a hierarchical resource selection process, which addresses the complex arrangement of resources and services among virtual organisations, institutions and entities. This selection process is complemented with the past quantitative and qualitative experiences of resource selection, as well as with a ranking of resources and services based on their reputation. GridEigenTrust uses trust and reputation as the dynamic and adaptive metrics to support their quality of service requirements. The framework also introduces a novel algorithm to evaluate Grid reputation on a more scalable level for large Grid environments. The algorithm combines global trust with the use of eigenvectors, which is based on the P2P EigenTrust algorithm [39]. Combining eigenvectors with a global trust value addresses the problems related to scalability and multiple contexts as encountered in other models [10, 11].

8.3.2.4 PathTrust

PathTrust [40] is a reputation model proposed for member selection in virtual organisations. The reputation model makes use of the relationships among the participant members to form a web of trust, and views reputation as a function of the inquirer and the queried. The algorithm used in PathTrust combines transitive trust with reputation ratings. The use of trust relationships among participants helps to guard against the faking of positive feedback. The trust relationship between two participants is formed when they interact with each other and each leaves a feedback rating after each transaction. The reputation can then be established as a function of all the ratings left from the interactions each individual has made. Each participant must register with the Enterprise Network Infrastructure (EN) to become a member of a virtual organisation, by providing some credentials. The EN also provides a centralised reputation service. When the VO dissolves, all members leave feedback ratings with the reputation server for other members to use. In PathTrust, the system is arranged as as fully connected graph among all the participants that are registered with the EN. Each edge has an associated weight that provides a relative measure of the trust one participant has in another. PathTrust also supports the growth of the system. The algorithm has been evaluated against the EigenTrust algorithm [39] and is shown to have benefits in attack resistance compared to models that view reputation as a function of the queried only.

8.4 Trust Classes and Ontologies

Grandison and Sloman [28] present a classification of trust in Internet services, relating to access to a trustor's resources, provision of a service by the trustee, authentication, delegation, or infrastructure. Josang et al. [37] also use this classification of trust when specifying trust semantics.

Access trust

Trust comes into play when a trustor allows a trustee to use resources he owns or controls, and these resources can be a software execution environment or an application service [5, 6]. For different types of access and resources being accessed, the trust level will be different. For instance, trusting an entity to read a file on the trustor's server is different from trusting the entity to execute code on the trustor's workstation. The latter case necessitates a higher level of trust in the trustee, since issues such as damage to the trustor's resources, as well as usage limits have to be taken into account. Abrams and Joyce implicitly map trust decisions to access control decisions. The resource access trust relationships can be used to specify authorisation policies, which can then be implemented using an operating system, a database access control mechanism, or firewall rules, among others. The authorisation policies specify the actions that a trustee can perform on the trustor's resources and the constraints that apply, such as the time periods when access is permitted.

Service provision trust

This form of trust involves the trustee in providing a service, that does not involve access to the trustor's resources. Examples where service provision trust needs to be established include application service providers. Service provision can relate to different trust attributes, as follows.

- *Confidence*—for example, trusting a web site to provide information which is not offensive. This type of trust maps into a form of access control and can be implemented by some Web browsers as a means to screen sites or content.
- *Competence* of the trustee—this differs from confidence trust, as confidence applies to entities that the trustor will use, while competence applies to entities that perform some action on behalf of the trustee.
- *Reliability* or *integrity* of the trustee—for example in e-banking, the customer trusts the bank to support mechanisms that will ensure that passwords are not divulged.

Identity trust

This type of trust relies on the certification of the trustworthiness of a trustee by a third party. Certifications are often used to authenticate identity or membership in Internet applications. This is a special case of service provision trust as the certification authority is providing a trust certification service.

Delegation trust

This involves the trustor trusting a trustee to make decisions on its behalf, with respect to a resource or service that the trustor owns or controls. For example, delegation is also a special form of service provision: a trust decision making service.

Context trust

Grandison and Sloman [28] use the term infrastructure trust to describe that the trustor must be able to trust the base infrastructure, namely himself (implicit trust) and the workstation, network and servers he uses. These may implement security and other services in order to protect the trustor's infrastructure. Moreover, Josang et al. [37] consider that besides infrastructures, insurance, the legal system, law enforcement and social stability are factors that the trustor deems necessary to be in place to support his transactions.

8.4.1 Trust Semantics

Josang et al. [37] classify trust semantics in a *specificity-generality* dimension and a *subjectivity-objectivity* dimension, as shown in Table 8.2. The semantic characteristics of ratings, reputation scores and trust measures are important in order for participants to be able to interpret those measures.

Table 8.2 Classification of trust and reputation measures [37]

	Specific, vector based	General, synthesised
Subjective	Survey questionnaires	ebay, voting
Objective	Product tests	Synthesised general score from product tests, D&B rating

A *specific* measure relates to a particular trust aspect, such as the timeliness of delivery, whereas a *general* measure represents an average of all the trust aspects. A *subjective* measure means that the agent provides a rating based on a subjective judgement, while an *objective* measure is determined using some formal criteria.

Subjective and specific measures are used, for example in survey questionnaires where people are asked their opinions on a range of specific issues. *Subjective and general* measures are used in eBay's reputation system[1] where buyers and sellers leave feedback (1 for positive, 0 for neutral and −1 for negative).

Objective and specific measures are used, for example, in technical product tests where the performance and quality of of the product can be objectively measured. For instance, washing machines can be tested according to energy consumption, noise, washing program features, among others. Meanwhile, *objective and general* measures can be, for example, computed as a vector of objective and specific measures. A general score can be derived from a weighted average of the scores for each characteristic considered. For example, the Dun and Bradstreet (D&B) credit rating is derived from a vector of objectively measurable company performance parameters. D&B is an international credit reporting service, which uses a two-part rating code it its business reports, for example 5A 4 [53]. The first part of the rating, *Financial Strength*, reflects the the company's tangible net worth, derived from the latest available audited financial statements. The second part of the rating, the *Composite Credit Appraisal*, indicates D&B's calculation of the level of risk associated with dealing with a firm. Codes range from 1 to 4, where 1 is the lowest risk. D&B uses a scoring system based on 30 key company data elements to assign a risk factor. These elements come from the payment data, financial data, other public records, such as court judgements, and special events such as a press release that may affect the company's trading position.

8.5 Summary

In this chapter we have introduced some of the main approaches to trust and reputation. The first half of this chapter discussed a variety of mechanisms developed for general agent based systems. In the second half of the chapter we introduced how the notion of trust and reputation have been used in P2P architectures and Grid computing. Finally, we described generally applicable work on trust classes and trust semantics that will be useful in applying trust and reputation in future SOC systems.

References

1. A. Abdul-Rahman and S. Hailes. Supporting trust in virtual communities. In *Proceedings of the 33rd Hawaii International Conference on System Sciences (HICSS 2000)*, page 6007. IEEE Computer Society, 2000.

[1] http://www.ebay.com

2. K. Aberer, P. Cudré-Mauroux, A. Datta, Z. Despotovic, M. Hauswirth, M. Punceva, and R. Schmidt. P-Grid: a self-organizing structured P2P system. *ACM SIGMOD Record*, 32(3):29–33, 2003.
3. K. Aberer, A. Datta, and M. Hauswirth. P-grid: Dynamics of self-organizing processes in structured peer-to-peer systems. In R. Steinmetz and K. Wehrle, editors, *Peer-to-Peer Systems and Applications*, volume 3485 of *Lecture Notes in Computer Science*, pages 137–153. Springer-Verlag Berlin Heidelberg, 2005.
4. K. Aberer and Z. Despotovic. Managing trust in a peer-2-peer information system. In *Proceedings of the tenth international conference on Information and knowledge management (CIKM 2001)*, pages 310–317, New York, NY, USA, 2001. ACM.
5. M. D. Abrams and M. V. Joyce. New thinking about information technology security. *Computers and Security*, 14(1):69–81, 1995.
6. M. D. Abrams and M. V. Joyce. Trusted computing update. *Computers and Security*, 14(1):57–68, 1995.
7. E. Adar and B. A. Huberman. Free riding on gnutella. *First Monday*, 5(10), 2000.
8. B. K. Alunkal, I. Valjkovic, G. von Laszewski, and K. Amin. Reputation-based grid resource selection. Workshop on Adaptive Grid Middleware (AGridM 2003), September 28, 2003, New Orleans LA, USA. To appear in Journal of Parallel and Distributed Computing Practices.
9. R. Axelrod and W. D. Hamilton. The evolution of cooperation. *Science Magazine*, 211(4489), 1981.
10. F. Azzedin and M. Maheswaran. Evolving and managing trust in grid computing systems. In *Proceedings of the IEEE Canadian Conference on Electrical & Computer Engineering (CCECE 2002)*, volume 3, 2002.
11. F. Azzedin and M. Maheswaran. Integrating trust into grid resource management systems. In *Proceedings of the 2002 International Conference on Parallel Processing (ICPP 2002)*, page 47, Washington, DC, USA, 2002. IEEE Computer Society.
12. S. Braynov and T. Sandholm. Contracting with uncertain level of trust. In *Proceedings of the 1st ACM conference on Electronic commerce*. ACM Press, 1999.
13. S. Braynov and T. Sandholm. Trust revelation in multiagent interaction. In *Proceedings of CHI 2002 Workshop on The Philosophy and Design of Socially Adept Technologies*, 2002.
14. V. Buskens. Social networks and the effect of reputation on cooperation. ISCORE Paper No. 42, Utrecht University, 1998.
15. Cambridge University Press. Cambridge Dictionaries Online. Available online at http://dictionary.cambridge.org.
16. C. Castelfranchi and R. Falcone. Principles of trust for MAS: Cognitive anatomy, social importance, and quantification. In *Proceedings of the International Conference of Multi-Agent Systems (ICMAS 1998)*, pages 72–79, 1998.
17. C. Castelfranchi and R. Falcone. Socio-cognitive theory of trust. Deliverable report D1, ALFEBIITE, 2001.
18. Cheskin Research and Studio Archetype/Sapient. eCommerce trust report. Technical report, Cheskin Research, 1999.
19. F. Cornelli, E. Damiani, S. De Capitani di Vimercati, S. Paraboschi, and P. Samarati. Choosing reputable servents in a p2p network. In *Proceedings of the 11th international conference on World Wide Web (WWW 2002)*, pages 376–386, New York, NY, USA, 2002. ACM.
20. N. Curtis, R. Safavi-Naini, and W. Susilo. X^2rep: Enhanced trust semantics for the xrep protocol. In *Applied Cryptography and Network Security (ACNS)*, volume 3089 of *Lecture Notes in Computer Science*, pages 205–219. Springer-Verlag Berlin Heidelberg, 2004.
21. E. Damiani, S. De Capitani di Vimercati, S. Paraboschi, P. Samarati, and F. Violante. A reputation-based approach for choosing reliable resources in peer-to-peer networks. In *Proceedings of the 9th ACM Conference on Computer and Communications Security*, Washington, DC, USA, November 2002.
22. B. Esfandiari and S. Chandrasekharan. On how agents make friends: Mechanisms for trust acquisition. In *Proceedings of the Fourth Workshop on Deception, Fraud and Trust in Agent Societies*, 2001.

23. R. Falcone and C. Castelfranchi. The socio-cognitive dynamics of trust: Does trust create trust? In *Proceedings of the workshop on Deception, Fraud, and Trust in Agent Societies held during the Autonomous Agents Conference: Trust in Cyber-societies, Integrating the Human and Artificial Perspectives*. Springer-Verlag, 2000.
24. R. Falcone and C. Castelfranchi. Social trust: A cognitive approach. In Cristiano Castelfranchi and Yao-Hua Tan, editors, *Trust and Deception in Virtual Societies*, pages 55–90. Kluwer Academic Publishers, Netherlands, 2001.
25. R. Falcone, G. Pezzulo, and C. Castelfranchi. A fuzzy approach to a belief-based trust computation. In R. Falcone, S. Barber, L. Korba, and M. Singh, editors, *Trust, Reputation and Security: Theories and Practice*, volume 2631 of *Lecture Notes in Artificial Intelligence*. Springer-Verlag, 2003.
26. D. Farenholtz and W. Lamesdorf. Transactional security for a distributed reputation management system. In *Proceedings of the Third Interantional Conference on E-Commerce and Web Technologies (EC-WEB 2002)*, volume 2455 of *Lecture Notes in Computer Science*, pages 214–223. Springer, 2002.
27. D. Gambetta. Can we trust trust? In *Trust: Making and Breaking of Cooperative Relations*, pages 213–237. Department of Sociology, University of Oxford, 2000.
28. T. Grandison and M. Sloman. A survey of trust in internet applications. *IEEE Communications and Surveys*, 3(4), Fourth Quarter 2000.
29. N. Griffiths. Task delegation using experience-based multi-dimensional trust. In *Proceedings of the 4th International Conference on Autonomous Agents and Multiagent Systems (AAMAS 2005)*, pages 489–496, New York, NY, USA, 2005. ACM Press.
30. N. Griffiths. Enhancing peer-to-peer collaboration using trust. *International Journal of Expert systems with Applications*, 31(4):849–858, 2006.
31. N. Griffiths, K.-M. Chao, and M. Younas. Fuzzy trust for peer-to-peer systems. In *Proceedings of P2P Data and Knowledge Sharing Workshop (P2P/DAKS 2006), at the 26th International Conference on Distributed Computing Systems (ICDCS 2006)*, 2006.
32. N. Griffiths and M. Luck. Cooperative plan selection through trust. In *Proceedings of Multi-Agent System Engineering: Proceedings of the Ninth European Workshop on Modelling Autonomous Agents in a Multi-Agent World*, volume 1647 of *Lecture Notes in Artificial Intelligence*, 1999.
33. M. Gupta, P. Judge, and M. Ammar. A reputation system for peer-to-peer networks. In *Proceedings of the 13th International Workshop on Network and Operating Systems Support for Digital Audio and Video (NOSSDAV 2003)*, pages 144–152. ACM, 2003.
34. S. P. Hargreaves-Heap and Y. Varoufakis. *Game Theory: A Critical Introduction*. Routledge, London, UK, 1997.
35. T. D. Huynh, N. R. Jennings, and N. Shadbolt. Developing an integrated trust and reputation model for open multi-agent systems. In *Proceedings of the 7th International Workshop on Trust in Agent Societies*, pages 65–74, New York, USA, 2004.
36. T. D. Huynh, N. R. Jennings, and N. Shadbolt. An integrated trust and reputation model for open multi-agent systems. *Journal of Autonomous Agents and Multi-Agent Systems*, 13(2):119–154, 2006.
37. A. Jøsang, R. Ismail, and C. Boyd. A survey of trust and reputation systems for online service provision. *Decision Support Systems*, 43(2):618–644, 2007.
38. R. Jurca and B. Faltings. Reputation-based pricing of P2P services. In *Proceedings of the Third Workshop on Economics of Peer-to-Peer Systems (P2PECON 2005)*, Philadelphia, USA, 2005.
39. S. D. Kamvar, M. T. Schlosser, and H. Garcia-Molina. The Eigentrust algorithm for reputation management in P2P networks. In *Proceedings of the 12th international conference on World Wide Web (WWW 2003)*, pages 640–651, New York, NY, USA, 2003. ACM.
40. F. Kerschbaum, J. Haller, Y. Karabulut, and P. Robinson. PathTrust: A trust-based reputation service for virtual organization formation. In *Proceedings of the 4th International Conference on Trust Management*, 2006.
41. B. Kosko. Fuzzy cognitive maps. *International Journal Man-Machine Studies*, 24, 1986.

42. D. M. Kreps and R. Wilson. Reputation and imperfect information. *Journal of Ecomonic Theory*, 27, 1982.
43. S. Kuhn. Prisoner's dilemma. The Stanford Encyclopedia of Philosophy (Fall 2003 Edition), Edward N. Zalta (ed.), available at http://plato.stanford.edu/archives/fall2003/entries/prisoner-dilemma/, 2003.
44. Z. Liang and W. Shi. Enforcing cooperative resource sharing in untrusted P2P computing environments. *Mobile Networks Applications*, 10(6):971–983, 2005.
45. Z. Liang and W. Shi. PET: A personalized trust model with reputation and risk evaluation for P2P resource sharing. In *Proceedings of the 38th Annual Hawaii International Conference on System Sciences (HICSS 2005)—Track 7*, page 201.2, Washington, DC, USA, 2005. IEEE Computer Society.
46. C.Y. Liau, X. Zhou, S. Bressan, and K.-L. Tan. Efficient distributed reputation scheme for peer-to-peer systems. In *Proceedings of the 2nd International Human.Society@Internet Conference (HSI 2003)*, volume 2713 of *Lecture Notes in Computer Science*, pages 54–63, Berlin Heidelberg, 2003. Springer-Verlag.
47. S. Marsh. *Formalising trust as a computational concept*. PhD thesis, Department of Computer Science, University of Stirling, 1994.
48. S. Marsh. Optimism and pessimism in trust. In H. Geffner, editor, *Proceedings of IV Ibero-American Conference on Artificial Intelligence (IBERAMIA 1994)*, pages 286–297. Addison-Wesley, 1994.
49. S. Marsh and M. R. Dibben. Trust, untrust, distrust and mistrust – an exploration of the dark(er) side. In P. Herrmann et al., editor, *iTrust 2005, Lecture Notes in Computer Science*, volume 3477, pages 17–33, Berlin Heidelberg, 2005. Springer-Verlag.
50. N. Mezzetti. A socially inspired reputation model. In *Proceedings of the 1st European PKI Workshop (EuroPKI 2004)*. Springer-Verlag, 2004.
51. L. Mui, M. Mohtashemi, and A. Halberstadt. A computational model of trust and reputation for e-businesses. In *Proceedings of the 35th Annual Hawaii International Conference on System Sciences (HICSS 2002)*, volume 7, page 188, Washington, DC, USA, 2002. IEEE Computer Society.
52. A. Oram, editor. *Peer-to-Peer: Harnessing the Benefits of a Disruptive Technology.* O'Reilly, Sebastopol, CA, USA, 2001.
53. R. A. Pagell and M. Halperin. *International Business Information: How to Find It, How to Use It.* Greenwood Publishing Group, 1998.
54. J. Patel, W. T. L. Teacy, N. R. Jennings, and M. Luck. A probabilistic trust model for handling inaccurate reputation sources. In *Proceedings of the Third International Conference on Trust Management*, 2005.
55. J. Patel, W. T. L. Teacy, N. R. Jennings, M. Luck, S. Chalmers, N. Oren, T. J. Norman, A. Preece, P. M. D. Gray, G. Shercliff, P. J. Stockreisser, J. Shao, W. A. Gray, N. J. Fiddian, and S. Thompson. CONOISE-G: Agent-based virtual organisations for the grid. In *Proceedings of the 1st International Workshop on Smart Grid Technologies*, 2005.
56. S. D. Ramchurn, D. Huynh, and N. R. Jennings. Trust in multi-agent systems. *The Knowledge Engineering Review*, 19(1):1–25, 2004.
57. S. Russell and P. Norvig. *Artificial Intelligence: A Modern Approach.* Prentice Hall, New Jersey, USA, second edition, 2003.
58. J. Sabater. *Trust and Reputation in Agent Societies.* PhD thesis, Universitat Aùtomata de Barcelona (UAB), Spain, 2003.
59. J. Sabater. Evaluating the ReGreT system. *Applied Artificial Intelligence*, 18, 2004.
60. J. Sabater and C. Sierra. A reputation model for gregarious societies. In *Fourth Workshop on Deception Fraud and Trust in Agent Societies*, pages 61–70, 2001.
61. J. Sabater and C. Sierra. Review on computational trust and reputation models. *Artificial Intelligence Review*, 24:33–60, 2005.
62. M. Schillo. *Trust and Deceit in Multi-agent Systems.* PhD thesis, Department of Computer Science, Saarland University, Germany, 1999.

63. M. Schillo, P. Funk, and M. Rovatsos. Using trust for detecting deceitful agents in artificial societies. *Applied Artificial Intelligence, Special Issue on trust, Deception, and Fraud in Agent Societies*, 14(8):825–848, 2000.
64. J. Scott. *Social Network Analysis: a handbook.* Sage Publications, London, UK, 2001.
65. S. Sen. Reciprocity: A foundational principle for promoting cooperative behavior among self-interested agents. In Victor Lesser, editor, *Proceedings of the First International Conference on Multiagent Systems*, pages 322–329. MIT Press, 1996.
66. S. Sen and P. S. Dutta. The evolution and stability of cooperative traits. In C. Caltelfranchi and L. Johnson, editors, *Proceedings of the First Intenational Joint Conference on Autonomous Agents and Multiagent Systems*, volume 3, pages 1114–1120. ACM Press, 2002.
67. M. Srivatsa, L. Xiong, and L. Liu. TrustGuard: Countering vulnerabilities in reputation management for decentralized networks. In *Proceedings of the 14th World Wide Web Conference (WWW 2005)*, pages 422–431. ACM, 2005.
68. R. Steinmetz and K. Wehrle. What is this “peer-to-peer” about? In R. Steinmetz and K. Wehrle, editors, *Peer-to-Peer Systems and Applications*, volume 3485 of *Lecture Notes in Computer Science*, pages 9–16. Springer-Verlag Berlin Heidelberg, 2005.
69. I. Stoica, R. Morris, D. Karger, M. F. Kaashoek, and H. Balakrishnan. Chord: A scalable peer-to-peer lookup service for internet applications. In *Proceedings of the 2001 Conference on Applications, Technologies, Architectures, and Protocols for Computer Communications (SIGCOMM 2001)*, pages 149–160, New York, NY, USA, 2001. ACM.
70. W. T. L. Teacy, J. Patel, N. Jennings, and M. Luck. TRAVOS: Trust and reputation in the context of inaccurate information sources. *Autonomous Agents and Multi-Agent Systems*, 12(2):183–198, 2006.
71. J. von Newmann and O. Morgenstern. *Theory of Games and Economic Behaviour*. Princeton University Press, 60th anniversary edition edition, 2004.
72. K. Walsh and E. Gün Sirer. Experience with an object reputation system for peer-to-peer filesharing. In *Proceedings of the 3rd conference on 3rd Symposium on Networked Systems Design & Implementation (NSDI 2006)*, pages 1–14, Berkeley, CA, USA, 2006. USENIX Association.
73. F. E. Walter, S. Battiston, and F. Schweitzer. A model of a trust-based recommendation system on a social network. *Journal of Autonomous Agents and Multi-Agent Systems*, 16(1):57–74, 2008.
74. A. J. Wells. *Grid Application Systems Design.* Auerbach Publications, Boca Raton, FL, USA, 2008.
75. M. Witkowski, A. Artikis, and J. Pitt. Experiments in building experiential trust in a society of objective-trust based agents. In R. Falcone, M. Singh, and Y. H. Tan, editors, *Trust in Cyber Societies*, volume 2246 of *Lecture Notes in Artificial Intelligence*, pages 111–132. Springer-Verlag, 2001.
76. M. Witkowski and J. Pitt. Objective trust-based agents: Trust and trustworthiness in a multi-agent trading society. In *Proceedings of the 4th International Conference on MultiAgent Systems (ICMAS 2000)*, 2000.
77. D. J. Wu and Y. Sun. The emergence of trust in multi-agent bidding: A computational approach. In *Proceedings of the 34th Annual Hawaii International Conference on System Sciences (HICSS 2001)*, volume 1, page 1041, Washington DC, USA, 2001. IEEE Computer Society.
78. L. Xiong and L. Liu. PeerTrust: Supporting reputation-based trust for peer-to-peer electronic communities. *IEEE Transactions on Knowledge and Data Engineering*, 16(7), 2004.
79. G. Zacharia and P. Maes. Trust management through reputation mechanisms. *Applied Artificial Intelligence*, 14(9):881–907, 2000.
80. G. Zacharia, A. Moukas, and P. Maes. Collaborative reputation mechanisms in electronic marketplaces. In *Proceedings of the Thirty-second Annual Hawaii International Conference on System Sciences*, volume 8, page 8026. IEEE Computer Society, 1999.
81. L. Zadeh. Fuzzy sets. *Information and Control*, 8, 1965.

Chapter 9
QoS-Aware Service Selection

James W. J. Xue and Stephen A. Jarvis

Abstract With the widespread use of the Internet, the number of web services that can provide similar functionality has increased rapidly in recent years. Web service selection has to be based on some non-functional attributes of the services, such as the quality of service (QoS). In this chapter, we use a server switching service that is commonly used in Internet hosting environments to explain how an agent can use a performance model to evaluate services and select the most suitable services among a number of functionally similar services returned by the service discovery. The various criteria that can be used to assess QoS are introduced in this chapter, including mean response time, throughput, system utilisation and others closely related to business such as revenue and operating costs. Service selection in the chosen case study depends on the quality and suitability of various switching policies, in other words, different switching policies can be selected depending on the QoS of the services and the run-time system state. Since the system performance can be evaluated using an analytic model, therefore, the QoS of services is assessed based on the output of the performance model.

9.1 Introduction

There are two key challenges in Semantic Web services. One is service advertisement and discovery, which has been discussed in a previous chapter. The second key challenge is service selection and composition, which has attracted extensive research in the literature [1, 9, 11, 12, 23, 24, 27, 29].

James W. J. Xue
Department of Computer Science, University of Warwick, Coventry, CV4 7AL, UK
e-mail: W.J.Xue@warwick.ac.uk

Stephen A. Jarvis
Department of Computer Science, University of Warwick, Coventry, CV4 7AL, UK
e-mail: S.A.Jarvis@warwick.ac.uk

N. Griffiths, K.-M. Chao (eds.), *Agent-Based Service-Oriented Computing*, Advanced Information and Knowledge Processing,
DOI 10.1007/978-1-84996-041-0_9,

Web services are usually described by WSDL [28] and published by registering the service using UDDI [25]. Current approaches for service publication and registration rely on static description of web service interfaces. The static description is sufficient for providing some information such as service functionality, service URL and the service namespace. However, other attributes such as QoS can not be accurately described as it is runtime environment dependent. A web service might work well in one scenario, whereas it might be a bad choice for another scenario. Therefore, it is crucial to select the most suitable service among many functionally similar services.

The goal for service selection is to find the best set of services available at runtime, taking into consideration end-user preferences and the execution context [23]. It is a challenge task as it is very difficult to predict the QoS of a given web service. The challenge arises partly because you may not able to trust the other party who could claim arbitrary QoS properties to attract interested parties, and partly because you lack knowledge of the environment within which it is executing, especially in some runtime contexts where many factors could affect the performance of the service. Moreover, dynamic evaluation of service is usually required as the run-time system state is changing. In addition, all customer system environments are different, thus it is difficult for the service provider to test the service for all scenarios. Therefore, it might be a good idea that the agents be able to evaluate the quality of a service in different customised environments using a performance model.

In this chapter, we use a server switching service usually used in Internet hosting centres to explain how an agent can use a performance model to evaluate and select the most suitable services among a number of functionally similar services returned by the service discovery. Service selection in the chosen case study depends on the suitability and quality of various switching policies, that is different switching policies can be selected depending on the QoS of the services and the run-time system state. Since the system performance can be evaluated using a analytic model, therefore, the QoS of services is assessed based on the output of the performance model.

9.2 Service Selection Procedure

Figure 9.1 is an illustration of the service selection procedure. First, when a client sends a service request, the agent searches for services that can provide the required capabilities in the registry and uses the matchmaker to match the user requirements (in terms of the functionality required) with all available services. The output from the service matchmaker is a number of functionally similar services. The agent needs to choose the most suitable service among those services based on some non-functional attributes such as the QoS of the services. As introduced earlier, it is very difficult to present QoS using a static description in WSDL. Therefore, the performance evaluation manager can play a important role in the service selection process. Evaluation can be made through an analytical model, simulation

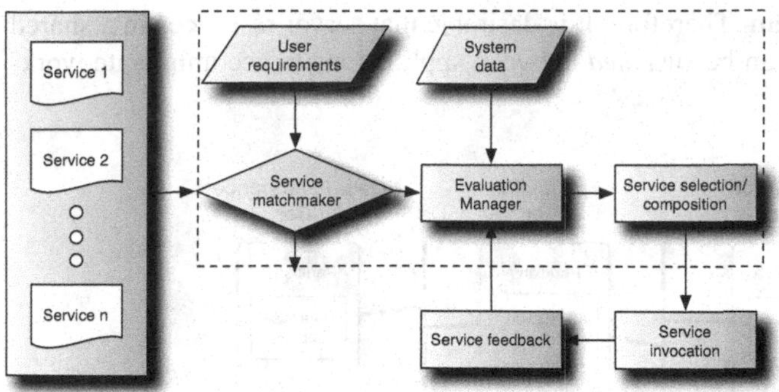

Fig. 9.1 System diagram of service selection

or the hybrid approach. The evaluation manager takes the system data such as system architecture configuration information, runtime workload demand, and feeds the data into the performance model for evaluation. The main benefit of the use of a performance model is that performance can be quickly evaluated without actual invocation of the services. Performance metrics of each model depends on the design of the model, with common metrics including mean response time, throughput and system utilisation. Some other performance metrics related closely to business include operational cost and system revenue.

Based on the performance evaluation results, the agent can choose the most suitable service and compose it when it is needed. When a service is selected and properly composed, it then can be called by the client. After service invocation, the user can give feedback of the service via a feedback (or recommendation) system. The *feedback* component in the framework is used for the purpose—to adjust the performance model and to dynamically adapt to user requirements.

In the next section, we use the server switching service as an example to explain how performance evaluation can be done and how the results can be used to assist web service selection.

9.3 Case Study—Selection of Switching Service

9.3.1 Server Switching in Internet Hosting Centres

Internet services are normally hosted in commercial hosting environments that are run by Internet Service Providers (ISPs). Workload demand for Internet services is usually very bursty [2,4,31], thus it is difficult to predict the workload level at a certain point in time. Therefore, fixed server configurations for a service are far from satisfactory for an application when the workload level is high; whereas it is potentially a waste of resource while the workload is light for the remaining applications supported by the system. Therefore, it is desirable that server resources in a shared hosting environment can be *switched* between applications to accommodate workload variation.

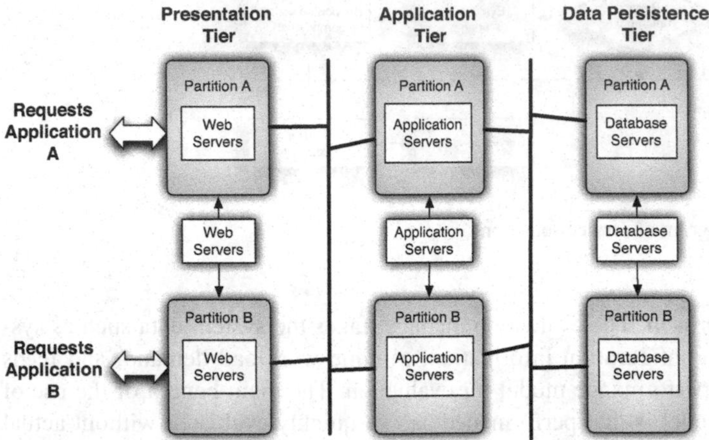

Fig. 9.2 Illustration of server switching in a multi-tier architecture

A server switching service is a service that can be employed by the ISPs to improve the Internet service and optimise the resource usage in the server centres. To employ a switching service, the ISPs need to assess the quality of the service, in other words, to assess the benefits of using the switching service. The quality of the switching service depends on the benefits it brings to the ISPs, thus, to assess the quality of a switching service, one needs to assess the improvement of the Internet services. There are a number of performance metrics to evaluate the quality of a switching service. From a request sender's perspective, mean response time is the main performance metric; from the ISPs' perspective, performance metrics include throughput, system utilisation and total generated revenue during a certain period.

Figure 9.2 is an illustration of how server switching happens in a distributed e-Business environment. The diagram assumes the ISP hosts two different Internet services, both of which require a multi-tier system architecture. The typical system configuration includes the presentation tier, application tier and data persistence tier. In each tier, a cluster of servers is used for processing the requests. In Figure 9.2, the cluster of servers in each tier is partitioned into two pools, each of which is responsible for each Internet application. When there is a need, some portion of servers at the same tier can be switched between pools to adapt to workload fluctuation.

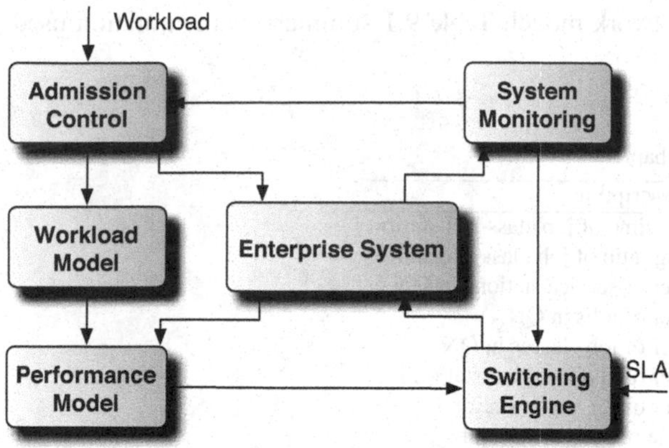

Fig. 9.3 Server switching procedure

9.3.2 Server Switching Procedure

Figure 9.3 shows how server switching works in a distributed e-Business environment. This diagram is a portion of Figure 9.1 and it corresponds to the *evaluation manager* component of Figure 9.1. In this diagram, there are some key components, including *admission control, workload model, performance model, system monitoring* and the *switching engine*. When requests arrive, they are controlled by the *admission control* component, based on the system information (e.g., system utilisation) from the *monitoring* component. The *workload model* takes as the input the allowed requests and builds a workload model based on the workload characteristics. The *performance model* then takes as input the output of the *workload model* and system architecture configuration and calculates the required performance metrics. These metrics are combined with system information from the monitoring facilities and fed into the *switching engine*, which then computes the benefits and penalties of all possible switches before making the final switching decision. In the following section, we show how to model the multi-tier Internet services using a queueing network.

9.3.3 Modelling Multi-tier Internet Services

A multi-tiered Internet service can be modelled using a multi-class closed queueing network [26, 30]. Figure 9.4 shows a model for a typical configuration of such applications. In the model, C refers to the client; WS, AS and DS refer to the web server, application server and database server respectively. The queueing network is solved using the MVA (Mean Value Analysis) algorithm [19], which is based on Little's law [17] and the Arrival Theorem [19,22] from standard queueing theory. In this section, we briefly describe how different performance metrics can be derived from the closed queueing network model. Table 9.1 summarises the notation used throughout this chapter.

Table 9.1 Notation used in this chapter

Symbol	Description
S_{ir}	Service time of job class-r at station i
v_{ir}	Visiting ratio of job class-r at station i
N	Number of service stations in QN
K	Number of jobs in QN
R	Number of job classes in QN
K_{ir}	Number of class-r job at station i
m_i	Number of servers at station i
ϕ_r	Revenue of each class-r job
π_i	Marginal probability at centre i
T	System response time
D_r	Deadline for class-r jobs
E_r	Exit time for class-r jobs
P_r	Probability that class-r job stays
X_r	Class-r throughput before switching
$X_r^{'}$	Class-r throughput after switching
U_i	Utilisation at station i
t_s	Server switching time
t_d	Switching decision interval time

Consider a product form closed queueing network with N load-independent service stations. $N = \{1, 2, \cdots, N\}$ is the set of station indexes. Suppose there are K customers and they are partitioned into R classes according to their service request patterns; customers grouped in a class are assumed to be statistically identical. $R = \{1, 2, \cdots, R\}$ is the set of class indexes. The service time, S_{ir}, in a multi-class closed queueing network is the average time spent by a class-r job during a single visit to station[1] i. The service demand, denoted as D_{ir}, is the total service requirement, which is the average amount of time that a class-r job spends in service at station i during execution. This can be derived from the Service Demand Law [18] as $D_{ir} = S_{ir} \cdot v_{ir}$; here v_{ir} is the visiting ratio of class-r jobs to station i. K_r is the total population of customers of class r. The total population of the network is thus defined as $K = \sum_r K_r$. The vector $\mathbf{K} = \{K_1, K_2, \cdots, K_R\}$ is used to represent the population of the network.

In modern enterprise systems, clusters of servers are commonly used in each application tier to improve server processing capability. Thus, when modelling those applications, we need to consider both -/M/1-FCFS and -/M/m-FCFS in each station. Suppose there are k jobs in the queueing network, for i = 1, ..., N and r = 1, ..., R, the mean response time of a class-r job at station i can be computed as follows [5].

[1] The terms *station*, *centre* and *node* have the same meaning, and are used interchangeably.

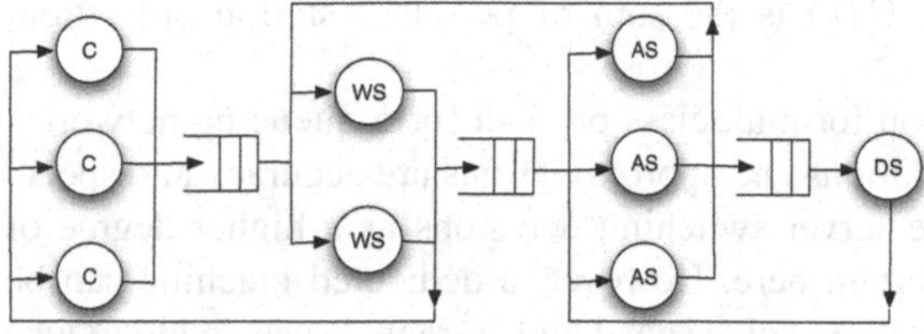

Fig. 9.4 A model of a typical configuration of a cluster-based multi-tiered Internet service. C represents customer machines; WS, AS and DS represent web servers, application servers and database servers, respectively

$$\overline{T}_{ir}(k) = \begin{cases} D_{ir}\left[1+\sum_{r=1}^{R}\overline{K}_{ir}(k-1_r)\right], & m_i = 1 \\ \dfrac{D_{ir}}{m_i}\left[1+\sum_{r=1}^{R}\overline{K}_{ir}(k-1_r)\right. \\ \left.+\sum_{j=0}^{m_i-2}(m_i-j-1)\,\pi_i(j\mid k-1_r)\right], & m_i > 1 \end{cases} \quad (9.1)$$

Here, $(k-1_r) = (k_1,\ldots,k_r-1,\ldots,K_R)$ is the population vector with one class-r job less in the system. The mean system response is the sum of mean response time of each tier.

For the case of multi-server nodes ($m_i > 1$), it is necessary to compute the marginal probabilities. The marginal probability that there are j jobs ($j = 1,\ldots,(m_i-1)$) at the station i, given that the network is in state k, is given by [5].

$$\pi_i(j\mid k) = \frac{1}{j}\left[\sum_{r=1}^{R}\frac{v_{ir}}{S_{ir}}X_r(k)\,\pi_i(j-1\mid k-1_r)\right] \quad (9.2)$$

Applying Little's law [17], the throughput of class-r jobs can be calculated,

$$X_r(k) = \frac{k_r}{\sum_{i=1}^{N} v_{ir}\overline{T}_{ir}(k)} \quad (9.3)$$

Applying Little's Law again with the Force Flow Law [18], we derive the mean queue length $\overline{K}_{ir}$ for class-r job at station i as below.

$$\overline{K}_{ir}(k) = X_r(k)\cdot\overline{T}_{ir}(k)\cdot v_{ir} \quad (9.4)$$

The starting point of this equation is $\overline{K}_{ir}(0,0\ldots,0) = 0, \pi_i(0\mid 0) = 1, \pi_i(j\mid 0) = 0$; after K iterations, system response time, throughput and mean queue length in each tier can be computed.

In multiclass product form queueing networks, per-class station utilisation can be computed using the following equation [19].

$$U_{ir}(k) = \frac{k_r D_{ir}}{\sum_i D_{ir}[1+\overline{K}_i(k-1_r)]} \quad (9.5)$$

and the total station utilisation $U_i(k)$ is the sum of per-class station utilisation, $U_i(k) = \sum_{r=1}^{R} U_{ir}(k)$.

The above is the exact solution for multiclass product form queueing networks. The trade-offs between exact solutions and approximations are accuracy and speed. We use exact solutions to guide server switching decisions as a higher degree of accuracy is believed to be important here. However, a dedicated machine can be used for the switching system itself, to solve speed and storage issues and to reduce the interference with the servers themselves. In our model, job class switching is not permitted.

9.3.4 Model Parameterisation

Once a performance model is built, it can be parameterised. The parameterisation involves collection and manipulation of sample data. Sample data to be collected includes service time S_{ir} of each type of request, and the visiting ratio v_{ir}. Since service demand $D_{ir} = S_{ir} \times v_{ir}$, only service demand of each request needs to be collected. Service demand of each request is difficult to measure, however, according to the service demand law [18], $D_{ir} = U_i / X_{ir}$, here U_i is the utilisation of service station i and X_{ir} is the throughput of job class r at station i. Therefore, we can measure U_i and X_{ir} (through monitoring utility or system logs) and calculate D_{ir} using the service demand law. In a real test-bed, we could drive the system utilisation to a required level by sending a large number of requests that are of the same type, and measure the resulting throughput. The service demand of each request can then be computed based on the service demand law.

9.3.5 Bottleneck Identification of Multi-tier Architecture

Bottlenecks are a phenomenon where the performance or capacity of an entire system is severely limited by a single component. This component is sometimes called the *bottleneck point*. Formally, a bottleneck lies on a system's critical path and provides the lowest throughput [6]. It has been shown in [3] that multi-class models can exhibit multiple simultaneous bottlenecks. The dependency of the bottleneck set on the workload mix is therefore derived. In an enterprise system there are normally different classes of jobs and the class mix can change at run-time. This suggests that there might be several bottlenecks at the same time and bottlenecks can shift from tier to tier over time. Therefore, system designers need to study the best server configuration to avoid bottlenecks during system capacity planning and provisioning, and ideally provide schemes to support dynamic server allocation during run-time.

9.3.5.1 Identification Methods

In [8], it is shown that the bottleneck for a single class queueing network is the station i with the largest service demand $S_i v_i$, under the assumption of the invariance of service time S_i and visiting ratio v_i and given routing frequencies. Considerable research exists [3, 8, 15, 16, 21] which studies bottleneck identification for multi-class closed product-form queueing networks as the population grows to infinity. For a finite population, the results in [10, 14] can be used. In this chapter we use the approach developed in [7], which uses convex polytopes for bottleneck identification in multi-class queueing networks. This method can compute the set of potential bottlenecks in a network with one thousand servers and fifty customer classes in just a few seconds.

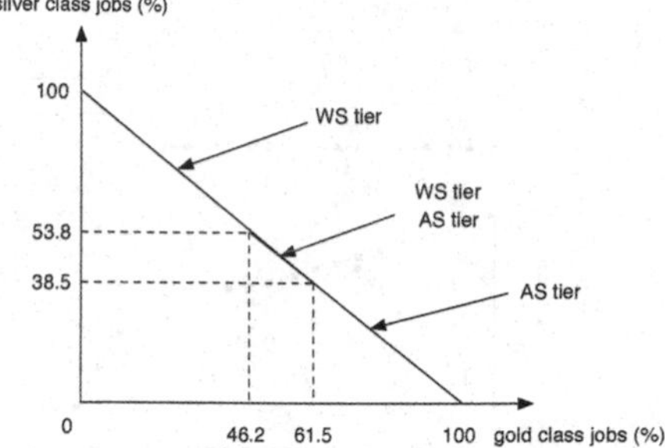

Fig. 9.5 Bottleneck of the two-class queueing network in pool 1

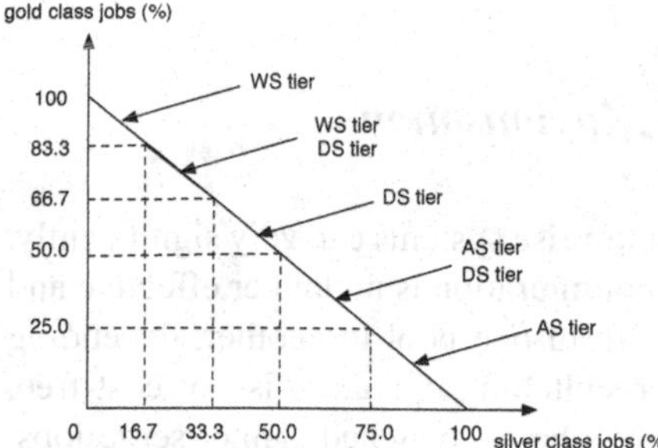

Fig. 9.6 Bottleneck of the two-class queueing network in pool 2

Figures 9.5 and 9.6 are the bottleneck identification results using convex polytopes for our chosen configurations for pool 1 and pool 2. Figure 9.5 shows that in pool 1, when the percentage of gold class jobs is less than 46.2%, the web server tier is the bottleneck; when it is between 46.2 and 61.5%, the system enters a *crossover points region*, where the bottleneck changes; when the percentage of gold class jobs in pool 1 exceeds 61.5%, the application server tier becomes the bottleneck.

Figure 9.6 shows the bottleneck identification in pool 2. It is more complex and is a good example of multiple bottlenecks and bottleneck shifting. In this case, when the percentage of silver class jobs is less than 16.7%, the web server tier is the bottleneck; when it is between 16.7 and 33.3%, both the web server tier and the database tier are in the *crossover* region; if the percentage of silver class jobs lies in the region 33.3–50.0%, the database tier becomes the bottleneck; when it is between 50.0 and 75.0%, the system enters another *crossover* region, where the application server tier and the database server tier dominate; and finally, if the percentage of silver class jobs exceeds 75.0%, the application server tier is the bottleneck in the system.

Figures 9.7 and 9.8 provide a clear picture as to how the utilisations corresponding to the workload mix changes in both pools. The two figures can also be used to verify the results in Figures 9.5 and 9.6.

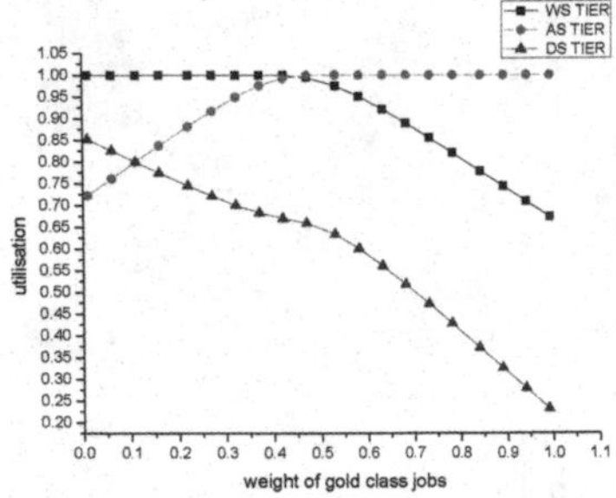

Fig. 9.7 Utilisation in pool 1

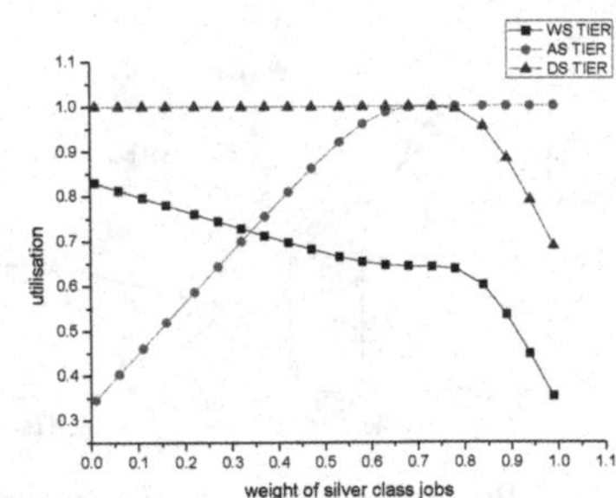

Fig. 9.8 Utilisation in pool 2

9.3.6 Server Switching for Revenue Maximisation

As previously highlighted, the workload in enterprise systems can vary significantly. It is therefore the case that one-time system configuration is no longer effective and it is desirable that servers be able to switch from one pool to another, depending on the load conditions. However, the server-switching operation is not cost-free, since during the period of switching the servers being switched cannot serve jobs. Therefore, a decision has to be made as to whether it is worth switching in terms of revenue maximisation.

9.3.6.1 Revenue Function

For a typical Internet service, a user normally issues a sequence of requests (referred to as a *session*) during a new visit to the service site. Intuitively, a request contributes full revenue if it is processed before the deadline[2] D_r. When a request r misses its deadline, it still waits for execution with a probability $P(T_r)$ and credit is still due for late, yet successful processing. As can be seen from Figure 9.9, when the response time $T_r < D_r$, then $P(T_r) = 1$; which means that the request contributes full revenue and the user will send another request. Suppose E_r is some time point, at which the request is dropped from the system. It is assumed in this chapter that when $D_r \leq T_r \leq E_r$, the request will quit the system with probability $P(T_r)$, which follows a uniform distribution (refer to Figure 9.10). If $T_r \geq E_r$, then $P(T_r) = 0$, which means that the request quits the system without contributing any revenue. The following equation is used for calculating P_r.

$$P(T_r) = \begin{cases} 1, & T_r < D_r \\ \dfrac{E_r - T_r}{E_r - D_r}, & D_r \leq T_r \leq E_r \\ 0, & T_r > E_r \end{cases} \tag{9.6}$$

The meaning of the above equation is that the longer the completion time of a job r exceeds its deadline, the more likely it is that the client will quit the system, thus approximating real-world client behaviour.

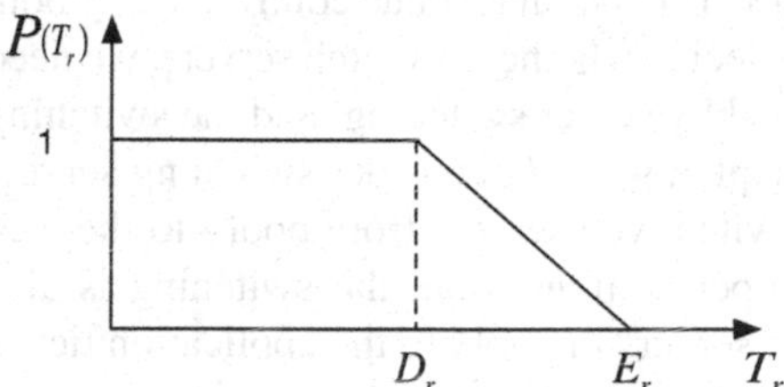

Fig. 9.9 Illustration of the relationship between job response time and the probability that the customer will remain in the system

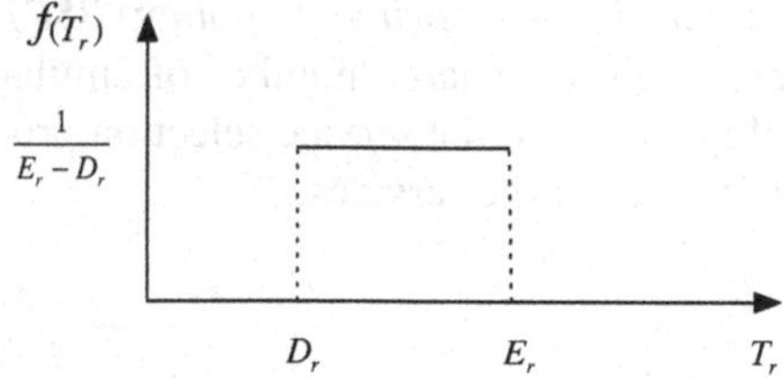

Fig. 9.10 Illustration of the relationship between the probability density function and request response time

[2] Soft deadline in lieu of hard deadline is used in this chapter.

9.3.6.2 Revenue Maximisation

Based on the revenue function, the revenue gained and lost by server switching can be calculated. Suppose some servers need to be switched from pool i to pool j. We use V^i_{loss} to represent the revenue loss in pool i. From the time that switching happens, the service capacity offered by server pool i starts to degrade. From Equation 9.7, the revenue loss in pool i can be derived.

$$V^i_{loss} = \sum_{r=1}^{R} X^i_r(k^i)\phi^i_r P(T_r)t_d - \sum_{r=1}^{R} X^{i'}_r(k^i)\phi^i_r P(T_r)t_d \tag{9.7}$$

The server switching itself takes time, during which neither pool i nor pool j can use the servers being switched. Only after switching time t_s, does pool j then benefit from the switched servers. During the switching decision interval time t_d, the revenue gain V^j_{gain} can be calculated as below.

$$V^j_{gain} = \sum_{r=1}^{R} X^{j'}_r\left(k^j\right)\phi^j_r P(T_r)\left(t_d - t_s\right) - \sum_{r=1}^{R} X^j_r\left(k^j\right)\phi^j_r P(T_r)\left(t_d - t_s\right) \tag{9.8}$$

Here, it is assumed the decision interval time $t_d > t_s$.

Our goal in this chapter is to maximise the ISP's total revenue contributed by both pool i and pool j. In other words, when we decide whether to switch servers, we need to compare the revenue gain and loss caused by server switching, and the switching is done only when $V^j_{gain} > V^i_{loss}$. In this chapter, we only consider switching servers between pools in the same tier (i.e., we switch web servers from pool i to the web server tier in pool j), although given proper configuration, the switching is also possible between tiers (i.e., switching web servers in pool i to the application tier in pool j).

9.3.7 Switching Policies

In this section, we describe two different server switching policies namely the *proportional switching policy (PSP)* and the *bottleneck-aware switching policy (BSP)*. In the real-world web service registry, there might be a large number of similar services in terms of the switching functionality, however, the service selection procedure discussed in this chapter is the same for each of the services.

9.3.7.1 Proportional Switching Policy

First, we consider a näive policy called the proportional switching policy (PSP). The policy switches servers between pools based on the workload proportion in both pools. Performance criteria for server switching is computed using the queueing network model; if the performance of the new configuration is better than the current one, then server switching is done, otherwise the server configuration remains the same. Algorithm 3 describes how the policy operates.

Input: $N, m_i, R, K_{ir}, S_{ir}, v_{ir}, \phi_r, t_s, t_d$
Output: Server configuration
for each i **in** N **do**
    $m_i^1/m_i^2 = K^1/K^2$
end for
calculate V_{loss} and V_{gain} using eq. 9.7 and eq. 9.8;
if $V_{gain} > V_{loss}$ **then**
    do switching according to the calculations;
    $S_{ir} \leftarrow S_{ir}^{'}$;
else
    server configuration remains the same;
end if
return current configuration.

Algorithm 3: Proportional Switching Policy.

Algorithm 3 is simple as it only considers the workload proportion. In fact, workload mix and revenue contribution from individual classes in different pools can also affect the total revenue. In the next section, we will introduce a new switching policy, which takes the above factors into account.

9.3.7.2 Bottleneck-Aware Switching Policy

Input: $N_r, m_i, R, K_{ir}, S_{ir}, v_{ir}, \phi_r, t_s, t_d$
Output: new configuration
while bottleneck saturation found in one pool **do**
    if found at same tier in the other pool **then**
        return;
    else switch servers to the bottleneck tier;
        $m_i \leftarrow m_i^{'}$ and $S_{ir} \leftarrow S_{ir}^{'}$;
    end if
end while
search configurations using Algorithm 5
return current configuration.

Algorithm 4: The Bottleneck-aware Switching Policy.

Here we describe a more sophisticated server switching policy called the bottleneck-aware switching policy (BSP), as described in Algorithm 4. BSP works in two phases: bottleneck identification and local search.

Input: $N_r, m_i, R, K_{ir}, S_{ir}, v_{ir}, \phi_r, t_s, t_d$
Output: best configuration
Initialisation: compute U_i^1, U_i^2
while $U_0^1 > U_0^2$ **do**
  if $m_0^2 > 1$ **then**
    $m_0^2 \downarrow, m_0^1 \uparrow; S_{0r}^2 \leftarrow S_{0r}^{2'}$;
    while $U_1^1 > U_1^2$ **do**
      if $m_1^2 > 1$ **then**
        $m_1^2 \downarrow, m_1^1 \uparrow; S_{1r}^2 \leftarrow S_{1r}^{2'}$;
        while $U_2^1 > U_2^2$ **do**
          if $m_2^2 > 1$ **then**
            $m_2^2 \downarrow, m_2^1 \uparrow; S_{2r}^2 \leftarrow S_{2r}^{2'}$;
            compute V_{loss} using eq. 9.7;
            $S_{2r}^1 \leftarrow S_{2r}^{1'}$;
            compute V_{gain} using eq. 9.8;
            if $V_{gain} > V_{loss}$ **then**
              store current configuration;
            end if
            compute new U_i^1, U_i^2;
          end if
        end while
        similar steps for $U_2^1 < U_2^2$
        $S_{1r}^1 \leftarrow S_{1r}^{1'}$;
        compute new U_i^1, U_i^2;
      end if
    end while
    similar steps for $U_1^1 < U_1^2$
    $S_{0r}^1 \leftarrow S_{0r}^{1'}$;
    compute new U_i^1, U_i^2;
  end if
end while
similar steps for $U_0^1 < U_0^2$
return best configuration.

Algorithm 5: The Configuration Search Algorithm.

Bottleneck identification. It first checks for bottleneck saturation in both pools. If both pools have bottlenecks at the same tier, two cases are considered: (*a*) if both of them are saturated, then no server will be switched; (*b*) if a bottleneck is saturated in one pool but not in the other, then the algorithm incrementally switches servers to the bottleneck tier and compares the new revenue with the value from the current configuration. If a potential switch will result in more revenue, then the configuration will be stored. The process continues until no bottleneck saturation in either pools or no more switching can be done from the other pool. Note that when bottleneck saturation is found, server switching in other tiers has little or no effect, thus it can be safely neglected.

Local search. If there is no bottleneck saturation in either of the pools, then the algorithm computes the server utilisation at all tiers in both pools and switches servers from low utilisation tiers to high utilisation tiers using a local search algorithm

(Algorithm 5). In both algorithms, superscripts represent pools and subscripts 0, 1, 2 represent the web tier, application tier and database tier respectively.

Algorithm 5 uses nested loops to search for possible server switches, starting from the web tier continuing to the database tier. It tries to explore as many possible switching configurations as possible. However, the algorithm will not guarantee that the best switching result (the global optimal) will be found, thus it is a best-effort algorithm. If we use m_0, m_1, m_2 to represent the total number of web servers, application servers and database servers in both pools respectively, in the worst case, the total number of searches made by Algorithm 5 will be $(m_0 - 2) \times (m_1 - 2) \times (m_2 - 2)$, therefore the time complexity is $O(m_0 \cdot m_1 \cdot m_2)$. For typical server configurations, m_0, m_1 and m_2 are not normally large, thus Algorithm 5 is feasible in practice. The time for each search iteration depends on the complexity of the underlying queueing network model, which in turn depends on the number of stations and the number of job classes (the dominant factor as shown in [16]). Enterprise systems are normally three-tiered ($N = 3$), and the number of job classes is normally small, depending on the classification criteria. Therefore, solving such a multi-class closed queueing network model is very quick, thus the same applies for each iteration in the searching algorithm. As shown later in this chapter, for our configuration, the average runtime of the algorithm is less than 200 ms on a 2.2 Ghz computer, which is considered acceptable.

For complex multi-class closed queueing network models, with thousands of stations and hundreds of job classes, the storage requirement for solving the models are very high. In our case, storage is also not an issue as the model is relatively simple. Moreover, using a dedicated machine for the switching engine can increase the searching speed, and also relax the associated storage requirement.

9.3.8 Proactive and Reactive Switching

In our proposed switching system, two approaches to server switching can be used—proactive switching and reactive switching. Proactive switching is motivated by identifying similar workload patterns over time (hours, days, weeks etc). Most Internet services have cyclical patterns. For instance, for real-time financial applications, the peak load normally appears at the beginning and the end of the market, and the load is lower during the remainder of the opening hours; it is also the case that Monday and Friday are busier than other weekdays. Based on historical workload patterns, and by applying some workload prediction techniques such as those introduced in [20], the server switching engine can re-allocate resources before the expected heavy workload arrives, and also, can save the costs of server switching during a heavily loaded period. However, due to uncertainties, workload demand can have huge variation and predictive inaccuracies can be introduced by the workload predictor, which are then passed to the switching engine, stimulating inappropriate or wrong decisions. Therefore, proactive switching is not perfect and it can at best hope to improve the overall performance during long term periods.

Reactive switching is more dynamic, based on run-time system parameters and can respond to system state changes quickly. The run-time data is collected via system monitoring tools, is reformatted, and is fed into the analytical model. The model is then solved and alternative switching decisions are compared. The proactive and reactive switching approaches can of course work together to optimise the overall system performance.

9.3.9 Admission Control

As described in the literature, admission control (AC) is necessary for busy Internet services in order to achieve the SLAs. When a system is overloaded, most ISPs simply reject less important requests. ISPs may give their customers compensation for the rejected requests, depending on the SLAs between themselves and their customers.

In this work, we also use a simple admission control scheme, in addition to the server switching policy, to maintain the number of concurrent jobs in the system at an appropriate level. When the workload is high, which in turn makes the overall system response time high, less important requests are rejected first. If requests in this category are rejected, but the overall response time still remains high, the AC scheme continues to reject jobs in the system, until the response time decreases to an acceptable level.

9.4 Performance Evaluation

9.4.1 Experimental Setup

We design and develop a simulator to evaluate the server switching approach in this chapter. Two applications are simulated, running on two logical pools (1 and 2). Each application has two classes of job (gold and silver), which represent the importance of these jobs. Both applications are multi-tiered and run on a cluster of servers. The service time S_{ir} and the visiting ratio v_{ir} are chosen based on realistic values or from those supplied in supporting literature.

Based on a real test-bed which we have access to, the application server switching takes less than five seconds and web server switching is relatively straightforward. Database server switching is more complex, however, it does not affect the switching policy itself. In this chapter, we assume that the switching cost for web servers, application servers and database servers is the same for simplicity. Experimental parameters used for our evaluation can be found in Table 9.2.

Table 9.2 Experimental parameters

		Pool 1		Pool 2	
		Silver	Gold	Gold	Silver
Number of servers	WS	4		5	
	AS	10		15	
	DS	2		3	
Service time(sec)	WS	0.07	0.1	0.05	0.025
	AS	0.03125	0.1125	0.01	0.06
	DS	0.05	0.025	0.0375	0.025
Visiting ratio	WS	1.0	0.6	1.0	0.8
	AS	1.6	0.8	2.0	1.0
	DS	1.2	0.8	1.6	1.6
Deadline (sec)		20	15	6	8
Exit point (sec)		30	20	10	12
Revenue unit		2	10	20	4

9.4.2 Evaluation Results

Experiments have been conducted for a number of different workload scenarios called *mixed workload*, *cross load*, *random load* and workload generated from real-world Internet traces. For each of these cases, we compare the results from our proposed bottleneck-aware server switching policy (BSP) with those from the proportional server switching policy (PSP) and the non-switching policy (NSP).

9.4.2.1 Mixed Workload

As described in Section 9.3.7.2, even if the total workload remains the same, system bottlenecks can shift among tiers depending on the workload mix. To study the system behaviour of different workload mixes, we choose a few key evaluation points illustrated in Figures 9.5 and 9.6. Two sets of experiments are run: 1) keeping the workload mix constant in pool 1 and altering the workload mix in pool 2, as shown in Figures 9.11, 9.12, and 9.13; 2) keeping the workload mix in pool 2 constant and altering the workload mix in pool 1 as seen in Figures 9.14, 9.15, and 9.16. The server switching time is set to 5 seconds and the switching decision is made every 30 seconds. We explain the impact of the workload mix on the total revenue for the NSP, and compare the results against the PSP and BSP policies.

From Figures 9.11, 9.12, and 9.13, it can be seen that when the workload mix in pool 1 is constant, Figures 9.11, 9.12 and 9.13 show similar patterns. The total revenue from both pools from NSP and PSP decreases when the percentage of silver class jobs in pool 2 increases from 10 to 40%. This is understandable as silver class jobs contribute less to the total revenue. When the percentage increases to 50%, there is a big increase in total revenue. Based on our observations, this is due to a lower response time in pool 2, which is less than E_r for gold class jobs in pool 2. When the percentage of silver class jobs is over 50%, although the response time

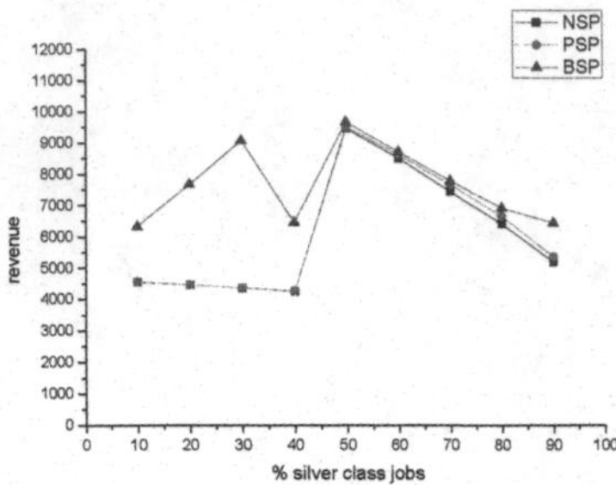

Fig. 9.11 The ratio of silver class jobs to gold class jobs in pool 1 is (80:20).The percentage of silver class jobs in pool 2 ranges from 10 to 90%

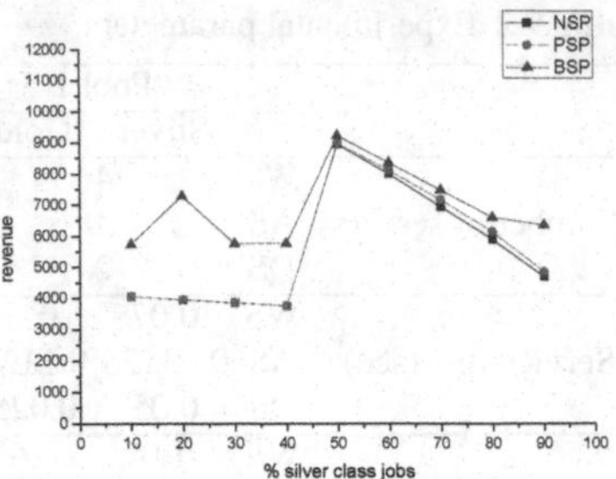

Fig. 9.12 The ratio of silver class jobs to gold class jobs in pool 1 is (60:40). The percentage of silver class jobs in pool 2 ranges from 10 to 90%

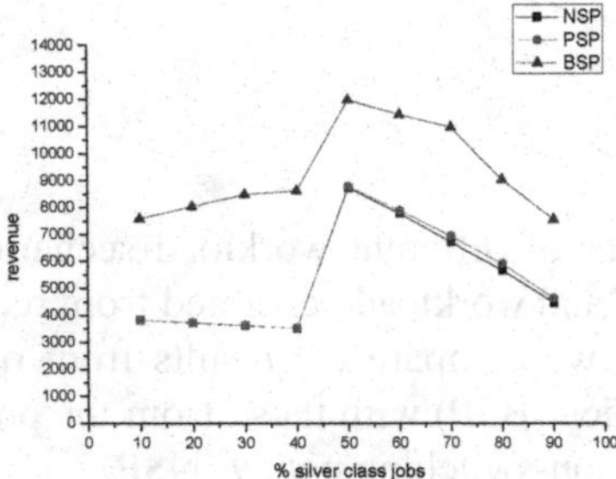

Fig. 9.13 The ratio of silver class jobs to gold class jobs in pool 1 is (20:80). The percentage of silver class jobs in pool 2 ranges from 10 to 90%

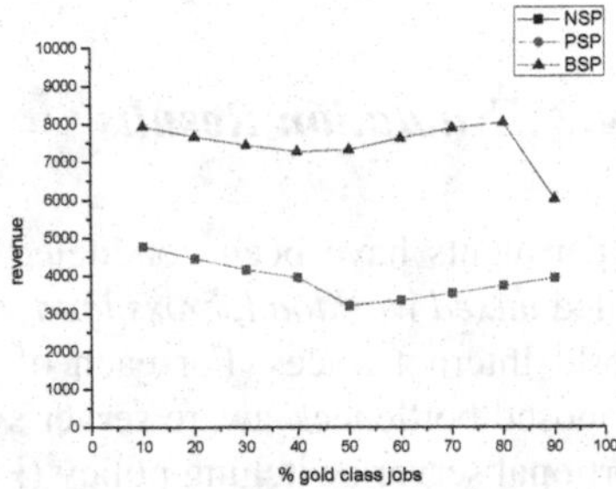

Fig. 9.14 The ratio of gold class jobs to silver class jobs in pool 2 is (80:20).The percentage of gold class jobs in pool 1 ranges from 10 to 90%

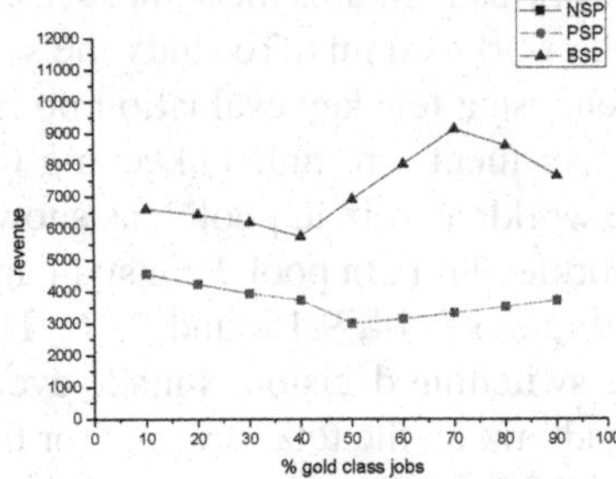

Fig. 9.15 The ratio of gold class jobs to silver class jobs in pool 2 is (60:40). The percentage of gold class jobs in pool 1 ranges from 10 to 90%

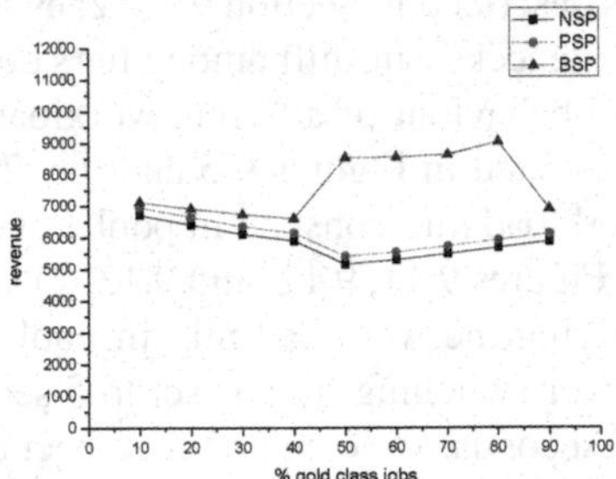

Fig. 9.16 The ratio of gold class jobs to silver class jobs in pool 2 is (20:80). The percentage of gold class jobs in pool 1 ranges from 10 to 90%

in pool 2 decreases, the total revenue again decreases due to the decreasing weight of gold class jobs. It can also be seen that Figure 9.11 has the highest revenue and Figure 9.13 has the lowest revenue among the three cases. This is due to the longer response time (within deadline) in pool 1 as a result of the percentage increases in gold class jobs in the pool. As we know, a longer response time results in less throughput, which then results in less revenue contribution.

In the second set of experiments, the workload mix in pool 2 is constant and the percentage of gold class jobs in pool 1 is altered. Figures 9.14, 9.15, and 9.16 also present similar patterns. The total revenue in all three cases decreases when the percentage of gold class jobs in pool 1 increases from 10 to 50%. The difference in revenue between BSP and the other two policies is smaller as the weight of gold class jobs increases. When the percentage is greater than 50%, the total revenue increases as the percentage of gold class jobs in pool 1 increases. We notice that the total revenue in Figure 9.16 is significantly higher than that in the other two cases. This is due to lower response time (below E_r) of both classes of jobs in pool 2, which can result in a significant increase in revenue.

In both sets of experiments, it can be seen that PSP and NSP have almost the same impact on total revenue for the one-time switching. The total revenue from NSP is always higher than those from the other two policies as the local search algorithm is employed in BSP and switching is done only when a better configuration is found.

9.4.2.2 Alternative Workload

In a web hosting centre, it is not uncommon that during certain periods the workload for one application is increasing while it is decreasing for another. This kind of crossover in workload can affect overall system performance. In this section, we conduct performance evaluation for two cases: (1) when the workload increases in pool 1 and decreases in pool 2; (2) when the workload increases in pool 2 and decreases in pool 1. In both cases, the workload mix for silver and gold class jobs in both pools is constant. The total number of concurrent users is set to a fixed number (200), which matches the value in Section 9.4.2.1. During evaluation, admission control is applied when necessary. Both sets of experiments are run for 570 seconds, during which 19 switching decisions are made. Tables 9.3 and 9.4 list the results for both sets of experiments.

In Table 9.3, we see that the workload in pool 1 increases by 10 each time from 10 to 200, while it decreases by 10 from 200 to 10 in pool 2. The total revenue from NSP is 88,093. If AC is not applied, the total revenue from PSP and BSP are 85,130 and 1,900,034, representing a −3.4% and a 115.7% improvement, respectively. When AC is applied, the total revenue from PSP and BSP are 85,130 and 211,947, representing a −3.4% and a 140.6% improvement, respectively. The negative impact from PSP is reasonable as the PSP is a näive switching policy, which simply allocates servers based on the workload proportion regardless of the performance results. Moreover, for each server switching, there is also a cost associated with it. Although during each run, the resulting revenue from PSP is higher than

Table 9.3 Load in pool 1 increases while it decreases in pool 2

Workload (P1, P2)	NSP	Without A/C PSP	Without A/C BSP	With A/C PSP	With A/C BSP
(20,190)	2,418	403	5,916	403	5,916
(30,180)	2,429	2,429	2,569	2,429	2,569
(40,170)	2,429	2,429	6,134	2,429	6,134
(50,160)	2,425	2,425	2,619	2,425	2,619
(60,150)	2,420	2,420	7,175	2,420	7,175
(70,140)	2,415	2,415	3,458	2,415	3,385
(80,130)	2,410	2,410	15,097	2,410	15,097
(90,120)	3,827	3,827	10,389	3,827	9,288
(100,110)	3,459	3,459	11,014	3,459	3,837
(110,100)	6,374	6,374	11,872	6,374	16,510
(120,90)	5,244	5,526	11,189	5,526	16,497
(130,80)	5,557	6,923	7,963	6,923	16,233
(140,70)	4,761	6,255	13,367	6,255	16,151
(150,60)	6,735	3,780	13,408	3,780	16,038
(160,50)	6,834	6,905	13,461	6,905	15,877
(170,40)	6,944	6,273	13,532	6,273	15,639
(180,30)	7,068	6,478	13,632	6,478	15,264
(190,20)	7,201	7,012	13,752	7,012	14,604
(200,10)	7,143	7,387	13,487	7,387	13,114
Total revenue	88,093	85,130	1,90,034	85,130	2,11,947
Improvement		−3.4%	115.7%	−3.4%	140.6%

from NSP, in the long term the overall improvement could be negative (note that PSP does not switch servers in each run). In this set of experiments, there is also a performance improvement when admission control is applied.

In Table 9.4, the workload in pool 1 decreases by 10 each time step from 200 to 10, while it increases in steps of 10 from 10 to 200 in pool 2. The total revenue from NSP is 83,289. Without AC, the total revenue from PSP and BSP are 105,698 and 127,469, representing a 26.9% and a 53.0% performance improvement, respectively. When AC is applied, the new total revenues are 105,698 and 117,808, representing a 26.9% and a 41.4% improvement. Note that with AC, the total revenue from BSP is less than it is in the no AC case. This is reasonable for light load situation (such as the chosen workload in this case) because the AC works before the BPS and if the workload results in system bottleneck saturation, the AC simply rejects requests. However, the saturation for current configuration can be relaxed in another configuration that is returned by the BPS, and the rejected requests will result in loss of revenue. We believe that when workload is high, due to switching cost, the overall revenue without AC will be less than in the AC case. To confirm this, we set the total number of users in both pools to 250. The total revenue from NSP is now 84,170. Without AC, it is 127,918 using PSP and 158,487 from BSP, representing a 52.0% and a 88.3% performance improvement. With AC, the total revenue from PSP and BSP are 127,918 and 161,550, representing a 52.0% and a 115.7% performance improvement. In conclusion, BSP always outperforms PSP in terms of

Table 9.4 Load in pool 1 decreases while it increases in pool 2

Workload (P2, P1)	NSP	Without A/C		With A/C	
		PSP	BSP	PSP	BSP
(20,190)	7,201	6,227	14,492	6,227	14,492
(30,180)	7,068	6,862	11,895	6,862	11,895
(40,170)	6,944	5,584	9,865	5,584	9,865
(50,160)	6,834	5,576	14,617	5,576	14,617
(60,150)	6,735	5,569	14,787	5,569	14,787
(70,140)	4,761	5,560	14,917	5,560	14,917
(80,130)	5,557	5,551	1,790	5,551	1,790
(90,120)	5,244	5,540	4,567	5,540	4,742
(100,110)	6,374	5,528	7,562	5,528	5,238
(110,100)	3,459	5,515	9,442	5,515	3,321
(120,90)	3,827	5,499	12,455	5,499	4,233
(130,80)	2,410	5,482	586	5,482	2,028
(140,70)	2,415	5,461	1,792	5,461	7,181
(150,60)	2,420	5,436	1,346	5,436	1,346
(160,50)	2,425	5,405	1,468	5,405	1,468
(170,40)	2,429	5,367	1,469	5,367	1,469
(180,30)	2,429	5,314	1,471	5,314	1,471
(190,20)	2,418	5,229	1,474	5,229	1,474
(200:10)	2,339	4,993	1,474	4,993	1,474
Total revenue	83,289	1,05,698	1,27,469	1,05,698	1,17,808
Improvement		26.9%	53.0%	26.9%	41.4%

revenue contribution. The AC doesn't always improve performance, depending on the workload intensity and workload mix.

9.4.2.3 Random Workload

In this section, we consider a more representative workload scenario—the random workload. The number of users in pools 1 and 2 are uniformly distributed between 20 and 200. Moreover, the workload mix in each pool is also random. In Sections 9.4.2.1 and 9.4.2.2, a thirty-second fixed switching decision interval is used. In this section the switching decision interval time is the same as the workload change interval time, which is also a random number uniformly distributed in a fixed range. Two cases are considered: (1) a short switching decision interval time uniformly distributed between 15 and 25 s; (2) a long switching decision interval time uniformly distributed between 25 and 55 s. In Sections 9.4.2.1 and 9.4.2.2, a 5 s fixed server switching time is used; we also alter the switching time (to 5, 10 and 15 s) and evaluate the performance impact of the switching cost on total revenue for the three different switching policies. We evaluate the performance of the three policies with and without the admission control scheme for each of the above cases. All the experiments run for approximately two hours, during which 1,000 switching decisions are made.

Table 9.5 Short decision interval for random load

Switching time	Metrics	Without A/C NSP	Without A/C PSP	Without A/C BSP	With A/C NSP	With A/C PSP	With A/C BSP
5 s	No. of switches	0	130	20	0	145	15
	Revenue (x1,000)	2,340	2,833	5,692	2,340	2,813	5,702
	Improvement (%)	0	21.1	143.3	0	20.2	143.7
	Improvement over non-ac (%)				0	−0.71	0.17
10 s	No. of switchcs	0	108	3	0	112	13
	Revenue (x1,000)	2,340	2,886	4,731	2,340	2,894	5,684
	Improvement (%)	0	23.3	102.2	0	23.7	142.9
	Improvement over non-ac (%)				0	0.27	20.2
15 s	No. of switches	0	101	3	0	106	3
	Revenue (x1,000)	2,340	2,928	4,730	2,340	2,937	4,783
	Improvement (%)	0	25.2	102.1	0	25.5	104.4
	Improvement over non-ac (%)				0	0.29	1.13

Tables 9.5 and 9.6 list the performance results for short and long switching decision intervals (thus switching decision interval time). As can be seen from Table 9.5, for different server switching times, both PSP and BSP perform better than NSP in terms of revenue contribution with and without AC. When no AC is applied, the improvements are 21.1 and 143.3%, 23.3 and 102.2%, 25.2 and 102.1% for the 5, 10 and 15 second switching times respectively. With AC, the improvement are 20.2 and 143.7%, 23.7 and 142.9%, 25.5 and 104.4%, for the three cases, respectively. Without AC, the numbers of switches are 130 and 20, 108 and 3, 101 and 3, for 5, 10 and 15 s switching times respectively. When AC is employed, the numbers are 145 and 15, 112 and 13, 106 and 3, respectively. As can be seen from both tables, the number of server switches decreases as the server switching time increases. This is because the increase in switching time makes server switching more costly, which results in fewer switches. PSP always implements more switches than BSP. Also, the total revenue from BSP decreases slightly whereas it increases using PSP as the server switching time increases. This is understandable since PSP makes switching decisions solely based on workload proportion, and it switches servers even though the performance improvement may be very small. BSP on the other hand tries to search for the best switching that results in more improvement at each switching step. We find that the configuration returned by BSP is usually much further from the current configuration (that not found by PSP), thus each BSP switching step is more costly than that from PSP. On average, for each switching step, the ratio of the improvement over the cost from BSP is greater than that from PSP. Thus, BSP results in more revenue than the PSP policy. Due to the nature of the random load, servers may need to be switched back to their original pool. As the switching time increases, the number of switches for both policies decreases, therefore the total revenue increases from PSP but decreases from BSP. However, BSP consistently outperforms PSP in terms of revenue contribution for all cases, and the improvement from BSP over NSP is more than four times that of PSP.

From Table 9.5, it can also be seen that when AC is employed, there is a considerable improvement (20.2%) when the server switching time is 10 s. The improvement for the other two cases is less pronounced. The table also shows that when AC is employed, PSP results in more switches in each case compared with the no AC case. We believe this is a result of the workload mix change, which is caused by the AC.

Table 9.6 Long decision interval for random load

		Without A/C			With A/C		
Switching time	Metrics	NSP	PSP	BSP	NSP	PSP	BSP
5 s	No. of switches	0	152	20	0	158	13
	Revenue (x1,000)	4,778	5,702	11,567	4,778	5,661	11,579
	Improvement (%)	0	19.4	142.1	0	18.5	142.4
	Improvement over non-ac (%)				0	−0.73	0.11
10 s	No. of switches	0	134	20	0	82	15
	Revenue (x1,000)	4,778	5,710	11,557	4,778	6,399	11,577
	Improvement (%)	0	19.5	141.9	0	33.9	142.3
	Improvement over non-ac (%)				0	12.1	0.17
15 s	No. of switches	0	119	3	0	80	15
	Revenue (x1,000)	4,778	5,832	9,539	4,778	6,436	11,566
	Improvement (%)	0	22.1	99.7	0	34.7	142.1
	Improvement over non-ac (%)				0	10.4	21.2

Table 9.6 presents similar results to those seen in Table 9.5. Without AC, the number of switches for PSP increases from 130 to 152, 108 to 134, 101 to 119 for 5, 10 and 15 s switching times, respectively; the number from BSP drops to 3 for the 15 s case, this trend can also be seen in Table 9.5. This is reasonable as longer switching interval times result in potentially better configurations, thus more switches. With AC, the number of server switches for PSP increases from 145 to 158 for the 5 s case, but decreases from 112 to 82, 106 to 80 for the other two cases; the numbers of switches from BSP are 13, 15, 15 for 5, 10, 15 s switching times, respectively. We believe that the workload mix (more weight for gold class jobs) in the long switching decision interval case will result in more potentially better configurations, and thus more switches.

The revenue improvement when using BSP is almost 142% for all the cases regardless of the use of AC (an exception is the 99.7% implement for the case when the server switching time is 15 seconds and no AC is employed). The reason for the latter decrease is the same as for the number of switches above. The total revenue improvement from PSP without AC are 19.4, 19.5 and 22.1% for the three switching time cases. With AC, the improvements are 18.5, 33.9, and 34.7%. The improvements are, however, much less than those from BSP regardless of the use of AC.

9.4.2.4 Workloads Generated from Internet Traces

The workloads used for our simulation are generated from real-world Internet traces [13]. Two Internet traces are used for the workloads in the two server pools in the experiments. The *EPA-HTTP* trace contains a day's worth of HTTP requests to the EPA WWW server located at Research Triangle Park, NC. The *SDSC-HTTP* trace contains a day's worth of HTTP requests to the SDSC WWW server located at the San Diego Supercomputer Centre in California. Workload characteristics (in terms of the number of requests in the systems) in both traces are extracted every five minutes. In this section, two switching decision intervals are considered: (1) a short switching decision interval—30 s; (2) a long switching decision interval—60 s. In Section 9.4.2.2, a 5-s fixed server switching time is used; we use different server switching times (5, 10 and 15 s) in this section and evaluate the performance impact of the switching cost on total revenue for the three different switching policies. We evaluate the performance of the three policies with and without the admission control scheme for each of the above cases.

Table 9.7 Short decision interval for workload from traces

		Without A/C			With A/C		
Switching time	Metrics	NSP	PSP	BSP	NSP	PSP	BSP
5 s	No. of switches	0	18	5	0	18	7
	Revenue (x1,000)	614	683.5	1,374	614	683.2	1447
	Improvement (%)	0	11.3	123.7	0	11.3	135.6
	Improvement over non-ac (%)				0	0	11.9
10 s	No. of switches	0	14	5	0	13	16
	Revenue (x1,000)	614	715	1370	614	714.7	1370
	Improvement (%)	0	16.4	123.2	0	16.4	123.2
	Improvement over non-ac (%)				0	0	0
15 s	No. of switches	0	13	16	0	13	24
	Revenue (x1,000)	614	648.7	569.1	614	648.7	1250
	Improvement (%)	0	5.6	−7.3	0	5.6	103.5
	Improvement over non-ac (%)				0	0	110.8

Tables 9.7 and 9.8 list the performance results for short and long switching decision intervals. As can be seen from both tables, for different server switching times, both PSP and BSP perform better than NSP in terms of revenue contribution with and without AC, except for the long interval case when the server switching time is 15 s. The improvement for PSP ranges from 5.6 to 16.4% whereas it ranges from 103.5 to 136% for BSP with one exception (−7.3%).

Table 9.8 shows that when the number of switches is the same (the number of switches for BSP is the same for different switching times), the longer the server switching time is, the less the performance improvement is. Table 9.8 also shows that the number of switches for PSP when the switching time is 5 and 10 seconds is the same; but when the switching time increases to 15 s, the number of switches decreases by 2 to 16, which results in a slight performance improvement. In Table 9.7, it can be seen that when the server switching time increases from 5 to 10 s, the number of server switches for PSP drops from 18 to 14, which results in slight performance improvement. When the switching time is increased to 15 s, the number of switches only decreases by 1. Since the switching cost has increased by 50%, the total revenue is reduced. Results from both tables are intuitive. Server switching is not cost-free, therefore, the performance improvement is closely related to how long a switching takes and the number of server switches. There is a trade-off between performance improvement and the number of server switches, and it depends on the decision interval and the server switching time. On the one hand, more switches results in more potential performance improvement, on the other hand, due to the switching costs involved, too many switches could result in less or negative improvement.

Table 9.8 Long decision interval for workload from traces

		Without A/C			With A/C		
Switching time	Metrics	NSP	PSP	BSP	NSP	PSP	BSP
5 s	No. of switches	0	18	5	0	18	7
	Revenue (x1,000)	1,228	1,369	2,750	1,228	1,369	2,899
	Improvement (%)	0	11.5	123.9	0	11.4	136.0
	Improvement over non-ac (%)				0	−0.1	12.1
10 s	No. of switches	0	18	5	0	18	7
	Revenue (x1,000)	1,228	1,367	2,747	1,228	1,366	2,894
	Improvement (%)	0	11.3	123.7	0	11.3	135.6
	Improvement over non-ac (%)				0	0	11.9
15 s	No. of switches	0	16	5	0	16	7
	Revenue (x1,000)	1,228	1,420	2,744	1,228	1,420	2,890
	Improvement (%)	0	15.6	123.4	0	15.6	135.3
	Improvement over non-ac (%)				0	0	11.9

For the chosen workload, when AC is applied, there is no performance improvement for PSP, and the overall improvement for BSP is approximately 12%. The exception is the last case in Table 9.7, where the improvement is 103.5% with AC but is negative without AC.

In conclusion, for certain workload scenarios, there is a trade-off between performance improvement and the number of server switches for different server switching times and switching decision intervals. The number of server switches depends on workload characteristics. Admission control schemes do not always improve performance for all workload scenarios.

9.5 The Selection of Switching Services

After extensive performance evaluation of the switching services, the agent can then choose the most suitable service among all services. The goal of each server switching service in the given example is to maximise the total revenue from both server pools. The performance results show that the BSP service outperforms the PSP service in terms of revenue contribution to ISPs, therefore, it should be chosen in the given scenario.

9.6 Summary

In this chapter, we first explain the importance of web service selection as the number of functionally similar services is increasing, hence, the agent has to choose the best one among those services based on some non-functional attributes such as the QoS of each service. The challenge of web service selection arise due to a number of factors. One important factor is that it is very difficult to assess the QoS of a service, especially in the real-time environment, where changing system state can affect the quality of the service. Another important factor that could affect the assessment of QoS is that some dishonest service providers over claim the quality of their services to attract more clients. This issue is closely related to reputation of service providers and trust between them and the agents (or the end users). Some approaches such as the introduce of user feedback (or voting) mechanisms can help to resolve the trust-related issues.

After general discussion of the procedure of service selection, we then use a server switching service as a case study to describe the service selection procedure. The focus of the case study is on performance modelling of the multi-tier Internet services and performance evaluation of various switching services employed in such as multi-tier architecture. As can be seen in this chapter, service selection after performance evaluation is straightforward, therefore, performance evaluation plays a very important role in web service selection. The development of performance models can be time-consuming, however, it is the service providers' responsibility to model their service and the targeted execution environments.

References

1. A. S. Ali, S. A. Ludwig, and O. F. Rana. A Cognitive Trust-Based Approach for Web Service Discovery and Selection. In *Third IEEE European Conference on Web Services*, 2005.
2. M. Arlitt and T. Jin. A Workload Characterization Study of the 1998 World Cup Web Site. *IEEE Network*, 14(3):30–37, 2000.
3. G. Balbo and G. Serazzi. Asymptotic Analysis of Multiclass Closed Queueing Networks: Multiple Bottlenecks. *Performance Evaluation*, 30(3):115–152, 1997.
4. P. Barford and M. Crovella. Generating Representative Web Workloads for Network and Server Performance Evaluation. *ACM SIGMETRICS Performance Evaluation Review*, 26(1):151–160, 1998.
5. G. Bolch, S. Greiner, H. de Meer, and K. S. Trivedi. *Queueing Networks and Markov Chains: modelling and performance evaluation with computer science applications*. Wiley, 2nd edition, 2006.
6. J. Y. L. Boudec. *Rate Adaptation, Congestion Control and Fairness: A Tutorial*, Nov 2005.
7. G. Casale and G. Serazzi. Bottlenecks Identification in Multiclass Queueing Networks Using Convex Polytopes. In *Modelling, Analysis, and Simulation of Comp. and Telecommunication Systems (MASCOTS)*, 2004.
8. P. J. Denning and J. P. Buzen. The Operational Analysis of Queueing Network Models. *ACM Computing Surveys*, 10(3):225–261, 1978.
9. D. A. D'Mello and V. S. Ananthanarayana. Quality Driven Web Service Selection and Ranking. In *Fifth International Conference on Information Technology (ITNG'08)*, 2008.

10. D. L. Eager and K. C. Sevcik. Bound Hierarchies for Multiple-class Queueing Networks. *Journal of ACM*, 33(1):179–206, 1986.
11. S. Galizia, A. Gugliotta, and J. domingue. A Trust Based Methodology for Web Service Selection. In *International Conference on Semantic Computing (ICSC'07)*, 2007.
12. Y. Gao, J. Na, B. Zhang, L. Yang, and Q. Gong. Optimal Web Services Selection Using Dynamic Programming. In *11th IEEE Symposium on Computers and Communications (ISCC'06)*, 2006.
13. Internet Trace. Internet Traffic Archive Hosted at Lawrence Berkeley National Laboratory. In *http://ita.ee.lbl.gov/html/traces.html*, 2008.
14. T. Kerola. The Composite Bound Method for Computing Throughput Bounds in Multiple Class Environments. *Performance Evaluation*, 6(1):1–9, 1986.
15. C. Knessl and C. Tier. Asymptotic Approximations and Bottleneck Analysis in Product Form Queueing Networks with Large Populations. *Performance Evaluation*, 33(4):219–248, 1998.
16. M. Litoiu. A Performance Analysis Method for Autonomic Computing Systems. *ACM Transaction on Autonomous and Adaptive Systems*, 2(1):3, 2007.
17. J. Little. A Proof of the Queueing Formula $L = \lambda W$. *Operations Research*, 9(3):383–387, May 1961.
18. D. A. Menasce and V. A. F. Almeida. *Capacity Planning for Web Performance: metrics, models,and methods*. Prentice Hall PTR, 1998.
19. M. Reiser and S. Lavenberg. Mean-value Analysis of Closed Multi-Chain Queueing Networks. *Journal of the Association for Computing Machinary*, 27:313–322, 1980.
20. J. Rolia, X. Zhu, M. Arlitt, and A. Andrzejak. Statistical Service Assurances for Applications in Utility Grid Environments. Technical report, Technical Report HPL-2002-155, HP Labs, 2002.
21. P. J. Schweitzer. A Fixed-point Approximation to Product-form Networks with Large Populations. In *2nd ORSA Telecommunication Conference*, 1992.
22. K. Sevcik and I. Mitrani. The Distribution of Queueing Network States at Input and Output Instants. *Journal of the Association for Computing Machinary*, 28(2), 1981.
23. M. Sun and F. Arbab. Qos-driven Service Selection and Composition. In *8th International Conference on Application of Concurrency to System Design*, 2008.
24. D. T. Tsesmetzis, I. G. Roussaki, I. V. Papaioannou, and M. E. Anagnostou. QoS awareness Support in Web Service Semantics. In *the Advanced International Conference on Telecommunications and International Conference on Internet and Web Applications and Services (AICT/ICIW'06)*, 2006.
25. UDDI. Universal Description Discovery and Integretion. In *http:// www.uddi.org*, 2006.
26. B. Urgaonkar, G. Pacifici, P. J. Shenoy, M. Spreitzer, and A. Tantawi. An Analytical Model for Multi-tier Internet Services and its Applications. *ACM SIGMETRICS Performance Evaluation Review*, pages 291–302, 2005.
27. L. Vu, M. Hauswirth, and K. Aberer. QoS-Based Service Selection and Ranking with Trust and Reputation. Lecture Notes in Computer Science, 2005.
28. WSDL. Web Serivce Description Language. In *http://www.w3.org/TR/ wsdl*.
29. P. C. Xiong and Y. S. Fan. QoS-aware Web Service Selection by a Synthetic Weight. In *Fourth International Conference on Fuzzy Systems and Knowledge Discovery*, 2007.
30. A. Zalewski and A. Ratkowski. Evaluation of Dependability of Multi-tier Internet Business Applications with Queueing Networks. In *International Conference on Dependability of Computer Systems (DEPCOS-RELCOMEX'06)*, 2006.
31. J. Y. Zhou and T. Yang. Selective Early Request Termination for Busy Internet Services. In *15th International Conference on World Wide Web, Edinburgh, Scotland*, 2006.

Chapter 10
Future Directions

Nathan Griffiths, Kuo-Ming Chao, Simon Miles, Sanjay Modgil, Nir Oren, Michael Luck and Kwei-Jay Lin

Abstract Given the distributed and dynamic nature of SOC, and the autonomy of the agents involved, it is inevitable that failures will sometimes occur. Such failures might be due to simple errors or bugs, or may be a result of explicit malicious behaviour on behalf of an agent. In this chapter we introduce a number of future directions that will support the management of SOC by defining and constraining interactions (contracts), assessing and reducing the risk of failure (trust and reputation), and defining the responsibilities of the agents involved (accountability).

Nathan Griffiths
Department of Computer Science, University of Warwick, Coventry, CV4 7AL, UK
e-mail: nathan@dcs.warwick.ac.uk

Kuo-Ming Chao
Department of Computer Science, Coventry University, Coventry, CV1 5FB, UK
e-mail: k.chao@coventry.ac.uk

Simon Miles
Department of Computer Science, King's College London, London, WC2R 2LS, UK
e-mail: simon.miles@kcl.ac.uk

Sanjay Modgil
Department of Computer Science, King's College London, London, WC2R 2LS, UK
e-mail: sanjay.modgil@kcl.ac.uk

Nir Oren
Department of Computer Science, King's College London, London, WC2R 2LS, UK
e-mail: nir.oren@kcl.ac.uk

Michael Luck
Department of Computer Science, King's College London, London, WC2R 2LS, UK
e-mail: michael.luck@kcl.ac.uk

Kwei-Jay Lin
Department of Electrical Engineering and Computer Science, University of California, Irvine, CA, USA
e-mail: klin@uci.edu

N. Griffiths, K.-M. Chao (eds.), *Agent-Based Service-Oriented Computing*, Advanced Information and Knowledge Processing,
DOI 10.1007/978-1-84996-041-0_10,

10.1 Introduction

In open systems there will always be a need for agents to be constrained or incentivised to act cooperatively [8]. Where agents have divergent goals there is a temptation to attempt to improve individual utility by rescinding commitments, overcharging, or reducing quality. Current service-oriented systems tend to either avoid addressing such issues, by restricting the agents involved to those from known trusted providers, or by providing only a partial solution using relatively simple trust and reputation techniques. In the long-term we see electronic contracts as being the foundation of an overall solution (introduced in Section 10.3). Electronic contracts, as per traditional paper contracts, allow the creation and enforcement of restrictions on agent behaviour. However, as described in Section 10.3, we are some way off from practical useable contract-based approaches. Moreover, even when practical electronic contract systems do exist, such contracts are unlikely to specify precisely all aspects of an interaction, but instead will focus on the main issues and likely areas of failure. Trust and reputation (introduced in Section 10.2) can be used in the short-term to provide a solution to constraining and influencing the behaviour of agents, and in the long-term will provide a fall-back for failures and circumstances that are not covered by electronic contracts. A related aspect of interactions is accountability (introduced in Section 10.4), which enables the identification of responsibility in the event of service failure. Such accountability supports reconfiguration to remedy failures, and can include mechanisms such as compensation.

10.2 Trust and Reputation

Trust and reputation, as discussed in Chapter 8, are a means for an agent to assess the likelihood that others will behave as desired and as expected. Several computational approaches to trust and reputation have been developed over recent years. At the most basic level trust is seen as a simple numerical assessment of the risk associated with interacting with others based on an agent's direct past experiences. Using these experiences simple update functions [25], probability assessments [36], and fuzzy logic [13] have all been used to estimate an agent's trustworthiness. Reputation combines this notion of trustworthiness from direct experiences with information from third parties to determine a richer notion of trust [1]. Many approaches take into account reputation information from third parties as a complement to direct experiences. For example, the mechanisms used in Regret [33], TrustNet [35], FIRE [15] and TRAVOS [36] all make use of reputation in this way. More details on these approaches can be found in Chapter 8. At present, however, there is no single trust and reputation mechanism that is widely used and generally accepted. Moreover, there is no widely accepted mechanism that is targeted at service-oriented systems, and although the existing mechanisms are clearly applicable to service-oriented systems, they do not fully address the needs of this domain. Each of the models proposed addresses the needs of a particular environment and, despite being of clear relevance, none has yet found widespread acceptance in the area of service-oriented computing.

Trust and reputation are fundamental to supporting decision making across the various processes in a service-oriented system, ranging from the initial selection of appropriate services, to managing runtime issues such as QoS and resource provision. Our view is that there are three important areas that require further work to enable trust and reputation to be fully integrated into service-oriented systems, namely, establishing agreement on the characteristics of services and interactions that can be monitored and managed using trust-based techniques, refinement of existing trust and reputation mechanisms to take account of such characteristics, and extending existing tools and technologies to support decision making based on trust and reputation. These areas can be viewed as giving rise to two main activities that are required to facilitate widespread adoption of trust and reputation in supporting decision making, namely standardisation and technology integration.

10.2.1 Standardisation

In order to increase the adoption and use of trust, some form of standardised information representation and communication mechanism is needed. There are several aspects to achieving such standardisation, but the most fundamental is to have a clearly defined information format and set of trust and reputation dimensions. Many existing approaches to trust consider interactions as being decomposed into several dimensions, such as cost, quality, reliability and so forth [13]. If trust and reputation are to be useful in open systems it is important for heterogeneous agents operating on different platforms and supplied by different vendors to consider the same dimensions, and for these dimensions to have appropriate semantics and representation. In particular, we need a common language and frame-of-reference for specifying the characteristics of services, agreements, and interactions such that suppliers' and consumers' expectations match, and are relevant to third parties who may be relying on information regarding the results of an interaction to make judgements about trust and reputation. Thus, we require all agents in a system to have a common understanding of characteristics such as cost, quality, reliability etc.

The first stage in achieving a widely applicable trust and reputation mechanism for service-oriented systems is to define an appropriate representation for describing service and interaction characteristics. In technical terms this is a relatively straightforward task, since the possible dimensions have been considered in detail by existing literature, and we are essentially concerned with selecting a subset of these and finding an appropriate representation language. At a management level, however, this is a non-trivial task requiring input from stakeholders and users to ensure that a suitable set of dimensions, along with appropriate semantics and representations are selected. Given the range of application domains for service-oriented systems this is a complex task, since we need to arrive at a suitable set of dimensions that is rich enough to represent agents' concerns and yet simple enough to enable sharing of trust and reputation information. For service aspects such as cost it is simple to envisage a commonly agreed unit of currency, for example, but for aspects such as quality and reliability it is more difficult to frame an agent's interests in a domain independent and commonly understood manner. Our view is that a promising solution is to combine existing domain specific characteristics with more general interaction descriptions. For example, quality might be described in terms of the proportion of interactions in which expectations were met, rather than focusing on precise service details. A common representation language and semantics is fundamental to enabling agents to exchange trust and reputation information without misinterpreting or corrupting the meaning of the information.

Based on an agreed representation of service and interaction characteristics, we need a commonly agreed mechanism for sharing such information. In particular, to enable agents to make judgements about trust and reputation we need a mechanism to support feedback and recommendations between agents. On the completion of an interaction (and potentially during service delivery) it is likely that both the service provider and consumer will update their own personal trust assessments of the other party, with respect to their behaviour during the interaction. If such information is shared, then other third parties can use it to refine their own assessments of the agents concerned. To enable third parties to effectively use such information not only do we require a common representation language, but we also require an agreed mechanism for the dissemination of information.

Reputation mechanisms can be categorised into centralised and decentralised, and it is also important to develop a standardised approach for acquiring and maintaining reputation information. Ideally, this would be done in a decentralised manner, such that no single agent (or group of agents) has overall control. Decentralisation reduces the risk of a controlling agent manipulating reputation information or being a bottleneck or single point of failure in the system. A centralised approach, however, is simpler and so a pragmatic approach may be to first deploy a centralised approach, and then move to decentralisation once scalability etc. becomes an issue. For example, a basic reputation scheme would be for all agents involved in an interaction to submit feedback to a central repository on completion of the interaction. Agents can then extract feedback from this repository to make trust and reputation assessments of the agents with whom they might interact. For example, if faced with a choice between two service suppliers who advertise similar characteristics, an agent might try to select the most reliable by looking at the feedback for the two suppliers to assess whether one is more likely to deliver the stated characteristics.

10.2.2 Technology Integration

For trust and reputation to be widely adopted in practical deployed service-oriented systems, the notions of trust and reputation need to be fully integrated into the tools and technologies that are used. This applies throughout the discovery, selection, composition, execution and management of services. Throughout this book we have have seen a variety of techniques and approaches for integrating agents and service-oriented computing, and the tools and technologies described can all be extended to support trust (and reputation). The most basic level at which trust needs to be incorporated is in QoS-aware service selection and composition. The most common approach to service selection and composition is based on business process flow using WSDL and BPEL4WS. Our view is that the first step to widespread utilisation of trust and reputation to support SOC is to integrate such concepts into these existing technologies. Once this is done, more advanced approaches, such as the multiagent service composition approach described in Chapter 3 can be extended to incorporate trust and reputation. From this base, tasks such as workflow management and maintaining QoS, as discussed in Chapters 4 and 9, can similarly incorporate trust and reputation. The key point is that to facilitate the adoption of trust-based techniques we need to identify the most widely used tools and technologies and augment or extend them to support trust. Doing so will, first, provide a short-term alternative to electronic contracts (as discussed in the following section), and second, in the long-term, provide a fall-back for situations and failures that are not covered by contracts.

Integrating support for trust and reputation into the tools and technologies that are used for service-oriented systems is reliant on the existence of a common representation language and semantics, as discussed above. Once such a representation is agreed, existing tools can be augmented to support this representation. For example, the WSDL descriptions of services offered might be required to specify particular service characteristics as defined by the representation. Similarly, when orchestrating services, the control and data flow can be specified in such as way as to ensure that the required characteristics are considered.

10.2.3 Further Challenges for Trust and Reputation

In addition to the integration of trust and reputation support into the tools and technologies used for service-oriented computing, there are a number of more general challenges to address in which trust and reputation are likely to be part of the solution. Two significant issues that will become increasingly important as service-oriented computing becomes more widespread are collusion and compliance.

Collusion occurs where two or more agents manipulate interactions and/or information to promote or demote particular agents or services. For example, an agent may give positive feedback after a negative experience in return for some payment. Agent can use a combination of their own experiences and the information provided by others in detecting collusion. Detection of collusion is an open problem in agent-based systems, and although initial work exists in particular areas such as centralised reputation systems [20] and online auctions [39] there is no general solution. Similarly, there is no mechanism for detecting collusion in service-oriented systems, and this is likely to be an important area of future research.

Compliance is concerned with ensuring that interactions proceed in accordance with the agreed characteristics. In a complex workflow, where there are several levels of sub-contracting, it can be difficult to ensure that the overall result meets the required criteria. For example, in a data analysis application where all services must meet certain accuracy and quality constraints it is difficult for the overall "customer" to ensure that all sub-contractors adhere to these constraints. The first issue, as discussed above, is to ensure that we have suitable languages for expressing the characteristics required of interactions, for example using an augmented version of BPEL4WS. The second issue is to ensure that appropriate monitoring is performed at run-time to ensure compliance with the specified workflow. Since there is no global agent, this again involves issues of trust as the only practical solution is for individuals to monitor compliance locally and trust the compliance information provided by others.

The final challenge for integrating trust and reputation into service-oriented computing is to ensure that there exist appropriate mechanisms for imposing sanctions on agents who rescind their commitments. Such sanctions are likely to be two-fold including a decrease in perceived trust and reputation and an explicit penalty or compensation mechanism, and both of these aspects require consideration. Existing approaches to trust and reputation typically include mechanisms by which the perception of an agent is decreased if they fail to fulfil their commitments. These mechanisms should be relatively straightforward to transfer to a service-oriented setting. However, little work has been done on establishing penalty or compensation mechanisms, and we see this a important issue. Firstly, some mechanism is needed for specifying the penalties that will be incurred under different circumstances (for example, there may be different penalties for being late to a complete failure to deliver). (Note that this is different to the notion of "compensation" in BPEL which is related to rollback of transactions rather than imposing penalties.) Secondly, a mechanism is required to ensure that such penalties when incurred are actually paid.

10.3 Contract-Based Systems

Simon Miles, Sanjay Modgil, Nir Oren and Michael Luck

In this section, we consider contract-based systems, their grounding on the concept of *norms*, and the infrastructure required to support them. Dynamic open systems of the kind envisaged for service-oriented architectures can be considered complex systems in which very many entities interact, usually with some individual or collective purpose. However, it has been argued [8] that agents interacting in a common society need to be constrained in order to avoid and solve conflicts, make agreements, reduce complexity, and in general to achieve a desirable social order. This is the role of *norms*, which represent what ought to be done by a set of entities (agents or services), and whose fulfilment can be generally seen as a public good when their benefits can be enjoyed by the overall society, organisation or group [7]. Research on norms and agents has ranged from fundamental work on the importance of norms in agent behaviour to proposing internal representations of norms [37], considering their emergence in groups of agents, and proposing logics for their formalisation (e.g., [32, 37]).

The easiest way to represent and reason about norms is by seeing them as built-in constraints, where all the restrictions and obligations of agents are obeyed absolutely without deliberation. In this view, the effort is left to the system designer to ensure that all agents respond in the required way and, consequently, that the overall system behaves coherently. However, this may result in inflexible systems that must be changed off-line when either the agents or the environment change. By contrast, if a dynamic view of norms is taken, in which agents are not assumed to obey norms in all cases, the flexibility of the overall system can be assured [40].

Norms are thus the mechanisms of a society to influence the behaviour of the agents within it. They can be created from different sources, varying from built-in norms to simple agreements between agents, or more complex legal systems. They may persist over different periods of time, for example until an agent dies, as long as an agent remains in the society for which the norms were issued, or just for a short period of time until a normative goal is satisfied.

10.3.1 Electronic Contracts

In situations in which the obligations, prohibitions and permissions that may affect agent behaviour in a normative system may not apply to societies as a whole, but to individuals within the society, they can be documented and communicated between agents in the form of *contracts*. Electronic contracts, mirroring the paper versions exchanged between businesses today, offer the possibility of dynamic, automatic creation and enforcement of such restrictions and compulsions on agent behaviour. In addition, in situations in which there are many contracts within a particular application, it can be difficult to determine whether the system can reliably fulfil them all; computer-parsable electronic contracts may allow such verification to be automated.

Modelling business service components belonging to different organisations (such as a Web Service, for example) as independent entities that are able to dynamically negotiate, commit to, enact and dissolve contractual agreements at runtime seems to be a sensible and natural option. Here, contracts may be used as a formal means to set out commitments, obligations, prohibitions, permissions, powers, duties, penalties and other conditions on the execution of the underlying process or workflow. Such software contracts can thus help to bridge the gap between formal legal documents between companies and their software implementations. In particular, they facilitate increased flexibility in deployed systems while at the same time they maintain a formal underpinning for service-service interaction, and make it possible to evaluate service execution in terms of compliance with the contract rather than behaviour according to shared program code.

There are two pre-requisites to realistically applying an electronic contracting approach in real-world domains. First, to exploit electronic contracts, a well-defined conceptual *framework* for contract-based systems, to which the application entities can be mapped, is needed. Second, to support the management of contracts through all stages of the contract life-cycle, we need to specify the functionality required of a contract management *architecture* that would underly any such system, leading to ready-made implementations for particular deployments of that architecture. We will consider the requirements of both the conceptual framework and the supporting architecture below.

10.3.2 Conceptual Frameworks for Contract-Based Systems

A conceptual framework is needed to describe a contract-based system, including the contracts themselves and the agents to which they apply. A number of useful operations may be performed on the framework specification of a given application. First, off-line verification mechanisms can check whether the contracts to be established obey particular properties, such as being achievable, given the possible states the world can reach. From this, and the contracts themselves, it is possible to determine which states are critical to observe during execution to ensure appropriate behaviour. A *critical state* of a contract-based system with regard to an obligation essentially indicates whether the obligation is fulfilled or fulfillable, e.g., achieved, failed, in danger of not being fulfilled, etc.

The framework specification can also aid in determining which processes are suitable for the administration of the electronic contracts through their lifetimes, including establishment, updating, termination, renewal, and so on. In particular such processes also include observation of the system, so that contractual obligations can be enforced or otherwise effectively managed; these processes depend on the critical states mentioned earlier. The selection of a process typically requires that certain agents take on specific roles. These roles in turn require that the agents have certain capabilities, which are in turn instantiated by specific components. Furthermore, only once these administrative processes exist may contract documents actually be used and enforced by the system.

10.3.3 Supporting Architectures for Contract-Based Systems

An effective architecture for contract-based systems should support multiple different ways of handling all stages of a contract's life cycle (for example, allowing for contracts to be negotiated, or imposed by the organisational hierarchy, allowing for both lax and strict contract enforcement, and the like). This would allow the architecture to be incorporated into a wider range of application domains and types of deployment than existing systems which mandate the use of a specific protocol. For example, there are different ways for agents to sign a contract, some useful in domains in which some centralised management components exist, such as using a trusted third party notary to manage the process and store the contract, while others are applicable in decentralised settings, such as all parties to the contract applying digital signatures to preserve its integrity. Similarly, an architecture should not constrain a designer in using a single approach for contract administration and management, but instead provide guidelines and useful building blocks from which complete systems may be created. This contrasts with specifications such as WS-Agreement and Web Service Level Agreement, where the specifications cover only part of a contract's administrative requirements [2, 24].

Moreover, it is valuable to aim for broad *observation* and *management* of obligations and prohibitions, so as to verify whether they are being complied with, to prevent failure when in danger of violation, and to take advantage of success when obligations are being easily met. Here, the critical states identified from a framework specification as those in which the status of a norm changes, can be used to focus observation and management of obligation fulfilment in accordance with a particular application.

10.3.4 Existing Work and Future Directions

Current deployments of e-business applications typically function in the following way: some overarching legal agreement between the relevant parties is signed by human representatives, with only the subsequent *implementation* of the resulting e-business links being developed and deployed in software [6]. This enables businesses to address particular (but basic) legal constraints, and at the same time to benefit from the opportunities afforded by new software tools. However, the approach suffers from some important limitations. First, there is often no explicit or formal connection between the initial legal agreement and the resulting software implementation. Second, legal agreements are typically general, covering the whole business collaboration, as opposed to particular aspects of that collaboration. For example, this might not address the specific aspects of a shipment of parts for aircraft engines, but might instead cover the agreement between businesses to supply parts in general. Related to this is a third limitation: legal agreements are typically fixed and restrict flexibility, yet the implementation of software contracts or agreements (and the supporting infrastructure) facilitates much greater flexibility than is possible in these legal documents. A key advantage of software contracts is that they can be modified dynamically at runtime, yet if the corresponding legal agreements do not permit this, then the benefits that might be gained from the software infrastructure are thus severely curtailed.

Although there is much existing work on contract-based systems, with significant research and development, we are still far from the development of practical usable contract-based approaches to e-business system design. In particular, approaches such as software by contract (and Microsoft INDIGO) are at a very low level and primarily address *method* correctness rather than higher level issues of service delivery, which is where the additional value, as described in this section, arises. Similar approaches, such as ebXML, allow only static contract patterns, which lose much of the flexibility and dynamism, as suggested above.

Concepts such as norms specifying patterns of behaviour for agents, contract clauses as concrete representations of dynamic norms, management or enforcement of norms being governed by other norms, and the like, are all already established in the literature [9–11, 23], but less work has been conducted on the development of practical system deployments for business scenarios. In particular, business systems operate in the context of wider organisational and inter-organisational processes, so that commitments, providing assurance over the actions of others, assume great importance. While potentially less flexible over the short term (as an entity should honour its commitments rather than performing any action it desires), explicit contracts provide just such commitments. They are therefore more appropriate for business systems than more flexible, less predictable ad hoc approaches [12,27].

Overall, the area of contract-based systems is very promising, but with much work remaining to transform the existing ideas into practical implementations.

Acknowledgement

The research described in this section is partly supported by the European Commission Framework 6 funded project CONTRACT (INFSO-IST-034418). The opinions expressed herein are those of the named authors only and should not be taken as necessarily representative of the opinion of the European Commission or CONTRACT project partners.

10.4 Service Accountability

Kwei-Jay Lin

When a service agent in SOC [5,16] delegates service functionalities to other service agents, it is imperative for the main agent to ensure that all external servers provide an acceptable and consistent level of performance, in order to meet the overall objective from its clients. The behaviour of each individual service in a service process must be clearly understood in order to resolve any responsibility issue if there is a service failure. Any ill-behaved service should be detected and may be replaced immediately to ensure the service quality. In other words, service agent systems should have simple-yet-effective mechanisms to conduct:

1. monitoring of services and diagnosis of possible faults and problems,
2. inspection and reasoning about the correctness of individual services, and
3. dynamic reconfiguration of services and service processes.

To provide a holistic solution to the above requirement, the framework of *service accountability* has been proposed in [41] as a means to monitor services, identify problems, and make remedies. Indeed, accountability needs have been defined constantly in the real world by many public institutions such as government agencies, hospitals and non-profit organisations as a comprehensive measure to provide operation transparency and to furnish a responsible attitude toward any unacceptable behaviour. We believe that accountability for agents and services should also be carefully studied in SOC by considering the unique characteristics in the service oriented paradigm. An accountability mechanism for service systems should clearly specify the expected behaviour, model inter-dependencies among service components, diagnose and identify faulty service agents, and defuse and recover from faults [28].

10.4.1 Introduction to Accountability

Accountability has become a major concern for business management in USA, especially after the ratification of the Sarbanes-Oxley Act of 2002 [34] (also known as the Public Company Accounting Reform and Investor Protection Act of 2002), which establishes new enhanced accountability standards for all public companies and public accounting firms. The PCAOB (Public Company Accounting Oversight Board) is given the responsibility of overseeing, regulating, inspecting, and disciplining accounting firms in their roles as auditors of public companies. The Act has made accountability a mandatory requirement for organisations. An effective quality management infrastructure is essential to maintain business integrity.

Horsch reports on results-based accountability for public institutions [14], and identifies the following design considerations for systems with accountability:

1. Objective: Outcomes that articulate what programs are to achieve;
2. Quality: Indicators to measure whether or not outcomes have been achieved;
3. Benchmark: Performance standards to assess how programs are progressing;
4. Monitoring: Data collection instruments to regularly obtain indicator data;
5. Feedback: Periodic collection and analysis of data for decision making and reporting.

Among the five design issues of an accountable institution, the first three are industry-specific, to be identified by the mission of a specific institution. With that, IT may be used to implement the last two elements: monitoring and feedback. This is particularly true for agent-based SOC systems since we can utilise the agent capability for intelligently monitoring services and analysing their behaviours. Through an agent-based SOC framework, we can offload the accountability management burdens from humans to agent infrastructure.

10.4.2 SOA Accountability

Service accountability means that services deployed (regardless of whether by human, machine or software) have the obligation to accept the responsibility of, i.e., *to account for*, all of their actions [22]. By imposing accountability on services, service clients are given transparency on service behaviours when conducting service collaborations. As a result, they may have better problem resolution capability when invoking accountable services.

Accountability in the context of computer decision systems has been analysed in [18] using four accountability attributes: *fault*, *causality*, *role* and *liability*. We now review these four accountability attributes from SOA's perspective.

- *Fault* in SOA is the result of a service execution which deviates from the client's expectation on the service. When a service is invoked, the service is expected to fulfil some functional and nonfunctional capabilities. If a service result does not comply with the *a priori* agreement, it is deemed to have a fault.
- *Causality* in SOA is a relationship between a fault and one or more services that produce the results directly or indirectly. In many cases, a fault in service execution can be the cause for another fault, resulting in a chain of faults.
- *Role* in SOA is a well-defined responsibility fulfilled by an agent during service execution. Service providers and service clients are the two most obvious roles in SOA. Other roles in SOA include service monitors, fault handlers, etc.
- *Liability* in SOA may include service replacement, process reconfiguration, and/or compensation transactions. In the simplest case, a faulty service is replaced by a capable service. It may also cause the service process to be recomposed with a different workflow. Finally, due to some erroneous actions that have occurred, a service system may need to initiate a compensation transaction to correct previous executions. Depending on the type of problem situation, different liability actions should be applied.

10.4.3 Accountable Service Computing Model

As shown in Figure 10.1, the key phases of accountable computing include *Detect*, *Diagnose*, *Defuse*, and *Disclose*. Each phase has its goals and artifacts. In this section, we discuss the issues in each phase.

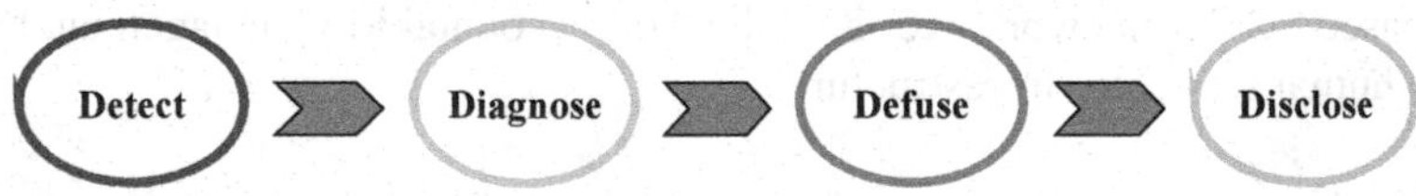

Fig. 10.1 Phases of accountability management

10.4.3.1 The Detection Phase

The detection phase is to implement the following tasks: (1) dynamically acquiring status on services and the environment, (2) computing the values of the relevant quality attributes, and (3) comparing the values of quality attributes to the threshold values identified in the SLA.

An accountable SOA system must first determine the expected behaviour in a service system. The criteria for determining acceptable behaviours are usually derived from the service interface, service policies, and service level agreement (SLA) that includes quality and constraints of services.

A policy in SOA is a formal statement representing assertions on the requirements of services. Examples of SOA policies are authentication requirements for sensitive information, and the predetermined response time for time-sensitive services, etc. Service providers and consumers define their policies on services. A service agreement is then derived as a mutual agreement on various quantifiable quality aspects of the service in order to enable runtime measurement and calculation. Quality attributes are defined with an acceptable range for normal service executions [18, 29]. Example quality attributes are availability, accessibility, and performance. The values of these quality attributes can be computed from measurements on services and the execution environment. For example, availability is defined as the percentage of time during which a service is available and performance can be measured by dispatch time and latency time.

Faults in service processes may be present at different system levels: including *platform level*, *service level*, and *process level*. The platform level includes the system hardware, middleware, resources, and communication network. The service level is defined by service invocations, service outputs, and QoS interfaces. The process level is defined by business process specification and service flow from the end-to-end point of view. An accountable system must detect all types of faults at all three levels. Measurements on services and environment can be gathered by various service monitoring methods such as [4, 26].

10.4.3.2 The Diagnosis Phase

Given some detected error or failure, an accountability support system must analyse the problems detected to identify the likely cause(s). A *cause* is defined as the fault origin of the erroneous behaviour or a situation (context) which has resulted in a failure.

We can classify causes into three classes: (1) causes arisen from problematic services, (2) causes arisen from malfunctioned infrastructure, and (3) causes arisen from invalid service invocations by clients. Causes of the first type are often found on poor behaviour of services such as "service not responding" and "unexpected service behaviour". Causes of the second type are similar to that found in conventional application system management. For example, service systems may be overloaded with an excessive number of invocations or network may be congested. Causes of the third type are related to invalid input values or parameters sent by clients, and incompatible input and output parameters between two interconnected services.

There are different ways to diagnose faults and to identify causes. A probabilistic model is reported in [41], which adopts the Bayesian network model to assess services upon the observation of some abnormal behaviour. The approach utilises monitoring agents and intelligent diagnosis methods, so that accountability is efficiently assessed. However, as in any probabilistic model, the result of assessing accountability and diagnosed results is not always correct. Additional checking is required to confirm the true cause of a fault.

Another way to conduct diagnosis is to use a statistical approach which utilises the history of service invocations and rules for determining the cause based on the observed abnormality. In this approach, we need to derive and define diagnosis rules from the statistical analysis on earlier occurrences of (*Abnormality Type*, *Cause Type*) pairs. The more comprehensive service logs are recorded, the more reliable diagnosis may be produced. Statistical studies have been reported in [3, 38].

10.4.3.3 The Defusing Phase

This phase is to resolve the problem determined from the diagnosis phase. The actual method of defusing problems largely depends on the type of the cause.

For faulty services, the defusing method is usually to replace malfunctioning services. The replacement can be for a service, a portion of a process execution path, or the whole process. A faulty service may be replaced by a compatible service which provides similar functionality and possibly stronger QoS (but with a higher cost). When replacing a portion of an execution path, the execution path is updated by considering the dependency between replaced services and their neighbour services. When replacing the whole process path, the path is re-composed without using the faulty service.

For causes from malfunctioning hardware, a defusing method must identify all services affected and exclude them from the new service process. After that, the system may reboot the middleware environment. For causes of the third type, e.g., invalid input parameters from clients, the defusing method is to request a new set of input values, or select another service that can accept the parameters correctly.

10.4.3.4 The Disclosure Phase

In real life legal matters, a liability is often imposed on the party that has caused a service failure. The disclosure phase is to apply a post-mortem remedy on the outcome of a failed service. The remedy may be to compensate the service client due to the damage from the service delivery failure, or to penalise the faulty server so that it is prevented from making similar problem in the future.

The former remedy may be carried out as compensating transactions for the client. For example, an aborted transaction may be restarted. An incorrect purchase may be returned and credited. A delayed payment transaction may need to be honoured with the original price and terms, even with extra discounts. Such remedy actions may be executed as "exception handling" transactions by a penalty decision maker in the accountability framework.

To penalise faulty servers (such as business process designers, service providers, network administrators, SOA middleware managers), the information about their unacceptable service record can be used to change the qualification or reputation of these services. The result of disclosure can be reflected in the service repository for future reference. That is, the causes for a certain abnormality, the effectiveness of defusing methods for the causes, and the reputation of services can be effectively utilised for future invocations.

10.4.4 Accountability System Components

To provide the functionality needed for accountable service computing, a component architecture for accountable service system is shown in Figure 10.2. The architecture consists of four components: *Monitor*, *Inspector*, *Handler*, and *Recorder*.

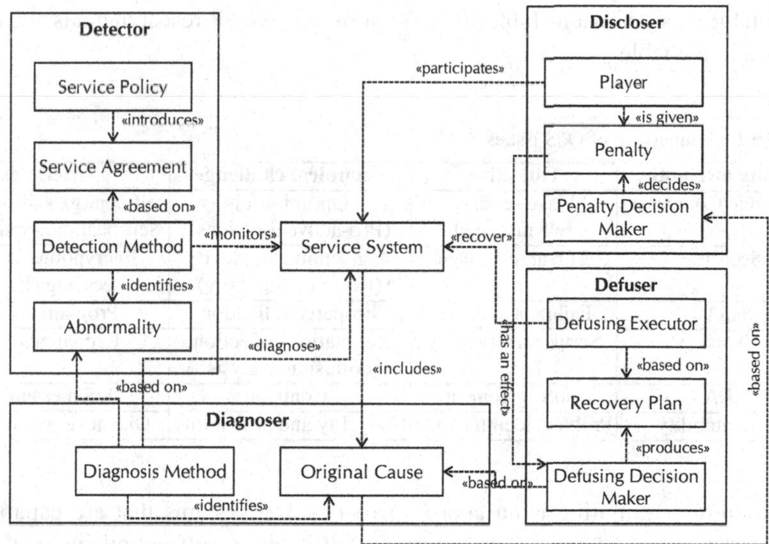

Fig. 10.2 Accountability components

The component *Monitor* is to detect abnormality of services. It consists of the following elements: Service Policy, Service Agreement, Fault Detector, and Abnormality. Based on the Service Policy, the Fault Detector provides ways to recognise

Abnormality by monitoring services, comparing current states to Service Agreement, and describing abnormal situations.

The component *Inspector* is to analyse the situations and identify the fault origin. It has elements of Diagnosis Conductor and Root Cause. For the errors detected, the Diagnosis Conductor identifies causes using its diagnosing methods, and produces a description of causes.

The component *Handler* is to recover a problematic services system from the causes identified. It consists of the following elements: Recovery Decision Maker, Recovery Plan, and Recovery Manager. Recovery Decision Maker generates a recovery plan on which the Recovery Manager defuses the fault causes. The recovery plan is defined with appropriate defusing methods for the types of causes and system management guidelines.

The component *Recorder* is to determine responsible players for the causes and relevant penalties for them. It utilises the following elements: Penalty Decision Maker, Service Provider, and Penalty. Penalty Decision Maker decides the specific penalty for responsible players.

10.4.5 Related Work

Many service quality management and assurance research subjects are related to accountability, as shown in Table 10.1. We summarise their research goals and technologies in the table.

Table 10.1 Comparison of QoS issues

Quality attributes	Objective	Technical challenge	Methods
Autonomic Computing	Make services self-managed	Optimisation (Pro-active decisions)	self-config., self-protection, Self-healing, -optimisation
Security	Threat resistance	Algorithm complexity (Resource integrity)	Encryption, firewalls, securing channels
Safety	Failure avoidance	Property validation	Program analysis
Trust	Service trustworthy	Reputation collection, collusion analysis	Recommendation
SLA	QoS agreement	Contract	QoS measurement
Accountability	Problem identification	Causality and probability	Diagnosis and reasoning

Autonomic computing is an approach to develop systems that are capable of self-management, and are self-configuring, self-healing, self-optimising, and self-protecting [17]. Each of the self-* methods is implemented with four operations in sequence; monitoring, analysing, planning, and executing. These operations are analogous to those defined in accountability. However, autonomic computing is motivated more from the demands for self management, whereas accountable service computing is motivated to provide reliable and stable services. Even if a service is managed in full autonomic manner, it may not be considered to be accountable because accountability demands clarification aspects and goals such as determining the responsible party for the given problem, which are not typically presented in autonomic computing.

Security in computing systems means protecting systems from unauthorised access, use, disclosure, disruption, modification, or destruction [31]. Security focuses on withstanding threats, whereas accountability considers diagnosing threats for security related problems and considers a comprehensive set of quality attributes beyond security. Hence, a secure service may or may not be accountable, but an accountable service is meant to be secure.

Safety in computer systems is a condition where theories and engineering approaches are defined to prevent foreseeable accidents and to minimise the result of unforeseen ones [21]. The primary concern of system safety is the management of hazards: their identification, evaluation, elimination, and control through analysis, design and management procedures. Safety conditions are often defined to detect the extreme values in the range of normal service output. In other words, an incorrect output may not qualify as a system safety concern. Safety definitely can be enhanced by accountable service computing, but it is only part of the objective for accountability management.

Trust is the subjective probability by which an individual expects that another individual performs a given action on which its welfare depends [19]. Services with a high trust value usually cause less problems during invocation. By choosing services with a high trust, service systems may be more stable on providing a high QoS; but it does not necessarily mean that the systems are accountable.

A service level agreement (SLA) is a specification of contracts between service providers and consumers and it is generally accompanied with contracts on QoS [30]. A SLA is focused on defining agreements between two parties, while accountability is to identify problems and resolve them based on the specification of SLA.

As observed in preceding discussions, some notions of accountability also appear in existing work on autonomic computing, trust, and SLA. However, accountability has a different motivation and objectives. Its main objective is on the fault identification and resolution for service processes. It presents a comprehensive management framework, deploys an accountability support architecture, and incorporates some fault diagnosis methodology.

10.4.6 Future Direction

Accountability is very important for agent-based SOC since agents in multi-agent systems rely on each other to complete their total functionalities. Agents must have the mechanism to assure others that they are accountable of their behaviour and performance, so that their clients may achieve specific end-to-end service objectives.

One of the most important issues for a practical support of accountability is *efficiency*. We need to facilitate the 4-D capabilities without a heavy system overhead.

We also need to have a good mechanism design so that it can respond promptly whenever a service fault occurs. Another practical issue is the completeness of the quality attributes. A real-life service-oriented system must manage many complex quality attributes. Some of them may not be detected by a single event, but must be reasoned in a holistic manner and/or compared with historical records. More research is needed to design innovative event detection and reasoning technologies for all types of accountable services.

Acknowledgement

The research described in this section is partly supported by the Tsinghua National Laboratory for Information Science and Technology (TNList), China. The opinions expressed herein are those of the named author only and should not be taken as necessarily representative of the opinion of Tsinghua University.

References

1. A. Abdul-Rahman and S. Hailes. Supporting trust in virtual communities. In *Proceedings of the 33rd Hawaii International Conference on System Sciences (HICSS 2000)*, page 6007. IEEE Computer Society, 2000.
2. A. Andrieux, K. Czajkowski, A. Dan, K. Keahey, H. Ludwig, J. Pruyne, J. Rofrano, S. Tuecke, and M. Xu. Web services agreement specification (ws-agreement). Technical report, Global Grid Forum, 2004.
3. L. Ardissono, L. Console, A. Goy, G. Petrone, C. Picardi, M. Segnan and D. T. Dupre. Enhancing web services with diagnostic capabilities. In *Proceedings of the Third European Conference on Web Services (ECOWS '05)*, page 182, 2005.
4. L. Baresi and S. Guinea. Towards dynamic monitoring of WS-BPEL processes. In *Proceedings of International Conference on Service-Oriented Computing (ICSOC 2005)*, pages 269–282, 2005.
5. M. Bichler and K. J. Lin. Service-oriented computing. *IEEE Computer*, 39(3):99–101, 2006.
6. B. Brauer and S. Kline. SOA governance: A key ingredient of the adaptive enterprise. Development technical report, Hewlett Packard, February 2005.
7. C. Castelfranchi, R. Conte, and M. Paolucci. Normative reputation and the cost of compliance. *Journal of Artificial Societies and Social Simulation*, 1(3), 1998.
8. R. Conte. Emergent (info)institutions. *Journal of Cognitive Systems Research*, pages 97–110, 2001.
9. C. Dellarocas. Contractual agent societies: Negotiated shared context and social control in open multi-agent systems. In *Workshop on Norms and Institutions in Multi-Agent Systems, 4th International Conference on Multi-Agent Systems*, 2000.
10. F. Duran, V. Torres da Silva, and C. J. P. de Lucena. Using testimonies to enforce the behaviour of agents. In *Proceedings of the AAMAS'07 Workshop on Coordination, Organization, Institutions and Norms in Agent Systems*, 2007.
11. A. Garcia-Camino. Ignoring, forcing and expecting concurrent events in electronic institutions. In *Proceedings of the AAMAS'07 Workshop on Coordination, Organization, Institutions and Norms in Agent Systems*, 2007.

12. M. Ghijsen, W. Jansweijer, and R. Wielinga. Towards a framework for agent coordination and reorganization, agentcore. In *Proceedings of the AAMAS'07 Workshop on Coordination, Organization, Institutions and Norms in Agent Systems*, 2007.
13. N. Griffiths. A fuzzy approach to reasoning with trust, distrust and insufficient trust. In *Cooperative Information Agents X*, volume 4149 of *Lecture Notes in Computer Science*, pages 360–374. Springer-Verlag, 2006.
14. K. Horsch. Results-based accountability systems: Opportunities and challenges. The Evaluation Exchange II(1), 1996. http://www.gse.harvard.edu/hfrp/eval/issue3/theory1.html
15. T. D. Huynh, N. R. Jennings, and N. Shadbolt. Developing an integrated trust and reputation model for open multi-agent systems. In *Proceedings of the 7th International Workshop on Trust in Agent Societies*, pages 65–74, New York, USA, 2004.
16. M. N. Huhns and M. P. Singh. Service-oriented computing: Key concepts and principles. IEEE Internet Computing, 2005.
17. IBM: An architectural blueprint for autonomic computing, 2006. http://www-01.ibm.com/software/tivoli/autonomic/
18. D. G. Johnson and J. M. Mulvey. Accountability and computer decision systems. *Communications of the ACM*, 38(12):58–64, 1995.
19. A. Josang, R. Ismail, and C. Boyd. A survey of trust and reputation systems for online service provision. *Decision Support Systems* 43, 2007.
20. R. Jurca and B. Faltings. Collusion-resistant, incentive-compatible feedback payments. In *Proceedings of the 8th ACM conference on Electronic commerce*, pages 200–209. 2007.
21. N. G. Leveson. Safeware: System Safety and Computers. Addison-Wesley, 1995.
22. K. J. Lin. Accountable services. In *Proceedings of the IEEE International Conference on e-Business Engineering (ICEBE)*, 2007.
23. F. Lopez y Lopez, M. Luck, and M. d'Inverno. A normative framework for agent-based systems. *Computational and Mathematical Organization Theory*, 12(2–3):227–250, 2005.
24. H. Ludwig, A. Keller, A. Dan, R. P. King, and R. Franck. Web service level agreement (WSLA), language specification. Technical report, IBM Corporation, January 2003.
25. S. Marsh. Optimism and pessimism in trust. In H. Geffner, editor, *Proceedings of IV Ibero-American Conference on Artificial Intelligence (IBERAMIA 1994)*, pages 286–297. Addison-Wesley, 1994.
26. G. Morgan, S. Parkin, C. Molina-Jimenez, and J. Skene. Monitoring middleware for service level agreements in heterogeneous environments. In *Challenges of Expanding Internet: E-Commerce, E-Business, and E-Government*, pages 79–83, Springer, 2005.
27. E. Muntaner-Perich, J. Lluis de la Rosa, and M. Esteva. Towards a formalisation of dynamic electronic institutions. In *Proceedings of the AAMAS07 Workshop on Coordination, Organization, Institutions and Norms in Agent Systems*, 2007.
28. H. Nissenbaum. Computing and accountability. *Communications of the ACM*, 37(1):72–80, 1994.
29. L. O'Brien, L. Bass, and P. Merson. Quality attributes and service-oriented architectures. Technical Note CMU/SEI-2005-TN-014, 2005.
30. M. Papazoglou. Web Services: Principles and Technology. Prentice Hall, 2007.
31. C. P. Pfleeger and S. L. Pfleeger. Security in Computing. Prentice Hall, 2003.
32. A. Ross. *Directives and Norms*. Routledge and Kegan Paul Ltd., 1968.
33. J. Sabater and C. Sierra. A reputation model for gregarious societies. In *Fourth Workshop on Deception Fraud and Trust in Agent Societies*, pages 61–70, 2001.
34. Sarbanes-oxley act (2002). http://www.sec.gov/about/laws/soa2002.pdf
35. M. Schillo, P. Funk, and M. Rovatsos. Using trust for detecting deceitful agents in artificial societies. *Applied Artificial Intelligence, Special Issue on trust, Deception, and Fraud in Agent Societies*, 14(8):825–848, 2000.
36. W. T. L. Teacy, J. Patel, N. Jennings, and M. Luck. TRAVOS: Trust and reputation in the context of inaccurate information sources. *Autonomous Agents and Multi-Agent Systems*, 12(2):183–198, 2006.
37. R. Tuomela and M. Bonnevier-Toumela. Norms and agreements. *European Journal of Law, Philosophy and Computer Science*, 5:41–46, 1995.

38. G. Wang, C. Wang, A. Chen, H. Wang, C. Fung, S. Uczekaj, Y. L. Chen, W. G. Guthmiller and J. Lee. Service level management using QoS monitoring, diagnostics, and adaptation for networked enterprise systems. In *Proceedings of the Ninth IEEE International EDOC Enterprise Computing Conference (EDOC '05)*, pages 239–250, 2005.
39. J.-C. Wang and C.-C. Chiu. Recommending trusted online auction sellers using social network analysis. Expert Systems with Applications 34(3):1666–1679, 2008
40. F. Zambonelli, N. Jennings, and M. Wooldridge. Organisational abstractions for the analysis and design of multi-agent systems. In *Proceedings of the First International Workshop on Agent-Oriented Software Engineering*, 2000.
41. Y. Zhang, K. J. Lin, and J. Y. Hsu. Accountability monitoring and reasoning in service-oriented architectures. *Journal of Service-Oriented Computing and Applications (SOCA)* 1(1), 2007.

Index